Statelessness after Arendt

Manchester University Press

Cultural History of Modern War

Series editors

Ana Carden-Coyne, Max Jones, Bertrand Taithe and Joanne Laycock

To buy or to find out more about the books currently available in this series, please go to: https://manchesteruniversitypress.co.uk/series/cultural-history-of-modern-war/

https://www.alc.manchester.ac.uk/history/research/centres/cultural-history-of-war//

Statelessness after Arendt

European refugees in China
and the Pacific during
the Second World War

Edited by Kolleen Guy and Jay Winter

MANCHESTER UNIVERSITY PRESS

Copyright © Manchester University Press 2025

While copyright in the volume as a whole is vested in Manchester University Press, copyright in individual chapters belongs to their respective authors, and no chapter may be reproduced wholly or in part without the express permission in writing of both author and publisher.

Published by Manchester University Press
Oxford Road, Manchester, M13 9PL

www.manchesteruniversitypress.co.uk

British Library Cataloguing-in-Publication Data
A catalogue record for this book is available from the British Library

ISBN   978 1 5261 8302 6   hardback

First published 2025

The publisher has no responsibility for the persistence or accuracy of URLs for any external or third-party internet websites referred to in this book, and does not guarantee that any content on such websites is, or will remain, accurate or appropriate.

EU authorised representative for GPSR:
Easy Access System Europe, Mustamäe tee 50, 10621 Tallinn, Estonia
gpsr.requests@easproject.com.

Typeset
by Deanta Global Publishing Services, Chennai, India

Contents

List of figures	*page* viii
List of contributors	x
Acknowledgements	xi
List of abbreviations	xii

Introduction – Kolleen Guy and Jay Winter   1

Part I: Perspectives on statelessness

Section I.I: Statelessness and the refugee predicament: a conversation

1	Statelessness and the burden of our times – Jay Winter	12
2	A response – Peter Gatrell	28

Section I.II: Telling the tale of refugees and the stateless

3	Some poems: statelessness and refugees – Peter Balakian	38
4	*Run* (refugee series) – Mary Behrens	46
5	'Nobody's children': families, internees, and refugees in Singapore and Australia during the Second World War – Eva de Jong-Duldig	52
6	Family memories of war and displacement: primary sources for a historian – Joy Damousi	75

Part II: Refugees and the stateless in Asia and the Pacific in the global Second World War

Section II.I: Varieties of refugee life and statelessness in China

7 War, memory, the state, and statelessness in China – Rana Mitter   96
8 The international politics of refugee settlement in Shanghai, 1937–56 – Meredith Oyen   111
9 Statelessness and its (sometime) benefits: the case of Russians in Harbin in the 1930s and 1940s – Sheila Fitzpatrick   133
10 'I have been a refugee all my life': refugees in China in the era of the Second World War – evidence from UNHCR individual case files – Peter Gatrell   151

Section II.II: Refugees and the stateless in Shanghai and beyond

11 'A right to the city': New Villages for the Commoners, the Nantao Safe Zone, and humanitarian internationalism in Shanghai, 1932–40 – Qian Zhu   170
12 Chinese Nationalists, Japanese occupiers, and the European Jewish refugees in Shanghai, 1938–41 – Gao Bei   186
13 Statelessness, national sovereignty, and German and Austrian refugees in China during and after the treaty port era – Sara Halpern   207
14 A moveable feast: the Mir Yeshiva from Vilna to Shanghai and beyond – Jay Winter   224
15 Agents of empathy – Kolleen Guy   247
16 From Shanghai to Australia: Jewish emigrés in the period of the Second World War – Seumas Spark   267

Section II.III: The end of cosmopolitan Shanghai

17 The rise and fall of US military power in China – Zach Fredman   290

Contents

18	From paradise to hell: the downfall of French interests in China – Christian Henriot	308
19	Out of Shanghai – Robert Bickers	333
	Conclusion: statelessness in the global Second World War – Kolleen Guy and Jay Winter	351
	Index	359

Figures

4.1	Mary Behrens, *Run*, 'Baby'.	*page* 47
4.2	Mary Behrens, *Run*, 'Boat'.	48
4.3	Mary Behrens, *Run*, 'Human trail'.	48
4.4	Mary Behrens, *Run*, 'Medusa'.	49
4.5	Mary Behrens, *Run*, 'Mother, child, flee'.	49
4.6	Mary Behrens, *Run*, 'Rug road'.	50
4.7	Mary Behrens, *Run*, 'Twirl'.	50
5.1	Alien Registration Form, Certificate No. 586 for Karl Duldig, © Duldig Studio Museum. Image courtesy of the National Archives of Australia. NAA: B6531, NATURALISED/1946 – 1947/ POLISH/DULDIG KARL.	58
5.2	Ludwig Meilich, 'Happy Birthday to Paul Schlesinger from his poker fellows', 1940, pen and ink, by Ludwig Meilich. © Tatura Internment and POW Camps Museum.	62
5.3	Alfred Figdor, 'POW – Fifth Column Luggage', cover of Camp 3D newsletter *Behind the Fence*, Sept. 1940–Sept. 1941. © Tatura Internment and POW Camps Museum.	63
5.4	Karl Duldig (1902–1986), *Fragment* 1940, redgum, h 44 cm; Collection: Newcastle Art Gallery, Australia 1962013; Photo: Karl Duldig.	64
5.5	Tatura children on a picnic, c. 1941. Photographer unknown.	65

Figures

ix

5.6 Karl Duldig (1902–1986), *Ring-a-ring-a-roses*,
1941, pen and ink, 30.3 × 21.0 cm, signed and dated
l. r. 'K. Duldig Tatura 1941'. © Duldig Studio Museum.   66
6.1 Photograph of Pandelis Klinkatsis, in uniform.
Source: Joy Damousi.   80
6.2 Sophia Damousi, alien registration form, 1957.
Series number: B78, Control Symbol: Greek/
Damousi Sofia. Image courtesy of the National
Archives of Australia. NAA: B78, GREEK/
DAMOUSI SOFIA.   89
14.1 Students and teachers of the exiled Mir Yeshiva
studying in the Sanctuary of the Beth Aharon
Synagogue, Museum Road, Shanghai. 1942.
Courtesy of Rabbi Jacob Ederman. United States
Holocaust Memorial Museum, photo no. 40211.   225
16.1 The Maehrischel clothes shop in Vienna. Source:
Jeannette Abrahams.   271
16.2 Poldi's business card, Shanghai. Source: Jeannette
Abrahams.   272
16.3 The Maehrischel family in Shanghai, c. 1941. Alfred
and Helene (front) with their three children; Karl,
Poldi, and Regina. Poldi is in the centre. Source:
Jeannette Abrahams.   274
19.1 Charles Archer, from *Holly Street Residents*.
Photograph © Tom Hunter, 1998.   348
20.1 Stateless Jewish children in Shanghai, 1946. Arthur
Rothstein. Source: Dr Ann Rothstein Segan, director
of the Arthur Rothstein Legacy Project.   357

Contributors

Peter Balakian, Colgate University

Mary Behrens, independent artist

Robert Bickers, University of Bristol

Joy Damousi, Australian Catholic University

Eva de Jong-Duldig, independent writer

Sheila Fitzpatrick, Australian Catholic University

Zach Fredman, Duke Kunshan University

Gao Bei, University of North Carolina, Wilmington

Peter Gatrell, University of Manchester

Kolleen Guy, Duke Kunshan University

Sara Halpern, Cardiff University

Christian Henriot, Aix-Marseille University

Rana Mitter, Harvard University

Meredith Oyen, University of Maryland, Baltimore County

Seumas Spark, Monash University

Jay Winter, Yale University

Qian Zhu, Duke Kunshan University

Acknowledgements

This book is a collective effort. The first steps were taken by students and colleagues at Duke Kunshan University. Thanks are due to student researchers Giulia de Cristofaro, Emily Gonzales, Susan Lin, Weifan Mo, Nino Nadirashvili, Leiyuan Tian, Meixuan Wang, Jingcheng Wu, and Shuhuai Zhang. Duke Kunshan University support staff Yifei Qi, Ruiyue Ma, and Eugenie Chao provided crucial administrative assistance. Jaden Chee, project research assistant, helped coordinate the international meetings at Kunshan, Barcelona, and Melbourne.

We are grateful to Cesar Alegre Alsina and the staff at the Institute for Educational Study Abroad Barcelona Center, and to Joy Damousi and Ebony Nilsson at the Australian Catholic University for their hospitality. Professor Rai Gaita kindly took the time to join our Melbourne meeting and to deepen our discussion of Hannah Arendt's ideas and their implications for our study of statelessness. We want, as well, to thank Sheila Fitzpatrick for sage advice at the final stage of editing this book.

For student research funding, we acknowledge Duke Kunshan University and the Duke Kunshan University Center for the Study of Contemporary China. The meetings that brought this project to fruition were generously funded by the Duke Kunshan University Humanities Research Center. Without the support of co-directors James Miller and Carlos Rojas, this book would never have seen the light of day.

Abbreviations

AHA	Academia Historica (the National Archives of Taiwan)
AJJDCA	American Jewish Joint Distribution Committee Archives, in Jerusalem
AJMFA	Archives of the Japanese Ministry of Foreign Affairs
BREM	Bureau for the Affairs of Russian Emigrants
CCP	Chinese Communist Party
CER	China Eastern Railway
CFCRA	China–Foreign Charity and Relief Association
CMA	Chongqing Municipal Archives
CNRRA	Chinese National Relief and Rehabilitation Administration
COC	French Garrison
CRB	Central Reserve Bank of China yuan
DP	Displaced person
EYD	Academia Historica (the National Archives of Taiwan), Executive Yuan Documents
FDA	French Diplomatic Archives, Courneuve
FDA Nantes	French Diplomatic Archives, Nantes
FDRLA	Franklin Delano Roosevelt Library and Archives
FMD	Academia Historica (the National Archives of Taiwan), Foreign Ministry Documents
FO	Foreign Office Papers, Kew
HC	Hannah Arendt, *The Human Condition*
HIA	Hebrew Immigrant Aid Society
HUA	Harvard University Archives
ICEM	Intergovernmental Committee for European Migration
ICRC	International Committee of the Red Cross
IGCR	Intergovernmental Committee for Refugees
IRO	International Refugee Organization

Abbreviations xiii

JACAR	Japan Center for Asian Historical Records
JDC	American Jewish Joint Distribution Committee
JDCA	American Jewish Joint Distribution Committee Archives, in New York
MOFA	Ministry of Foreign Affairs (Chinese)
NAA	National Archives of Australia
NARA	United States National Archives and Records Administration
NVC	New Villages for the Commoners
PCIRO	Preparatory Commission of the International Refugee Organization
PRC	People's Republic of China
ROC	Republic of China
RSL	Returned Services League of Australia
RSSAILA	Returned Sailors', Soldiers', Airmen's Imperial League of Australia
SMA	Shanghai Municipal Archives Collection
SMC	Shanghai Municipal Council
SMR	South Manchurian Railway Company
TLIA	Livelihood Improvement Association
TNA	The National Archives, Kew
UNHCR	Office of the United Nations High Commissioner for Refugees
UNRRA	United Nations Relief and Rehabilitation Administration
USHMM	United States Holocaust Memorial Museum
USHMMA	United States Holocaust Memorial Museum Archives
WCC	World Council of Churches
WJCC	World Jewish Congress Collection

Introduction

Kolleen Guy and Jay Winter

In December 2019, the editors of this book visited the Shanghai Jewish Refugees Museum. It was built around the remains of a synagogue, Ohel Moshe, established by Russian immigrants in 1907. In the late 1930s and early 1940s, approximately twenty thousand mostly Austrian and German Jews joined them in Shanghai. The history of this community of refugees has attracted scholars from many different parts of the world.[1] What the editors saw was that there was room for further research placing this story in comparative perspective.

One way forward was to bring out the striking differences and similarities in the forced arrival of German and Austrian internees in Australia. These men, women, and children came from the same social milieux as did the refugees in Shanghai. In 2008, the great Australian historian Ken Inglis launched a project on a parallel topic, and one of the editors of the current book helped see it through to publication after Ken's death in 2017. That study was original in that it was exhaustive, in the sense that it was based on an archival account of every single individual internee who came to Australia from Britain or Singapore and on what happened to them after the war.[2]

In the Shanghai Jewish Refugees Museum, there is a list of Jews who came to China in the years after 1938. Our first thought was to follow the methodology of Inglis's research and to collect as much information as possible on as many individuals as we could find. One of the editors invited her students at Duke Kunshan University to participate in the project. They began the research in 2020, at

2 — *Statelessness after Arendt*

the onset of the COVID-19 pandemic. In August 2021, we invited international scholars who specialised in the history of the period to help us conceptualise the comparison of different refugee groups in Asia and the Pacific during the Second World War. We developed a framework for analysis based on Hannah Arendt's idea of statelessness elaborated in her *Origins of Totalitarianism*. Our agenda was to reinterpret the history of refugees in terms of a challenge to the Arendtian approach to statelessness. Their exclusion from the political domain, we claim, was both crippling and incomplete. What if we found first, *pace* Arendt, that there was a middle ground between full citizenship and the ostracism of statelessness? And secondly, what if during this liminal period, the stateless themselves forged pathways to freedom despite the fact that they had no formal or legal claim to rights?

In the two years that followed, students and scholars continued to work on both questions. We present in this book the cumulative results of their work. The central claim of Part I, 'Perspectives on statelessness', is that there are in the discursive space between statelessness and citizenship cultural forms that frame and drive forward collective and individual efforts to perform both the miseries and the achievements of those unmoored from settled social and political life. As we show throughout the book, there is a continuum not only between those with and without rights, but also between refugees and the stateless. These are not hermetically sealed categories but porous and malleable states of being.

In Section I.II of this book, titled 'Telling the tale of refugees and the stateless: Languages of displacement', we show how people in many parts of the world struggled to comprehend their predicament. Their efforts were expressed in different ways that we term 'languages of displacement'. Language, including words, gestures, performances, and artefacts of many kinds, frames the complex memories of those who, during the course of their lives, lived in flight from persecution. These cultural forms also framed the memories of their descendants.[3] They used poetry, the visual arts, and storytelling at the family level and at the level of published narratives, including history, to make sense of their lives. We present instances of each of these strategies of remembrance in this section.

Our intention in this part of the book is to explore the cultural forms created by the inhabitants of what Peter Gatrell terms

Introduction 3

'refugeedom', wherever they reside and whatever their status. The Second World War is but one chapter in the history of war and displacement in the twentieth century and after. Refugees and the stateless today (2024) construct, with different emphases and inflections, narratives that are similar to those in the past. In this field, comparative history is not an option; it is a necessity. While our principal focus is on the period of the Second World War, we deal with issues in the second part of this book that span the twentieth century and beyond.

Pulitzer-prize winning poet Peter Balakian's voice is that of a man holding in his hands what he terms the 'filaments' of the history of his once stateless Armenian family. His poems explore the way traumatic memory sticks in the dreams and words of generations of survivors of the Armenian genocide. Artist Mary Behrens provides a visual dimension to our understanding of the lives of those caught in 'refugeedom'. She captures fragmentary images of the terror of families fleeing with children, and provides echoes of what Balakian offers in his poetry. We then show in the case of two families – Eva de Jong-Duldig's stateless family and Joy Damousi's refugee family – how those who had been children in flight tell stories of vulnerable and unsettled lives. In sum, this section sets our book in a comparative global framework, and puts the flesh of artistic and literary creativity on the bones of the Arendtian conversation in which we engage in Part I.

Why does a global framework matter? The primary focus of Arendt's work was on Europe and on the failure of the nation-state system to protect minority rights in the 1920s and 1930s. What happens, we ask, when we focus on a similar stateless population in other parts of the world, in particular Asia and the Pacific? What we find is that statelessness is context-dependent; to be stateless in China is not at all the same as to be stateless in Czechoslovakia. The very weakness of sovereignty in China accounts for its attractiveness as a safe-haven for the stateless. The history of those who had found refuge in Shanghai and then lost it after 1945 tells us much about the different trajectories and treatment of the stateless in different parts of the world. As we have already noted, it also discloses strategies of survival that resemble those developed by the stateless in other parts of the world both before and after the Second World War. Resemblance is not replication; each stateless population

4 *Statelessness after Arendt*

writes its own transnational story. Only a global approach can do justice to such a multifaceted phenomenon.[4]

In Part II of the book, we turn explicitly to Asia, the Pacific, and the Antipodes. There, we explore varieties of statelessness in China and in other parts of Asia in the 1930s and during the global Second World War. There is no one story of statelessness in China, but many different forms of statelessness, including exclusion from the official history of the period. In Section II.II, we narrow our focus to Shanghai, and present facets of the experience of statelessness in this unique city, one of the few that did not require that new residents have a visa before entering it.

Here we explore the fate of a substantial community of Jewish people who escaped persecution and death. Some were observant; others were not. In either case, their cultural resources helped fuel their resilience under very straitened circumstances. They were helped materially by prominent Jewish families in Shanghai and by international supporters, in particular the American Jewish Joint Distribution Committee. Together they ran cafés, theatres, schools, and hospitals; published newspapers; organised sporting clubs; ran synagogues; and kept intact the sense that they were the authors of their lives. Their acts said that they were a people with a collective identity, a common cause, and had a future they themselves were determined to forge. Through these efforts, stateless people engaged in a kind of politics long before they reached the threshold of freedom. Here is a global story that needs to be told in a global context; focusing exclusively on Europe or North America is no longer an option in this field of research.

Section II.III is titled 'The end of cosmopolitan Shanghai'. Here we explore the unravelling of the unusual world of compromised sovereignty in China in the 1940s. One reason why European refugees and the stateless flocked to Shanghai was that that city was cosmopolitan in a legal sense. When the war against Japan came to an end, the city of Shanghai was, legally and politically, re-nationalised. The old privileges of European powers disappeared, and so did the place refugees and the stateless occupied in it. When the captains and the kings departed, the vast majority of foreigners in China – refugees, the stateless, and those in between – were forced to go.

In Europe and the Atlantic world, there were massive population movements too, but none of them mirrored the unique situation in

Introduction 5

China and in the Pacific. This section demonstrates that changing power structures over the period 1937–49 determined the fate of the stateless in China, first presenting a safe-haven and then shutting it down. The families of the children shown in the last image in the book had to leave Shanghai, not because the Chinese people were ungenerous, but because the new Chinese state broke with the past.

Section II.III of this book shows that when we turn away from Europe and the Atlantic, and investigate refugee lives in Asia and the Pacific region, we encounter systems of compromised sovereignty that framed both the positive and negative facets of refugee life. Imperialism made Shanghai a safe-haven in the late 1930s for refugees. But Shanghai – and the rest of Asia – changed when imperial domination, Japanese, British, French or Dutch, came to an end after the Second World War. The decline of imperial power did not make the place of refugees in this region more secure; on the contrary. The stateless had to leave. That is one important point highlighted in the last section of this book.

In our conclusion, we return to Arendt's original contribution, and suggest ways of going beyond her pioneering work. Not all refugees were (or are) stateless, and not all of the stateless were (or are) refugees, but they all shared the experience of being unmoored in a world of states. This book shows how men and women in parts of Asia and the Pacific region in the period of the Second World War responded to the challenges of statelessness and struggled to regain what Charles Maier calls their 'civic anchorage'.[5]

No one book can do justice to the varied history of refugees and the stateless in the Asian theatre of the Second World War. What we offer is an array of studies that permit comparison with the many valuable works that have appeared on the topic in the European and North American context.[6] Much has been gained from recent writing on warfare and its consequences from a transnational, comparative, and global framework. We hope we point the way forward to further scholarship in the transnational history of refugees, the stateless, and displaced people in the century of total war.[7]

There is a clear and present need today to recognise the special features of statelessness that continue to haunt our world. This book aims at escaping from a focus limited to Europe and North America, and instead addresses the global nature of refugee flows

6 *Statelessness after Arendt*

during the period of the Second World War.[8] Only by adopting such a broad comparative view can we do justice not only to the circumstances faced by the stateless, but also to their human agency in surviving and transcending statelessness.[9]

Notes

1 Marcia Reynders Ristaino, *Port of Last Resort: The Diaspora Communities of Shanghai* (Stanford, CA: Stanford University Press, 2001); David Kranzler, *Japanese, Nazis, and Jews: The Jewish Refugee Community of Shanghai* (New York: Ktav Publishing, 1988); Steve Hochstadt, *Exodus to Shanghai: Stories of Escape from the Third Reich* (New York: Palgrave Macmillan, 2012). Among memoirs, see Sigmund Tobias, *Strange Haven: A Jewish Childhood in Wartime Shanghai* (Urbana, IL: University of Illinois Press, 1999); Samuel Iwry, *To Wear the Dust of War* (New York: Palgrave Macmillan, 2004); Ursula Bacon, *Shanghai Diary: A Young Girl's Journey from Hitler's Hate to War-Torn China* (Milwaukie, OR: Milestone Books, 2004); Irene Eber (ed.), *Voices from Shanghai: Jewish Exiles in Wartime China* (Chicago, IL: University of Chicago Press, 2008).
2 Ken Inglis, Seumas Spark, Jay Winter, with Carol Bunyan, *Dunera Lives: A Visual History* (Melbourne: Monash University Publishers, 2018); Ken Inglis, Bill Gammage, Seumas Spark, Jay Winter, with Carol Bunyan, *Dunera Lives: Profiles* (Melbourne: Monash University Publishers, 2020).
3 Jay Winter, *War beyond Words: Languages of Remembrance from the Great War to the Present* (Cambridge: Cambridge University Press, 2017).
4 On statelessness in Europe today (2024), see the website of the European network on statelessness at https://www.statelessness.eu/. Accessed 20 November 2024. On the United Nations Human Rights Commission's work in this field, see their website 'Global focus' at https://reporting.unhcr.org/spotlight/statelessness. Accessed 20 November 2024. On the Middle East and North Africa, see the MENA statelessness website at https://www.statelessmena.com/. Accessed 20 November 2024. See too the Institute on Statelessness and Inclusion (ISI) website at https://www.institutesi.org/pages/covid19_and_statelessness. Accessed 20 November 2024. There are many other similar initiatives with a global perspective.

Introduction

5 Charles Maier, 'On *Statelessness: A Modern History*, the Francesco Guicciardini Prize Forum', *Cambridge Review of International Affairs*, 36, 1 (2023), pp. 109–12.

6 In particular, see Mira Siegelberg, *Statelessness: A Modern History* (Cambridge, MA: Harvard University Press, 2020).

7 On the transnational, see Jay Winter (ed.), *The Cambridge History of the First World War*, 3 vols. (Cambridge: Cambridge University Press, 2014).

8 For an up-to-date discussion of statelessness in Asia, see Michelle Foster, Jaclyn Neo, and Christopher Sperfeldt (eds), *Statelessness in Asia* (Cambridge: Cambridge University Press, 2024).

9 On the term 'agency' and its use in historical research, see Anna Yu Krylova, William Sewell, Judith Walkowitz, and Geoff Eley, 'The Agency Dilemma', *American Historical Review*, 128, 2 (2023), pp. 883–937.

Part I

Perspectives on statelessness

Section I.I

Statelessness and the refugee predicament: a conversation

1

Statelessness and the burden of our times

Jay Winter

'Wohl dem, der keine Heimat hat; er sieht sie noch im Traum.'
'Blessed is he who has no homeland; he sees it still in his dreams.'

Hannah Arendt[1]

Samuel Johnson, the story goes, once said that every time he reflected on moral problems, it was like climbing slowly up a mountain; and every time he did so, he saw Plato coming down the other side. With respect to the problem of statelessness, the descending thinker whom we encounter is Hannah Arendt. She set the terms of our conversations about statelessness, including this one.

This book engages time and again with her thinking on statelessness. We first outline her position on the problem of the *Heimatlosen*, those without a nationality or those without citizenship or both. We then consider ways in which the stateless themselves found political, cultural, and social answers to their predicament. We do so in a different framework from that usually associated with Arendt's work. By choosing the domain of Asia, the Pacific, and the Antipodes in the period of the Second World War, we show that statelessness varied in different theatres of war and that the stateless themselves in these areas constructed pathways out of their loss of citizenship during and after the war that differed in some respects from those of refugees in Europe. Essential to their efforts was the construction and performance of new narratives of their lives as people with the courage and capacity to live what Arendt, following Aristotle, termed a political life.[2] The nascent politics of the stateless, we argue, constituted a third way between citizenship and statelessness, one recognised in part by Hannah Arendt herself in her 1958 publication *The Human Condition*.

The Arendtian divide

Hannah Arendt's diagnosis of the plight of the stateless is at the heart of her analysis of the crisis of interwar Europe. The collapse of the political order established after the Great War arose, she believed, from the degeneration of states whose citizens were equal under the law to inegalitarian nations. The racial character of these nation-states crystallised at a time of imperial expansion before 1914[3] and undermined the Paris peace settlement of 1919 by exposing the impossibility of maintaining its commitment to protecting the rights of national minorities. From 1918 onwards, millions of men and women lost the protection of citizenship and were forced to seek shelter in other countries. They then came to constitute what Arendt termed the burden of our times, since no state was prepared to take them in. The Nazi seizure of power in 1933 only worsened the already existing problem of statelessness. Arendt herself was one of these bearers of the bad news that the international order, with Europe at its centre, was built on quicksand.[4] There was more than a touch of bitterness in her account of the fate she shared with millions of innocent stateless people. That is why the line of poetry I cite at the beginning of this chapter can be read in different ways; irony, after all, is saying one thing and meaning another. Can we really believe that those who had to flee their homeland are happy to dream about what they had lost?

The structure of this introductory chapter is straightforward. First, we consider Arendt's powerful description of the fate of the stateless in the period after the First World War. We will then discuss how the stateless acted to survive statelessness and then to move beyond the imprisonment their status inflicted on them. While the injuries of their descent into statelessness were ineradicable, what Arendt would call their political life began long before they achieved citizenship and safety in the post-1945 period. Aspects of her own life and thought support this revision of her early interpretation of statelessness. This book is, therefore, both an homage to Arendt, as the major theorist of statelessness, and an effort to go beyond

14   *Perspectives on statelessness*

the interpretation of statelessness she published in *The Origins of Totalitarianism* in 1951.[5]

Statelessness: Arendt's diagnosis

Statelessness, Hannah Arendt wrote, turns civilised people into savages. The distinction forced on millions of people in the inter-war period and beyond is between those excluded or outcast from political society and those embraced by a polity whose public life gives their individual lives a meaning, a significance, a destination. The stateless, she wrote, are without profession, without citizenship, without an opinion that counts, 'without a deed with which to identify' themselves, without the capacity to express themselves, and to act 'upon a common world'. In sum, their lives lose 'all significance'.

What remains to those who lose 'legal personality' are

> those qualities which usually can become articulate only in the sphere of private life and must remain unqualified, mere existence in all matters of public concern. This mere existence, that is, all that which is mysteriously given us by birth and which includes the shape of our bodies and the talents of our minds, can be adequately dealt with only by the unpredictable hazards of friendship and sympathy, or by the great and incalculable grace of love, which says with Augustine, '*Volo ut sis* (I want you to be)', without being able to give any particular reason for such supreme and unsurpassable affirmation.[6]

Beyond such acts of grace in private lives is a world of collective creativity in the public sphere that the stateless cannot touch, share, or enjoy.[7] No claim to natural rights or human rights can affect their exclusion from the political community. Once expelled from the political world, they are deprived completely of agency, and progressively descend into becoming a mass of people whose existence has no meaning other than that they can be incarcerated, used for labour like beasts in the field, and destroyed when no longer useful. 'The survivors of the extermination camps, the inmates of concentration and internment camps, and even the comparatively happy stateless people could see ... that the abstract nakedness of being nothing but human was their greatest danger.'[8]

Statelessness and the burden of our times   15

The problem of what to do with the stateless undermined the rule of law and transformed the police powers of the nations faced with handling them. A person without a state was 'an anomaly for whom there is no appropriate niche in the framework of the general law'. He was therefore 'an outlaw by definition' and 'completely at the mercy of the police, which itself did not worry too much about committing a few illegal acts in order to diminish the country's burden of *indésirables*'.[9] In other words, the state, 'insisting on its sovereign right of expulsion, was forced by the illegal nature of statelessness into admittedly illegal acts'.[10] Inevitably, the police took on powers well before the Second World War to deal with the stateless independently of both law and political instructions. The greater the flow of refugees, the more completely were the police 'emancipated' from both.[11]

Here was one of the sources of the totalitarian temperament, in so-called democracies as well as in dictatorships. In sum,

> The clearer the proof of their inability to treat stateless people as legal persons and the greater the extension of arbitrary rule by police decree, the more difficult it is for states to resist the temptation to deprive all citizens of legal status and rule them with an omnipotent police.[12]

The phenomenon of camps preceded the interwar crisis of statelessness. Indeed, it arose out of the policing of indigenous populations during the expansion of imperial rule at the end of the nineteenth century. But by the 1930s, and emphatically after the declaration of war in 1939, in many countries, including Britain, France, Germany, and Russia, it became clear that 'the only practical substitute for a nonexistent homeland was an internment camp. Indeed, … this was the only "country" the world had to offer the stateless.'[13]

What Arendt showed was the extent to which the stateless exposed the fragility of the European legal system. The very presence of the stateless destabilised the status of resident aliens. 'Once a number of stateless people were admitted to an otherwise normal country, statelessness spread like a contagious disease. Not only were naturalized citizens in danger of reverting to the status of statelessness, but living conditions for all aliens markedly deteriorated.'[14] Worst of all, for Arendt, was that the only stable or safe status the stateless could seek was to become criminals. Then they

16 *Perspectives on statelessness*

would be judged and punished according to the only laws of their country of residence applicable to them. Here is Arendt's formulation of the way statelessness turned the stateless into pariahs:

> The stateless person, without right to residence and without the right to work, had of course constantly to transgress the law. He was liable to jail sentences without ever committing a crime. More than that, the entire hierarchy of values which pertain in civilized countries was reversed in his case. Since he was the anomaly for whom the general law did not provide, it was better for him to become an anomaly for which it did provide, that of the criminal.[15]

Those stateless people who were not criminals had no rights at all. Here is the point at which Arendt came to her celebrated conclusion.

> We became aware of the existence of a right to have rights (and that means to live in a framework where one is judged by one's actions and opinions) and a right to belong to some kind of organized community, only when millions of people emerged who had lost and could not regain these rights because of the new global political situation.[16]

That situation applied not only to the Jews, the homeless people par excellence, but also to minorities turned refugees without a homeland and without another state prepared to welcome them. Statelessness was not only a condition, but also a symptom of the failure of the international system during the period of the two world wars.

Varieties of statelessness

Individuals and political groups did lose their citizenship before the First World War, but we can date from 1914 the emergence of statelessness as both a condition suffered by millions and a challenge to the state system that emerged from the world conflict.

After 1914, statelessness was a house of many mansions, most of them dangerous. Lacking the protection of a state made it difficult for those who had fled from their homeland to secure the right of entry into another state or the right to work there, once admitted. People without papers were easy targets for criminals who knew that going to the local police carried risks of arrest and deportation.

Statelessness and the burden of our times   17

To remedy some of these problems, the League of Nations issued what were termed 'Nansen passports', named after the Norwegian High Commissioner for refugees. His first objective was to protect approximately eight hundred thousand Russian emigrés who had lost their citizenship by fleeing Bolshevik Russia. Later in the 1920s, Armenians, Assyrian, Bulgarian, and Turkish refugees were issued with Nansen passports, and others benefited from them. This passport did not guarantee the right to return to the country of origin, but it did act, solely for purposes of official identification, as a letter of transit for displaced persons. In this respect, the League of Nations was acting as a surrogate legal entity, though not a state.

Not all refugees were stateless, and not all stateless people were refugees. But all of these unmoored men, women, and children were people who did not fit into the state system established through the peace treaties following the Great War. One major reason why so many people were in difficulty was that the minority protections embedded in the peace treaties meant only as much as sovereign states wanted them to mean. In most cases, state sovereignty trumped the treaties, propelling even more people out of their homelands to seek shelter in a world where the nineteenth-century freedom of movement had come to an end. The gates came down in the United States in the early 1920s, and after the onset of the world financial crisis in 1929, economic turmoil bred political turmoil, leading in the following decade to a massive increase in the flow of refugees, in particular from Germany, Spain, and China.[17]

War began in China before it engulfed Europe in 1939, but in the aftermath of the Allied victory in 1945, the problem of displaced people became even more difficult to handle. Statelessness was a condition folded into the overall refugee problem, with a consensus forming around the idea that, while refugee flows are inevitable, the stateless should all be converted into national citizens. In the seventy-five years since the end of the Second World War, no such conversion has taken place.

Transcending statelessness

As Mira Siegelberg has shown, the problem of statelessness entered into political theory at the same time as it became a perennial

18 *Perspectives on statelessness*

headache in international politics.[18] Hannah Arendt's writings on refugees and on totalitarianism hinge on her presentation of a radical distinction between citizenship and statelessness. She lost the first in 1933 and lived in the second for eighteen years. This was the period in which she wrote her first major intervention in political theory, published in Britain as *The Burden of Our Times*, and in the United States as *The Origins of Totalitarianism*.

In 1972, in Arendt's later years, her close friend Mary McCarthy pointed out to her in an open debate in Toronto that her *modus operandi* is like that of Aristotle. Her first step is to make a radical distinction, one that bifurcates the world, and then to see where the distinction she establishes leads.[19] Arendt agreed completely. There is no better instance of her Aristotelian approach than her treatment of statelessness and citizenship. They stand opposed to each other as do night and day, sickness and health, life and death.[20]

And yet, while her devastating diagnosis of statelessness as a disease produced by a failed political order stands the test of time, there is much more to say about the liminal space occupied by stateless men and women ejected from their homelands without finding a shelter abroad. As we shall show in a moment, in *The Human Condition*,[21] Arendt herself provided a number of suggestions about how the stateless acted politically even before they achieved citizenship.

This book focuses on that middle ground, that no-man's-land of living without formal rights, and suggests that the stateless themselves were by no means inert or silent. They had a voice. They were to a degree, and with substantial assistance from allies, the authors of their own recovery.

The boundaries of the political

There are two ways of constructing the story of how the stateless overcame their predicament. The first follows French philosopher Jacques Rancière[22] and others[23] who develop a performative interpretation of rights. That is, they suggest that those without rights develop, through protest, a political language that performs the injustice of their deprivation. They stage their rightlessness as a jarring dissensus over who should be heard in the political arena,

Statelessness and the burden of our times

and often (though not always) 'enact' equality despite their exclusion from the community of those with rights. Politics start here, as a dispute over inequality, and not, as in Arendt, as a conversation among equals. For Rancière, rights emerge through a contest between opposing views as to who should have the right to define the boundary between what Aristotle terms the political life (*bios politikos*) and mere life (*zoē*). The threshold for entering the political domain is not fixed, but is approached through the language and action – that is, the praxis – of those initially excluded from the political realm.

Rancière did not contest Arendt's assertion that in the 1930s, those without rights lost 'the entire social texture in which they were born and in which they established for themselves a distinct place in the world'.[24] What he could not accept was her claim that they thereby had lost 'all human relationships'. She put this claim in no uncertain terms: when men and women lost their citizenship, as she did in the 1930s, and when sovereign states made it impossible for them to find a safe harbour where they could be protected by the laws of another state, they were effectively expelled 'from humanity altogether'.[25] Here we see the imprint of Arendt's Aristotelianism in defining the good life, the life in which human beings realise their full potential, as the political life. Viewed from Greek or Roman practice, statelessness resembled banishment. Having annoyed powerful enemies, Ovid was sent to live in a land where they spoke a language he did not understand. No language; no politics.[26]

The poignancy of Arendt's argument arose out of her deep awareness that she herself had survived the Nazis' expulsion order not only from Germany but from humanity. Where Rancière parts company with her is over whether the stateless, under various circumstances, actually do enter the political arena even without the right to do so. By challenging their exclusion from the political world, they perform and sometimes even shift the boundary that Arendt takes as given.

This is the sum and substance of Rancière's paradoxical claim that 'the Rights of Man are the rights of those who have not the rights they have'. By this, he means that those excluded from the political realm are humans who have the right to act politically by disputing their exclusion and by embodying the contradictions of the arrangements that exclude them. Their disturbing presence

20 *Perspectives on statelessness*

among those who are not excluded highlights the injustice of their condition. They show that thinking about rights means thinking about wrongs. By questioning the boundaries of the political, such stateless men and women show that they too live a political life.[27] Starting as pariahs, the stateless transform themselves into the carriers of dissensus over the central question as to who has the right to have rights. This is the first step on their road to freedom.

Liberating narratives

The second step is also embedded in seizing control of language, through seizing the right to tell the story of chaotic times. This is much more difficult than it may appear, since Arendt herself accepted that traditional narratives of the past have been exploded by the violence of our times. In this respect, she followed faithfully a path already sketched by her friend Walter Benjamin, like her a stateless exile in France. He had given some of his most powerful unpublished writings to Arendt, who, thirty years after his suicide in 1940, was responsible for their publication.[28] In these papers were major statements about history, memory, and storytelling. Historian Reinhard Koselleck, like Arendt a student of Heidegger, formalised later some of the issues that Benjamin and Arendt confronted. In Koselleck's words, our ideas of historical time are framed by the coupling of the sphere of experience – the past – and the horizon of expectations – the future.[29] What happens, Benjamin, Arendt, and Koselleck asked, when these two are severed irrevocably?

In *The Human Condition*, published in 1958, seven years after *The Origins of Totalitarianism*, Arendt accepted that her essential linkage of freedom with sovereignty left out millions of human beings. Their fate was a dark one: 'the simultaneous presence of freedom and non-sovereignty, of being able to begin something new and of not being able to control or even foretell its consequences, seems almost to force us to the conclusion that human existence is absurd'. And yet, she admitted, crucially for our study, that human beings still retain the 'freedom to act' despite the fact that 'the actor never remains the master of his acts'. This admission opens up the space for what I term the nascent autonomy of the stateless. What if 'our notion that freedom and non-sovereignty are

Statelessness and the burden of our times

mutually exclusive' is false or perhaps incomplete? What if we fail to see that 'the capacity for action' does indeed 'harbor within itself certain potentialities which enable it to survive the disabilities of non-sovereignty?'[30]

If so, Arendt continues, we might find a way out of a meaningless existence through 'the interrelated faculties of action and speech which produce meaningful stories as fabrication produces use objects'.[31] Here is the opening we explore in this book. Storytelling is the precondition for political life, open to the stateless as much as it is to the citizen. Here we follow the insights of anthropologist Michael Jackson: collectives exist through the stories they tell about themselves in a conflict-ridden world.[32]

Political theorist Seyla Benhabib has further developed this argument. She shares with Arendt the view that recounting the story of one's life and that of one's world is an essential human activity, without which we cannot preserve our identities. Those who have lived a fragmented political life, one in which citizenship was lost and statelessness endured, Benhabib writes, told their stories in new ways. Both Arendt and Benjamin believed that the storyteller in our times must dive below the surface to find 'whatever pearls could be recovered from the debris'.[33] From these fragments, the storyteller creates what Benhabib terms a 'redemptive narrative', in the sense of 'redeeming the memory of the dead, the defeated and the vanquished by making present to us once more their failed hopes, their untrodden paths, and unfulfilled dreams'.[34] Whether or not either Arendt or Benjamin would have accepted Benhabib's word 'redemptive', both held the view that, for the stateless, the art of storytelling was essential to the arts of survival.

Others have developed Benhabib's argument even further to claim that the stateless and refugees, having endured the 'moral shock' of 'radical evil', use storytelling to reconstruct their own 'political subjecthood'.[35] Here they draw on other parts of Arendt's writings, in which there are many references to the arts of storytelling. 'With speech and action', Arendt wrote, 'we insert ourselves into the human world'.[36] During the unstable years of statelessness, Arendt knew very well that doing so entailed risks, but she was unrepentant in her view that the stateless should not hide who they were. That is the source of her identification, in the 1930s and 1940s, with the Zionist movement. Its adherents stood up proudly as Jews and, she believed, had to fight Hitler as Jews. They had to stand up and be counted, not only as human beings, but also as Jews, the primary target of the Nazis. To do so was an act of storytelling, one that outcasts like Arendt turned into a political necessity. In a sense, much of her writing is a creative refashioning of the story of her own life, from statelessness to freedom. What pariahs like her achieved was the 'artistic transposition of individual experiences'.[37]

Julia Kristeva, among other writers and cultural critics, sees storytelling as an intrinsically political act.[38] Listening to or reading a story, individuals enter what Arendt called 'a space of appearance' shared with those who hear it or read it. The framing of such a space 'pre-dates and precedes all formal constitution of the public realm'.[39] Storytelling informs and to a degree frames the construction and operation of the political domain itself.

Critical theorist Judith Butler takes a similar line when exploring what she calls 'postnational forms of political opposition' to 'the massive problem of statelessness'.[40] In conversation with Gayatri Spivak, Butler uses the term 'postnational' to characterise the efforts of those without rights to develop 'forms of resistance, agency and counter-mobilisation that elude or stall state-power'.[41] Butler cites the example of Hispanic undocumented migrants in the United States insisting on singing in Spanish the American national anthem, much to the annoyance of then American President George W. Bush. When they sing 'what so proudly we hailed', the 'we' thus affirmed in song by those without rights is the 'we', that band of equals, in Arendt's terms, capable of acting within the political domain. Following Rancière's argument, Butler notes that

> They have no right of free speech under the law although they're speaking freely, precisely in order to demand the right to speak freely. They are exercising these rights, which does not mean that they will 'get' them. The demand is the incipient moment of the rights claim, its exercise, but not for that reason its efficacy.[42]

The route out of statelessness is forged outside of the political realm by those not entitled to act politically; their proto-political existence emerges from that 'state of the social that takes form in discourse and other modes of articulation, including song'.[43] Those lyrics and harmonies perform the contradictions of statelessness.[44]

Conclusion

In effect, what Arendt achieved in *The Human Condition* is a softening of the rigid distinction she drew in *The Origins of Totalitarianism* between statelessness and citizenship. Already in the late 1950s, Arendt provided clues to the exploration of a third pathway, that of the emerging or nascent autonomy of the stateless. That pathway is the subject of this book.

We draw upon this reading of Arendt to suggest that her ideas both help us diagnose the injuries of statelessness and suggest ways in which men and women imagined their way out of it. The forms of their creativity are writ large in this book. As Seumas Spark notes in Chapter 16, over two thousand German and Austrian internees were deported from Britain to Australia in 1940. They were deemed 'enemy aliens' and constituted a potential security threat, since the Nazis may have harboured spies among these mostly Jewish refugees. The fear behind this decision, approved by Churchill himself, was part of the panic induced by the disaster of Dunkirk. Invasion was a possibility, and so was the presence in Britain of a hidden 'fifth column' of Nazi agents. Now we see this decision as a fantasy, but no one could be sure at the time that all German- or Austrian-born refugees in Britain were what they said they were: anti-Nazi.[45]

In July 1940, these internees sailed from Liverpool to Australia on the transport ship the *Dunera*. While at sea, three internees, all stateless, wrote on toilet paper a constitution to frame their lives to come in internment camps. In doing so, they were seizing the narrative and making it into their own.[46] When the organisers of a theatre in Shanghai wondered how far they could go in criticising their past and present governors, they were probing the boundaries of their own political existence. When stateless people in Harbin found ways to use statelessness strategically, they were shaping the system from which they had been excluded.

This book is, then, an account of the ways in which stateless people in Asia, the Pacific, and the Antipodes found particular stories to tell about themselves and the people around them. Not all stories were transformative, but the fact that some individuals and groups fashioned new identities out of older ones, or permanently broke with their own past, gave them the material to link together what

24 *Perspectives on statelessness*

had been severed – the sphere of their experiences and the horizon of their expectations.

The framework of this study may be seen as twofold in character. First, we show the power of Arendt's diagnosis of statelessness, etched with acid on the pages of *The Origins of Totalitarianism*. Secondly, we draw on other and later elements of her thought, in particular from her 1958 study *The Human Condition*, to recover the tale of the entry of the stateless into a form of politics growing organically out of the social construction of stories. Arendt is right in assuming that politics is a way of exchanging stories about the perennial and yet tragic search for freedom. Who better than the unfree to imagine a world other than the one into which they have fallen?

The problem remains, though, that discourse alone cannot break the stranglehold on rights that keeps the stateless permanently vulnerable or in various forms of bondage. Following Michel de Certeau, our study shows that not all social practices can be collapsed into discourse.[47] Social and cultural mobilisation of many kinds, mostly at the local level, put flesh and bones on the discursive claim to rights. Many of these sub-national or transnational forms of activism took place in cities where large migrant populations lived. Shanghai is one such metropolitan centre in which we can trace the transition from statelessness to new forms of political mobilisation.

There is much to be learned from the history of refugees in Asia and the Pacific that is not visible in work on the stateless in Europe. A state system torn up by Japanese imperialism had a very different character than that torn up by fascism and communism in Europe. The room for manoeuvre exploited by 'agents of empathy', in Kolleen Guy's terms,[48] was perhaps greater in Asia than in Europe, where the hegemonic power of the Nazi empire strangled many attempts to help the stateless. During the Second World War, American racism and heightened chauvinism made the plight of the stateless pale in comparison to the need to defend the well-being of the home population. The complex mix of liberalism and illiberalism in the British Empire and the Commonwealth in the 1940s is a story with its own special aspects. The problem of the Russian stateless in Asia also showed unique features that Sheila Fitzpatrick has studied. In sum, a shift in the centre of gravity of the study of

Statelessness and the burden of our times   25

statelessness and refugee life to Asia, the Pacific, and the Antipodes has opened up new sources, new conversations, and new enquiries we hope other scholars will explore in future.[49] After all, what is the purpose of pioneering comparative studies like this one, if not to present a point from which to move on?

Notes

1　Hannah Arendt, *Heureux celui qui n'a pas de patrie: Poèmes de pensée*, trans. François Mathieu (Paris: Payot, 2015), pp. 102–3. The English translation is by Jay Winter.

2　On that term in Aristotle, see Richard Mulgan, 'Aristotle and the Value of Political Participation', *Political Theory*, 18, 2 (1990), pp. 195–215.

3　Caroline Elkins, *Legacy of Violence: A History of the British Empire* (London: Bodley Head, 2022).

4　Hannah Arendt, 'We Refugees', *Menorah Journal*, 21 (1943), pp. 69–77.

5　The British edition, published by Secker & Warburg in 1951, was titled *The Burden of Our Times*. The American edition was published by Schocken Books in the same year. Citations here are from the American edition, hereafter cited as '*Origins*'.

6　*Origins*, p. 302. On this phrase, see Lyndsey Stonebridge, *We Are Free to Change the World: Hannah Arendt's Lessons in Love and Disobedience* (London: Jonathan Cape, 2024), ch. 4.

7　Serena Parekh, 'Hannah Arendt and the Ontological Deprivation of Statelessness', in her *Refugees and the Ethics of Forced Displacement* (London: Routledge, 2016), pp. 82–103.

8　*Origins*, p. 300.

9　Ibid., p. 283.

10　Ibid., p. 284.

11　Ibid., p. 287.

12　Ibid., p. 290.

13　Ibid., p. 284.

14　Ibid., p. 285.

15　Ibid., p. 286.

16　Ibid. pp. 296–7. See also Hannah Arendt and Ruth Martin, 'Nation-State and Democracy', *Arendt Studies*, 1 (2017), pp. 7–12.

17　On interwar refugees, see Peter Gatrell, *The Making of the Modern Refugee* (Oxford: Oxford University Press, 2013); and Claudena M. Skran, *Refugees in Inter-War Europe: The Emergence of a Regime* (Oxford: Clarendon Press, 1995). The word 'regime' is problematic. See

Davide Rodogno, *Night on Earth* (Cambridge: Cambridge University Press, 2022).

18 Myra Siegelberg, *Statelessness: A Modern History* (Cambridge, MA: Harvard University Press, 2020).

19 McCarthy's point is published in Melvyn A. Hill (ed.), *Hannah Arendt: The Recovery of the Public World* (New York: St Martin's Press, 1979), p. 338. For the link with Aristotle's method, see Andrea Falcon, 'Aristotle's Theory of Division', *Bulletin of the Institute of Classical Studies*, in Supplement, no. 68, Aristotle and after (1997), Supplement, pp. 127–46.

20 On Arendt's tendency to make radical distinctions that go too far, see Martin Jay, 'Women in Dark Times: Agnes Heller and Hannah Arendt', in his *Force Fields: Between Intellectual History and Cultural Critique* (New York: Routledge, 1993), pp. 61–70.

21 Hannah Arendt, *The Human Condition* (Chicago, IL: University of Chicago Press, 1958), 2nd ed. 1998 (hereafter cited as 'HC').

22 Jacques Rancière, 'Who Is the Subject of the Rights of Man?', *South Atlantic Quarterly*, 103, 2/3 (2004), pp. 297–310.

23 Andrew Schaap, 'Enacting the Right to Have Rights: Jacques Rancière's Critique of Hannah Arendt', *European Journal of Political Theory*, 10, 1 (2011), pp. 22–45; and James D. Ingram, 'The Subject of the Politics of Recognition: Hannah Arendt and Jacques Rancière', in G. Bertram, R. Celikates, C. Laudou, and D. Lauer (eds), *Socialité et reconnaissance: Grammaires de l'humain* (Paris: L'Harmattan, 2006), pp. 229–45.

24 *Origins*, p. 293.

25 Ibid., p. 297.

26 See David Malouf, *An Imaginary Life* (London: Chatto & Windus, 1978).

27 Rancière, 'Who Is the Subject', pp. 302–3.

28 Walter Benjamin, *Illuminations*, trans. Harry Zohn (New York: Harcourt, Brace & World, 1969), edited and with an introduction by Hannah Arendt.

29 Reinhart Koselleck, *Futures Past: On the Semantics of Historical Time*, trans. Keith Tribe (New York: Columbia University Press, 2004).

30 HC, pp. 235–6.

31 Ibid., p. 236.

32 Michael Jackson, *The Politics of Storytelling: Violence, Transgression and Intersubjectivity* (Copenhagen: Museum Tusculanum Press, 2002).

33 Seyla Benhabib, 'Hannah Arendt and the Redemptive Power of Narrative', *Social Research*, 57, 1 (1990), pp. 167–96.

34 Benhabib, 'Hannah Arendt', p. 139.

35 Cindy Horst and Odin Lysaker, 'Miracles in Dark Times: Hannah Arendt and Refugees as "Vanguard"', *Journal of Refugee Studies*, 34, 1 (2019), pp. 71–2.

36 HC, p. 177.

37 Ibid., p. 50.

38 Julia Kristeva, *Hannah Arendt: Life is a Narrative*, trans. Frank Collins (Toronto, ON: University of Toronto Press, 2000); Lisa J. Disch, 'More Truth Than Fact: Storytelling as Critical Understanding in the Writings of Hannah Arendt', *Political Theory*, 21, 4 (1993), pp. 665–94; and Monika Krause, 'Undocumented Migrants: An Arendtian Perspective', *European Journal of Political Theory*, 7, 3 (2008), pp. 331–48.

39 HC, p. 199.

40 Judith Butler and Gayatri Chakravorty Spivak, *Who Sings the Nation-State? Language, Politics, Belonging* (Oxford: Seagull Books, 2008), p. 41.

41 Ibid., p. 42.

42 Ibid., p. 64.

43 Ibid., p. 65.

44 Ibid., p. 66.

45 Ken Inglis, Seumas Spark, and Jay Winter, with Carol Bunyan, *Dunera Lives: A Visual History* (Melbourne: Monash University Publishers, 2018), pp. 41–72.

46 Ken Inglis et al., *Dunera Lives: A Visual History*, pp. xviii, 69, 85–91.

47 Michel de Certeau, *The Practice of Everyday Life*, trans. Steven Rendall (Berkeley, CA: University of California Press, 1984).

48 We leave aside here Arendt's distaste for empathy as the enemy of action. To measure or to refute her argument would require an essay in itself.

49 On today's parallels, see Masha Gessen, '"The Right to Have Rights" and the Plight of the Stateless', *New Yorker*, May 2018; and Jeremy Adelman, 'Pariah: Can Hannah Arendt Help Us Re-Think the Global Refugee Crisis?', *Wilson Quarterly*, 40, 2 (Spring 2016); Megan Bradley, 'Rethinking Refugeehood: Statelessness, Repatriation, and Refugee Agency', *Review of International Studies*, 40 (2014), pp. 101–23; Patrick Hayden, 'From Exclusion to Containment: Arendt, Sovereign Power, and Statelessness', *Societies without Borders*, 3 (2008), pp. 248–69; Siobhan Kattago, 'Statelessness, Refugees, and Hospitality: Reading Arendt and Kant in the Twenty-First Century', *New German Critique*, 46, 1 (2019), pp. 15–40; and Tara Zahra, 'The Return of No-Man's Land: Europe's Asylum Crisis and Historical Memory', *Foreign Affairs*, 22 September 2015.

2

A response

Peter Gatrell

Jay Winter invites us to engage with Hannah Arendt's insights on statelessness. He begins with her reflections on statelessness and then goes on to consider how stateless people managed to resolve their predicament 'by constructing pathways' that enabled them to resolve their loss of nationality and/or citizenship. Of prime importance in that regard was the 'construction and performance' of narratives that demonstrated their capacity to make a political life for themselves in unpromising and threatening circumstances. He suggests that we can advance scholarship on these issues by adopting a non-Eurocentric focus and concentrate instead on (East) Asia and the Pacific. I return to this point later.

The first section of Jay Winter's interpretation tracks Arendt's argument about the transformation of Europe after 1918 and the crystallisation of a system of rights based on nationality. As she put it, 'only nationals could be citizens' entitled to the protection and membership of the state. The consequences of being cast out from membership proved devastating. Aristide Zolberg developed these insights in a classic article in which he examined the impact of the dissolution of empires, including the exposure of minorities to the nation-state building projects of successor states in East-Central Europe. In a brief coda, he extended the analysis to national liberation movements in the modern era and hence to the Global South, where minority social groups were likewise exposed. Minorities and stateless persons faced everyday hostility and political exclusion, including their denationalisation and expulsion. Zolberg maintained that refugees were 'fortunate' in finding an escape route, even though their escape did not bring an end to suffering

A response

and uncertainty. Crucially, he argued, this generic political process manifested itself in specific forms and outcomes and hence needed to be contextualised.[1]

Zolberg's political analysis took Arendt as its starting point, but he was less concerned with the agency of refugees, preferring instead to concentrate on structural change, whereas Arendt had already outlined a different agenda in her chapter on 'Action' in *The Human Condition*, as Jay Winter explains in the second part of his introductory chapter. She opened with an epigram from her friend Isak Dinesen: 'All sorrows can be borne if you put them into a story or tell a story about them.' Arendt developed this idea in her discussion of action and initiative: 'In acting and speaking, men show who they are, reveal actively their unique personal identities and thus make their appearance in the human world while their physical identities appear without any activity of their own in the unique shape of the body and sound of the voice.' Action is about disclosing oneself as distinct and unique. But 'action and speech require the surrounding presence of others': action is relational. Accordingly, she then proceeded to talk about the power that is generated by 'the living together of people'.[2]

Lyndsey Stonebridge picks up this point in her important book on statelessness and refugees, where she reflects on Arendt's brief incarceration in the notorious French camp in Gurs in Southwestern France. Stonebridge suggests that Gurs served Arendt as a place to 'tell stories' within a specific enclosed community. Ultimately, the camp became a site of refugees' agency with the potential to transcend refugeedom.[3] She follows up with a broader argument about the meaning of statelessness and refugeedom in the modern world, including an insistence – here, she recalls Edward Said and others – on twentieth-century displacement as a distinct phenomenon compared to pre-1900 exile. Statelessness was a political and an existential condition and is not to be romanticised as a kind of cosmopolitan way of being in the world.[4]

Here I want to ask about the conditions, particularly the bureaucratic-legal conditions, that created or undermined the scope for refugees to assert themselves as a collective, of people 'living together', and joined in a common cause. One can quite easily make the case that post-1945 displaced persons (DPs), like Spanish Civil War refugees in Gurs internment camp in the 1930s, succeeded in

30
Perspectives on statelessness

forging a kind of political community. DPs developed a sense of solidarity in their collective refusal to repatriate, in other words to opt for statelessness rather than regain their former nationality in countries whose political complexion and structure they rejected. The refugee studies literature provides abundant examples of political self-expression and the crystallisation of a political community in sites of incarceration.[5]

What happened to storytelling when the international refugee regime adopted the legal instrument known as the 1951 UN Convention on Refugees? Here, the condition of being recognised as a refugee and thus entitled to seek protection and assistance required the individual to demonstrate a 'well-founded fear of persecution'.[6] Persons who claimed refugee status presented themselves before an official such as an eligibility officer who determined the validity or otherwise of their claim to refugee status. Everything hinged on whether the official believed that claim; specifically, did the story told by the refugee carry conviction? It was not enough for the refugee to assert a broad claim based on the prevailing political conditions in the country of origin. One had to tell a credible and consistent personal story, not rely on a generic account or a template. Hence the importance of providing accurate biographical information, sufficient to permit a forensic investigation of the case and a verdict that satisfied the prescription of the refugee regime.

My point, therefore, is about the status of the singular narrative, the insistence that one's story be uniquely credible, even if other refugees experienced similar persecution. Did the encounter between official and refugee nevertheless enable refugees to draw attention to systematic and general conditions – that is, the possibility of making a connection between the singular and the generalisable? Refugees wrote letters and petitions to the post-war International Refugee Organisation and to its successor, the Office of the UN High Commissioner for Refugees (UNHCR), and sometimes situated their own circumstances within a broader frame of reference, such that their personal story provided an opportunity to refer to the situation of others who could not testify. But this was a tangential rather than an integral element of the claim.[7]

In reading UNHCR confidential case files, one is regularly reminded of the agony and uncertainty of persecution and displacement and the painful necessity to recount details of suffering.

A response 31

Granted, there was scope to describe personal adventure and self-realisation (and sometimes to embellish the narrative or to choose not to disclose certain aspects), albeit that the individual was expected to stick to the facts. In recounting a story of persecution and flight, and in seeking greater security, refugees understood that their interlocutor exercised enormous power. There was little exchange or interaction, and certainly not between equals. Ultimately, they had to provide answers to the formulaic questions that were set by those who held power over them. If this was 'performative' (pace Jacques Rancière, quoted by Jay Winter), it left limited room for refugees to write the script. At the same time, it is worth emphasising that the refugee regime required that someone in authority should pay attention to them and make a response to what refugees affirmed. This imperative to listen is consistent with what Arendt (and Seyla Benhabib in turn) deemed to be significant and meaningful.[8]

To be sure, refugees and stateless persons exercised political imagination and judgement when they 'wrote upwards'.[9] The case files assembled by UNHCR disclose several examples. In March 1953, Hungarian merchant seaman Janos S. explained that he had left the country of his birth and arrived in Denmark in 1948 where he had found work without difficulty. Five years later, he was jobless and destitute:

> As I am in connection with many of the same situation as me suffering under the weight of the stigma 'Stateless DP' and I understand fully the state of mind of my 'fellow prisoners' between the various 'Iron Curtains' existing all over the world, ready to commit even foolishness in order to belong to a 'State' where justice and fairplay necessary for our rehabilitation sincerely prevail and our constructive enthusiasm, technical knowledges, sense of honour and duty based upon 1000 years old national traditions are not considered 'unwanted sweepings' to be thrown into the dustbin ... I propose [that] their sufferences [be brought] to an end by letting them cooperate in building up a 'State' of their own in the form of a 'Reservation' following the noble example of the USA where by Constitution there was given a place to the Indians under the Sun. I have many practical ideas for solving this question of the Refugees.[10]

Writing in these terms, he unwittingly echoed the writings of international lawyers who between the two world wars entertained

32   *Perspectives on statelessness*

alternative visions of political organisation in the form of 'nonstate entities' and 'personalities', as Mira Siegelberg has shown.[11]

Jay Winter's remarks are an invitation to rethink statelessness from a distinct geographic and temporal perspective, namely 'the domain of Asia, the Pacific and the Antipodes in the period of the Second World War', parts of the world that escaped Arendt's discussion of refugees and stateless persons, although she had plenty to say about the violence associated with decolonisation in the Global South.[12] In practice, the following chapters mainly address the European origins of statelessness, as it affected Europe's Jews together with White Russians. Can we stretch the canvas to accommodate other dynamics? In terms of institutional responses to mass displacement – in other words, the emergence and operation of the international refugee regime – there is now a considerable literature that points out its Eurocentric origins.[13] We should acknowledge, too, the contributions of scholars who are now rethinking mass displacement from a non-European perspective, including the impact and legacies of colonial rule, the situation of overseas Chinese, and the interests and claims of regional actors as well as inter-governmental organisations and those who interrogate contemporary non-European reflections on statelessness, including on the part of refugees themselves, such as those who moved from East to West Bengal in the wake of the Partition of India in 1947.[14] Perhaps most fundamentally, we should now consider (or reconsider) what it means to connect Europe and Asia through a focus on the contours and the cultural representation of mass population displacement, on the reassertion of state sovereignty in different settings, on different incarnations of the refugee regime, and on the mobility not just of stateless persons but also of aid workers and other peripatetic actors who crossed continents.

One final point: Jay Winter speaks of 'pathways', which one can take to have a figurative as well as a literal meaning. It might be helpful to think of the pathway as a learning process in which both officials and refugees/stateless persons acquired and shared knowledge as to the options that were available to them. Valuable work is now being done to explore these issues and initiatives.[15]

Nevertheless, without wishing to discount the inventiveness and 'agency' shown individually and collectively by refugees, it also behoves us to underline the constraints imposed by states and other actors in the international and regional incarnations of the refugee regime. This emerged clearly in the efforts of DPs and others who sought resettlement in a third country: apart from having a 'good story' to tell, it was imperative to be sponsored and to have no disability or criminal conviction that normally would be a disqualification from being admitted. In the latter case, the barriers erected by prospective host states and maintained by immigration officers were insuperable.[16] What is more, resettlement brought its own challenges and disappointments as well as adventures and opportunities: some disillusioned refugees opted for repatriation and thereby resolved statelessness on their own initiative. They had a different story to tell.[17]

Notes

1 Aristide Zolberg, 'The Formation of New States as a Refugee-Generating Process', *The Annals of the American Academy of Political and Social Science*, 467 (1983), pp. 282–96.
2 Hannah Arendt, *The Human Condition* (Chicago, IL: Chicago University Press, 1958), pp. 175, 179, 188, 201.
3 Peter Gatrell, Anindita Ghoshal, Katarzyna Nowak, and Alex Dowdall, 'Reckoning with Refugeedom: Refugee Voices in Modern History', *Social History*, 46 (2021), pp. 70–95.
4 Lyndsey Stonebridge, *Placeless People: Writing, Rights, and Refugees* (Oxford: Oxford University Press, 2018), pp. 50, 58–60. See also Edward Said, *Reflections on Exile and Other Essays* (London: Granta Books, 2001); Miriam Rürup, 'Lives in Limbo: Statelessness after Two World Wars', *Bulletin of the German Historical Institute*, 49 (2011), pp. 113–34. On pre-1900 manifestations and limitations of asylum, see Delphine Diaz, *En exil. Les réfugiés en Europe, de la fin du XVIIIe siècle à nos jours* (Paris: Gallimard, 2021); Stephanie DeGooyer, 'Resettling Refugee History', *American Literary History*, 34 (2022), pp. 893–911.
5 The classic study is Liisa H. Malkki, *Purity and Exile: Violence, Memory, and National Cosmology among Hutu Refugees in Tanzania* (Chicago, IL: Chicago University Press, 1995). See also Kirsten McConnachie, 'Camps of Containment: A Genealogy of the Refugee Camp', *Humanity: An International Journal of Human Rights, Humanitarianism, and Development*, vii (2016), pp. 397–412. On DPs' political agency, see Katarzyna Nowak, *Kingdom of Barracks: Polish Displaced Persons in*

Allied-Occupied Germany and Austria (Montreal, QC: McGill-Queen's University Press, 2023).

6 The Convention stipulated that it applied to a refugee who, 'As a result of events occurring before 1 January 1951 and owing to well-founded fear of being persecuted for reasons of race, religion, nationality, membership of a particular social group or political opinion, is outside the country of his nationality and is unable or, owing to such fear, is unwilling to avail himself of the protection of that country; or who, not having a nationality and being outside the country of his former habitual residence as a result of such events, is unable or, owing to such fear, is unwilling to return to it.' It committed signatory states not to return such persons against their will (non-refoulement). The complete text is available at https://www.unhcr.org/media/28185. Accessed 10 July 2023.

7 'I tell my story because people need to hear it. I tell my story because it is not just my own story, and because there are many like me who can no longer tell their stories', as Afghan refugee Abdallah put it. Quoted in Cindy Horst and Odin Lysaker, 'Miracles in Dark Times: Hannah Arendt and Refugees as "Vanguard"', *Journal of Refugee Studies*, 34 (2021), pp. 67–84 (p. 78). On the IRO regime and refugee testimony, see Ruth Balint, *Destination Elsewhere: Displaced Persons and Their Quest to Leave Europe after 1945* (Ithaca, NY: Cornell University Press, 2021); on the UNHCR, see Peter Gatrell, 'Raw Material: UNHCR's Individual Case Files as a Historical Source, 1951–1975', *History Workshop Journal*, 92 (2021), pp. 226–41.

8 Seyla Benhabib, 'Hannah Arendt and the Redemptive Power of Narrative', *Social Research: An International Quarterly*, 58 (1990), pp. 167–96.

9 Martin Lyons, 'Writing Upwards: How the Weak Wrote to the Powerful', *Journal of Social History*, 49 (2015), pp. 317–33.

10 Fonds UNHCR 17, Records Relating to Protection, Sub-fonds 1, Individual Case Files, Archives of the United Nations High Commissioner of Refugees, IC11515.

11 Mira Siegelberg, *Statelessness: A Modern History* (Cambridge, MA: Harvard University Press, 2020), pp. 94, 182–3. See also Natasha Wheatley, 'Spectral Legal Personality in Interwar International Law: On New Ways of Not Being a State', *Law and History Review*, 35 (2017), pp. 753–87.

12 Samuel Moyn, 'Hannah Arendt among the Cold War Liberals', *Journal of the History of Ideas*, 84 (2023), pp. 533–58.

13 B. S. Chimni, 'From Resettlement to Involuntary Repatriation: Towards a Critical History of Durable Solutions to Refugee Problems', *Refugee*

Survey Quarterly, 23 (2004), pp. 55–73. See also Lucy Mayblin, *Asylum after Empire: Colonial Legacies in the Politics of Asylum Seeking* (London: Rowman & Littlefield, 2017).

14 Glen Peterson, 'The Uneven Development of the International Refugee Regime in Postwar Asia: Evidence from China, Hong Kong and Indonesia', *Journal of Refugee Studies*, 25 (2012), pp. 326–43; Laura Madokoro, Elaine Lynn-Ee-Ho, and Glen Peterson, 'Questioning the Dynamics and Language of Forced Migration in Asia: The Experiences of Ethnic Chinese Refugees', *Modern Asian Studies*, 49 (2015), pp. 430–38; Meredith Oyen, 'The Right of Return: Chinese Displaced Persons and the International Refugee Organization, 1947–56', *Modern Asian Studies*, 49 (2015), pp. 546–71; Milinda Banerjee, 'The Partition of India, Bengali "New Jews", and Refugee Democracy: Transnational Horizons of Indian Refugee Political Discourse', *Itinerario*, 46 (2022), pp. 283–303. On the refugee regime in post-Partition India and the situation of stateless persons, see Vazira Fazila-Yacoobali Zamindar, *The Long Partition and the Making of Modern South Asia: Refugees, Boundaries, and Histories* (New York: Columbia University Press, 2007).

15 Magdalena Kmak and Heta Björklund (eds), *Refugees and Knowledge Production: Europe's Past and Present* (London: Routledge, 2022); Simone Lässig and Swen Steinberg, 'Knowledge on the Move: New Approaches toward a History of Migrant Knowledge', *Geschichte und Gesellschaft*, 43 (2017), pp. 313–46.

16 Concerted international efforts might bring about a change of heart, as happened with elderly Russian refugees in China during the UN campaign for World Refugee Year in 1959–60. See Peter Gatrell, *Free World? The Campaign to Save the World's Refugees, 1956–1963* (Cambridge: Cambridge University Press, 2011).

17 For a discussion of contemporary repatriation in the Global South and its implications in relation to Arendt's original insights on statelessness, particularly concerning refugees who advance claims on their country of origin, see Megan Bradley, 'Rethinking Refugeehood: Statelessness, Repatriation, and Refugee Agency', *Review of International Studies*, 40 (2014), pp. 101–23.

Section I.II

Telling the tale of refugees and
the stateless

3

Some poems: statelessness and refugees

Peter Balakian

Editorial note

Peter Balakian's poetry is a meditation on suffering and statelessness, the visceral core of this book. He offers us a language of dislocation, providing insights into the intergenerational transfer of memories of persecution, flight, and mourning. His words capture images and sounds to which memories are attached, memories of the time when his family was trapped in the Armenian Genocide of 1915. His words are family passports, clutched to the chests of stateless refugees on their journeys far from their homes. Those fleeing the Nazis in the 1930s followed in their footsteps.

Balakian's poetry burnishes 'filaments' of history, the history of twentieth-century statelessness. In 'Ellis Island', he conjures up images of his deported grandmother's 'stockings that walked to Syria in 1915', and 'a porcelain cup blown into the desert'. As she arrives at Ellis Island, the taint of death lingers as the sea gulls are 'gnawing' on the dead. The site of entry into a safe-haven is polluted by the suffering of all those who have perished and survived.

In 'Coming to Istanbul', the poet returns to his father's native city, and is haunted by the ghosts of the dead and exiled Armenians and finds traces of generations of Turkish persecution. The plaque to murdered Armenian journalist Hrant Dink puts him into one timeframe, the 'trompe d'oeil' of Turkish thugs places him into another, and he calls out with irony for his 'lost family' to greet him in their city. In 'Home', he captures the journeys of his diasporan family in the in the aftermath of the Armenian genocide as his imagination wanders the pathways of his family's global flights. He

Some poems 39

evokes his uncle's escape from Anatolia to Australia, and then to London to Kolkata and back, 'never returning to the Armenian village on the Black Sea'. Such is the shadow of displacement inscribed in his poetry.

Poet's statement

From Homer to Heaney, history has been a preoccupation of poets. My own work has been at times focused on my family's experience in the Armenian Genocide. In poems and prose over various books, I've imagined the experiences of my family in the aftermath of this catastrophe. As a poet, my interest in writing about refugees and stateless people migrating along 'global pathways', as Jay Winter has put it, has been a vitalising force in my imagination. I've imagined my grandparents in flight from mass violence; fleeing genocide; living in liminality. I've been engaged in what the literary scholar Marianne Hirsch calls 'post memory', a psychological and imaginative condition in which writers and artists are preoccupied or obsessed with a particular history and historical events that have preceded their lives.[1] Some postmemory poets include Robert Hayden, Derek Walcott, and Rita Dove writing poems about the history of African enslavement in the United States and the Caribbean; Robert Lowell writing about early Protestant New England history; Seamus Heaney writing poems about the plight of Irish Catholics under British rule; Adrienne Rich writing about the oppression of women in patriarchal history.

Between 1915 and 1918, the Ottoman Turkish government massacred and deported more than two million Armenians – Ottoman citizens who were living on their historic Armenian homeland mostly in Eastern Turkey. Armenian women children and men were force marched, raped, abducted, and massacred throughout the country while Turkey was fighting in the First World World War on the side of the Central Powers.[2] For context, I note briefly some facts about my family's history.[3] My paternal grandparents – the Balakians and the Panosyans – fled Constantinople (now Istanbul) in the summer of 1922 after the Armenian Genocide had decimated the Armenian population of the capital, and the Greek loss in the Greco-Turkish war of 1922 had also dimmed life for Christians in Turkey. My

40   *Perspectives on statelessness*

great-grandfather Murat Panosyan was a wealthy coal mine owner and merchant. He and his wife and family of seven children lived in a stately late-nineteenth-century Queen Anne–style house looking out on the Bosphorus in the Scutari section of the city. Their homes and wealth were all confiscated by the Turkish government, and almost all of them fled with the clothes on their backs and their diplomas in their pockets. My grandmother Koharig and her sister Arusyag and their children, which included my father, who was then two years old, found refuge in the French Alp town of Collonge Sous Salève, where they lived until my grandfather, Diran Balakian, who was a physician, could find a hospital in the United States that would allow him to join their staff once he passed his medical boards in his newly adopted country. In 1924, my grandfather landed at a hospital in Indianapolis where he was preparing to pass his medical boards in his fifth language – English – at the age of forty-six before he moved to New York City where his family joined him in 1926, eventually settling on the corner of 116th Street and Broadway, where my grandfather also had his private practice. His profession provided him with a pathway to a new life.

My mother's family, the Aroosians and Shekerlemedjians, were in the textile and silk business in the crossroads city of Diyarbakir in Southeastern Turkey. The Shekerlemedjians were prosperous traders and textile merchants who traveled between Greece and Syria and had numerous dry-goods stores in the Diyarbakir province. My grandmother's Nafina's entire family, from two-year-old nieces to seventy-five-year-old parents and her husband Hagop Chilinguirian, were massacred in the first weeks of August 1915. My grandmother and her two small daughters ages four and two (Gladys and Alice) survived a death march into the deserts of Northern Syria and arrived in Aleppo in the fall of 1915 – a city rampant with famine, disease, and dead and dying Armenian survivors. For five years, she worked as a seamstress before accruing the funds to emigrate to the United States, entering through Ellis Island for Paterson New Jersey, where she married my grandfather, Bedros Aroosian. My mother Arax was the second of their two daughters. Given these histories, I have or have had family on every continent except for Africa.

Poems create rhetorical gestures, metaphoric entanglements, conceits, and layered renderings in probing and representing some filaments of historical events. Poems that grapple with history often

Some poems

41

deal with collisions between past and present, and such poems can pitch a voice that is at once public and private. Poems can offer a view, a vision, a visceral sensation, a probe and representation, an emotional insight into a historical moment or, in my case, an experience of one's ancestors.

These three poems embody filaments of history: my grandmother's arrival at Ellis Island, my coming to Istanbul for the first time in 2013 (the capital city from which my family was expelled, and their wealth confiscated), and a poem that takes on my sense of my family's diasporan history and its impact on me.

Ellis Island[4]

The tide's a Bach cantata.
The beach is the swollen neck of Isaac.

The tide's a lamentation of white opals.
The beach is free. The Coke machine rusted out.

Here is everything you'll never need:

hemp-cords, curry-combs, jade and musk,
a porcelain cup blown into the desert

stockings that walked to Syria in 1915.

On the rocks some ewes and rams
graze in the outer dark.

The manes of the shoreline undo your hair.
A sapphire ring is fingerless.

The weed and algae are floating like a bed,
and the bloodless gulls –

whose breaths would stink of all of us
if we could kiss them on the beaks –

are gnawing on the dead.

Coming to Istanbul[5]

Follow the gaze of Athena
down a cistern where water glows.

Follow silver snakes along Marmara
and Golden Horn.

Walk over the black plaque for Hrant Dink
smack in the street in Shishli.

Follow the ferry-waves to Üsküdar –
where your father was born,

where your uncle returned
incognito from prison –

Drink the split bourbon voice of Ray Charles
in the café in Taxsim

under the red flags of star and moon
guns to the head, wild prayer –

streets banging with pots and pans –
rage at the dictator.

Walk by in oblivion and terror
an American, an Armenian, black shirt

under the olive-trellised restaurant
hotel rooftop light-rinsed Bosphorus

hot raki fumes in the throat
under the wind-umbrellas

and boutique-class facades of Beyoglu
galleries of blue mosaics, magenta carpets –

the Ottoman historian pours you
tahn and wine into the sunset.

Some poems   43

Follow the lights on the bridge
into the chandelier of the sky

trompe l'oeil of Gray Wolves
voices of Turkish friends in the stone.

Follow ghost signs midnight cab
smashed café windows

night-sea journey of beloveds
Byzantine dirt smoke roads

past Tobacco Regie and sultana crates –
Haydarpasha of Armenian-soul death hour.

Lost family come greet me in your city.

Home[6]

Driving Route 20 to Syracuse past pastures of cows and falling silos

you feel the desert stillness near the refineries at the Syrian border.

Walking in fog on Mecox Bay, the long lines of squawking birds
    on shore,

you're walking along Flinders Street Station, the flaring yellow
    stone and walls of windows where your uncle landed after he fled
    a Turkish prison.

You walked all day along the Yarra, crossing the sculptural bridges
    with their twisting steel,

the hollow sound of the didgeridoo like the flutes of Anatolia.

One road is paved with coins, another with razor blades and ripped
    condoms.

Walking the boardwalk in January past Atlantic City Hall, the
    rusted Deco ticket sign, the waves black into white,
you smell the grilled cevapi in the Bascarsija of Sarajevo,

44 *Perspectives on statelessness*

and that street took you to the Jewish cemetery where the weeds
  grew over the slabs and a mausoleum stood intact.
There was a trail of carnelian you followed in the Muslim quarter
  of Jerusalem

and picking up those stones now, you're walking in the salt marsh
  on the potato fields,
the day undercut by the flatness of the sky, the wide view of the
  Atlantic, the cold spray.

Your uncle stashed silk and linen, lace and silver in a suitcase on a
  ship that docked not far from here; the ship moved in and out of
  port for years, and your uncle kept coming

and going, from Melbourne to London to Kolkata and back, never
  returning to the Armenian village near the Black Sea.

The topaz ring you passed on in a silver shop in Aleppo appeared
  on Lexington off 65th;
the shop owner, a young guy from Ivory Coast, shrugged when you
  told him you had seen it

before; the shuffled dust of that street fills your throat and you
  remember how a slew of
coins poured out of your pocket like a slinky near the ruined castle
  now a disco in

Thessaloniki where a young girl was stabbed under the strobe lights –
  lights that lit the

sky that was the iridescent eye of a peacock in Larnaca at noon,
  when you walked into the

church where Lazarus had come home to die and you forgot that
  Lazarus died

because the story was in one of your uncle's books that were
  wrapped in newspaper in a suitcase and
stashed under the seat of an old Ford, and when he got to the border

he left the car and walked the rest of the way, and when you pass
  the apartment

Some poems 45

on 116th and Broadway – where your father grew up
  (though it's a dorm now) –
that suitcase is buried in a closet under clothes, and when you walk
  past the security guard

at the big glass entrance door, you're walking through wet grass, clouds
  clumped on a hillside, a subway station sliding into water.

Copyright by Peter Balakian

Notes

1 Marianne Hirsch, *Family frames: Photography, Narrative, and Postmemory* (Cambridge, MA: Harvard University Press, 1997).
2 Peter Balakian, *Burning Tigris: The Armenian Genocide and America's Response* (New York: HarperCollins, 2003).
3 For a fuller account, see Grigoris Balakian, *Armenian Golgotha*, trans. Peter Balakian with Aris Sevag (New York: Alfred A. Knopf, 2009); and Balakian, *The Black Dog of Fate: A Memoir* (New York: Basic Books, 1997).
4 'Ellis Island' in *June-tree: New and Selected Poems* (New York: HarperCollins, 2001).
5 'Coming to Istanbul' in *No Sign* (Chicago, IL: University of Chicago Press, 2022).
6 'Home' in *Ozone Journal*, 2015 (Chicago, IL: University of Chicago Press, 2015).

4

Run (refugee series)

Mary Behrens

Editorial note

Run is a series of images conveying the 'ragged and terrifying experience of refugee flight'. The series is Behrens's attempt, as an artist, to express empathy with the plight of people on the run from violence and war.

Many of these people are stateless. But their status matters less than their predicament. Being on the run while trying to protect children is an agonising fate; all that one can do is to pass the children through the barbed wire denying them free entry to a safe-haven.

This work raises difficult questions about our subject position as we view these images. Where do aesthetics begin or end, she asks? What do we feel when we confront images of terrified flight? Every chapter in this book returns to this problem. Statelessness challenges our visual, as well as our moral, imagination; seeing these images may enable us not to look away when a child is passed through a barbed-wire barrier.

Artist's statement

Run

I began the series of mixed-media collages titled *Run* in 2018. The Syrian war was raging. Thousands of civilians were trying to flee to safer ground. The media were filled with images of terror and destruction, and I felt an urgency to create art from the toxic brew of news and imagery I was absorbing each day.

Run (refugee series)

Unlike many photojournalists and war photographers whose work I admire – Gilles Peress,[1] Sebastiao Salgado,[2] Nick Ut[3] – I am not interested in creating lush reflections or, in Salgado's case, *tableaux* of the dispossessed and the war-torn. My work does, however, engage with the same questions their work raises.

Is it acceptable to create, to re-imagine, photographs that might be considered 'beautiful', 'compelling', or 'informative', without exploiting their human subjects/victims?

Where do aesthetics begin or end? What feelings do viewers experience while gazing at images of trauma from a safe and privileged distance?[4]

It is not vital to the work that each piece be described or historically contextualised. What matters is the collective sense of *having* to run, *having* to flee one's home.

My work is not autobiographical, but family history – my father fled Nazi Germany in 1939 – has always grounded my interest in re-imagining history through an aesthetic lens.

Run is a series of appropriated images gathered from history books, the internet, and other media sources. The images are laser

Figure 4.1 Mary Behrens, *Run*, 'Baby'.

Figure 4.2 Mary Behrens, *Run*, 'Boat'.

Figure 4.3 Mary Behrens, *Run*, 'Human trail'.

Run *(refugee series)*

Figure 4.4 Mary Behrens, *Run*, 'Medusa'.

Figure 4.5 Mary Behrens, *Run*, 'Mother, child, flee'.

Figure 4.6 Mary Behrens, *Run*, 'Rug road'.

Figure 4.7 Mary Behrens, *Run*, 'Twirl'.

ink prints on paper. The originals were altered by fragmentation and distortion then re-assembled in a grid measuring 36" × 22". The collaged pieces are wrapped in plastic 'bandages' (in fact, shipping tape), giving each piece a reflective, ambiguous surface – a counterpoint to the traditional photographic surface.

Through its materiality, I hope that the work conveys what I imagine as the ragged and terrifying experience of refugee flight. The series is my attempt, as an artist, to express empathy with the plight of people on the run from violence and war.

Notes

1 On Gilles Peress, see his photographs in *Village Destroyed: War Crimes in Kosovo* (Berkeley, CA: University of California Press, 2001).
2 Sebastião Salgado, 'Exodus Migrations against All Odds', *Aperture*, 163 (Spring 2001), pp. 1–19.
3 On Nick Ut's Vietnam photography, see Nancy K. Miller, 'The Girl in the Photograph: The Vietnam War and the Making of National Memory', *JAC*, 24, 2, *Special Issue, Part 1: Trauma and Rhetoric* (2004), pp. 261–90.
4 Susan Sontag, *Regarding the Pain of Others* (New York: Picador, 2003).

5

'Nobody's children': families, internees, and refugees in Singapore and Australia during the Second World War

Eva de Jong-Duldig

'Tatura ist ein paradies' (Tatura is a paradise)[1]

I was a child in a family of stateless people deported from Singapore to Australia in 1940. Between the ages of two and four, I lived with my mother and father, Karl and Slawa Duldig, in a detention camp in Northern Victoria. This chapter offers a personal point of view on what happened to my family and others who fled Austria after the Anschluss of 1938. We found a home in Singapore, but in 1940, we were deported to Australia on the refitted luxury liner the *Queen Mary*, and held as internees in Camp 3 at Tatura in Northern Victoria during the war. I draw on my own family memories, as well as on conversations with other internees, family documents, and other archives on this period.

Driven from our Viennese home by the rise of Nazism and the growing persecution of Jews, my family and other refugees from Germany and Austria who wound up in Camp 3D near Tatura in September 1940 were indeed fortunate. While they did not realise this at the time, only a few months later, Singapore and the Malay Peninsula, their previous temporary home, fell to the advancing Japanese forces. There is, therefore, a distinct possibility that had we been allowed to remain in Singapore, we may have suffered a tragic fate. The fall of that city was bloody and brutal, and many of the civilians who remained under Japanese occupation were interned under difficult conditions.

'Nobody's children' 53

The exact number of internees removed from the Straits Settlements to Australia in 1940 is open to conjecture.[2] This chapter, however, is principally concerned with my family and other Jewish refugees who were brought to Australia on the *Queen Mary* as 'enemy aliens' and subsequently detained in Camp 3D, Tatura.[3]

While some of the experiences of this group were indeed similar to those of other refugees displaced by the Second World War, there were also marked differences. The differences were due mainly to the circumstances over which they had no control, but also to the capacity of these people to respond to their situation as it arose. This response was often initiated by the group itself, but sometimes also by individuals. These initiatives were not always successful, but they displayed courage, resilience and resourcefulness – qualities which held many of these people in good stead when eventually they remade their lives in post-war Australia.

Among many skilled and highly qualified refugees were musicians, artists, engineers, lawyers, accountants, teachers, nurses, dressmakers, a watchmaker, a monumental stonemason, and a milliner. With few exceptions, they had arrived in the Straits Settlements after 1938. For instance, artists Julius and Tina Wentscher came to Bali in 1931. Following travel in China and Hong Kong and realising they could not return, they moved to Java, then Bangkok, and finally Singapore in 1936. All newcomers, within two weeks of arrival, needed a guarantee of employment in the colony or they would be sent on to Shanghai.

The largest family group was the ten members of the Seefeld family, spread over three generations. Gerhard Seefeld, later Camp Leader in Tatura, had lived in Singapore since the 1920s and worked as an import–export merchant representing British, Canadian, and American firms. His Singapore-born children were British citizens. Gerhard's brother Helmut, and his father Professor Arthur Seefeld, formerly Professor of Dentistry and the Superintendent Head Physician of Dentistry in the General Hospital in Hamburg, Germany, and their families had arrived shortly before the war.

Paul Schlesinger, later Deputy Camp Leader in Tatura, arrived in Singapore with his wife Gertrude and teenage daughter Eve in 1938. In Vienna he had been a member of the Vienna Stock Exchange, and his wife ran a gymnastics school. They were both

Perspectives on statelessness

outstanding bridge players, and Gertrude was a member of the victorious Austrian Bridge Team in the 1937 World Championships.

My uncle Dr Leo Duldig practised law in Vienna before fleeing to Belgium after the *Anschluss* with his wife Stefanie and teenage son Arthur. He became joint Deputy Leader in Tatura with Paul Schlesinger. Leo and Stefanie's daughter Irene and her Belgian husband, Hendrik Gutwirth, whose family business had a branch in Singapore, sponsored their stay in Singapore. Irene also persuaded my parents, the sculptor Karl Duldig (Leo's younger brother), and my mother, the artist and inventor Slawa Horowitz-Duldig, to come to Singapore, where they founded an art school. My father also completed important commissions while my mother restored valuable paintings in the Singapore municipal collection.[4]

Some of the refugees had originally left Europe for Shanghai – a unique destination where no visa or landing permit was required. When their ship docked en route in Singapore, a few seized on employment opportunities offered there or elsewhere in the Straits Settlements. The Austrian civil and industrial engineer Otto Gottlieb and the accountant and graphic designer Alfred Figdor obtained positions in the British Mining Company, which had sites all over the Malay Peninsula.

The musician Werner Baer had been arrested in Berlin and imprisoned in Sachsenhausen on *Kristallnacht*. His wife Ilse secured his release on condition they leave Germany immediately for Shanghai. When the ship docked en route in Colombo, Werner answered an advertisement for a music teacher in Singapore. Ilse's father had already prepared his daughter for probable emigration and, contrary to her own academic ambitions, insisted she learn dressmaking, which enabled her to earn a living, first in Singapore and later in Australia.

Initially, even though the refugees, including my family, had arrived in Singapore holding German papers, they could move about freely; however, after the outbreak of the Second World War, parole restrictions were imposed on all German and Austrian refugees. The small numbers did not warrant harsh measures such as those implemented in Great Britain, but further restrictions were imposed on them while a long-term solution was sought. They were no longer allowed to travel from the Settlements, change address, be absent from home for more than twenty-four hours, possess arms

'Nobody's children'   55

or cameras, or approach any prohibited area or naval or military base without notifying the Registrar of Aliens to obtain special permission. People with motor vehicles could only use them to take children to school, for essential shopping, or in case of sickness. While these restrictions were trying, they did not significantly affect their lifestyle.[5]

By June 1940, the Germans were advancing all over Europe and, as the presence of German and Italian nationals in Singapore became 'incompatible with security',[6] the Governor of the Straits Settlements asked the Australian authorities to accept these people for safe custody in Australia. By July 1940, the Australian Government had agreed to this request.

Over the ensuing months, protracted correspondence took place between the Straits Settlements Government, Singapore, the Colonial Office in London, and the Australians.[7] The principal figures involved were the Colonial Secretary Stanley W. Jones and the Rt. Hon. Lord Lloyd, Secretary of State for the Colonies. There were two main issues: the first was the decision to arrest and intern the 'enemy aliens'; the second was the decision to deport them to Australia. Contemporary documents appear to confirm that both the decision to arrest the group of 'anti-Nazis' and the decision to deport them for internment in Australia were taken by the Straits Settlements administration without the approval of their London-based superiors.[8] Before they were interned, the Singapore refugees had been given one other alternative – they were free to go to a country outside the British Empire, but in the current situation with the world at war, this was totally unrealistic, and unsurprisingly nobody was able to take advantage of this.

On 22 July, first notice of their impending deportation came from the Jewish Refugee Relief Committee, an organisation established by the local, principally Sephardic, Jewish community to assist Jewish refugees arriving from Europe. The letter stated, 'It is practically certain that within three weeks all German, Austrian and Italian Jewish refugees, including women and children, will be interned and will be sent out of the country, and they are therefore advised to make arrangements accordingly.'[9]

At that time my father was working on a major commission for Aw Boon Haw, a Chinese entrepreneur and philanthropist and founder of Tiger Balm ointment. My father engaged the services of

56 *Perspectives on statelessness*

solicitor John Eber, of the firm Chan and Eber, to appeal against the deportation order. The affidavit stated 'We are Polish; our families are currently in Poland; we own property in Poland and our brothers are serving officers in the Polish army'.[10] Further, it stated that although the Duldig family had entered the colony on German passports, these were invalid as Germany had stripped their Jewish citizens of their rights as citizens. Other interventions were attempted through the family's connections in the British Admiralty, the Municipality of Singapore, the diplomatic corps, and Aw Boon Haw. The initial appeal was turned down, and on 29 August 1940, the Colonial Secretary officially refused the appeal. On 3 September, my family was among those who received notification that 'you will be removed from the colony in two weeks'.[11] The final instructions arrived on 11 September 1940,

> to attend at the Sikh Barracks Pearls Hill (off New Bridge Road), at 8 a.m. on 18.9.40 ready to proceed to internment ... Bring only hand luggage with you. Your heavy baggage will be brought to the Sikh Police Barracks between 9 a.m. and 4 p.m. on 15.9.40 by you personally for inspection. A reasonable amount of personal baggage only will be allowed, and cases of furniture, crockery and so on, will not be permitted.[12]

In spite of these clear instructions, my mother made representation through the family doctor to take my cot to Australia. On 14 September, Dr E. Laidlaw Thomson wrote:

> Mrs Karl Duldig has asked me to write to you in order to find out whether there is any possibility of her being able to take the baby's cot with her to Australia, as her child is only 2 and a half years old and has not been sleeping well for some time. The question is this, children get into certain habits and there is no doubt she is going to give her parents some trouble if her bed is changed.[13]

Permission was granted.

Hoping to be released on parole, my father obtained letters of introduction from his Chinese friends in Singapore to the Chinese community in Australia, and my mother obtained a letter of appreciation from the Municipality of Singapore. Gerhard Seefeld met the Secretary of Defence in Singapore and was assured that the refugees would be released and paroled in Australia. Even though his children were British citizens, the whole family was nevertheless interned. Otto Gottlieb, who had been joined in Malaya by his wife Johannah and toddler daughter Ruth, had applied for British citizenship, but the documents were not issued in time, so they were interned. Paul and Gertrude Schlesinger wanted to protect their daughter Eve, then only 16, and arranged her marriage to Alfred Huntley, a 36-year-old Royal Navy Volunteer Reserve Officer. The marriage secured Eve a new identity and British nationality.[14] It saved her from internment in 1940, but it would be many years before parents and daughter saw each other again.

On 18 September 1940, 266 internees assembled for the first time and were transported to St John's Island for the night. Next day, we were transferred to the *Queen Mary*, which was anchored in deep water nearby. Reflecting on the loss of freedom, my father wrote:

> This loss of freedom became clear to me when, after our assembly on St John's Island, we were marched one behind the other to fetch something for the night from our luggage. ... That was the first day of my imprisonment. ... The day of departure came, the day of the END ... as we gathered below I see before my eyes the beautiful sight of the sea and Singapore, Singapore which in such a short time left the deepest impressions on me.[15]

The Guard of Transport W1 (*Queen Mary*), from the Gordon Highlander regiment, were surprised when 'the dangerous enemy aliens' included old people and children. Assigned cabins on C deck, the internees enjoyed comfortable second-class accommodation, meals, and amenities.[16] Were it not for regular testing of the newly installed cannons and overall apprehension, it could almost have been a holiday cruise.

After eight days at sea, the ship entered Sydney Harbour on 25 September 1940. It quickly became apparent that the parole assured in Singapore was an empty promise. Our disembarkation was supervised by more than one hundred soldiers, naval officers, and police officers. Each internee was photographed, fingerprinted, and assigned an identification number, which was to be used in all future communication. Their personal dossier also included their age, profession, religion, and nationality (Figure 5.1).

The arrival of the *Queen Mary* and its unusual passengers was reported in the local press, and film footage was shown in the daily newsreel cinema screenings.[17] One journalist wrote,

58 Perspectives on statelessness

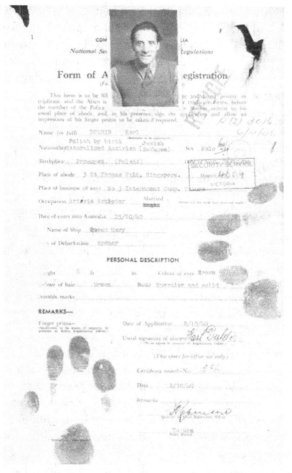

Figure 5.1 Alien Registration Form, Certificate No. 586 for Karl Duldig, © Duldig Studio Museum. Image courtesy of the National Archives of Australia. NAA: B6531, NATURALISED/1946 – 1947/POLISH/DULDIG KARL.

'Luxury' internees have disembarked in Sydney on their way to a country internment camp … The internees are Germans, Eurasians and Italians. They will be kept in Australia for the duration … Police and naval launches supervised the transfer of the internees from the liner to a ferry boat in mid-harbour.[18]

My family and all the other internees were taken to a railway siding where the railway platform was lined by armed soldiers.

'Nobody's children'   59

Armed guards were in each carriage and the windows could only be slightly opened. We were now effectively prisoners in a far-off land, totally isolated from everything and everyone we had known. Whereas I was too young to be affected at the time, for the adults, the loss of freedom must have weighed heavily on them, especially as it was contrary to the assurances they had been given before our deportation.

After a long train journey, we alighted in Albury, New South Wales, and were transported in covered army trucks to an internment camp located in central Victoria, halfway between Rushworth and Tatura. Newly constructed on land acquired from a local farmer, the camp was intended to confine prisoners of war, enemy aliens, and others whose nationality or activities made them a possible threat to the security of Australia. We *Queen Mary* internees were housed in Compound D, one of four identical compounds which made up a diamond-shaped camp site. Armed soldiers marched up and down the corridors which divided the four compounds, while manned watchtowers, equipped with searchlights, were erected on all four corners of the barbed wire perimeter of the camp. The personal recollections from other internees describe facilities that were utterly primitive; the unlined huts were very cold in winter and very hot in summer and did not cater for families that included small babies and the elderly. The worst of the winter was over, but, after living in the tropics, nobody was prepared for the brisk cold winds during the day and the still colder wintry nights.[19]

Every compound had eight barracks, each containing twelve small rooms. The communal facilities included a large kitchen, a mess hut, and a laundry, as well as separate washing and ablution blocks for men and women. A makeshift hospital was supervised by a qualified nursing sister. The inhospitable camp was in stark contrast to the peaceful rural scene outside the barbed wire, where horses grazed in lush green fields and giant gum trees dotted the landscape. The *Queen Mary* internees were the first to be housed in this camp.

If any hope remained in the minds of the internees that they might be released on parole, it was quickly dashed when, immediately after their arrival, an officer addressed them in German: 'Here you are and here you will stay. For this, you have to thank Hitler

60 *Perspectives on statelessness*

and his friends.'[20] There was clearly no ambivalence in Australia about our status as enemy aliens.

On 29 September, the day after their arrival at the camp, a document titled 'Re: – Jewish Refugees' was sent to the Commandant of the Internment Camp and signed by G. Seefeld, Camp Leader. It read in part,

> Our small children in the age from six weeks onwards and our aged people up to 80 years are definitely not able to stand the hardship of living under such conditions. In the whole Empire no children, women and old people were interned at all and to our knowledge no Jewish Refugees are interned in the Commonwealth of Australia.[21]

Four further group appeals were sent in the first three months after our arrival, and personal appeals were also lodged by individual internees.[22] As well as repeating the assurances they had been given of release on parole in Australia, the appeals stressed the injustice of their imprisonment as they were genuine Jewish refugees, and, applying the principle that they were 'juridically stateless', they stated that they believed they would be under the protection of the British Government.[23] At this stage of international hostilities, however, none of the three jurisdictions (Great Britain, the Straits Settlements, and Australia) was prepared to take responsibility for our predicament and therefore all these petitions were virtually dismissed. The situation was at a total impasse, and this prompted Rabbi Danglow, the Chief Rabbi in Melbourne, who also held an official position in the Australian armed forces, to write to Prime Minister Menzies describing the internees as 'nobody's children'.[24] Adding to our distress, we refugees no longer had contact with our relatives in Europe, and even the censored correspondence with friends in Singapore also ceased.

Possibly underlying the reluctance of the Australians to release Jewish internees was an endemic racism initially evident in the appalling treatment of Indigenous people in the early years of British Colonial rule. During the gold rushes of the nineteenth century, it also surfaced towards Chinese miners, and in 1901, the Australian Parliament adopted the White Australia Policy, which was not abolished till 1966. The Second World War heightened the language of racism, and racist propaganda was often initiated by the Returned Sailors', Soldiers', Airmen's Imperial League of Australia (today

'Nobody's children'   61

known as the Returned and Services League of Australia (RSL)). The attitude of Australian Jewry was also ambivalent. While the internees were supported by Jewish welfare organisations, other influential Jewish voices objected to an influx of a large group of foreign-speaking co-religionists which posed a threat to their stable status within the predominantly Anglo-Saxon Australian community.[25]

We 'enemy alien' internees did, however, have some staunch and influential supporters. Petitions were signed by prominent church and community members advocating against the 'ill-informed propaganda directed at refugees'.[26] From the outset, stalwart support was forthcoming from the Governor General, Lord Gowrie, while Ada Constance Duncan, Director of the Victorian International Refugee Emergency Council, also advocated for our release. In response to this, an Aliens Tribunal was set up in November 1940, allowing refugees to appeal their categorisation. Practical aid came from the Christian churches, the Society of Friends (Quakers), and the YMCA. Nevertheless, negative public opinion took the view that the refugees were lucky to have found a safe-haven.

In spite of their justified anger and frustration, the internees quickly organised their lives in the camp. They drew up work rosters to share the daily routines. My uncle Leo Duldig ordered the supplies; my father was responsible for 'sport and amusements', and Alfred Figdor ran the canteen. Women took turns to cook and wash, while the men handled the heavy work around the camp. Fresh food was plentiful and there were excellent cooks among the internees. Lolo Jacobowitz and Inge Rosenfeld, both trained teachers, organised a kindergarten for the younger children (including me), and the older children were sent to Melbourne for schooling.

The internees initiated many activities to relieve the boredom of their imprisonment and as far as possible normalise their predicament. In November 1940, Hans Blau, a gifted musician, organised a revue, *Tatura Melody*, to which the guards were invited. Ludwig Meilich sketched Paul Schlesinger and his friends playing bridge, while chess was also popular (Figure 5.2). Alfred Figdor illustrated the front cover of the camp newsletter (Figure 5.3). My father drew up a landscape plan to beautify the surroundings and, together with other men, planted flower seeds in garden beds between the huts.[27] He also wrote to the authorities asking for equipment to

Figure 5.2 Ludwig Meilich, 'Happy Birthday to Paul Schlesinger from his poker fellows', 1940, pen and ink, by Ludwig Meilich. © Tatura Internment and POW Camps Museum.

build a tennis court and posted a notice – 'Founding of the tennis club. Today at 8.15h in the mess hall, all ladies and gentlemen who are interested in tennis are invited.'[28] His poster for a football match is dated '7.V1. 1941'. A head my father carved from firewood with an axe is now in the Newcastle Art Gallery[29] (Figure 5.4). Sometimes locals took women and children on outings to the nearby Waranga Basin, and generally we were well treated by the guard and workforce of the camp (Figure 5.5). When Ilse Baer fell ill, the camp authorities insisted she have an egg every day to make her stronger.[30] A Rabbi travelled from Melbourne to officiate at the wedding of Lotte Calm and Hans Fischer.[31]

The fact that there were so many young children among the internees played a significant role. We had first come to the attention of authorities on arrival in Sydney. An overseeing officer reported:

> Nearly all the children are very young, many of them babes in arms. Perambulators, push carts, etc., were very much in evidence at disembarkation. [In light of] The fact that the children were so young and that a few of the old people were in indifferent health, I thought it would be advisable to consult the Medical Authorities and ask for a trained nurse to accompany the internees by rail.

This had been agreed to.[32]

'Nobody's children'

Figure 5.3 Alfred Figdor, 'POW – Fifth Column Luggage', cover of Camp 3D newsletter *Behind the Fence*, Sept. 1940–Sept. 1941. © Tatura Internment and POW Camps Museum.

Understandably our parents were concerned about the effect of confinement on us children and tried to normalise our lives (Figure 5.6). When Ruth Gottlieb turned five, Otto Gottlieb built her a doll's pram out of packing cases. It had been beautifully decorated with Australian motifs by another internee. Professor George Fink (Funk) has treasured all his life the miniature 'Torah' his grandfather, Manny (Emanuel) Weiss, fashioned from an old cigar box, pieces of scrap metal, cloth, and paper. Inside the tiny Torah 'scrolls'

Figure 5.4 Karl Duldig (1902–1986), *Fragment* 1940, redgum, h 44 cm; Collection: Newcastle Art Gallery, Australia 1962013; Photo: Karl Duldig.

Figure 5.5 Tatura children on a picnic, c. 1941. Photographer unknown.

was a small piece of paper inscribed with the most sacred prayer in Judaism in fine Hebrew calligraphy.[33] My father cut down to size a racquet for me to play on the court he had built, little knowing that one day I would compete at Wimbledon. Every birthday was celebrated with gusto, and we children could play happily and wander freely around the camp site. This constant interaction with us children and our activities distracted the adults' anxiety about the war and relieved their boredom.

Figure 5.6 Karl Duldig (1902–1986), *Ring-a-ring-a-roses*, 1941, pen and ink, 30.3 × 21.0 cm, signed and dated l. r. 'K. Duldig Tatura 1941'.
© Duldig Studio Museum.

The plight of the children also eventually softened the hearts of the bureaucrats and helped break the impasse of our imprisonment. Though he did not refer directly to the children, in June 1941 Dr Herbert Vere Evatt, a former High Court Judge and spokesperson for the Labor parliamentary opposition, raised the matter of the ultimate fate of the internees.[34] This elevated the profile of the situation

'Nobody's children' 67

in Parliament, and the Minister for the Army, Percy Spender, wrote a memorandum in response:

> I am concerned with the young people included in this batch, some I am informed of tender years. Nothing is said as to their particular problems. I would be glad if ... reference is made to these internees from the Straits Settlement [*sic*], and in particular to what action is proposed (a) generally (b) in relation to very young internees. It seems heartless that they, i.e. the young people, should be held within present captivity during the rest of the war.[35]

Serious consideration was first given to the release of the internees in August 1941, when a Cabinet Agendum was drafted which took in not only the Singapore internees, but also 1,500 mostly German and Austrian internees who had arrived on the transport ship the *Dunera* from England in September 1940. It did not go unnoticed that the majority of these arrivals were Jewish, and some reticence was evident in allowing such a large number of Jews into the community. The fact that the internees included a significant number of Jewish women and children complicated matters further, as the Army had to find a humane way to deal with them and of absorbing them into the community at a time of war. It was, however, the change of government in October 1941 that led to a resolution of the matter of the 'enemy alien' internees.

The previous Menzies coalition government was replaced by a Labor government, and responsibility for the internees fell on the new Deputy Leader of the party and Minister for the Army, Frank Forde, who assumed overall discretionary power. Security concerns were paramount, but it is also possible that antisemitism played a role, and an incident in Camp 3 in September 1941 may have influenced the final decisions.

The *Queen Mary* internees came from diverse social and educational backgrounds. Their attitude to Judaism was similarly diverse – most were secular Jews, a few were strictly observant, and some held Zionist views, while still others would normally not have identified themselves as Jewish at all. The fact that we were interned as a cohesive group in Australia not only united us in our Judaism, but also in our dealings with authority. Ironically, our Jewish roots, specified on racial terms by Hitler, which had forced us to flee from

68   *Perspectives on statelessness*

Europe in the first place, were now providing us agency towards our liberty.

On the evening of 28 September 1941, exactly one year after we internees had first arrived at the camp, a riotous disturbance took place. The exact circumstances are clouded by the differing accounts given by the protagonists and the army officers who witnessed the incident. However, underlying the disturbance was the fact that there were a few Nazi sympathisers housed in our family compound alongside the Jewish internees. A riot ensued when German internees in the adjoining compound drilled along the fence line, sang Nazi songs, and gave the Hitler salute. This deliberate provocation caused a violent reaction, which escalated when a Nazi from our compound gave the Hitler salute. The next day the situation intensified until eventually shots were fired into the air by the guard to quell the disturbance.[36]

The incident demonstrated that the Jewish internees were determined to defend themselves at risk of punishment – a reaction that was thought uncharacteristic for Jews and was totally unexpected by the army. The reaction of the guard under Commandant, Major James Sproat, and the Group Commandant, Lieutenant-Colonel William Tackaberry, showed at the very least a decided ignorance of the experiences of Jews under Nazism in Germany and Austria. In a memorandum of 29 September, Tackaberry left no room for doubt as to who was at fault:

> The compound concerned has given a great deal of trouble during a period of several months, and the Jews therein are continually asking for the removal of the Nazis and Fascists who are interned with them. I am of the opinion that the disturbance of last night and today was a planned demonstration in order to advance their case for the removal of the Nazis and Fascists. None of the Jews, including the Compound Leader, evinced any desire to help the Camp Commandant to restore order. On the other hand, the Internees in the other Compounds dispersed quickly when ordered to do so, and the Compound Leaders were very helpful. ... I am of the opinion that the people in 'C' Compound singing the German songs, were doing so merely in relaxation and not with any intent to 'bait' the Jews.[37]

An independent enquiry was launched by the Honourable Mr Justice Gavan Duffy, who concluded: 'Both sides are ready to swear

'Nobody's children' 69

to the most contradictory stories with the utmost assurance and it would require, in our opinion, a Solomon to arrive at any really satisfactory conclusion.'[38]

The Army had been forewarned as early as December 1940 that trouble could ensue between the Nazis and so-called 'Anti-Nazis' living in the same compound, but it had failed to act. The riot escalated tensions, and the Jewish internees ultimately succeeded in their demand for the removal of all Nazi and fascist internees from Compound D. The incident did, nevertheless, further sour an already tense relationship between the Camp Leaders, Gerhard Seefeld and Paul Schlesinger, and Camp Commandant Tackaberry. Seefeld and Schlesinger refused to take any responsibility for the protest against the Nazis, and consequently Tackaberry dismissed them. The internees were asked to elect new leaders, but to his dismay, they promptly re-elected Seefeld and Schlesinger.

In November 1941, Irene Gutwirth successfully interceded with the Minister of the Army for the release of her father, my uncle Dr Leo Duldig (Deputy Camp Leader) and his family – much to the chagrin of my father, Leo's brother. In February 1942, Leo wrote from Melbourne, 'The mills of destiny are grinding slowly yet the more precisely.'[39] His words proved to be prescient.

The World War had arrived in the Pacific and South-East Asia. Japan attacked Pearl Harbor on 7 December 1941, drawing the United States into the conflict. The Japanese forces were making substantial inroads in South-East Asia. On 15 February 1942, Singapore, the impregnable strategic outpost of the British Empire, fell to the advancing Japanese army. Then, on 19 February, the Japanese air force bombed Darwin and for the first time Australia was under direct attack from a foreign power.

Australia was now faced with an imminent Japanese invasion as well as a severe shortage of manpower. This dire situation substantially accelerated the release of the *Dunera* and *Queen Mary* internees into the Australian community, and the mobilisation of able-bodied men from internment, speculated upon by the British Home Office for some time, soon became a reality. Responsibility for this process was largely assigned to Major Julian Layton. Layton initially worked for the Central British Fund for German Jewry and had a long history of successful intervention on behalf of internees in Great Britain.[40]

70   *Perspectives on statelessness*

Arriving in Australia in March 1941 on assignment from the British Home Office to find a solution to the problem of interned German and Austrian refugees, Layton faced considerable opposition from the Australian Army and others. He was, however, supported by the Governor General, Lord Gowrie, and, after October 1941 by the Minister for the Army, Frank Forde. In the first months of 1942, Layton arranged for the men from the *Dunera* interned in Tatura to pick fruit in the Goulburn Valley. The *Queen Mary* internees were soon subsumed into the larger *Dunera* cohort. The fruit-picking detachments were reformed in April 1942 to become the 8th Employment Company of the Australian Military Forces under the command of Captain Edward Renata Broughton.[41] Broughton, one of only two coloured officers in the Australian Army, had himself experienced discrimination on racial grounds and went out of his way to advocate for the motley group of soldiers who came under his command. He is fondly and respectfully remembered.[42]

Enlistment meant release from internment, though not from statelessness. While they were neither Australian nor British citizens, the internees were now part of the Australian Army. Consequently, they were not bound by the restrictions reserved for other enemy aliens and were effectively free residents of the Commonwealth of Australia. A bizarre situation prevailed, however, as the wives and children (including me) of the eighty-five male Singapore internees who joined the armed forces had to remain in internment. Legally, as noted by historian Paul Bartrop, we were still subject to an arrangement with the Straits Settlements which, after the fall of Singapore on 15 February 1942, no longer existed.[43] Recognising the absurdity of this situation, it was not long before a steady stream of wives and children from the camp were released and allowed to go to Melbourne, though my mother and others still had to report to the local police every week.

Of all the places from which internees were sent to Australia, which included Britain, Iran, and Palestine, only the Straits Settlements refused to take Australian internees back following their release.[44] Whether this abandonment played a part in our thoughts about the future is not certain, but nearly all of the *Queen Mary* internees settled in Melbourne and remained there for the rest of their lives. This had no parallel in any of the other groups of overseas internees sent to Australia. For example, of the original

'Nobody's children' 71

2,500 *Dunera* internees, more than two-thirds had left Australia by 1946. My family remained stateless till 1946 when we were granted Australian citizenship, six years after our arrival in Australia.

The post-war boom economy was good for Australia, and we *Queen Mary* internees were direct beneficiaries of this. We were able to integrate into society, and many made a significant and lasting contribution to Australia – a contribution which has also characterised generations of our descendants.

Reflecting on this period in my family story, I believe that being kept together as a family unit protected us from the worst features of internment. By comparison, the men from the *Dunera* interned in Australia were totally deprived of family support and had to rely entirely on their own resourcefulness and the support of the larger cohort. It was therefore perhaps harder for them to handle the twist of fate that had brought us all to Australia, but nevertheless we all shared the stress of leaving our loved ones behind to an uncertain fate in Europe.

I was incredibly fortunate to have loving and creative parents who shielded me from the reality of our predicament, and I never knew the anguish of so many children – literally 'nobody's children' – who were separated from their parents during the 1939–45 war. In recounting this episode in my life, I realise even more deeply than before that I was one of the lucky ones, a resident of a place my father called 'paradise'.

Acknowledgements

Thanks are due to the following: Melinda Mockridge, Seumas Spark, Angela James, Paul Bartop, George Fink, Miriam Gould, and Ruth Simon.

Notes

1 Karl Duldig (1902–1986), First line of poem, 1941; Duldig Studio Archives.
2 For different estimates, see: Frank Forde, Minister of the Army's estimate in National Archives of Australia (NAA) A 2676, 1234. Carol Bunyan's figure is 266–221 from Germany, Austria, and other countries

of Eastern Europe and forty-five from Italy. Personal communication of M. Mockridge to the author, 1 August 2022.

3 Melinda Mockridge, *Art behind the Wire* (Melbourne: Duldig Gallery Inc., 2014), p. 6.

4 Eva de Jong-Duldig, *Driftwood: Escape and Survival through Art* (Melbourne: Arcadia, 2017), pp. 109–40.

5 Notice – Director, Special Branch, Straits Settlements Police to Slawa Duldig, 'Restrictions for Enemy Aliens on Parole', Singapore, 4 December 1939. Duldig Studio Archives Inv. No. 7088.02.

6 Letter by Jones to Prime Minister R. Menzies, 20 September 1940, NAA: A1608, file J20/1/3. See Paul Bartrop, 'Incompatible with Security: Enemy Alien Internees from Singapore in Australia, 1940–1945', *Australian Jewish Historical Society Journal*, 12, 1 (1993), p. 152, n. 15.

7 The National Archives (UK), CO 323/1799/1. 'Straits Settlements' 1940–1941. Records of the Colonial Office, Commonwealth and Foreign and Commonwealth Offices.

8 Seumas Spark, unpublished 'notes' on the file CO 323/1799/1, TNA.

9 Letter, Jewish Refugee Relief Committee, Singapore, 22 July 1940. Duldig Studio Archives, Inv. No. 7080.

10 Correspondence, Chan and Eber to Special Branch Straits Settlements Police, Permission for Duldigs to remain in Singapore, Singapore, 23 July–19 August 1940. Duldig Studio Archives, Inv. No. 7077.

11 Special Branch, Straits Settlements Police to Karl Duldig, Notice of removal from colony, Singapore, 3 September 1940. Duldig Studio Archives, Inv. No. 7068.02.

12 Special Branch, Straits Settlements Police to Mr and Mrs Duldig, Notice to proceed to internment, Singapore. Duldig Studio Archives, Inv. No. 7070.

13 Dr Laidlaw Thomson on behalf of Slawa Duldig, Singapore, 14 September 1940. Duldig Studio Archives, Inv. No. 7092.

14 Kate Garett, *Family Lost and Found: The Story of the Schlesingers*, https://www.dunerastories.monash.edu/dunera-stories/232-story-of -the-schlesingers.html. Accessed 3 October 2022.

15 Karl Duldig, *Tatura Diary*, 30 December 1941, Duldig Studio Archives.

16 For the printed menus of passengers, see Mockridge, *Art behind the Wire*, pp. 5–6.

17 'More Internees Arrive', *Cinesound Review* newsreel, released October 1940, National Film and Sound Archives Title No. 108998.

18 *Daily Telegraph*, 28 September 1940, p. 5.

19 de Jong-Duldig, *Driftwood: Escape and Survival through Art*, p. 147.

'Nobody's children'   73

20 Draft letter from internees to the Governor-General, Lord Gowrie, 1941, copy, Duldig Studio Archives. See Mockridge, *Art behind the Wire*, p.6.

21 Copy of part of an appeal to the Governor-General, Lord Gowrie, 2 March 1941, signed by G. Seefeld, Dr L. Duldig, and P. Schlesinger, Duldig Studio Archives.

22 Australian Archives MP 385/4, file 1940/ 242, 'Internees from Abroad. Applications for Release', Mr K. Arndt and 170 others, Internment Camp No.3, Tatura, to the Colonial Secretary, Government House, Singapore, 28 October 1940. Quoted in Bartrop, 'Incompatible with Security', p. 154, n. 21.

23 Statement and Petition, 7 November 1940 to Prime Minister, The Rt. Hon. R. G. Menzies, copy, Duldig Studio Archives. See also Mockridge, *Art behind the Wire*, p. 8.

24 Australian Archives MP 508/1, file 255/ 702/ 981, 'German and Austrian Internees mostly of Jewish Faith', Rabbi Jacob Danglow (St Kilda, Victoria) to Prime Minister R. G. Menzies, Melbourne, 17 January 1941. Quoted in Bartrop, ibid., p. 155, n. 25.

25 Ken Inglis, Bill Gammage, Seumas Spark, and Jay Winter, with Carol Bunyan, *Dunera Lives: vol. 2. Profiles* (Melbourne: Monash University Publishing, 2020), pp. 250–2.

26 'Treatment of Refugees – an Appeal for Justice – Cruel Propaganda', *Sydney Morning Herald*, 1 August 1940. Quoted in Mockridge, *Art behind the Wire*, p. 10.

27 Landscape plan of Tatura Camp, 6 March 1941. Duldig Studio Archives Inv. No. 7273.

28 Notice, Duldig Studio Archives, uncatalogued.

29 Karl Duldig, 'Fragment', Collection Newcastle Art Gallery. Photograph, Collection Duldig Studio, Inv. No. 6149.

30 Miriam Gould, 'Ilse: The Story of a Remarkable Life', *Australian Jewish Historical Society Journal*, 25, 1 (2020), p. 117.

31 Mockridge, *Art behind the Wire*, p. 32. Photo of the wedding of Lotte Calm and Hans Fischer (Collection Ruth Simon).

32 Australian Archives MP 729 / 6, file 63/ 401/ 201, 'Straits Settlements', Captain A. R. Heighway to Director of Personal Services, AHQ, Melbourne, 30 September 1940. Quoted in Bartrop, 'Incompatible with Security', p. 153, n. 17.

33 See George Fink's presentation in 'Laugh But Don't Forget', a Duldig Studio webinar celebrating the 80th anniversary of the arrival of the Queen Mary internees in Australia (2022). https://duldig.org.au/80th anniversary event/. Accessed 15 May 2023.

74 *Perspectives on statelessness*

34 Australian Archives MP 729 / 6, file 63/ 401/ 335, 'Overseas Internees Pt l', H. V. Evatt to Minister for the Army, 28 June 1941. Bartrop, 'Incompatible with Security', p. 157, n. 37.

35 Ibid., Ministerial Direction from P.C. Spender, Minister for the Army, 8 August 1941. Bartrop, 'Incompatible with Security', p. 157, n. 38.

36 Bartrop, 'Incompatible with Security', pp. 159–61.

37 Australian Archives MP 70/ 1, file 36/101/45, 'Internees – Disturbances 1941', Army memorandum *(Disorders at No. 3 Camp, Tatura)* for General Officer Commanding, Southern Command, no date. Confidential memorandum from Lieutenant-Colonel W.T. Tackaberry *(Disturbance in 'D' Compound. No 3 Camp)*, 29 September 1941. Bartrop, 'Incompatible with Security', p. 161, n. 61.

38 Ibid. General Officer Commanding, Southern Command, to Secretary, Military Board (Confidential), no date. Bartrop, 'Incompatible with Security', p. 162, n. 62.

39 de Jong-Duldig, *Driftwood*, p.164.

40 See 'Julian Layton, Stockbroker and Soldier', in Inglis et al., *Dunera Lives, volume 2*, pp. 22–46.

41 See Chapter 16 for the way military service helped former internees integrate into Australian society.

42 See 'Edward Broughton, Soldier and Bookmaker', in Inglis et al., *Dunera Lives, volume 2*, pp. 3–21.

43 Bartrop, 'Incompatible with Security', p. 163.

44 Ibid., pp. 164–5.

6

Family memories of war and displacement: primary sources for a historian

Joy Damousi

In 'We Refugees', Hannah Arendt's powerful discussion of the psychological and cultural experience of displacement, we are taken to the heart of the stateless condition. In this haunting and chilling essay, Arendt raises fundamental questions of agency, disempowerment, and the control or otherwise by refugees of their circumstances and destiny. Written in 1943, the picture Arendt presents is bleak, desperate, and haunting. Stateless refugees not only lose their identities, Arendt suggests, but they are also forced to renounce their own histories and personal narratives – and in doing so, relinquish their identity, their core self.[1]

In this chapter, I expand on the theme of retaining the historical narrative while meditating on the interplay of history and memory and my own course as a historian of memory, migration, and the aftermaths of war. Shaping, possessing, and ultimately determining the historical and personal story is central to the experience of the migrant, the stateless person, and the refugee. There is no shortage of memoirs that recall these experiences. This has become a rich genre where writers, poets, and creative artists have powerfully reflected on the physical, psychological, and emotional state that displacement generates.[2]

Having grown up in a familial context where history is fundamental and central to retaining a sense of self and identity following dislocation, my own practice as a historian has been informed by this need to retain and re-remember this past. Oral storytelling has been the way in which I learnt and heard about my family history. Controlling and not losing the historical narrative

76 *Perspectives on statelessness*

intergenerationally is another aspect of the need to keep family memories and histories alive through generational change in a new country.

War and its aftermaths have been a major theme in my own scholarship, and this is squarely a product of these stories and my own family histories. While my most recent work on Greek migration in the aftermath of war and then child refugee histories have come to the fore, the storytelling and memories that I grew up with as a child have made a deep impression on me. These memories passed down were fragmented, out of context, without chronology and framework. But the colour and drama through which these were conveyed to me appealed to my inquisitiveness and sensitivities. It drove me to learn more about the fragments I heard and to pursue the meanings of them – a quest which continues to this day.

These intergenerational stories are not passively received but circulate in communities and, as they are passed on, create new narratives and interpretations. The narrative of the stateless, displaced, and migrant can continue to cast a shadow within families. In some contexts, these memories are often expunged and denied in the public arena. In the public sphere, such stories are often left untold and rendered illegitimate. The key connection here is the right to tell the story of periods of turbulence in what Jay Winter describes in Chapter 1 in this volume as 'seizing the right to tell the story of chaotic times'.[3] And it is in storytelling that there is liberation and some potential for political engagement and political life. The art of storytelling was so fundamental to survival that it can also be seen as an act of empowerment. The 'third way', as Winter characterises it[4] – the act of capturing narratives and making them one's own, such as processing them in historical texts – provides links with the past and the future of these inherited stories for new generations.

A focus on storytelling raises the question of the context these stories told and articulated. Who and what is the audience? And how is this memory and storytelling used and for what purpose? In this chapter, my focus is the familial, the intimate, the everyday. This is in sharp contrast to other circumstances where stories are told such as the legal, bureaucratic, or governmental – described by Peter Gatrell in his chapter – where storytelling is framed with different imperatives and agendas and in sharply different historical contexts.[5]

Family memories of war and displacement 77

I consider familial stores that circulate in the private sphere that as historians we seek to make public. In translating these for a wider public, they become political: the assertion of a cultural identity that is not easily recognised or identified in the prevailing culture. In the context of the assimilation era in Australia immediately after the Second World War, where the government objective was to deny such identities and narratives, and ethnic storytelling, this becomes deeply politicised. In this context, it is only the familial narrative that can incubate the story telling of the dispossessed. It is also the familial that provides new narratives of empowerment and new cultural identities into the future. Stories of war, violence, poverty, and starvation resonate with different meaning in a new context, but these narratives do forge new beginnings of how these stories can empower and how they can endure.

I begin with an anecdote. I first heard about the Holocaust when I was about 8. I recall my mother Sophia talking about how the Nazis would raid villages in Northern Greece in her hometown of Florina when she was just a little older than I was. She talked about the survival strategies of civilians and of deprivation and violence. Her narrative, told with great power and force, was one of resilience and strength.

Her most striking descriptions were (and still are) of how she witnessed the obliteration of the Jewish community of the small town of Florina in 1943. She was thirteen. Tragically, 295 Jewish residents (as I later discovered) were deported. Fully 84 per cent of the Jewish population in the town vanished, thus ending four centuries of harmonious co-existence between my Greek ancestors and our Jewish neighbours. These scenes were terrifying and enduring in my mother's memory. She was keen to pass on details of this witnessing to her impressionable daughter as she did not want her memories lost in the passage of time in her own displacement after the war through her migration to faraway Australia. Her story was told as a morality tale about evil, with passionate political comment and with a very deep sense of melancholy and loss.

If the nuance of a history lesson was lost on me as a child in receiving my mother's visceral framing of her memory, the emotional force of the narrative immediately stuck. I found myself externalising (and perhaps internalising) these stories through child's play and my invented survival games of war. I would imaginatively roam the house ducking bullets, armies, and the stampede of Nazi invaders. By propping up a sheet with broom sticks in the dining room of our home, I would escape into my imaginary haven and hence to safety. I would try to replicate the sound of German boots, which would reverberate in my imagination; my mother's narrative would repeatedly feature this sound of war as it had an indelible and enduring imprint on her memory of terror and fear. In these games, I would perform her history, her experience of war – or at least as I interpreted those experiences as a child.

That was in 1969. Very little, if anything, was taught in mainstream Australia about the Holocaust at that time. 'Memory', 'testimony', and 'oral history' were words of the future. But my mother and I were not to know that our conversations were poised at the cusp of a moment in time, for only a few years later, from the early 1970s, the memory boom and oral history would burst onto the history profession and take the writing of the history of the Holocaust, the histories of the First and Second World Wars, and other themes of war in dramatically new directions. The visceral elements of war, the day-to-day experience of civilians, and the dramatic dislocation it caused were inescapably part of my growing up. They have remained historical questions for me.

I begin with this anecdote to explore how such family memories can become the primary sources not only for constructing a family narrative of displacement, but also for providing a frame for my work writing on the histories of war and its aftermaths, from an emotional, political, social, and cultural perspective.

The nexus I wish to explore is that between family memory, war, and my work on the emotions of grief, loss, and mourning in war. The specific focus is not the Holocaust stories, for these were not directly familial, devasting as they were to hear as a child. It is the death of my uncle, Pandelis Klinkatsis, during the Greek Civil War in 1949. My mother Sophia's ongoing grief continues through her relentless search for Pandelis' son, called Victor, who was born out of wedlock in 1945. Sophia has never met Victor – the one remaining connection of the past to her dear lost brother – but she has continued to search for his whereabouts. The sources that piece this story together are many and varied, and I draw on a range of materials and three perspectives to bring this family memory of dislocation together.

Family memories of war and displacement 79

First, oral history is the basis for much for this story. As with many family war stories, the narrative is fragmentary. In the chaos of war, the fate of family members is not easily traced and is often lost forever. These are tales of snippets of biography, research dead ends, with specific details lost over time.[6] This gap of knowledge becomes part of how mourning for those lost remains open-ended and unresolved, with only raw emotions and memory for those left to grieve. This absence in the oral testimony of my mother is filled with mourning for that which can never be retrieved: a full and detailed account of the events of wartime experience.

Second, the theme of emotions and war are manifest in this story through two expressions of love: sibling love between my mother and her brother, and romantic love between Pandelis and the mother of his child, Lottie, a Viennese woman he meets and falls in love with in Vienna under Nazi occupation. After the war, Lottie and Victor migrate to America without any further connection to Pandelis' family. Separation of lovers and children borne out of wedlock are a major part of all wars, and this thread is a crucial aspect of this story.[7]

The third theme relates to this, and that is the wider phenomenon of separation, displacement, and migration during the Second World War and after it. During the war, from 1942 to 1945, Pandelis, a tailor's assistant, travelled to Vienna from Greece, where he met Lottie. He returned to Greece when the Red Army arrived, leaving Lottie and Victor behind. By then he had been conscripted into the Greek Army. After the war, my father and mother migrated to Australia in 1956 and 1957 respectively, in the wave of massive post-war immigration from Greece, in numbers historically unprecedented until that time. How are war memories remembered and what emotions are expressed when these memories are transplanted to another place and passed onto future generations? Memory studies have informed analyses of the war and the civil war, but there is space for a fuller exploration of the emotions within this memory.[8] While I was born in Australia, the experience of displacement was palpable, and the stories of war have never left our family.

Other than oral storytelling, the other way in which the memory of displacement is kept alive in a transnational world is through photography. There are a few photographs that remain of Pandelis, but most of them are of him in the Greek military hospital (Figure 6.1). There

Figure 6.1 Photograph of Pandelis Klinkatsis, in uniform. Source: Joy Damousi.

are multiple copies of these photographs. When Sophia migrated to Australia, these were the photographs she took – these were the ones she remembers him by. They are the only way I would ever know my uncle, and the story surrounding his death.

This line of enquiry takes us to the heart of the social and cultural aspects of displacement and dislocation created by war. It is an example of how storytelling and memory can create a social

Family memories of war and displacement   81

community drawing on the family but also wider cultural narratives. These perspectives are absent from Arendt's formulations. While political rights are her focus, she captures despair in 'We Refugees' without consideration of the social and cultural domain and how these communities can provide agency, memory, and, through it, empowerment. In the 'Rights of Man', it is exclusively in political communities where she searches for the place of 'rights' and not beyond this sphere.

What is the role of the historian in this as both the receiver and disseminator of historical storytelling about displacement? Is the role to go beyond Arendt by discussing the role of displaced people in producing new historical stories? For those of us whose families' stories of displacement have shaped us, we have also in turn shaped the narrative. The generational aspect of storytelling remains unexplored in Arendt's work. But it is often here where stateless and displaced communities have found great strength and empowerment through the passing down of stories and memories to the next generations.

Discussions of intergenerational storytelling are not new. In her pioneering work on postmemory, Marianne Hirsch has written eloquently of issues of what she refers to as the 'guardianship' of Holocaust memory by subsequent generations. Hirsch highlights the issues that arise with the appropriation of memory. She notes the challenges of how memory can be transmitted to those who did not experience the event first hand. To distinguish these memories from the recall of participants, she coined the term 'postmemory', and explains how in recalling her own inherited memories and those like hers, she characterised herself as part of the postmemory generation.[9] She describes how the stories of her parents 'crowded out' her own memories of childhood, and she remembered these more than she recalled her own memories. Further, she also recalled as a child how she 'imagined myself into the lives they were passing down at me'.[10] These were also mediated memories, she notes; the stories were narratives that were told and retold, read, and heard.[11]

Hirsch further argues that postmemory refers to the relationship of the 'generation after', bearing the personal, collective, and cultural trauma of those who came before. But these traumas were so deep that they appeared 'to constitute memories in their own right'. Postmemory connection to the past was thus actually mediated not

82   *Perspectives on statelessness*

by recall but 'by imaginative investment, projection, and creation'.[12] Hirsch warned that this risks one's own memories being displaced, 'even evacuated', by our ancestors. 'These events happened in the past, but their effects continue into the present', she noted.[13] She argues that postmemory is not a 'movement, method, or idea'; it is a 'structure of inter- and trans-generational return of traumatic knowledge and embodied experience'.[14] The 'process of intergenerational transmission' has become an important 'explanatory vehicle and object of study' in American slavery and other subjects. Postmemory is not an identity position but a generational structure 'of transmission embedded in multiple forms of mediation'.[15] Photographic images are central to her analysis.[16] It is through photography, she argues, that we have 'the clearest articulation of what we fantasize and expect of surviving images from the past: that they have a memory of their own that they bring to us from the past; that that memory tells us something about ourselves, about what/how we and those who preceded us once were; that they carry not only information about the past but enable us to reach its emotional register'.[17]

For Hirsch, the stateless in particular have different memories. The term for Hirsch connotes not only dispossession and negation but also release and liberation, which she characterises as 'contradictory associations'.[18] Arendt, she believes, is part of our postmemory.[19] Yet there are problems, she argues, with Arendt's formulation that rights can only be acquired through national belonging and citizenship. Hirsch notes that national belonging does not guarantee rights: 'both stateless people and persecuted national minorities suffer from the lack of rights'. Hirsch rightly believes that the debate on rights is centred on 'the foundational right that grants the possibility of having rights'. Is it basic humanity that is meant to guarantee this right in Arendt's view, or is it, as Stephanie DeGooyer and others argue in 'The Right to Have Rights', 'the membership in a political community that must first be acquired before that right can be claimed'?[20] Hirsch believes it is the latter. But what does it mean, she asks, 'to have rights, given the fragility of political community?'[21]

Furthermore, Hirsch notes, how, if rights claims are based on the membership of a political community, does the work of creating that community become the basis for those who participate?[22] But communities are formed culturally and socially by narratives

Family memories of war and displacement 83

through intergenerational storytelling. Arendt discusses how, in her view, the stateless belong to no community. This is the 'calamity', as she sees it. But she has great confidence in what belonging to a political community provides.[23]

Hirsch provides an invaluable frame through which to connect postmemory with storytelling and new narratives of displacement. The memories that I discuss in this chapter are not memories that overshadow my own, and of course, they are not my memories. They are stories which I have inherited. They sit alongside mine and form a parallel memory growing up. I am of course not disengaged from them. They sparked an interest in storytelling and the past, but also a subliminal obligation, even a burden of guilt, and a visceral response to these stories. Postmemory is not identical to memory. But as Hirsch notes, it does 'approximate memory in its affective force and psychic effects'.[24] As a child, I was given and provided with fragments, isolated stories, snippets of events of the vagaries and violence of war and its aftermath. As a historian, I have tried to make sense of these and produce new narratives, interpretations, and perspectives on these memories. It is a re-telling of these stories to make them public and re-work them and so produce a narrative that is embedded within the social and the cultural and within communities.

Childhood memories

The story of my uncle's perilous fate during the Greek Civil War has been a dominant narrative within my family.[25] In October 1949, in the closing month of the Greek Civil War, my uncle, Pandelis Klinkatsis, aged twenty-four, was killed stepping on a landmine in Northern Greece. Fighting for the Greek Government against the communist insurgents, he was conscripted into the Greek army in 1945. Born in Florina in 1924, very close to where the most intensive fighting of this war took place, he had been wounded several times during his term as a soldier and had periods of convalescence in the military hospital in Athens, recuperating from war wounds. Each time he would return to battle. The fatal blow came in the last months of 1949, when he took that devastating last step. The announcement of his death was sent by telegram to his immediate

84 *Perspectives on statelessness*

family. His death was mourned by his younger siblings – his two younger sisters – Sophia, my mother (born 1930), and Fanni, my aunt (born 1926) – and his brother, my uncle, George (born 1934). His parents, Yannis and Petroula (both born 1901), were overcome by grief. His death devastated the family.

The backdrop to this story is the Second World War itself, and the inescapable events that have also been embedded within family memory. The German occupation of Greece began in April 1941 and ended in 1944. Bombing raids took place over many towns, and locals ran to bomb shelters for safety. The Greek Resistance that had emerged was a target for the Germans, and the guerrilla war was also being fought against the andartes – the resistance fighters – whom they aimed to destroy. The impact on the civilian population of this conflict was brutal and devastating. The anti-guerrilla campaign led to over a thousand villages being razed, with a million Greeks seeing their homes looted and burned down. More than twenty thousand civilians were killed or wounded, shot, hanged, or beaten by the German armed forces.[26] In Northern Greece, the impact of this campaign was the worst. Up to March 1944, military raids alone in Western Macedonia, where Florina is situated, affected eighty-five thousand people.[27]

These events have defined my family history through the memories of my mother, who was a child at the time. Children had to learn how to survive in a world of destruction and violence, as this had become a normal way of life. The emotions of fear and terror dominated Sophia's childhood memories of war. The fickle aspect of life and death was embodied within this fear. Sophia recalls the way in which seeking refuge in bomb shelters was terrifying, arbitrary, and confusing. In the chaos of sporadic bombs dropping and landing, the fear and terror of death loomed large. The deaths of neighbours and friends have never been erased, but she was one of the fortunate children who survived with her immediate family intact. These childhood experiences were retold through the eyes of an adult, but as a child, I immediately identified with that child survivor.

But it was Pandelis' death that overshadowed all my mother's recollections of her wartime experience. Sophia's story amplifies the telling observations made by Leonore Davidoff of the 'life long effect' of the loss of a sibling in childhood.[28] Children have their

Family memories of war and displacement

own mourning to do, which can be manifest as anger, sadness, frustration, fear, and irritability. Stephen Bank and Michael Kahn perceptively observe how a sibling's death 'ends only a life; it does not end a relationship'.[29] Over time, the politics of how Pandelis died and which side caused his death has dissipated. The enduring memory instead has now been distilled to an emotional response: the loss and mourning of a much loved and adored son and brother.

Before Pandelis served in the army, he was in Vienna between 1942 and 1945. There, he met an Austrian woman, whose name we only have as Lottie. They had a son, Victor, born in 1945 in Vienna. She travelled to New York with her son in 1947 and had arranged to meet him there after the war. Pandelis' death ended any further contact the family had with Lottie and Victor.

Why would Pandelis travel to Vienna under the Nazis? His residence in Vienna coincided directly with the active recruitment for foreign labour in the Reich. Over this time, the Germans relied increasingly on foreign workers, with a total of ten million working in the Reich by 1945. By then, one out of every five workers employed was a foreigner.[30]

By the end of 1942, only around ten thousand Greek workers had registered to work in the Reich, despite a relentless campaign to recruit them. Some may have gone as a last resort to stave off starvation. The reputation of Greek workers was very poor: it was one of a reluctance to work, absenteeism, the 'biggest good-for-nothings'. Some too were prepared to demonstrate their hostility to National Socialism. Even worse were the connections with German women. There was an overt anti-German and anti-Nazi attitude among many of the Greek workers. It was a source of horror that German women were in liaison with Greek men, and that pregnancies were reported. Greek workers were 'a headache' for the Germans and delivered low productivity.[31]

It is unknown whether Pantelis, at the age of eighteen in 1942, went to Vienna because he succumbed to pressure after the call to sign on, or because he was drawn to the possibility of work in the midst of grinding poverty and deprivation. There appears to be no political motivation, although impregnating a German woman was seen as a serious affront to the Germans. It was considered to be disrespectful, dishonourable, and a deliberate act of insult to Germany. There is also the issue of how the news of impregnating a woman

86   *Perspectives on statelessness*

out of wedlock was received by the family. Under ordinary circumstances, this would have been considered shameful. But Pandelis' safe return was all that mattered to Sophia, and, it appears, to his parents. Sophia as his close confidante was told first about his romantic entanglements, and then he told his parents. It was war, opined my mother, and these things happened in war. The story of how Lottie and Pandelis apparently met perhaps softens the tale of shame or humiliation of bearing a child out of wedlock. After a bomb attack, Pandelis was buried by rubble, from where Lottie retrieved him and saved his life. The romance of this story provides an explanation for the circumstances of their intimate relationship.

What is known is that Pandelis left Greece suddenly, abruptly, and with little explanation. Whatever the cause of his departure, finding his presence in Vienna has been elusive. Since he was not married, locating Lottie – even if they lived at the same place – would not have been documented on his record of residence; her details could only be found if we knew her full name. The only tentative connection arising is that the name of a tailor – K. Tuma – who was recorded at the same address where Pandelis lived, which might imply that Pandelis may have lived with this employer if he in fact worked as a tailor. This occupation, needless to say, was not the basis of recruitment of foreign labour into Vienna. Judging from the two photographs of Pandelis at that time, he did not appear to have worked in industry.

The fragmentation of families and search for missing members remains a hallmark of the legacy of war. There are still fragments to be connected in this story, and the search for Sophia's nephew continues. Lottie's exodus to the United States with two-year-old Victor is the last detail to date of their whereabouts. A deep longing to make connection may never ever happen. Wars created such unknowns. But without closure, the fate of Pandelis' lover and her child remains a mystery that speaks to the emotional wound of Sophia's brother's loss that remains unhealed.

Two forms of commemoration, closely connected to emotions and war, are the place of gravesites and photographs in family memories.

The first is the gravesite. In 2009, Sophia returned to the village of Amohouri where the family graves stand. Here she restored the tombstone for Pandelis, where she provided a photograph and

Family memories of war and displacement   87

attended to the gravesite as it had gone into disrepair, in order to honour and to further grieve Pandelis' memory and her loss.

The second is the collection of photos of Pandelis my mother took with her to Australia. Not only are these photographs central to keeping a remembrance alive, but also there are many taken when Pandelis was a soldier, so his memory is closely linked to the circumstances of his death. Only these photographs remain of him. They are a source of both remembrance and loss in Australia. They are a means through which Pandelis' story is told and re-told. The photos of Pandelis, as with all family photographs brought from Greece, have been kept in biscuit tins and shoeboxes. From time to time, when the family have gathered together, these are passed around and discussed. Sophia would identify the faces, places, and times of another life with colourful descriptions. The story about Pandelis was a reoccurring one in the family narrative that would ebb and flow around the photographs of him and those of Lottie. These would begin with Pandelis' untimely death, and then go back in time before his passing as a most adored brother, and finally return full circle to the importance of never forgetting this family story.

Memory and loss

In the immediate years following Pandelis' death, Sophia worked on the family tobacco farm. In 1954 she became engaged to George Damousi; in 1955 they married, and in 1956 Sophia gave birth to their first daughter, Mary, my eldest sister. In November 1957 she left Greece, never to return permanently. The link to Pandelis on the issue of emigration was not that Sophia may have sought to leave behind the devastation of his death and start life anew. On the contrary, his memory was one of the enduring links that connected Sophia back to Greece rather than a reason to move away from it.

Pandelis did however symbolise another narrative of migration for Sophia. When he confided in her that he hoped to join Lottie in the United States after the war, he promised that she, his adoring sister, would join them. Whether this was a genuine proposition or ever feasible soon became irrelevant. But Sophia's migration to Australia would have carried with it the shadow of the journey that

88 *Perspectives on statelessness*

never took place – the one where she would start a new life in the United States with her beloved brother, his son, and soon to be wife, Lottie.

The future after the war turned out to be in stark contrast to this imagined life, one that was shaped by the powerful absence and yet presence of Pandelis. The other shadow that is widely cast is the search for Victor. It is the pursuit of a connection with the loss and grief of Sophia's brother, the one embodied remaining connection to him, and which continues over sixty years after Sophia's migration to Australia. Migration to Australia after the war did not lead to these stories being expunged, but in some ways the retention of them was even more important, as the family narratives of war could have been erased or retained.

A part of the remembering this family history is connecting with Victor and hearing his war story and the ramifications of it. This quest may never be realised given the small fragments of information available of Victor's whereabouts. The emotional wound of loss remains.

Resettlement came with its challenges. The haunting image that Arendt paints while limiting the agency of the stateless nevertheless captures the visceral experience of the stateless. There is anger, fear, resentment, and loneliness embedded within the experience of migration. My parents arrived in Australia during the height of the assimilation period between 1945 and 1972 (Figure 6.2). Over these years, it became official policy for immigrants to assimilate into Australian culture and attempt to make them 'New Australians'. I could see how this was a great failure of policy as we occupied two worlds: internally as migrants, within the family where past histories and memories were fiercely kept alive; and externally, where assimilation was premised on such memories and past histories being extinguished. Arendt captures these tensions dramatically when she talks about how beneath the optimism shown by the stateless is the 'hopeless sadness of assimilationists'.[32] Optimism, hope, and sadness can co-exist and there is no question that many aspects of the war migration story should be told through success and resilience. What remained a constant was the need to retain historical memory through re-telling this story.

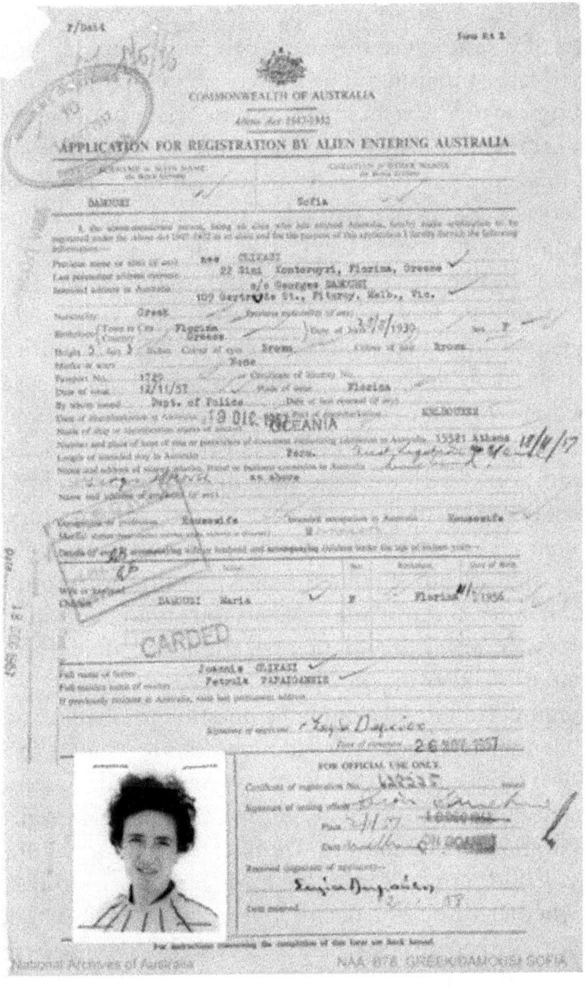

Family memories of war and displacement

89

Figure 6.2 Sophia Damousi, alien registration form, 1957. Series number: B78, Control Symbol: Greek/Damousi Sofia. Image courtesy of the National Archives of Australia. NAA: B78, GREEK/DAMOUSI SOFIA.

Familial memories

The familial is shaped and formed through these memories, shaping the social and establishing a connectedness. Towards this end, how are these memories and histories passed onto the next generation? What narratives are told? A few years ago, the cover of a book I had just finished, *Memory and Migration in the Shadow of War*, on memories of war amongst the Greek community in Melbourne, had arrived from the publishers. I was discussing the cover of it with my two siblings, which was an image of two Nazi guards ushering the German army on its way to Salonica in 1941. As we observed the striking image on the book, my twelve-year-old niece asked casually, 'What is a Nazi?' We paused. The silence expanded. None of us rushed to occupy the space. Her grandmother was not there to fill the void with her tales of courage and resilience. We, the second generation, did not have a quick narrative, handy and ready to be easily digested by a blooming teenager, with her enquiring mind, already unleashing endless questions. She sensed our unease.

'Why don't you want me to know?' she asked, perplexed by our uncomfortable silence. As custodians of the family memory of war, my siblings and I feel we have inherited a responsibility – some would say burden – to now construct an emotional history of war for the next generation. We as yet have no narrative. It remains a work in progress. But the interpretations I offer of the migration story in *Memory and Migration* serves to continue the storytelling, give it a new framework and interpretation, and allow for bringing communities together in a new way.

Turning full circle, and examining questions of memory, war, and childhood, my latest book, *The Humanitarians*, explores the history of child war refugees and the efforts on their behalf by humanitarians to save, evacuate, assimilate, and adopt children in war. It raises several questions including who speaks on behalf of children, how, and why. Children of all refugees have their stories told on their behalf: whether to be evacuated, saved, assimilated, or adopted – or some or all these aspects. The rights of children are beyond the remit of Arendt's formulation, but stories about children were told to help liberate and, if possible, save them from statelessness and navigate their future towards citizenship. Despite the various declaration of rights throughout the twentieth century, these remained elusive in the twentieth and into the twenty-first centuries. The story of children displaced and made stateless by war is perhaps the most poignant given it speaks to the future. But in recent times, the push has been to capture children's narratives and storytelling as a form of agency, empowerment, and the forging of community.

Family memories of war and displacement 91

Arendt's formulations may seem anachronistic at times in the dichotomy of stateless and citizenship she establishes. But story-telling gives us another avenue through which to explore displacement. Within the familial context, we can see how the circulation of memory and storytelling can empower and create new stories, both within families and outside of them.

I began this chapter with the theme of children in war – of my mother's own violent dislocation and displacement as well as her witnessing war, and myself as a child witness of her own memories. This resonates perhaps most explicitly with family histories and the primary source of my evolution as history, connecting emotional histories, displacement, migration, gender, and trauma. Gone are the children's games and the playing out of family war stories. Over several decades, however, the link to retain historical narratives remains. The interpretations of my mother's experiences are now replaced by academic tomes arguing for the complexity of war and its multifaceted meanings: for a deeper understanding the shadow war has cast. It remains a life-long pursuit.

Notes

1 Hannah Arendt, 'We Refugees', in Jerome Kohn and Ron H. Feldman (eds), *The Jewish Writings by Hannah Arendt* (New York: Schocken Books, 2008), pp. 264–74.
2 See for the use of such memoirs in Joy Damousi, '"We Are Still Alive": Refugees and Loneliness', in Katie Barclay, Elaine Chalus, and Deborah Simonton (eds), *The Routledge History of Loneliness* (London: Routledge, 2023), pp. 471–83.
3 See Chapter 1 in this volume.
4 Ibid.
5 See Chapter 10 in this volume.
6 For a discussion of such fragments, see Phillipe Sands, *East West Street: On the Origins of 'Genocide' and 'Crimes Against Humanity'* (New York: Alfred Knopf, 2016).
7 Claire Langhamer, *The English in Love: The Intimate Story of an Emotional Revolution* (Oxford: Oxford University Press, 2013); Marilyn Lake, 'Female Desires: The Meaning of World War II', in Joy Damousi and Marilyn Lake (eds), *Gender and War: Australians at War*

92 *Perspectives on statelessness*

in the Twentieth Century (Cambridge: Cambridge University Press, 1995), pp. 60–80.

8 See Riki van Boeschoten, 'The Impossible Return: Coping with Separation and the Reconstruction of Memory in the Wake of the Civil War', in Mark Mazower (ed.), *After the War Was Over: Reconstructing the Family, Nation, and the State in Greece, 1943–1960* (Princeton, NJ: Princeton University Press, 2000), pp. 122–41.

9 Marianne Hirsch, *The Generation of Post-Memory: Writing and Visual Culture After the Holocaust* (New York: Columbia University Press, 2012), p. 4.

10 Ibid., p. 4.

11 Ibid., p. 4.

12 Ibid., p. 5.

13 Ibid., p. 5.

14 Ibid., p. 6.

15 Ibid., p. 35.

16 Ibid., p. 36.

17 Ibid., p. 52.

18 Marianne Hirsch, 'Stateless Memory', *Critical Times*, 2, 3 (December 2019), p. 417.

19 Ibid., p. 420.

20 Ibid., p. 421.

21 Ibid., p. 421.

22 Ibid., p. 421.

23 Hannah Arendt, 'The Rights of Man', *Modern Review*, 3, 1 (Summer 1949), pp. 28, 30.

24 Ibid., p. 31.

25 For further discussion of this family history, see Joy Damousi, 'In Search of Victor: Transnationalism, Emotions and War', in Claire Langhamer, Lucy Noakes, and Claudia Siebrecht (eds), *Total War: An Emotional History* (Oxford: Oxford University Press, 2020), pp. 157–76.

26 Mark Mazower, *Inside Hitler's Greece: The Experience of Occupation 1941–1944* (New Haven, CT: Yale University Press, 1995), p. 155.

27 Ibid., p. 183.

28 Leonore Davidoff, *Thicker Than Water: Siblings and their Relations, 1780–1920* (Oxford: Oxford University Press, 2012), p. 308.

29 Quoted in ibid., p. 333.

30 Edward L. Homze, *Foreign Labor in Nazi Germany* (Princeton, NJ: Princeton University Press, 1967), p. 153.

31 Ibid., pp. 75–7.

32 Arendt, 'We Refugees', p. 272.

Part II

Refugees and the stateless in Asia and the Pacific in the global Second World War

Section II.I

Varieties of refugee life and statelessness
in China

7

War, memory, the state, and statelessness in China

Rana Mitter

On 3 September 2015, Tiananmen Square, at the heart of Beijing, was filled by an enormous parade. Missiles, tanks, and marching soldiers all made their way past thousands of gathered spectators from China and abroad. The event commemorated the seventieth anniversary of the end of the Second World War in Asia, and stood in stark contrast to the elegiac tone of many of the memorials in Europe in the preceding spring. On the anniversary of the liberations of Auschwitz in January 1945, or VE Day in May, there was a strong sense that the end of a narrative had been reached: veterans and survivors attending a seventieth anniversary in the knowledge that far fewer would reach an eightieth. In contrast, in China, while veterans stood at the centre of the parade, there was a much stronger sense that the military display was part of a definition of a new China, rather than a farewell to the old one.

The Chinese event was distinctive in another important way. The parade was the first ever national public commemoration of China's role in the Second World War in which the collective effort of the nation, rather than the role of the Chinese Communist Party (CCP), was at its heart. In particular, it included veterans of the Nationalist (Kuomintang) as well as communist armies that had fought against Japan, an act of historical inclusion that partially reversed the binary division between Nationalist losers and communist victors in the civil war that ended with the victory of Mao Zedong in 1949. The parade fell on the third of three new holidays that had been created in 2015 as part of a new veneration for China's wartime role. And it was a major date in a process that had been taking place over a much longer period of time – some thirty years or more – in which China's attitude toward memory of its wartime participation changed profoundly, and with significant consequences for its domestic and international politics.

The robust, even insistent, assertion of state identity was central to the narrative that that the Chinese party-state, the People's Republic of China (PRC) under the Chinese Communist Party (CCP), wished to project in 2015. Hannah Arendt's reflections on statelessness referred in significant part to the exclusion of categories of people from the seeming certainties of the modern nation-state. China's turbulent twentieth-century history certainly provided many of the circumstances which also shaped Arendt's: war, revolution, and ideological currents that had consequences in shaping polities and their policies toward individuals. Refugee flight, which shaped Europe in the wartime era, also shaped China during the Second World War, as did the displacement of huge numbers of refugees in the years after it.[1] However, there is a significant difference in the way in which the state – and ideas of 'statelessness' – come together in the shaping of modern Chinese political identity. Rather than the declaration of a section of the population as separate from a defined state, instead China's nationalism draws on an often seemingly very rigid definition of state identity precisely because it fears that the underpinnings of the modern Chinese state are dangerously fluid and less able to bear the load of national identity formation than the task demands. It can seem that the Chinese state is not so much worried that people might become stateless, but that the state itself might do so.

In this context, the creation of collective memory of the Second World War matters profoundly in China today. It is brought up ever more frequently as China seeks to make its position known in the world. In disputes in the East and South China Seas, in designing patriotic education, in producing films and television programmes, China refers back, again and again, to the war. China's own memory of war is unique among any of the Allied Powers. The United States remembers it, in Studs Terkels' evocative but ironic phrase, as 'the good war', when GIs were shipped to Europe and Asia to bring liberation. Britain remembers its war as a time when it resisted bombing and invasion and stood tall against the Nazis (with Japan playing a supporting role). From 1945 onward, the USSR defined its war as the 'Great Patriotic War', and Putin's Russia has made demeaning comments about the Soviet war record a matter for criminal proceedings, as well as pursuing spurious comparisons with the previous war during its brutal invasion of Ukraine. France has converted its story of occupation into one of resistance.

China is the only major Allied belligerent to have shifted its position about the meaning of the wartime years almost entirely during the course of the post-war era. For the first half of the Cold War, under Mao Zedong, official China spoke relatively little about the war years, and when it did, concentrated almost entirely on the record of the Chinese Communist Party and the importance of the war in bringing the CCP to power. From the 1980s onward, the war became a more and more central part of the Chinese official discourse, appearing everywhere from textbooks to museums to television soap operas. During this process, the scope of China's understanding of the war expanded significantly, with the most notable example being the way in which the communists' old opponents, the Nationalists, were brought back into the narrative of the war; from the 1980s, the Nationalist contribution to the defeat of Japan was much more prominently discussed in a China ruled by the CCP.[2] This process was, in large part, a way of tying the idea of a nation forged in war to the state that emerged during and after that war, and eliding differences between the Nationalist Chinese state that survived on the mainland until 1949 and the communist one that has been dominant ever since.

Imagining the Chinese state during wartime

How has Chinese nationalism been defined in the long state-formation of China in the past century and a half, ever since the arrival of Western imperial powers in China? In his now-classic study of the origins of the nation as an 'imagined community', Benedict Anderson wrote of the way in which the newspaper could be used as a means of creating the nation's narrative, the ability to participate in an ongoing story in which various 'characters' would appear, disappear, and re-appear on a regular basis.[3] The visual memory of war in China is likewise part of a still-ongoing attempt to define an imagined community when the state that encompasses that community still seems like a work in progress.

War, memory, the state, and statelessness in China   99

The origins and nature of Chinese nationalism have been deeply contested in the last few decades. As the constructed nature of that nationalism is more acknowledged, the role of print culture and the media have become central in explaining that construction, and the introduction of a mass-produced, mass-circulation visual imaginary through the medium of newsprint is an essential part of our new understanding of the formation and propagation of nationalism.[4] It is fitting, then, that perhaps the greatest crisis of Chinese nationalism in the last century, the war against Japan, should have been such a powerful occasion for the emergence of a visual imaginary that fuelled visions of what the nation might be.

The use of the visual to construct an idea of the nation through its wartime experience is not an innovation of the late twentieth century. Rather, the experience and presentation of war in early-twentieth-century China was profoundly shaped by the encounter with the modern, and, in particular, the dark side of the modern. The transnational currents of modernism that shaped the Italian Futurists also contributed to a fascination with dynamism and speed in the early period of the Republic (1912–49). The constant experience of warfare did a great deal to darken this enthusiasm, but even when war broke out with Japan in 1937, there was a strong conviction that the war itself might be the source of a form of national renewal: Chiang Kai-shek, the Chinese leader, had declared in 1938 that

> the only goal of the War of Resistance and the Revolution is to rebuild the country. To achieve this goal, we need to implement five types of reconstruction. The first is spiritual reconstruction, the second is material reconstruction, the third is social reconstruction, the fourth is political reconstruction, and the fifth is military reconstruction … only then can a modern nation be truly established.[5]

In that respect, there was a great deal of similarity between the agenda of the two deadly rivals for power in China, the ruling Nationalists and their communist opponents. Both aspired to a type of modernity derived from the ostensible agenda of the Enlightenment, with scientific progress and an attachment to rationality as the paths to bringing China out of the 'traditional' past, often at great psychological and aesthetic cost to China's heritage. Chiang's Nanjing regime painted itself as the embodiment of a kind of technological

100   *Refugees and the stateless in Asia*

modernity which would transform China into an industrialised, prosperous nation-state which had regained its own political and economic autonomy.[6] This vision of modern development was often too dismissive of or brutal toward the elements of Chinese society, such as popular religion, which did not fit into it. Both parties also placed themselves in opposition to a strong anti-rational strain in Japanese modernity which was fuelled by mystical ideas of 'national essence'. However, the Nationalist party's narrative of a new China emerging through technological modernity could not remain as it was after 1937. The reality of war with Japan was retreat, devastation, refugee flight, and the wholesale moving of the machinery of administration to Wuhan, and then Chongqing. However, the party could not abandon the old narrative of modernity and progress either, not least because it would surrender yet more legitimacy to their rivals and uneasy partners, the communists.

The determination to create some sort of order in the representation of the war effort by the Nationalists and China's writers and artists had profound effects in the fields of journalism, fiction, and drama.[7] The visual aspects of the war were also carefully reordered for public consumption. By the 1930s, China had a sophisticated and widespread print culture, which made extensive use of photographs as well as illustrations and cartoons.

'Historical statelessness'

Thus far, there is a similarity in China's mid-twentieth-century narrative to that of other major belligerent nations at the time. The state defined itself in large part through its performance of war, as did Britain, Germany, Japan, and the United States at a similar time. In doing so, it created the circumstances in which a defined state could choose to exclude certain groups, in the way critiqued by Arendt. However, after the revolution of 1949, the story of the war against Japan did not become the kind of all-encompassing 'Great Patriotic War' seen in the USSR for at least some of the post-1945 period. In contrast, the political dynamics of the Cold War meant that in Mao's China, public memory of the war against Japan was confined to the experience of a very limited section of the population. The story of Mao's base area, with its capital in the remote city of

War, memory, the state, and statelessness in China 101

Yan'an, became representative of the entire country's war, a narrative of guerrilla warfare combined with land reform which enthused the peasantry for communist rule. This was deeply exclusionary, however. A large proportion of the population was left 'historically stateless'; that is, that those who had lived either in the Nationalist government's zone of control, or under Japanese occupation, were regarded as irrelevant to the historiography that dominated after 1949. The wartime resistance state of which they had been part was, essentially, elided from public consideration. It was only in the early 1980s that there was a significant change in this narrative, and the Nationalist contribution to the defeat of Japan was given a higher profile within China; the reasons for this were various, including the deaths of Mao and Chiang, the desire to force Japan into providing financial aid for China and to reduce Tokyo's diplomatic clout in the region, and the ideological void where Maoism had previously been. This has led to a new nationalist dynamic between state and society, in which the Chinese Communist Party has officially sponsored a new remembering of aspects of the war that had been previously forgotten or obscured (such as the museum commemorating the Rape of Nanjing in 1937–38, which was formally opened only in 1985), and wider society has responded in various ways, such as paintings, novels, and reportage writing on the war years.[8] This public response can be confrontational, as in Shanghai in 2005, where public demonstrations took place protesting perceived slights by the Japanese in their own remembering of the war (such as the adoption of textbooks which underplayed the gravity of Japanese war crimes in China).[9] These demonstrations were endorsed by the government, but then hastily suppressed when it appeared that public sentiment was over-enthusiastic in its anti-Japanese feeling.

Nonetheless, the widening emphasis on the War of Resistance in China in the last two decades has not been primarily the product of a xenophobic rise in anti-foreign nationalism, but rather an attempt to integrate China's narrative of the war into a wider context. China, of all the major powers involved with the Second World War, was the only one not to have used the period after 1945 to come to terms with the meaning either of victory or defeat. The ability, finally, to talk about the war some four decades later meant that the new interest in the subject was in large part an attempt to 'normalise' China's discussion of the war. The use of public monuments and

102 *Refugees and the stateless in Asia*

art, such as in the establishment of the Memorial Museum of the War of Resistance to Japan in Beijing, was part of that normalisation/globalisation process. By coming to terms with the meaning of the war, China was also seeking to resolve a set of questions which has occupied it ever since the late nineteenth century: the ability to define precisely what sort of state China should be, and how that reconstruction of statehood relates to its history as an empire. In the twentieth century, the Chinese state has variously been a declining empire, a weak Republic, and a stronger People's Republic. Its geobody has also shifted during that time, particularly during the Japanese invasion of the 1930s and 1940s. All of this has meant that the state was placed under constant pressure to define itself, and that mechanisms had to be found to create a sense of a unified state. The trajectory of the People's Republic in the era since Mao has shown a significant engagement with the history of the wartime period, in particular, demonstrating that it has played a part in the shaping of the Chinese nation-state.

In most European states, coming to terms with the aftermath of the Second World War is an entirely mainstream political project. China is different. During the Mao era, the most notable difference was the relative absence of the war from popular discourse. It was not wholly absent – during the Cultural Revolution, memory of the Sino-Japanese War was used as part of a wider ideological education – but it was not prominent. Many of the tropes that have become central to contemporary Chinese understandings of World War II date from the 1980s or later: the Nanjing Massacre, the bombings of Chongqing, and the disputes over the meaning of the Cairo and Potsdam declarations among them (the latter being wartime conferences where the fate of Asia was discussed and decided). Essentially, under Mao, it was difficult to address the record of the Nationalists (Kuomintang) who led the resistance to Japan, since doing so would necessitate admitting some positive role for the party of Chiang Kai-shek, who would become the sworn enemy of the PRC after the civil war ended in 1949, when the Nationalists fled to Taiwan. The Nationalist wartime state became a non-state as far as the CCP was concerned.

Yet from the 1980s, the desire to find a new unifying narrative for China after the Cultural Revolution was a pressing concern for the PRC, and as a result the Chinese Communist Party (CCP) chose

War, memory, the state, and statelessness in China   103

to create museums, textbooks, and films that would encourage a new consciousness of that period as a means of creating a sense of national identity. The use of art and culture to do this was not a new tactic. In the 'Talks at the Yan'an Forum on Literature and Art' (1943), Mao Zedong had declared:

> Literature and art are subordinate to politics, and the first and fundamental problem in China today is resistance to Japan ... Petty bourgeois writers and artists are an important force in China among the various forces constituting the united front in literature and art ... It is therefore a particularly important task to help them overcome their shortcomings and win them over to the front that serves the masses of workers, peasants and soldiers.[10]

The Yan'an Forum on Literature and Art took place in the midst of the darkest period of China's war against Japan. The China of eight decades later seems unimaginably far from the wartorn country at the heart of a revolutionary storm that would bring Mao's communists to power. In the midst of national crisis, Mao called to writers and artists to embrace an artistic style which would acknowledge that 'in every class society ... without exception, political criteria are always placed ahead of artistic criteria'.[11] The ideas that underpinned the talks shaped the interpretation of art and literature for the decades that Mao ruled. Today's China seems to have abandoned class and revolution as political categories. Yet in at least one area, that of public artefacts and art, there are recognisable connections between the aesthetics of the past and the present. By the term 'public art' I mean artwork, usually of a political nature, that has been commissioned by the state for mass, often organised and directed, consumption. Although such statues, pictures, monuments, and museums were not created to be seen as freestanding works of art, they and the institutions that hold them deserve serious consideration as artistic works and art institutions, which draw on, but also adapt the overarching criteria for the consideration of art in communist China which Mao laid down at Yan'an.

Public art has been used to bolster a new narrative about the significance of China's war against Japan (the War of Resistance to Japan, the term most commonly used in China for the anti-Japanese War in the China Theatre of World War II, which lasted from 1937 to 1945). The techniques used suggest a globalised form

104   *Refugees and the stateless in Asia*

of public art that seems to draw more on examples in the West and on China's indigenous traditions, and which is at odds with a more explicitly regional Asian identity, for example of the type that emerged in the revolutionary Maoist era. The interpretation of public art and architecture in modern China has become a growing field of analysis in the last two decades, with one of the best-known examples being Wu Hung's examination of the semiotics of Tian'anmen Square.[12] China's museums have also come under scrutiny as institutions where the state shapes interpretations of aesthetic value. Tamara Hamlish has interpreted 'collective memory in Beijing's Palace Museum' as part of 'an understanding of museums as structured ritual spaces within which visitors engage in carefully choreographed ritual practices – generating a limited range of both personal and collective memories'.[13] Hamlish's analysis deals with a premodern building emphatically not designed originally for public view (the Imperial Palace in Beijing, generally known as the Forbidden City), which has been reconverted to modern use as a museum. Nonetheless, she makes a point about the palace in its role as museum that is of great relevance to the analysis of the public art established by the reform-era (i.e. post-Mao) Chinese government: that 'the Chinese imperial collections were envisaged as part of a global cultural heritage, one instance of the collective memory of the horrors of feudalism and imperial rule that is shared by all nations'.[14] One should note that this global role was of course envisaged by the modern curators of the museum, not the imperial dynasty which originally commissioned the palace.

Similarly, the establishment of memorial museums of the wartime experience are designed to fit into a global agenda and summon up horrors (the Rape of Nanjing, bacteriological warfare in Manchuria) that will have cognates elsewhere (the Holocaust, the Blitz, the Bataan death march). In that respect, the search for global cognates, China's museums of wartime experience do parallel institutions which, at first glance, seem far removed from their concerns, such as the Ming palaces of the Forbidden City.

However, although these institutions were not established as showcases for works of art in the classic sense, it is clearly meaningful to consider them as art institutions in their own right. An important part of the creation of a modern 'public' in China in the early twentieth century was its exposure to artworks and institutions whose appearance had been created with aesthetic considerations in mind. The Republican era (1911–49) saw a new artistic style which combined traditional Chinese styles with techniques acquired from Europe; artists such as Xu Beihong exemplified this style. At the same time, Republican governments also displayed their modernity by sponsoring public events which sought to create a link between art and a mass viewing public. One of the new-style artists, Gao Jianfu, was put in charge of organising China's 'first government-sponsored national art exhibition in 1929'.[15] Form and function also came together in the use of art in public settings.

The two factors which would change the way in which state-sponsored art related to its public were the dictates of total war, and the consequent success of a Maoist regime which prioritised political imperatives over aesthetic ones for the creation of successful artwork – and crucially, used its immense coercive power to transmit those values to the viewing public. The Yan'an talks were not a simple turning-point when the political suddenly became the arbiter of artistic worth in China; they represented a symbolic moment that crystallised trends that had been growing as part of the Maoist vision of art and its purpose.

There is, of course, considerable overlap between the aesthetics of public art in the West and in China. Much of the Chinese public art under discussion here bears the clear marks of modernism and of Western-derived genres such as socialist realism. Memorial museums of Japanese atrocities in Nanjing and Fushun push hard at emotional boundaries, as they include real skeletons along with dioramas and aestheticised displays (such as dioramas and social realist paintings). The very direct representation of atrocity in this way is perhaps rarer in the Western iconography of war. This contrast should not be overstated; there were also highly subtle and figurative artistic visions of the War of Resistance from Chinese artists such as Feng Zikai. Yet the difference does exist, and it may be in part the product of a continuing expectation that a public should be expected to be mobilised and politicised by what it sees, rather than merely horrified or moved, and for that, direct exposure to atrocity is a necessary counterpart to figurative display.[16] There is a clear purpose at work here: the use of history to create a sense that a strong state is a necessary protection to prevent such atrocities happening in future.

106   *Refugees and the stateless in Asia*

In practice, how do public institutions in China today draw on the War of Resistance in seeking to define the nation-state? One of the key sites is the Memorial Museum of the War of Resistance, located in Beijing at the Marco Polo Bridge, the site of the outbreak of fighting between Chinese and Japanese troops that triggered war in 1937. The museum is a major, national-level institution built at great expense. Its style of self-presentation is notably hybrid, showcasing the mixture of global and local, modern and premodern, that influences China's aesthetics more widely today. Although it is a museum in the sense that it contains artifacts that are on display, the term 'memorial' [jinianguan] in its title is perhaps more appropriate, as it also contains displays, such as a statue of the unknown soldier, designed to engender an emotional rather than an analytical response.

Nonetheless, the museum repays examination as an art institution, whose own design shows a carefully thought-out combination of various different artistic traditions which have shaped the modern Chinese aesthetic sensibility, and have been transmitted to the viewing public. Most eyecatching, perhaps, are images in the style most associated with communist regimes: socialist realism, a style simultaneously modern but anti-modernist. However, the revival of recent interest in China's premodern artforms is also shown in the traditional temple bells on display (doubling here as 'alarm bells' in case of invasion). Furthermore, the more abstract elements of modernism are also on display, such as the stylised figures of the Chinese people resisting the invaders. In a museum dedicated to the memory of a national struggle in which China was portrayed as fighting to preserve its traditions as well the benefits of modernisation, architecture and artifacts which pay tribute to these different parts of China's art-historical heritage are deployed in a carefully planned piece of design. Most notably, limited but real contributions by the Nationalists to the defeat of Japan are highlighted in the museum; the 'historical statelessness' of the Nationalist regime is being amended.

Perhaps least noticeable, and therefore worth singling out, are the ways in which significant elements of the aesthetic and narrative which was constructed by the Nationalist government to represent the war in the 1930s and 1940s have been reappropriated by the CCP in the present day: the instability of the state's self-definition

War, memory, the state, and statelessness in China 107

is elided by the assertion of a continuity across very different political periods. As in the visual imaginary created during wartime, the body is at the centre of the new public art. Furthermore, as with its predecessor, the depiction of the body in the museums and public art is coded masculine in defiance, and coded feminine in victimhood. The image of the unknown soldier, and the faces of the resistance, are frequently men, and when women are portrayed, it is in a style cognate with men. In contrast, images of victimhood, for instance during the Rape of Nanjing, tend to be feminised.[17]

One aspect that is crucial to the use of such public art is response; this type of institution lacks value if it cannot help define the state to the people. It has always been a mainstay of political art, as the Yan'an talks make clear, that it must engender a response in the viewer, and the socialist realist techniques that marked much art of the socialist bloc were designed for that purpose. The grassroots nature of much of the communist revolution also meant that participation in popular artforms became central to their effectiveness.[18] The memorial museums and the art associated with them are very much designed with popular participation in mind. The museum's location on the outskirts of the city means that the vast majority of visits are organised trips from schools and work units, and that interpretation is heavily directed not just by the signs and explanations, but also by the tour guides. Although the specific dictates of Mao's Yan'an talks about the need for class struggle are no longer part of the ideology of contemporary China, the explicit linking of politics and art that underpin the talks are still very much in the minds of those who create displays and monuments of this sort. This continuing ideological commitment implies that in any dispute between an aesthetic and political decision about interpretation, the political must still come first. This imperative makes China relatively distinctive even in an age of greater regional and global interaction.

Conclusion

The state is still a work in progress in China. Its self-presentation is shaped by its attempts to assert its identity in many forms, of which collective memory of the War of Resistance is only one. Nonetheless,

108 *Refugees and the stateless in Asia*

that element repays close attention. Not only is it connected to one of the most active and problematic aspects of contemporary Chinese politics (relations with Japan), but it is also exposed to a wide number of viewers who are given a strong steer about how they should appreciate it, and who are shaped by the highly politicised history of twentieth-century China. The artistic, architectural, and monumental elements of memory of war are linked directly to the wider, popular experience of how art is both politicised and aestheticised within China, and show the lasting grip of assumptions from Mao's Yan'an talks.

The content of public monuments and institutions that focus on the war between two of Asia's greatest powers stresses the importance of a historical *division*, rather than commonality, within the region. China is no longer the sort of top-down society that it was under Mao, though it remains highly controlled under Xi Jinping, yet the state's understanding of the purpose of memorialisation of war is still strongly linked to Maoist (and before that, Leninist) ideas of an artwork's aesthetic qualities lying in large part in their ability to achieve political mobilisation. The context of public art in Japan, India, and other Asian liberal democracies (Taiwan, but not, for instance, Singapore) is different from that in China in that their publics are less explicitly taught and encouraged to assess art in a political context. Nor, in China, is there meaningful space in public discussion to critique artworks and institutions that are sponsored by the state. Naturally, democracies and other Asian nations also put forward political agendas in their public art, and are not always open to dissent over interpretation. However, there is a degree of difference in kind in the case of China: while the types of public art and their uses have changed and widened in recent years, the response that the state expects from those who view them, and the aesthetic criteria that are assumed to underpin them, still hark back to an earlier China where propaganda was a central part of the state's self-justification. Even in the twenty-first century, the state continues to take a strong interest in the political message of public monumentality and art, and in doing so reflects the legacy of the agenda that Mao laid down in the hills of Yan'an over sixty years ago.

This is not surprising. The Chinese state is now, as it has been for a century and a half, unsure about how solid its own conception of

War, memory, the state, and statelessness in China   109

the state is, and how far it is accepted by its own people. Arendt was concerned with the way in which groups of people could be definitionally excluded from the state. China today is still not sure how soundly defined its own state is in the first place. Previously the CCP excluded the histories of people who were part of the non-communist state narrative from the brassy certainties of national self-definition in the Mao era. Since the 1980s, more of those 'historically stateless' people, such as those who resisted Japan in the Nationalist areas during the Second World War, have been reincorporated into the state's definition of who can be included. The appearance of those Nationalist veterans in Tiananmen Square in 2015 shows that the process is real. But these definitions are never final or completely stable, any more than is the shape of China's state.

Notes

1 On displacement and refugee policy in wartime China, see Stephen MacKinnon, *War, Refugees, and the Making of Modern China* (Berkeley, CA: University of California Press, 2008); for post-war China, see Rana Mitter, 'Relocation and Dislocation: Civilian, Refugee, and Military Movement as Factors in the Disintegration of Postwar China, 1945–49', *Itinerario*, 46, 2 (2022), pp. 193–213.

2 On war memory in Mao-era China, see Chan Yang, *World War Two Legacies in East Asia: China Remembers the War* (New York: Routledge, 2018). On the period since the 1980s, see Rana Mitter, *China's Good War: How World War II Is Shaping a New Nationalism* (Cambridge, MA: Harvard University Press, 2020).

3 Benedict Anderson, *Imagined Communities: Reflections on the Origin and Spread of Nationalism* (London: Verso, 1991).

4 See, for instance, Barbara Mittler, *A Newspaper for China? Power, Identity, and Change in Shanghai's News Media, 1872–1912* (Cambridge, MA: Harvard University Press, 2004).

5 Hans J. van de Ven, *War and Nationalism in China, 1925–1945* (London: Routledge, 2003), p. 219.

6 William C. Kirby, 'Engineering China: Birth of the Developmental State', in Wen-hsin Yeh (ed.), *Becoming Chinese: Passages to Modernity and Beyond* (Berkeley, CA: University of California Press, 2000), pp. 152–3.

7 Chang-tai Hung, *War and Popular Culture: Resistance in Modern China, 1937–1945* (Berkeley, CA: University of California Press, 1994).

110 *Refugees and the stateless in Asia*

8 See Sheila Jager and Rana Mitter (eds), *Ruptured Histories: War and Memory in Post-Cold War Asia* (Cambridge, MA: Harvard University Press, 2007).
9 See, e.g., Jessica Chen Weiss, *Powerful Patriots: Nationalist Protest in China's Foreign Relations* (New York: Oxford University Press, 2014).
10 Bonnie S. McDougall (ed.), *Mao Zedong's 'Talks at the Yan'an Conference on Literature and Art': A Translation of the 1943 Text with Commentary* (Ann Arbor, MI: Michigan Papers in Chinese Studies, 1980), p. 76.
11 McDougall, *Mao Zedong's*, p. 78.
12 Wu Hung, 'Tiananmen Square: A Political History of Monuments', *Representations*, 35 (Summer 1991), pp. 84–117.
13 Tamara Hamlish, 'Global Culture, Modern Heritage: Re-membering the Chinese Imperial Collections', in Susan A. Crane (ed.), *Museums and Memory* (Stanford, CA: Stanford University Press, 2000), p. 139.
14 Hamlish, 'Global Culture', p. 150.
15 Craig Clunas, *Art in China* (Oxford: Oxford University Press, 1997), p. 204.
16 Here, Foucault's analysis of the way in which visible punishments in Europe (torture, execution, etc.) were moved into the hidden confines of the prison in the modern era is relevant: see Michel Foucault, *Discipline and Punish: The Birth of the Prison*, trans. Alan Sheridan (Harmondsworth: Penguin, 1991), chapter 2.
17 Personal observation at Nanjing Massacre Museum site.
18 Hung, *War and Popular Culture*, ch. 6.

8

The international politics of refugee settlement in Shanghai, 1937–56

Meredith Oyen

In 1937, the city of Shanghai was overrun with refugees. Over the next few years, this state of affairs would be novel only in scope. The Japanese attack that swept through the city en route to the Chinese capital of Nanjing led to the creation of hundreds of thousands of displaced Chinese citizens. They fled their homes and frequently clamoured at the blocked entrances to the International and French Settlements in the city, straining local aid organisations and overflowing existing shelters.[1] As one editorialist wrote in 1939 in the *Shanghai Post and Mercury*,

> This international city's reputation of being a place of refuge is a matter of pride to those who have grown up with it, who have seen the Russian colony – refugees and emigres from a country in the turmoil of revolution – gradually become a part of the working life of Shanghai ... and who have seen the hundreds of thousands of Chinese who, on many occasions in the past two decades, have clamored at the gates for sanctuary.[2]

At the same time, the city emerged as a haven for new Jewish refugees from Europe, as the increase in Nazi restrictions and violence against their communities forced those with the means to seek escape in one of the few parts of the world yet open to them. Of course, Shanghai was only nominally open to refugees. The internationally governed sectors initially gathered support among Jewish community leaders and offered housing and assistance. By 1938, however, fears of being overrun by foreign refugees and dwindling resources led to efforts to limit European refugee arrivals. As one editorialist put it in early 1939, 'Shanghai can't save the world,

112   *Refugees and the stateless in Asia*

worse luck'.[3] The Japanese advance into Southeast Asia added a final complication as ethnic Chinese from across the region fled their homes and returned to family homesteads across China to wait out the conflict.[4]

These refugees from conflicts near and far challenged existing aid programs, charitable responses, and local authorities. The Japanese attack on Pearl Harbor further complicated official responses, as remaining British and American nationals found themselves relocated to internment camps and international sources of funding (like support for housing and soup kitchens provided by the American Jewish Joint Distribution Committee) ceased. In 1943, Japanese authorities commanded that all stateless refugees arriving after 1937 relocate to a small area in the Hongkou region of Shanghai, later termed the 'Shanghai ghetto'. Though dissimilar from the Jewish ghettos of Europe that preceded the outbreak of war there – it did not collect all the Jewish citizens of Shanghai, and some non-Jewish and non-European residents remained in place – it created tensions within the population of stateless European refugees and concerns about Japanese plans if the Allies did not win the war quickly. When the end of the war did come in August 1945, displaced and stateless persons in the city fell into a number of disparate categories, including internally displaced Chinese refugees, longstanding stateless Russian refugees, stateless Central European Jews, and externally displaced Chinese. These groups came to international attention, but they were not alone: there were also stranded Italian sailors, abandoned Korean and Taiwanese of undetermined nationality (if no longer Japanese citizens), and numerous other individuals whose experiences with global war left them far from home.[5]

The war had fundamentally reshaped China's relationship with its residents, including these thousands of non-citizen migrants who had made their homes in China and thousands more stateless refugees who sought protection there. As the Japanese withdrew, foreign officials remanded large swaths of territory they once controlled back into Chinese hands. The unsettled status of the citizens and residents of China created a unique dilemma for a weak and rebuilding Chinese government, and the city of Shanghai exposed all of these challenges at once. After decades divided into an international concession, a French Concession, Japanese territory, and Chinese old town, the war ended foreign rule and brought

The international politics of refugee settlement 113

the city back together under the authority of the Chinese government. Under the auspices of newly established international bodies like the United Nations Relief and Rehabilitation Administration (UNRRA), rebuilding a country and government after the ravages of war included a monumental task of managing this diverse body of people.

Stateless Central European Jews often receive the lion's share of the attention in histories of post-war refugee policies in Shanghai.[6] Their connection to the international Holocaust combines with an increasing interest in China in its role as a saviour for these people stemming from the work and recent expansion of the Shanghai Jewish Refugees Museum. However, the Chinese response to these refugees, and the cooperation with international organisations designed to aid Second World War displaced persons, proved inextricably linked with at least two of the other populations noted above: Russians (both Whites and Jews) who fled to China during and after the Bolshevik Revolution and did not seek citizenship in the Soviet Union; and displaced overseas Chinese from Southeast Asia who maintained nominal Chinese citizenship but whose lives remained bound to their places of residence abroad. All three populations lingered in Shanghai and other major ports in China after the war and sought assistance to either make their lives in China or resettle abroad, and at no point did the Republic of China government really address them as wholly discrete problems in the way Western histories and memory tend to do.

Solving the refugee, displaced person, and stateless resident problem in China after the Second World War became an international effort in cooperation with the Chinese government. Foreign assistance to China came through several international organisations in succession: the United Nations Relief and Rehabilitation Administration, the Intergovernmental Committee on Refugees (IGCR), the International Refugee Organization (IRO), and finally the United Nations High Commissioner for Refugees (UNHCR). Collectively, their work provides a useful window into how the post-war Chinese government pursued decolonisation, sought legitimacy through engagement with international organisations, and navigated the challenges of hosting a large and diverse population of stateless people in the context of demobilisation. They also offer a reminder not to view one of these groups completely in isolation,

114   *Refugees and the stateless in Asia*

because the big picture of refugee aid meant the fates of all these displaced persons were to some extent intertwined.

Stateless in Shanghai: the early dilemma of international refugees

Even before the war had ended, UNRRA and its Chinese-run counterpart, the Chinese National Relief and Rehabilitation Administration (CNRRA), began developing programs and plans for assisting in China's recovery from the war. UNRRA spent more money in China than anywhere else, though the bulk of its activities dealt with direct relief, health, agriculture, industry, transportation, and flood control.[7] Aid to displaced persons concentrated on four groups: internally displaced persons (often provided assistance through other food and direct relief programs as well as through rehabilitation of domestic transportation); overseas Chinese who had fled to China during the war; Chinese stranded outside the country who wanted to return to China; and Europeans stranded in China.[8] For UNRRA's purposes, this last category focused largely on the stateless Central European Jews who fled to China.

That stateless European population posed real dilemmas for the Chinese government in the wake of war. The Chinese government sought to remove anyone from China who did not have a claim to citizenship, thus eliminating some of the taint of colonialism from major cities like Shanghai and limiting the number of indigent souls fighting for limited charitable resources. With this task in mind, in late November of 1945 the Chinese Interior and Foreign Affairs Ministries promulgated a new set of regulations relating to one of these core groups of residents: Germans and stateless ex-Germans. It stated in part that:

> Germans, former Austrians, and German Jews in recovery and free China, who did not commit any of the offenses enumerated in (2) hereof [spying or collaborating with Japan], shall be repatriated unless the Ministries of Interior and Foreign Affairs sanction their further stay in China. Before their repatriation, however, they may submit a substantial shop guarantee provided by Chinese or foreigners and apply to the provincial and Municipal Governments for sanctioning their further stay in China. Those unable to supply a

The international politics of refugee settlement   115

guarantee shall be segregated under the administration of competent provisional and municipal governments.[9]

This announcement caused an uproar among stateless Jews resident in China. Having no claim to German citizenship and no longer holding valid German or Austrian passports, they found it offensive to be grouped in alongside non-Jewish Germans, some of whom were Nazi Party members or sympathisers. They also had no particular desire to return to Germany; in many cases, the International Tracing Service revealed they had little or no family left in Europe that had survived the war, and they had little reason to expect their former German neighbours would welcome them back or treat them well after their return. That said, most likely did not hope to stay in Shanghai either. They were divided between hoping for resettlement in the United States, Australia, Canada, or similar settler societies or moving to Israel to aid the efforts to create a Jewish homeland there.[10] The repatriation order interfered with all of these plans.

The announcement led to backlash and negotiation from representatives of international organisations aiding refugees. At first, the position of the Chinese government on the stateless refugees appeared especially rigid. There was no immediate push to enforce the measure, but in the months that followed, many Shanghai newspapers reported on it. The *Shanghai Herald* ran an article in January of 1946 that quoted Chen Kuo-lien of the Shanghai Office of the Ministry of Foreign Affairs saying, 'Many of the Jews here were smuggled into Shanghai at a time when the Chinese National Government was unable to exercise its right of sovereignty in this city.' He continued to note that they'd be lenient with these refugees, but they saw no reason why they could not safely return to a de-Nazified Germany.[11] UNRRA took the lead on repatriation, which they completed with CNRRA overseeing temporary housing, employment, and negotiations with the Chinese government over temporary residence permits. But UNRRA and CNRRA had no mandate to help refugees resettling in a new country. Instead, those refugees had to appeal to the Intergovernmental Committee on Refugees (IGCR) based out of Europe. It was the IGCR that would take the lead on negotiating with the Chinese government for special status for stateless European Jews.

116   *Refugees and the stateless in Asia*

Moses W. Beckelman of the IGCR made a three-month journey to China in the first half of 1946 to survey the situation on the ground there as well as learn directly from Chinese Ministry of Foreign Affairs (MOFA) officials what the Chinese policy on stateless refugees would be. Beckelman was an ideal choice for the conversation. A social worker from New York, he had spent the first years of the Second World War employed by the JDC in Vilna assisting refugees there before relocating to Morocco to head a UNRRA refugee camp. In 1945 he rose to the level of assistant director of the IGCR, and he traveled widely in support of their operations.[12] In his initial conversations with representatives at MOFA, his Chinese interlocutors, Dr Nai-kuang Kan and Nan-Ju Wu, stressed the status of stateless European refugees as illegal immigrants: 'advantage had been taken of China's inability at the time to enforce her rights, that if application had been made to Chinese consular representatives at that time visas would not have been granted'.[13] Both Beckelman and representatives of the American Jewish Joint Distribution Committee (JDC) who met with Chinese MOFA representatives came away with the sense that their Chinese counterparts were deeply empathetic with the plight of the refugees and very much interested in working with international organisations like IGCR and the JDC to find workable solutions to the problem of refugees.[14] The rhetoric about illegal immigration, however, served its own purpose: to reinforce as clearly as possible that the future of these migrants lay outside of China. Whether they repatriated as suggested in the initial order for Germans in China, or resettled abroad with the assistance of the IGCR, they needed to make their homes outside of China. Classifying them as illegal immigrants made clear that remaining in place and making a life in China was not one of their options. Beckelman had a second theory, however, about the reason for the pronouncement. A major part of the UNRRA mandate on displaced persons in China concerned repatriating overseas Chinese back to their pre-war homes in Southeast Asia, and many of those countries were under the control of the very Western European powers concerned with Jewish refugees. He wondered if 'the Chinese government hopes to trade the privilege of allowing refugees from Germany to remain in China against the extension of the right of the displaced Chinese to return to countries of pre-war residence'.[15]

The international politics of refugee settlement 117

From this starting point, Beckelman oversaw a series of negotiations that centred around ensuring that stateless refugees would be allowed to leave China voluntarily, not as a part of a forcible repatriation program alongside non-Jewish (or potentially pro-Nazi) German migrants. Their formal agreement in March included the time to facilitate resettlement elsewhere and the conditions under which refugees might be allowed to remain in China.[16] The task that followed was one of finding ways to manage the refugees' needs while they were still in China awaiting their departure, as well as arranging destinations and transportation. When UNRRA closed operations in China, it reported having successfully repatriated approximately twenty-one thousand overseas Chinese; provided aid to some fifteen thousand Europeans, repatriating or resettling five thousand; and helped over eight thousand Chinese return to China from homes around the world.[17]

Managing these different populations through the work of UNRRA/CNRRA also created its own controversies. By agreement, aid for displaced and stateless Europeans in China did not filter through CNRRA or come out of the Chinese allotment of relief funds; instead, this aid was managed separately.[18] On the ground, operations relied heavily on the work of the JDC, which had representatives in China before, during, and after the war. The fact that the aid funnelled through separate channels, however, gave rise to complaints about equality, and especially that European refugees had access to better housing, more calories, improved healthcare, and other advantages. Dr T. F. Tsiang, the former educator and government official who served as the first director of CNRRA, raised these concerns with his counterpart at UNRRA. In response, UNRRA Director Benjamin Kinzer replied,

> it is not the intention of UNRRA to create 'examples of inequality' on Chinese soil ... Instead of seeing the standard of living of the European refugees lowered to the standard of destitute Chinese, it is our earnest endeavor to aid you to raise the living standards of the Chinese people.[19]

Concerns about inequitable aid followed international efforts to aid refugees in China throughout the decade after the war, however, reinforcing the need for international organisations to embrace care for displaced Chinese on the same terms as displaced Europeans.

118 *Refugees and the stateless in Asia*

China, overseas Chinese, and the founding of the International Refugee Organization

As UNRRA began to wind down operations and consider what organisations might continue facets of its work, interested nations launched the Preparatory Commission of the International Refugee Organization (PCIRO). PCIRO would address refugee resettlement as a placeholder until enough governments signed the new constitution of the IRO to allow it to come into force. In the global context of 1947, however, recruiting international support for the IRO was not an easy task. As the United Nations fractured into camps that would align with the brewing Cold War in Europe, participation in the IRO took on new meaning. The Western powers, led by the United States, spearheaded recruitment to the project, running quickly up against reluctance from their counterweight, the USSR. The USSR had proved to be a greater recipient of than contributor to UNRRA projects, but it maintained both great power status and a distinct preference for solving the DP problem with repatriation over resettlement. As a result, it took part in the many discussions leading up to the creation of the IRO before ultimately rejecting the constitution and refusing participation. The USSR dispute with IRO plans was rooted in the idea of the changed mission of the IRO. Instead, the USSR 'emphasized that in their view all men of goodwill, since the defeat of the Axis Powers, could return to their home countries; quislings, war criminals, traitors, Fascists, and undemocratic elements who opposed governments of their countries should not receive any assistance from an international organization'.[20] In other words, the idea that refugees who opposed the communist governments in the USSR or the Eastern bloc should be helped to move to a new country as exiles offended these governments and threatened to politicise the program to aid DPs.

To counter the votes of the USSR if it joined the organisation, or to avoid charges that it was an all-Western coalition if it did not, officials in the United States and the United Kingdom involved in the founding grew determined to ensure that China joined the organisation. Their arguments in favour of Chinese participation fell along similar lines. Most importantly, the unfinished business of both overseas Chinese repatriations and resettling stateless European refugees required international support. China alone could not convince

The international politics of refugee settlement   119

Southeast Asian nations to accept returning overseas Chinese, and the financial costs of the refugee population without international support to maintain them would stretch Chinese resources to the breaking point. There was an expected annual contribution to the work of the IRO by each signatory government, and that requirement certainly caused anxiety to a Chinese government facing rapid inflation, ongoing recovery from the last war, and a growing civil war. But that money would be spent regardless on refugee support, and if spent through the IRO, the contributions would go farther. Additionally, there was an appeal to the legitimacy of the struggling Nationalist regime: China had been 'an active member of all important international organizations' and derived benefits from participation, particularly in the case of UNRRA. Refusing to participate, similarly, could blow back against the government and tarnish its international reputation. The US government also appealed to the mythology of China's wartime status as one of the 'five great powers' and the prospect of ongoing support from the United States as one of the ROC's most important allies.[21]

Though all persuasive arguments, China's ultimate decision to join the IRO cannot be separated from the challenge overseas Chinese repatriation posed to Chinese officials. Repatriating displaced overseas Chinese posed a unique problem both to China and to the international organisations that stepped forward to help. This population was not stateless – especially not in the sense of Central European Jews or Russian refugees who had been stripped of their original passports from their country of origin. Chinese nationality law affirmed their status as Chinese citizens, and the IRO agreement with the Republic of China explicitly highlighted that the IRO was only the authority for protecting refugees who were not ethnically Chinese, even if it ultimately aided displaced Chinese.[22] However, displaced overseas Chinese in China had longstanding residency in countries of Southeast Asia. Often they owned property or businesses there; sometimes they had families there. In many cases, European colonial governments had given the stamp of approval to their residency, but that approval and sometimes the documentary proof of it vanished in the war and the wave of decolonisation that followed. To Hannah Arendt, statelessness entailed the loss of home and the loss of government protection.[23] Displaced overseas Chinese had lost their homes, but not the protection of the Chinese

120 *Refugees and the stateless in Asia*

government. However, the Chinese government was impotent to restore them to their homes.

The difficulties inherent in the overseas Chinese repatriation project became very clear under UNRRA. Early in the repatriation process, UNRRA tried to begin negotiations for returns with each of the Southeast Asian governments, then turn over the efforts to the Chinese Embassy or representatives to finalise the arrangements or continue the talks. Within those talks, 'the Chinese principle that Overseas Chinese are always Chinese here worked a disservice to many'.[24] Rising nationalism, combined with post-war economic difficulties and concerns about the reach of Chinese Government influence through its expatriate community, made the returnees particularly unwelcome in many countries. Most countries declared themselves willing to accept the Chinese residents in principle, but the reality was that strict guidelines prevented many from returning. To facilitate the process of re-entry, the organisation issued those Chinese meeting the repatriation guidelines set by their former residences a general UNRRA visa as a travel document, intended to save the receiving country from having to conduct independent inspections in China for each traveller. Ultimately, Singapore, Malaya, Burma, British North Borneo, Sarawak, Thailand, and French Indochina accepted the UNRRA visa; Indonesia (then still the Dutch East Indies) and the Philippines refused it. Between 1 September 1946 and 1 July 1947, 20,893 overseas Chinese were repatriated through the efforts of the UNRRA, but more than twenty-five thousand still waited for repatriation.[25] As a result a large number of individuals' status remained unaddressed upon the inauguration of PCIRO.

The PCIRO took over displaced persons operations from the UNRRA in July 1947. The Constitution of the IRO included in the definition of refugees not only victims of fascist and Nazi regimes, but also Spanish Republicans and 'persons who were considered refugees before the outbreak of the Second World War, for reasons of race, religion, nationality, or political opinion'.[26] Two immediate problems existed: first, the overseas Chinese did not fully meet the definition of a refugee under the IRO constitution, but PCIRO would take over this work by agreement with the Chinese government. Second, a large number of emigrant Russians long resident in China would become eligible for aid under the new organisation.

The international politics of refugee settlement   121

Because UNRRA had not provided aid or relief, but only facilitated travel, supporting an expanded population of eligible refugees would require a substantial expansion of the China office budget.[27] The Shanghai office of the IRO was headed by Jennings Wong, a veteran of the Shanghai office of the CNRRA and someone very familiar with the landscape of refugee affairs in China. In 1948, Wong informed ROC government authorities that the funds were available to expand the work of his IRO office to include displaced Russians.[28] Thus the IRO would balance three sometimes competing mandates for repatriation and resettlement: those addressing stateless Jewish refugees, stateless Russian displaced persons, and overseas Chinese whose citizenship did not match their country of residence.

The International Refugee Organization at work in China

The lifespan of the IRO in China covered another signficant event: the founding of the People's Republic of China on 1 October 1949. The reigniting Chinese civil war complicated an already difficult situation for displaced persons in China. As Jewish refugee Horst Eisfelder observed,

> We thought that everything would return to normal, that we'd get back to the business in the heart of town, that things would settle down and we'd have a nice quiet life … But a few months later, we began to realize that things were not going to be all right. There was rapid inflation and enormous corruption under the Kuomintang regime, the Nationalists. The Communists were getting stronger in the north and marching south. Nobody got anything back again from the Communists, and we realized we couldn't stay there indefinitely.[29]

The civil war had several distinct effects on the project. First, it hurt the ROC's ability to keep up with its obligation to provide financial support. While still in the PCIRO planning stages, negotiations began for China to commit its funds mostly in local currency or in-kind supplies, but even that grew difficult as the Chinese currency underwent rapid, out-of-control inflation.[30] The second problem was logistical: moving armies and ongoing warfare made access to ports for transport difficult, and more than once the retreating

122   *Refugees and the stateless in Asia*

Nationalist forces temporarily occupied an IRO camp, interfering with the repatriation process.[31] The third effect of the civil war on IRO activities can be seen in the increased sense of urgency. White Russians – Russian emigrants who had opposed the founding of the Soviet Union – especially seemed to face imminent risk under a new government.[32] Finally, the civil war's outcome meant a final, significant hurdle: there would be a new government in China to work with. The fact that the IRO office in China had survived the civil war at all was due in part to the overseas Chinese repatriation program, as even an inexperienced new Chinese government recognised that stopping it would damage overseas Chinese opinions of the new government.[33] However, what did not change was the extent to which continued cooperation between any Chinese government officials and the IRO required continued progress on resettling European refugees and repatriating overseas Chinese, so despite these challenges, there is initially a surprising continuity in operations across the 1949 divide. Between 1947 and the Shanghai office's official closure in 1956, IRO work in China focused on three projects: helping migrants repatriate to their countries of origin (which included the overseas Chinese project), assisting with visas and transport for migrants bound for entirely new countries of asylum, and monthly relief donations to pay for food, housing, healthcare, and other necessities while refugees waited on visas and exit permits.[34]

As a critical reason explaining why China joined the IRO in the first place, overseas Chinese repatriations remained a high priority for everyone involved in refugee work. Over its lifetime, the IRO succeeded in repatriating 11,122 overseas Chinese to their countries of origin, but rapidly changing conditions in the Southeast Asian nations contributed to the longstanding reticence to receive returning Chinese. In July of 1950, William Collison of the IRO office in Hong Kong reported small movements to Burma, but that Singapore and the Malayan Union had blocked new arrivals. The Malayan emergency, a guerrilla war between the British government in Malaya and the Malayan Communist Party, had been 'blamed entirely on the Chinese'. Similarly, an approach to French authorities on the subject of repatriations to Indochina might be required, 'since a good portion of the trouble in Saigon and other cities in Indo-China is blamed on the Chinese'.[35] Meanwhile, developers in

The international politics of refugee settlement   123

Sarawak and North Borneo sought Chinese labourers to assist in their economic revival, creating competition between former residents and new immigrants for limited opportunities. In Indonesia, a complex situation developed in which Taiwanese residents of Indonesia had been shipped off to Australia by the Japanese army against their will; IRO hoped to use the negotiations to return them to Indonesia as a precedent for further overseas Chinese admissions, though with limited success. As of 1950, the Geneva office wrote to IRO Hong Kong to explain that

> our immediate desire in regard to the Overseas Chinese is to discover what programme is feasible within the lifetime of the organization, to plan the active completion of this programme, and to dispose as may be possible at the earliest time of the residual responsibilities which it is obvious through no fault of our own we cannot complete.[36]

Alongside this repatriation work, the IRO worked to resettle European refugees abroad. Finding countries willing to issue visas proved the greatest challenge for relocation efforts. Visas came predominantly from traditional countries of immigration: the United States first and foremost, but after that Australia, Brazil, Canada, Argentina, and the rest of Latin America. All of these countries accepted refugees in finite numbers, however, and with a degree of selectivity that left 'hard cases', the aged and infirm particularly, behind. As the civil war drew to a close in 1949, 4,500 Jewish refugees were evacuated from Shanghai to Israel and other countries where they had visas. Another seven hundred repatriated to Germany and Austria and other destinations in Central Europe.[37] The United States amended its 1948 Displaced Persons act with a special provision saving four thousand visas for Shanghai refugees, but the US consulate that issued such visas closed in China in 1949.[38] The founding of the communist government inspired refugee workers on the ground to break with procedure, and ship out a group of 106 hopeful refugees with family connections that could act as guarantors in the United States. They followed a not uncommon route for IRO refugees out of Shanghai: they boarded a train for Tianjin, then a ship to Hong Kong, and another to San Francisco. Upon arrival, there was no provision in the law that would allow them to land without entry visas, so they were transferred under guard across the country to Ellis Island. After repeated delays, the US government agreed they

124   *Refugees and the stateless in Asia*

would be admitted to the United States as Displaced Persons under the amended law, but they had to be processed in Germany.[39] 'We're going back to a country where our people were gassed after we fled from persecution ... We'd go back to nothing but graves and bitter memories', one refugee lamented.[40] These 106 people arrived in late 1950 at an IRO-run DP camp in Germany just over a decade after they fled, having since traveled all the way around the world and learned more than they'd ever cared to know about the intractability of American immigration bureaucracy.[41]

Stateless Russians in China posed additional problems for IRO operations. For one thing, statelessness among this group was a reality but not always technically true. In the 1940s, some Russians became convinced that their best claim to survival was to accept the offer of Soviet citizenship, only to seek an opportunity to relinquish it when the war ended and pressures mounted for Soviet citizens to return to the Soviet Union. As one Russian migrant explained, 'I cannot get along with Soviet papers as regards certain employment positions, I have no desire of repatriating to Russia, my parents are non-Soviet and I took Soviet papers due to an error of mine that every Russian would be compelled to do so sooner or later.'[42] Russians born in China of emigré parents sometimes held Chinese citizenship as well, which they had to renounce to apply for a Soviet passport.[43] Russian refugees who had been particularly active in anti-communist activities in Shanghai seemed in particular danger as the Chinese communists came to power, launching an effort by the IRO to screen and relocate five thousand to six thousand Russians to a camp outside China for further processing. After debating options with the British (including a number of British colonial territories),

> Authority for a temporary haven in the Philippines for 5,000 refugees from Shanghai was generously provided by the Philippine Republic as a result of negotiations between the IRO and the Philippine Republic at a time when efforts to secure such haven in other parts of the world were without success.[44]

US officials made arrangements to use a former US military base on Tubabo Island off the coast of Samar in the Philippines. From there, Australian and American consular officials would screen refugees for visas to either country, though fully clearing the camp would

The international politics of refugee settlement 125

take years, not the few months promised Philippine officials.[45] And the lingering problems of refugee resettlement out of the Samar camp had another affect on the interconnected work of the IRO. While trying to complete overseas Chinese repatriations in 1950, the IRO office in Geneva commented, 'As regards the Philippines, taking into account the Samar situation, we feel that an approach from here to the Government would not only be worthless, but even prejudicial at this time.'[46] The challenge of relocating White Russians from Samar effectively shut down any willingness on the part of the Philippines to accept overseas Chinese repatriations from the IRO.

The international politics of refugee relief changed significantly through the political events in China of 1949. As the outcome of the war became clear in 1948, the government of Israel sent a consular official to China to issue entry visas, and the IRO facilitated transportation to the new country. Over three thousand Jewish refugees left China in the space of a few months in 1948, overwhelmingly to Israel.[47] By the early 1950s, the restrictions on visas for Israel lifted further to allow more refugees to leave China. Walter Citrin, the Israeli immigration officer in Hong Kong, commented in 1952 that 'the situation of the Jews in China is a perilous one … the Israeli Government, the Jewish Agency and their Jewish organisations, including the JDC, must make an all-out effort' to evacuate them. Most of the Jewish refugees remaining in China by the early 1950s could be claimed by Russia, which carried with it the spectre of communist China cooperating to repatriate them to the Soviet Union without their consent. In fact, the People's Republic of China by and large did not interfere with the IRO's efforts to resettle even Soviet passport holders to capitalist countries, though it did seem to keep track of the numbers.[48]

Despite the continued IRO presence in Shanghai, so few foreign consulates remained in China to issue visas that the mechanics of leaving increased in complexity. In the early 1950s, refugees still trying to leave China would write to a consulate in Hong Kong for a certificate promising a visa on arrival, and then use that certificate to apply for an exit visa.[49] Settling financial affairs, completing physical exams, and booking travel to Hong Kong all had to be accomplished with precisely choreographed timing. But over the course of the 1950s, despite the Korean War, despite China's political and economic isolation, and despite the departure of personnel connected to the US or Republic of China governments, the

126   *Refugees and the stateless in Asia*

IRO office in Shanghai soldiered on, creating a partnership with the China Travel Service to arrange visas and transit through Hong Kong on to new homes abroad.[50] Mass movements abroad became impossible to effect, but continued small movements of individuals and family groups trickled out over the next few years. By the mid-1950s, the refugees still registered with the IRO were mostly the unmoveable 'hard cases', and a significant percentage of the IRO Shanghai office's work involved distributing funds for their support. The extent of these payments, and the standard of living they support, had been a frequent point of contention between Chinese officials and IRO administrators for years; under the equalising effects of the communist government, the controversy only deepened.

The IRO began the process of liquidating its assets and transferring its caseload in the early 1950s, handing over its affairs to the UN High Commissioner for Refugees by 1952. The Far East headquarters in Hong Kong shifted from the IRO to the UNHCR, and many branch offices of the IRO within China closed down. The IRO office in Shanghai remained open, becoming effectively the Shanghai branch of the UNHCR, but correspondence within China generally continued to use the IRO name. Colonel M. C. Liang became the director, having been involved in refugee work in China for a decade without having the ties to ROC authorities that forced the original director, Jennings Wong, to follow the Nationalists out of China to Taiwan. Liang stayed with the office, acting as an intermediary between the new government and the old refugee organisation until 1956, when he formally resigned and requested that the office be taken over by the Chinese People's Relief Association.[51]

Too many citizenships or none at all: the UNHCR in Hong Kong

When the IRO finally closed down in China, the remaining European refugees – stateless or otherwise – would have to correspond with UNHCR in Hong Kong to gain access to international assistance. All of the overseas Chinese that could be repatriated had left, and most of the Europeans who would ever move on had similarly gone. But in the 1950s there was a new Chinese refugee crisis engaging the UNHCR as Chinese nationals fled the new communist government

The international politics of refugee settlement   127

and arrived in Hong Kong. From 1949 through the early 1960s, over a million Chinese arrived in Hong Kong. They left first for political reasons, if they aligned with the departed Nationalists, and later for economic reasons, as the Great Leap Forward gave way to famine in the countryside. Like the overseas Chinese displaced by the Second World War, they could not be considered 'stateless' because, even having 'lost' their homes, they retained the potential of government protection. However, the government that could protect them was separate from the government that controlled their homes. UNHCR conducted an extensive legal study to determine whether they met the status of refugees such that they could receive aid under the UNHCR mandate. UNHCR employed Norwegian legal scholar Dr Edvard Hambro to investigate the problem and answer the question, but even his answer was not simple. Because the Republic of China claimed all overseas Chinese as its citizens, Chinese refugees in Hong Kong were not really refugees – they maintained a government to which they could appeal. However, because they were physically in Hong Kong, and Hong Kong authorities recognised the government of the People's Republic of China, that avenue of appeal was closed to them. With no easy solution, Hambro argued that this population were largely bona fide refugees who were not under the UNHCR mandate, but should receive assistance anyway on humanitarian grounds.[52]

The UNHCR in Hong Kong continued to support stateless Europeans leaving China, and left the aid for the large and increasingly desperate refugee population all around it to private humanitarian organisations. It appeared that just as in the early days of displaced persons work after the Second World War in Shanghai, the Europeans received support from international organisations above and beyond anything provided to indigent Chinese. The waning days of the IRO Shanghai office took place in this context, where the politics of citizenship overwhelmed the question of who was most in need. In the tense environment of both Asian decolonisation and the Cold War, all of these decisions on refugee aid carried consequences.

Acknowledgement

Research for this chapter was partially funded by a Sosland Fellowship at the United States Holocaust Memorial Museum (hereafter USHMM).

128　　　　*Refugees and the stateless in Asia*

Notes

1 Christian Henriot, 'Shanghai and the Experience of War: The Fate of Refugees', *European Journal of East Asian Studies*, 2 (2006), pp. 219–20.
2 'Jewish Refugees from Europe to Number some 4,000 by End of March', 29 January 1939, *Shanghai Times*, 284, 2971, Reel 4, Shanghai Municipal Archives Collection (hereafter SMA), USHMM.
3 '1000 More Refugees', editorial in the *Shanghai Post & Mercury*, 30 January 1939, 287, 2971, Reel 4, SMA, USHMM.
4 Xie Peibing (ed.), *Zhanhou Qianfan Huaqiao Shiliao Huibian 1M* (Taipei: Guoshiguan, 2003), p. 1.
5 The challenges presented by some of these categories are discussed here: Q-127-8-284 Songbu Jingbei Silingbu Waishichu Guanyu dui Rijun tezhong qiaomin, bai'e, Youtairen guanli banfa ji jingweibu 2nd waishi suotanhui jilv, deng, 11 October 1945, Shanghai Municipal Archives, Shanghai, PRC (hereafter SMA-Shanghai).
6 The historiography of the European communities in China is split between recent scholarly studies inspired by Robin Cohen's work on diasporas, which analyse their experiences as a 'victim diaspora', and oral histories and family memoirs, which have flourished in the last twenty years. For the former, see Marcia Reynders Ristaino, *Port of Last Resort: The Diaspora Communities of Shanghai* (Stanford, CA: Stanford University Press, 2001); Arieh J. Kochavi, *Post-Holocaust Politics: Britain, the United States, and Jewish Refugees, 1945–1948* (Chapel Hill, NC: University of North Carolina Press, 2001); David Kranzler, *Japanese, Nazis, and Jews: The Jewish Refugee Community of Shanghai* (New York: Ktav Publishing, 1988); Michael R. Marrus, *The Unwanted: European Refugees in the Twentieth Century* (New York: Oxford University Press, 1985). For the latter, see Sigmund Tobias, *Strange Haven: A Jewish Childhood in Wartime Shanghai* (Urbana, IL: University of Illinois Press, 1999); Samuel Iwry, *To Wear the Dust of War* (New York: Palgrave Macmillan, 2004); Ursula Bacon, *Shanghai Diary: A Young Girl's Journey from Hitler's Hate to War-Torn China* (Milwaukie, OR: Milestone Books, 2004); Irene Eber (ed.), *Voices from Shanghai: Jewish Exiles in Wartime China* (Chicago, IL: University of Chicago Press, 2008).
7 The broad scope of UNRRA's work in China is summarised in George Woodbridge, *UNRRA: The History of the United Nations Relief and Rehabilitation Administration*, vol. II (New York: Columbia University Press, 1950), pp. 371–453.
8 Woodbridge, *UNRRA*, p. 492.

The international politics of refugee settlement 129

9 'China Acts Against Germans', *North China Daily News*, Shanghai, 17 December 1945, DPs – European S-1121-0000-0118, United Nations Archives, New York, NY (hereafter UN Archives).

10 The American Jewish Joint Distribution Committee surveyed Central European refugees in Shanghai in early 1946, and only 2.4 per cent wished to remain in China. That said, the survey was conducted after this clear communication that they were not welcome to stay in China, and that might have skewed the results. American Jewish Joint Distribution Committee, Statistical Analysis of 13,475 Refugees in Shanghai, China as of 1 January to 31 March 1946, AJ43/699 File 55/2, Reel 3, Records of the International Refugee Organization (hereafter IRO),USHMM.

11 Letter to Mr. Howard from Beckelman, February 1946, AJ43/699 File 55/2, Reel 3, IRO, USHMM.

12 'Moses W. Beckelman, JDC Director-General, Dies of Heart Attack', 12 December 1955, *Jewish Telegraphic Agency Daily News Bulletin*, 22, 238. https://www.jta.org/archive/moses-w-beckelman-j-d-c-director -general-dies-of-heart-attack. Accessed 15 May 2023.

13 Summary of Conversation at Chinese Ministry of Foreign Affairs, 26 February 1946, AJ43/699 File 55/2, Reel 3, IRO, USHMM.

14 Draft summary of Chinese Government Position Regarding Refugees from Nazi Persecution Found in Shanghai upon the Liberation of the City in August 1945, 26 June 1951, Folder: China. 1948–52 (G45-54_ CC_003_0044 (1), JDC Archives.

15 M.W. Beckelman to Herbert, 27 January 1946, AJ43/699 File 55/2, Reel 3, IRO, USHMM.

16 Text of Statement Agreed Upon Between M.W. Beckelman, Intergovernmental Committee on Refugees, and Mr. Wu Nan-Ju, Ministry of Foreign Affairs, for issue by Mr. Beckelman as a News Release, 8 March 1946, AJ43/699 File 55/2, Reel 3, IRO, USHMM. In the interim, the CNRRA offered to provide the guaranty required for Germans and Austrians to remain in China. Memo to J. Franklin Ray, Jr. from Benjamin H. Kizer, Monthly Report No. 3, 20 March 1946, RG-67.059 UNRRA China Office, China Office Reports, UNRRA Records, USHMM.

17 Woodbridge, *UNRRA*, p. 492. UNRRA completed repatriations but did no resettlement; to the extent that European refugees were resettled from China, it was through the work of the JDC with funding through IGCR.

18 Memo to J. Franklin Ray, Jr. from Benjamin H. Kizer, Monthly Report No. 3, 20 March 1946, RG-67.059 UNRRA China Office, China Office Reports, UNRRA-USHMM. In his scathing recounting of KMT poli- cies during the takeover of Taiwan, US diplomat George Kerr claimed

130 *Refugees and the stateless in Asia*

that the CNRRA operations were deeply corrupt and that the requirement that aid be funnelled from UNRRA through CNRRA was both
unusual and deeply political. See George H. Kerr, *Formosa Betrayed*
(Boston, MA: Houghton Mifflin, 1965), ch. 8.

19 Memo from Benjamin Kinzer to T. F. Tsiang, 13 February 1946, DPs-
Europeans-Accounts S-1132-0000-0047, UNNRA, UN Archives.

20 Louise W. Holborn, *The International Refugee Organization: A
Specialized Agency of the United Nations, Its History and Work 1946–
1952* (London: Oxford University Press, 1956), p. 31.

21 CNRRA Memo, International Refugee Organization, 7 December
1946, 642/0049, Guojinanminzuzhi Zhinan (11-INO-05758), Ministry
of Foreign Affairs Archives of the Republic of China, Academia
Sinica, Taipei, Taiwan (hereafter MOFA Taipei); Washington Embassy
to Nanjing MOFA, Telegram 4571, 15 April 1947, 642/0049,
Guojinanminzuzhi Zhinan (11-INO-05758), MOFA Taipei.

22 Hungdah Chiu, 'Nationality and International Law in Chinese
Perspective', *Maryland Series in Contemporary Asian Studies* (2014);
113-00149-04(1) Zhongguo Zhengfu yu Lianheguo Guoji Nanminzushi
Xieding, n.d., Ministry of Foreign Affairs Archives of the People's
Republic of China, Beijing, PRC (hereafter MOFA Beijing).

23 Hannah Arendt, 'The Rights of Man', *Modern Review*, 3, 1 (Summer
1949), pp. 26–7.

24 Katrine R. C. Greene, 'Repatriating China's expatriates', *Far Eastern
Survey*, 17, 4 (25 February 1948), p. 45.

25 Greene, 'Repatriating China's Expatriates', p. 46.

26 Holborn, *The International Refugee Organization*, p. 584.

27 Preparatory Commission International Refugee Organization Far East
Monthly Operational Report, July 1947, IRO Reports S-1121-0000-
0156, UNRRA, UN Archives.

28 Jennings Wong to Dr George Yeh, 2 June 1948, 642/0058,
Guojinanminzuzhi Zhinan, MOFA Taipei.

29 Horst Eisfelder, quoted in Antonia Finnane, *Far from Where? Jewish
Journeys from Shanghai to Australia* (Melbourne: Melbourne University
Press, 1999), pp. 182–3.

30 Letter from Jennings Wong to Dr George Yeh, Vice Minister MOFA,
16 April 1948, 642/0056, Guojinanminzuzhi Zhinan (11-INO-05765),
MOFA Taipei; Draft Provisions Concerning Payments of China's
Contributions to IRO, 1948, FO 371/72052, The National Archives
of the United Kingdom, Kew, UK (hereafter TNA:PRO); Telegram,
Shanghai to Foreign Office, 2 December 1948, FO371/2086C,
TNA:PRO.

The international politics of refugee settlement 131

31 Savinggram to Mayor, Municipal Government of Amoy, from Horner H. C. Chen, IRO Amoy Suboffice, 11 March 1949, 642/0063, Guojinanminzuzhi Zhinan (11-INO-05773), MOFA Taipei; Letter to George Yeh from William N. Collison, 22 July 1949, 642/0065, Guojinanminzuzhi Zhinan (11-INO-05774), MOFA Taipei.

32 Minutes, Emergency Measures being considered for the evacuation of Jewish and White Russian DPs, FO 371/72086B, TNA: PRO.

33 Hua Dong Xun, [Fujian] Guanyu nanmin chuguo chuli banfa, 20 September 1950, 113-00125-01(1), MOFA Beijing.

34 Laura Madokoro, *Elusive Refugee: Chinese Migrants in the Cold War* (Cambridge, MA: Harvard University Press, 2016).

35 Memo to Andrew G. Findlay from William N. Collison, 1 July 1950, Guojinanminzuzhi Yuandongju jieshu gogzuo de youguan qingkuang, 113-00075-04(1), MOFA Beijing.

36 Letter to Findlay Andrews, From IRO Geneva, 19 June 1950, Guojinanminzuzhi Yuandongju jieshu gogzuo de youguan qingkuang, 113-00075-04(10), MOFA Beijing.

37 UN Advisory Committee on Refuges, Report of the High Commissioner on Emergency Aid to Refugees with Special Reference to Problems of Coordination and the Situation of Refugees in China, 28 July 1952, FO 371/101546, TNA: PRO.

38 United States Displaced Persons Commission, *Memo to America: The DP Story, the Final Report of the U.S. Displaced Persons Commission* (Washington, DC: Government Printing Office, 1952), pp. 37–9.

39 Kevin Ostoyich, '"Back on Straw": The Experience of Shanghai Jewish Refugees in Bremen after Escaping German National Socialism, Enduring a Japanese "Designated Area", and Fleeing Chinese Communism', *Studia Historica Gedanensia*, 5 (24 July 2014), p. 115.

40 Ernst Elguther, quoted in James R. Ross, *Escape to Shanghai: A Jewish Community in China* (New York: The Free Press, 1994), pp. 252–3.

41 Memorandum from IRO group leader, 15 June 1950, FO 127 Shanghai, Box 675, Papers of Harry S. Truman (HST papers), Truman Presidential Library, Independence, MO (HST Library).

42 Q131-4-1730, Shanghaishi jingchaju xingzhengchu guanyu wai-qiao shenqing yuguoji juliuzheng zhi gonghan ji diaocha baogao, SMA-Shanghai.

43 Shanghaishi jingchaju xunling, Shijingxing (35) zi di 3333 hao, 7 March 1946, Q131-5-9082 Shanghaishi jingchaju chuli Sulian qiaomin bai e fenzide juliu dengji he gui zai Zhongguohuifu Sulianji guiding jing suoshe fenju de xunling, SMA-Shanghai.

132   *Refugees and the stateless in Asia*

44 'White Russian Refugees in China', 6 February 1950, Shanghai Cases Samar, Box 53, RG 278, National Archives and Records Administration of the USA, College Park, MD (hereafter NARA College Park).

45 IRO Executive Committee, 3rd Session, 26 January 1949; Telegram from Shanghai to Foreign Office, 18 January 1949, FO 371/78187, TNA:PRO; Holborn, pp. 423–5.

46 Letter to Findlay Andrews, from IRO Geneva, 19 June 1950, 113-00075-04(10) Guojinanminzuzhi yuandongju jieshu gongzuo de youguan qingkuang, MOFA Beijing.

47 Holborne, *The International Refugee Organization*, p. 422.

48 For example, a report to MOFA Beijing counted 5,336 people who were sent to capitalist countries, 3,736 of which were Soviet or stateless Russians. Youguan Lianheguo nanmin gaoji zhuanzhi 'Shanghai zhi' jiankuang, 113-00287-01(1) Chuli he jieshu Lianheguo guojinanminzuzhi Shanghai zhi wenti June 1953–September 1956, MOFA Beijing.

49 Notes on Conference between Mr. Walter Citrin, Israeli Immigration Officer in Hongkong, and Mr. Charles H. Jordan and Mr. Henry L. Levy, 16 June 1952, China 1948–52, China Subject Matter, Geneva 45–54, Online Archives of the JDC.

50 Letter to IRO atten. Col. MC Liang from Fred Chow, CTS, 5 January 1951, Q-368-1-804 Zhongguo luxingshi Tianjin fenshe 1951 nian yu Lianheguo Guojinanminzuzhi yuandongju laiwang wenshu Pages 1–100, SMA-Shanghai.

51 MOFA to Consuls in China, 6 September 1956113-00287-01(1) Chuli he jieshu Lianheguo Guojinanminzuzhi Shanghai zhi wenti June 1953–September 1956, MOFA Beijing. Liang's resignation was arranged in advance, and he was convinced to step down. Ibid., MOFA to Shanghai, telegram 215, 16 January 1956.

52 The full report is published as Edvard Hambro, *The Problem of Chinese Refugees in Hong Kong* (Leyden: A. W. Sijthoff, 1955).

9

Statelessness and its (sometime) benefits: the case of Russians in Harbin in the 1930s and 1940s

Sheila Fitzpatrick

Are rights, or even the right to possess them, dependent on citizenship conferred by a nation state? In the mid-twentieth century, Hannah Arendt argued that they were, and that their deprivation – the condition of statelessness – left individuals bereft not only of citizenship but also of agency, personhood, and significance in the world.[1] In effect, though she did not use the word in this context, this constituted something like the 'atomisation' (breaking of familial, community, and other sub-state bonds) that she saw as a consequence of totalitarianism.

This argument was put forward in a context where millions of people from the 'civilised' world (Arendt's distinction, to distinguish them from the pre-rights status of, say, indigenous people under imperialism) had recently become stateless. The Russian Revolution of 1917, resulting in mass emigration from the educated classes and the Soviet cancellation of citizenship of those who emigrated, was the first major producer of statelessness in the wake of the First World War. Norwegian Fridtjof Nansen's office at the League of Nations organised the so-called 'Nansen passport' for this group, which allowed them to reside without citizenship but in comparative security in various European countries. Then, in the 1930s, Nazi Germany forced the emigration and loss of citizenship of Jews, including Hannah Arendt herself, who was formally stateless after her departure from Germany in 1933 until her naturalisation as a US citizen in 1951.

The argument about statelessness which Hannah Arendt joined in the 1940s and 1950s was partly a legal–philosophical argument about whether individuals had 'natural rights' that preceded and outranked their rights as citizens of nation states.[2] Arendt thought that the twentieth century had proven that they did not. A subsidiary theoretical argument, though not one in which Arendt engaged directly, was whether the rights and status conferred on an individual by membership of an organisation other than a nation state (be it a guild, a trade union, or an extraterritorial enclave) counted. Arendt implicitly dismissed this idea.

Even more salient, in the immediate post-war situation, were the practical arguments about what protection could and should be offered to those who found themselves involuntarily stateless. One obvious theoretical solution was that international organisations (the League of Nations, the United Nations and its subsidiaries) should be the agent of legal and other protection for stateless persons, as in the case of the Nansen passport before the 1939–45 war. In practice, of course, this was easier said than done. In Arendt's book, the focus on protection by international organisations was well and good, but not enough to solve the problem; she preferred a framework where nation-states were barred from removing citizenship from their members.

Arendt's approach to the question of statelessness was, as always, idiosyncratic, drawing simultaneously on her philosophical training, her personal experiences, and her political activism in a left-wing Jewish context. A natural polemicist, she was more likely to point to the evil and folly of governments and laws in dealing with the statelessness problem than to the ability of the stateless to make their way somehow through the minefields of a world of nation-states. To be sure, her own life experience might have been used as a counter-example to the argument of necessary atomisation through statelessness: in Paris from 1933, and even more in New York from 1941, she was an active and visible figure within active and visible German/Jewish/leftwing diasporas, using words like 'the tribe' and 'the Band' to describe the lively and close-knit émigré communities in which she moved.[3] To say that statelessness had deprived Hannah Arendt herself of her personhood or agency was, on the face of it, supremely implausible.

The aim of this paper is not, however, to convict Arendt of lack of logic but rather to point out that a different approach to statelessness is possible than the philosophical/legal/polemical one that

Statelessness and its (sometime) benefits 135

she used. If we look empirically at *de jure* statelessness in a variety of historical circumstances in the twentieth century, it becomes clear that the significance of the de jure status for the de facto stateless varied considerably from case to case. Often it was a disadvantage, but sometimes not. Moreover, the benefits of agency, personhood, and an established place in the world conferred, in Arendt's view, only by state citizenship, seem also in various circumstances to have been available via membership of formal or informal communities that were not states. I will approach this as an empirical question in this paper, but it could also be raised as a theoretical objection to Arendt's argument.

In Arendt's approach to citizenship, states have all the agency and individuals have none. In practice, however, we find exceptions to this rule. Individuals can sometimes game the system on citizenship, as on most matters where states, at first glance, hold all the cards. Such individuals may 'view passports instrumentally, in terms of status and security rather than as symbols of national loyalty and belonging'.[4] In the Displaced Persons (DP) camps in Germany after the Second World War, for example, Soviet and East European DPs were often able to register under false nationalities/ citizenships, claiming to have lost their documentation during the war. The main motive for doing this was to avoid repatriation, and, for Soviet Russians, a common false claim was to be stateless emigrants ('White' Russians). Whole teams of helpers, sympathetic to their desire to avoid repatriation to the Soviet Union, laboured to fabricate the 'stateless' documents that would support these claims.[5] This was a situation in which statelessness was regarded as a more advantageous situation than Soviet citizenship.

The case study I will use in this chapter for examining the variety of real-world consequences of the legal status of statelessness is that of 'White' Russians in Manchuria – refugees from the Russian Revolution who had settled in Harbin and other parts of Manchuria along the Russian-built Chinese Eastern Railway in the 1920s and remained there, for the most part, until after the Second World War. Unlike the DP camp communities, which were short-lived, the Russian diaspora in Manchuria had a degree of permanency and settled self-organisation. The Russian community in Harbin was not a state, to be sure, but it had rights as a community – recognised by the League of Nations Convention on the International Status

136   *Refugees and the stateless in Asia*

of Refugees,[6] but sometimes also by laws within the different state structures that existed in Manchuria from the 1920s to 1940s, and these rights conferred similar benefits to the ones Arendt associated only with state citizenship. Within this community, all the Russians were *de facto* emigrants, but only some of them had the legal status of statelessness, since there were other citizenship and quasi-citizenship options available, sometimes more advantageous than *de jure* statelessness and sometimes less. Individual Russians moved in and out of the legal status of statelessness as the balance of advantage shifted. For the historian, there is another kind of advantage: it is possible at any given time to compare the situation of the *de jure* stateless with those that were only *de facto*.

Russian Harbin

At the turn of the twentieth century, Imperial Russia had built the Chinese Eastern Railway, an offshoot of the Trans-Siberian Railway that ran from Chita to Vladivostok, to open up Manchuria to Russian trade and influence. Harbin and other smaller towns that sprang up along the railway were Russian in every sense, since the territory around the railways was a Russian concession. The Harbin of the early twentieth century was to all appearances a Russian city, with Russian architecture, street names, department stores, and cultural institutions. With its abundance of Russian Orthodox churches, its 'onion-domed cupolas, empire-style façades, wide boulevards and touches of *Art Nouveau*', it looked not only overwhelmingly Russian in the 1920s but also appeared as a cosmopolitan, as opposed to provincial, Russia. Russian Harbin was multicultural, with Russian-speaking Jews, Tatars, Ukrainians, and Poles among its residents. This not only reflected the make-up of the Russian Empire from which they had come, but also the fact that for ethnic minorities, Manchuria offered an escape from the discrimination that was intensifying in the Western regions of the country. Harbin's Russianness was more likely to be referred to with the broader term *rossiiskii* (covering inhabitants of Russia, regardless of ethnicity), rather than the narrower ethnic designations of Russians, *russkii*. But it became the centre not just of a complex Russian (and Russian-Empire) society but also of a

Statelessness and its (sometime) benefits 137

lively Russian cultural scene that to a large extent cut across ethnic sub-groups.[7]

Russians in Harbin lost their extraterritorial privileges in 1920, meaning that they were subject to Chinese courts and police. Formally speaking, political organisation was illegal for Russians in Harbin, and even non-political meetings and unions had to be registered with the local Chinese authorities. But the Chinese were in fact tolerant of politics that were irrelevant to their concerns, and a variety of Russian political associations – monarchist, fascist, and veterans – flourished on a semi-legal basis.[8] A similar disconnect between the formal and informal situation existed with regard to such everyday matters as street names and signage, with Chinese municipal authorities trying to replace Cyrillic with Chinese and Russian merchants often simply ignoring their ordinances.[9] The railway was, as ever, the core of Harbin's economy. Under Soviet ownership after the collapse of Imperial Russia, it was formally co-administered by Russians and Chinese in the 1920s, but in fact Russians retained the dominant role until the arrival of the Japanese, to whom the railway was sold in 1934.

It is extremely difficult to make definitive statements about Russian rights in Harbin in the 1920s, given the multitude of competing authorities: in addition to the railway administration and Harbin's municipal government, the local warlord, Zhang Zuolin, was a player, as was Peking (the formal seat of Chinese national government), while Britain, the United States, and Japan, as well as the Soviet Union, all exercised intermittent pressure. The formal situation as articulated by any of these authorities did not necessarily coincide with the actual situation on the ground, and in addition it was a constantly evolving situation as the Chinese population of Harbin increased exponentially through the 1920s and 1930s, and the Russian population declined, at first proportionately and then, in the 1930s, absolutely.[10] According to Russian retrospective accounts, the *de facto* rights and indeed privileges of Russians were to a large extent preserved throughout the 1920s, while China-focused accounts stress the legal curtailment of former rights and the rise of Chinese nationalism in Harbin.[11]

To compound the complications, Soviet influence in Harbin was offset by an influx of tens of thousands of 'White' (anti-Red) Russians in the early 1920s, many of them officers of the White

138   *Refugees and the stateless in Asia*

Armies recently defeated in the Russian Civil War. As of the end of the 1920s, 'Whites' and 'Reds' were almost equally balanced in Harbin's Russian population.[12] The White influx helped to turn Russian Harbin from an outpost of empire to a diaspora, although this process was complicated by the continuing presence (via the railway administration and powerful Soviet consulate) of the Soviet Union. In the 1920s, Harbin was home to one of the largest concentrations of Russian emigrants in the world, and the only one that could claim to be an actual Russian city, despite its geographical location outside Russia. Because of the 'Red' presence, however, some purists in the Russian diaspora refused to acknowledge its diaspora status on the grounds that true statelessness required a founding trauma, like the Jews' expulsion from Egypt.[13]

I have used the word 'Russians' as shorthand, but in fact both statuses – Soviet and stateless – were available to all Russian-speaking former citizens of the Russian empire, including those who did not identify as ethnically Russian. Jews were one of the major groups in this category, often regarding themselves as members both of the Russian diaspora and the Jewish one.[14] In the words of Sam Moshinsky, son of a prosperous Shanghai Russian-Jewish business family,

> Often we were called White Russians, because we were also economic refugees from the Soviet Revolution. But the difference between us and other White Russians was that the White Russians were supporters of the Czar, and of course quite anti-Semitic. We were White Russians to the extent that we fled from the Revolution but we weren't White Russians like they were because our whole cultural situation was different. So we grew up in separate communities.[15]

In Harbin, there was probably less separateness up to the end of the 1920s, but tensions developed with the increase of antisemitism in Russian nationalist circles and the rise of an influential Russian Fascist Party in Harbin.[16] In the wake of the scandalous murder of the pianist son of a prominent Harbin Russian-Jewish businessman, Simon Caspé, in the early days of the Japanese occupation, Russian Jews were much more likely to leave Harbin for Shanghai and other coastal cities,[17] even though it was not the Japanese themselves causing problems for Jews,[18] but rather local Russian nationalists and fascists.

Statelessness and its (sometime) benefits   139

The Russian-speaking Turko-Tatar community was another group of former Russian Imperial citizens well represented in Harbin. The status of the local Tatars received a boost during the Japanese occupation of Manchuria, since the Japanese saw them as warrior descendants of the thirteenth-century Mongol leader who imposed tribute on many Russian settlements, Chinghiz Khan.[19] But no hard and fast barriers separated the Tatars from other Russian speakers in Harbin. The barrier was between the Russian speakers – few of whom bothered to learn anything but street Chinese – and the local Chinese population.

In 1929, the Japanese took over Manchuria, establishing what is often described as the puppet state of Manchukuo that co-existed with the conspicuous presence of the Japanese military. This put an abrupt end to previous dynamics in Harbin, partly by quashing the Chinese nationalists who had been chipping away at historic Russian dominance in the city. White Russians were inclined to welcome the Japanese, who for their part saw potential utility in the Russians' anti-communism and hostility to the Soviet Union.[20] The Russian Fascist Party, already a significant force in Harbin's Russian community, was a natural ally of the Japanese, although the relationship was not without tension. The Asano unit, manned by Russian volunteers and later draftees, was set up within the Manchukuo army in 1938 for cross-border espionage and sabotage across the Soviet border.[21] Some of the lustre went off the White Russian/Japanese association, however, when Japan signed a non-aggression treaty with the USSR at the beginning of the 1940s; and in the course of the Second World War, a patriotic upsurge among Russians increased support for the Soviet Union and caused alienation from Japanese.[22]

Harbin's Russian population, even many Whites, greeted the Soviet Army warmly when it occupied the city in 1945: 'in my mind, these were Russian troops – not Soviet troops', the daughter of a former White Russian officer recalled.[23] The short period of Soviet occupation, before responsibility was handed over to the Chinese communists, was very productive in strengthening and, where necessary, re-establishing Russian cultural and educational institutions, simultaneously reinforcing pride in the Russian tradition and adding a mild and non-confrontational Soviet component that seems to have been easily assimilated by the local Russians.[24] But in the

140 *Refugees and the stateless in Asia*

post-war period, as the communists extended their control over the country, culminating in the creation of the People's Republic of China in 1949, the Russians in Manchuria saw the writing on the wall ever more clearly: the new Chinese rulers had no use for them and would prefer to see them go. A steady stream of emigration took Russians from Harbin to countries like the United States and Australia from the late 1940s, followed in the mid 1950s by the large-scale repatriation of Russians to the Soviet Union, recruited for Khrushchev's Virgin Lands schemes, which spelled the end of Russian Harbin.

Through all these political vicissitudes, the stubborn continuity of Russian culture in Harbin is striking. In the memoirs of Russian musicians, ballet dancers, and the like, the change of state authorities often rates little more than a passing mention. A violinist's memoirs note some 'shaking' of Harbin's 'peaceful and measured' musical life with the Japanese invasion, but his string quartet continued to perform unhindered up to 1945 and beyond, as did Harbin's symphony orchestra.[25] Russian operetta flourished under the Japanese and Soviets alike.[26] The race-track set up by the Chinese Eastern Railway administration early in the twentieth century existed as a Russian institution 'under all regimes up to 1949', regardless of conflicts between Japanese and Chinese in the late 1920s over whose flag should fly there.[27] And in Russian schools, as late as the early 1950s, schoolboys were wearing the same 'dark, sturdy, military-style school uniforms with a cap' and closely cropped hair as their grandparents had done in Imperial Russia, and studied the heroic exploits of the Cossacks, who in earlier times were among those who had guarded Harbin's Chinese Eastern Railway.[28] Even in the 1950s, Harbin's Russian adolescents were reading Russian books in the Central library, seeing Soviet films at the Soviet clubs, listening to Russian operetta at the club of the (Russian) Churin department store, playing volleyball, and skating in winter, as one fond memoirist recalled.[29] Migrating to (in her eyes) hopelessly uncivilised Australia in the 1950s, she was always grateful that she had had the chance to grow up as a cultured Russian in Harbin.[30]

Memories are, of course, an unreliable guide to the past as it was actually experienced. However, the survival, in later emigration, of a collective identity – *harbintsy* – for the Russians who had lived there; the continuing nostalgia for a lost way of life for

Statelessness and its (sometime) benefits 141

which Harbin, not St Petersburg or Moscow, was the exemplar; and the regular reunions in emigration of alumni of Harbin's Russian schools and universities[31] provide abundant evidence that Russian Harbin, a non-state entity, provided its members with much of the sense of agency and belonging that Arendt considered unique to state citizenship.

Passports and citizenships

The empirical question of the meaning of *de jure* statelessness for the *de facto* stateless can only be answered by a close examination of the laws and practices related to passports and citizenship for Russians in Manchuria. All of Harbin's Russian-speaking residents had formally lost their old state membership with the collapse of Imperial Russia in 1917.[32] But the Soviet Union offered Soviet passports to all the Russians in Harbin, and up to 1924 essentially required those who worked on the railway to take them. Those who chose not to take the Soviet passports, including most of those who had arrived in Harbin in the early 1920s after the defeat of the White armies, became stateless. These, however, were not the only possibilities. Some took Chinese passports, either from the local Manchurian warlord Zhang Zuolin (in whose armies some former Whites served) or from Peking. Successful businessmen often found a way of acquiring a foreign citizenship – French, Swiss, British, Portuguese, and so on. Some of Harbin's Russian Jews acquired passports of the new state of Lithuania (formerly part of the Russian Empire with a large Jewish population).[33]

While the Soviet and stateless groups were more or less equally balanced in the 1920s, under Japanese occupation in the 1930s and 1940s, the balance shifted against the Soviet and in favour of the émigré group and the number of Soviet passport-holders dropped to under ten thousand in 1937 and under two thousand by 1940, while the number of Russians registered as stateless held relatively steady, even rising by six thousand at the end of the 1930s.[34] This was the direct result of Japanese policy to give a measure of self-administration to 'Stateless' under the Bureau for the Affairs of Russian Emigrants (BREM), set up in 1934 to administer Russian affairs in Manchukuo.[35] BREM's remit extended to employment

142   *Refugees and the stateless in Asia*

cards, residence permits, schools, and travel documents. Russians who chose not to register with it thus exposed themselves to discrimination with regard to distribution of goods and travel visas, permission to hold meetings, access to education, and employment. Only those registered with BREM as stateless Russian emigrants enjoyed these quasi-citizenship privileges. (This category included Russian-speaking Jews and members of the Tatar community, which were still distinguished as separate entities but came under BREM's jurisdiction.[36]) Russians who were Chinese passport holders were also under pressure to register with BREM, and in 1942–43, they were all automatically transferred to the status of emigrants.[37]

BREM was defined by statute as an 'administrative organ' of the Manchukuo government whose competence included the direction of all emigrant associations and 'the defence of the legal, economic and cultural interests' of individual emigrants and adjudication of conflicts between them. Financed by a 1 per cent levy on its registered members, it was a 'peculiar kind of emigrant government', in the words of a Shanghai newspaper, whose competence covered the gamut from finances to culture and included an arbitration department with twelve appointed judges for settling emigrant disputes.[38] Formally headed by a series of White generals, its most powerful executives came from the Russian Fascist Party, notably Mikhail Matkovsky, who headed both the powerful Administrative and Railways Departments (the fact that Matkovsky, as was later revealed, was actually a Soviet agent as well as a fascist adds another twist to an already tangled story).[39]

BREM's significance was underlined by the fact that, according to a official statement on governance, Russian emigrants were one of the five basic nations of Manchukuo, along with Manchurians, Mongols, Koreans, and Japanese. Formally speaking, this conferred on them 'all the political rights and obligations of citizenship' in Manchukuo.[40] The independence of its jurisdiction was (no doubt unintentionally) underlined by a by-product of Japanese/ Manchukuo racism – the provision that, as non-Asians, Russians were not subject to the Manchukuo legislation on family law that applied to the other national groups, but 'would be ruled entirely according to their own laws',[41] that is, presumably, BREM's arbitration courts. Thus, in the context of Japanese occupation of Manchuria, Russians acquired a status of quasi-citizenship of

Statelessness and its (sometime) benefits 143

Manchukuo – as long as they were willing to register as 'stateless Russian emigrants' with BREM.

This must be qualified by the fact that Manchukuo's sovereignty – hence its ability to confer citizenship – was never firmly established; most foreign powers regarded it simply as a puppet state of Japan, and its long-awaited Constitution was never issued.[42] Moreover, during the Second World War, BREM lost its quasi-governmental status and was downgraded to 'an auxiliary organ of the administrative apparatus of Manchukuo', subordinate to a planned government department of Russian affairs (which, to be sure, seems never to have been created in fact).[43]

BREM was not the only example of the advantages of statelessness for Russians in China in the 1930s and 1940s. In the International Settlement and French Concession of Shanghai stateless Russians (both ethnic Russians and Russian Jews) enjoyed a different kind of privilege during the years of the Second World War. As Russian-Jewish emigrant Sam Moshinsky observed, in Shanghai of the 1940s, Russian nationality provided 'a protective mantle' as far as the Japanese were concerned.[44] When the Japanese interned the British and other opponents of the Axis power, they left the stateless Russians alone (which for those working, for example, in the Shanghai Municipal Police meant an opportunity for promotion).[45] Even more important was the fact that stateless Russians were exempt from the wartime internment that was the fate of citizens of the Western Allies. Whereas before the war, it had been a social advantage for a Russian woman to marry a British or American man, thus acquiring his citizenship, during the war this turned into a disadvantage, as it meant the women were liable to be interned along with their husbands.[46]

So far, our story has focused on the benefits that Russian in China emigrants derived from statelessness in various situations. But there were also circumstances in which it was Soviet passports that conferred the advantage. In the 1920s, only Soviet or Chinese citizens had the right to work on the Chinese Eastern Railway, the region's major employer. Almost twenty thousand according registered with the Soviet consulate in Harbin to receive these documents – which, although referred to as 'passports', actually did not entitle the bearer to move to or reside in the Soviet Union, but were,

144   *Refugees and the stateless in Asia*

as stated on the front page, 'residence permits' for Manchuria, valid for a year and renewable. 'Although some took Soviet passports out of sympathy with the revolution, most ... did so for practical rather than political reasons. They did not want to be stateless, especially in the turbulent times in which they lived.'[47]

In the mid 1930s, after the sale of the China Eastern Railway to the Japanese, many Russians with Soviet passports – an estimated thirty thousand families, many of them former employees of the CER and the associated network of schools and hospitals – decided to repatriate to the Soviet Union. This, as it turned out, was a disastrous decision, as in less than two years, the Great Purges had designated the group as a whole as a security risk, and most were swept into Gulag,[48] but it was still an option not available to the stateless. However, the situation of the Soviet passport-holders who remained in Manchuria deteriorated sharply in the era of BREM, when non-registered Russians – a disproportionate number of whom were probably Jewish, given the dominance of Russian fascists and nationalists in BREM – were subject to many forms of discrimination. In Hailar (a Russian town not far from Harbin on the Chinese Eastern Railway), the houses of Soviet passport-holders were made conspicuous in the 1940s by small wooden boards hung on their front gates with 'USSR' painted on them in red letters.[49] It was not surprising that by 1936, almost two thousand Russians in Manchuria had given up their Soviet passports and registered as stateless Russian emigrants with BREM.[50]

The tide turned again in 1945, when the Japanese were defeated in the Second World War, and the Soviet Army moved into Harbin and other parts of Manchuria. Once again, young Russian emigrants were eager to obtain Soviet passports, which were freely issued by the Soviet consulate in Harbin, which had essentially taken over BREM's role as registerer of Russians in Manchuria. (BREM, meanwhile, was closed down and many of its leaders, particularly the Russian Fascist Party members – including Soviet spy Matkovsky! – were arrested by Soviet security agencies and shot). As before, these documents did not entitle their holders to live in the Soviet Union. But many newly-patriotic Russians (including children of former Whites) were now eager to repatriate, which required application for real Soviet passports, whose issuance took time and required individual investigation. Repatriation of Russians from Shanghai

Statelessness and its (sometime) benefits

started in 1946–47, but it was not until around 1954 that the way for mass repatriation was open in Harbin, by which time many had already emigrated to North America or Australasia.[51]

While individual and family decisions about citizenship were sometimes made on ideological grounds, pragmatism was equally strong, and many Russians were savvy enough to game the system. Nor was this a one-off process. Many Harbin Russians changed their citizenship status, sometimes more than once, in response to shifting external circumstances. The Russian-Jewish violinist Vladimir Trakhtenberg, a resident of Harbin, initially had a Soviet passport but at some point swapped this for a Lithuanian one, which he was able to retain even while registered with BREM. This did not save him from surveillance by BREM agents, however, who took critical note of his continuing ties with the Soviet consulate (which included importing Soviet sheet music for his music store in Harbin).[52]

On the other side of the political spectrum was Kazimir Savitsky, a White Russian engineer of monarchist/fascist sympathies whose firm anti-Soviet views led him to answer BREM's question (a standard one in its questionnaire) as to why he had not repatriated to the Soviet Union with the blunt comment that 'I hadn't lost my mind'. He nevertheless took Chinese citizenship in the 1920s, probably to qualify for a job on the Chinese Eastern Railway, before in the 1930s registering with BREM as stateless. With the coming of the Soviets, he switched again; as his son remembered in an interview in 2019, 'in 1945 there was a change. You had no option but to take the [Soviet] passport'.[53] There were, in fact, other options, but this had become the advantageous one.

Conclusion

Statelessness was the worst of all possible worlds, in Hannah Arendt's scheme. In Harbin and other Russian settlements in Manchuria in the 1930s and 1940s, however, it was often the best option available. If you had a Chinese passport, you were encouraged to give it up. If you had a Soviet passport, you were subject to all kinds of exclusion and penalty. But if you were a 'stateless' person registered with BREM, you qualified as a member of one of

146 *Refugees and the stateless in Asia*

the five nationalities making up Manchukuo; in other words, it was your pathway to rights.

That is not the only situation where the formal status of 'Stateless' was the best of the available options. In the DP camps of Europe after the Second World War, it was the safe option for Russian speakers, who might otherwise be classified as Soviet and forcibly repatriated. To be sure, there was the concomitant disadvantage that 'stateless' Russians might be seen as Nazi collaborators, since that is what many of them had been during the war. But that disadvantage faded quickly as far as the Allies were concerned, as the end of the Second World War merged into the beginning of the Cold War, and anti-communism replaced anti-Nazism as the order of the day. For Russian speakers applying to settle, for example, in Australia, statelessness was the best choice, as acknowledging possession, even former possession, of a Soviet passport might suggest undesirable links with communism.[54]

It may be argued that these advantages of statelessness were simply temporary anomalies in exceptional circumstances. But circumstances are often exceptional. What is constant in history's changing circumstances is that the individuals involved do their best to make the best of them with the material at hand, including varieties of official documentation. This applies also to Hannah Arendt, who, with her communist second husband Heinrich Blücher, was perfectly aware of the possibility of manipulating the system and savvy enough to do it effectively: when Jewish refugees were told to register with the local prefecture by the new Vichy regime after the fall of France, she sensibly advised friends against it, since that meant providing an address that could lead subsequently to arrest.[55] Despite her strictures against the Nansen passport as conferring no specific right to live anywhere, and hence no real rights, she apparently procured a Nansen passport in 1940–41 that made her officially (not just *de facto*) 'stateless' and, together with an emergency US visa, enabled her and her husband to leave for the United States in May 1941.[56] Statelessness was, as Arendt pointed out, a terrible misfortune for many mid-twentieth-century refugees, but sometimes it was also a status that brought its own benefits – not least for around fifty thousand Russians whose registration as stateless emigrants in Manchukuo won them quasi-citizenship rights for a decade.

Notes

1 See Hannah Arendt, 'The Rights of Man', *Modern Review*, 3, 1 (1949), also Hannah Arendt, *Origins of Totalitarianism*, and lectures of 1953 and 1955 cited Mira Siegelberg, *Statelessness: A Modern History* (Cambridge, MA: Harvard University Press, 2020), pp. 205–9. The claims for loss of personhood through statelessness become more explicit in the 1950s, e.g. 'those who became stateless lost contact with humankind along with the loss of their citizenship', 1955 lecture, cited Siegelberg, *Statelessness*, p. 207.

2 On these discussions, see Siegelberg, *Statelessness*, ch. 3.

3 See Elisabeth Young-Bruehl, *Hannah Arendt: For Love of the World* (New Haven, CT: Yale University Press), pp. 113, 136, 273, and passim. For more evidence on the solidity of her membership of a cosmopolitan, mutually reinforcing, New York–based, intellectual-cum-friendship community, as well as of the strength of her personal sense of self within a network of likeminded friends, see Carol Brightman (ed.), *Between Friends: The Correspondence of Hannah Arendt and Mary McCarthy 1949–1975* (London: Secker & Warburg, 1995).

4 Elena Barabantseva and Claire Sutherland, 'Diaspora and Citizenship: An Introduction', *Nationalism and Ethnic Politics*, 7, 1 (2011).

5 See Sheila Fitzpatrick, *White Russians, Red Peril: A Cold War History of Migration to Australia* (Melbourne: Black, Inc., 2021), particularly pp. 44–5.

6 Claudena M. Skran, *Refugees in Inter-War Europe: The Emergence of a Regime* (Oxford: Larendon Press, 1995).

7 See my book *White Russians*, pp. 75–99 and 124–32 (quotation from p. 79).

8 S. V. Smirnov, *Rossiiskie emigrant v severnoi Man'chzhurii v 1920–1945 gg.* (Ekaterinburg: GOU VPO, 2007), pp. 39–40.

9 See James Carter, *Creating a Chinese Harbin. Nationalism in an International City, 1916–1932* (Ithaca, NY: Cornell University Press, 2019), pp. 145–6.

10 As of 1923, Russians constituted 48 per cent (down from 64 per cent in 1913) of Harbin's total population of 68,549, as against the Chinese 49 per cent. As of 1929, when the total population had risen to 160,670, Russians were down to 36 per cent (though with absolute numbers almost unchanged) while Chinese had risen to 61 per cent. By 1940, Russian numbers were down by twenty thousand, now a bare 8 per cent of the total of 457,980, of which 86 per cent were Chinese. Olga Bakich, 'Russian Emigres in Harbin's National Past: Censuses and Identity', in Dan E. Ben-Canaan, Frank Grüner, and Ines Prodöhl (eds),

148 *Refugees and the stateless in Asia*

Entangled Histories: The Transcultural Past of Northeast China (Cham: Springer, 2014), pp. 86–96.

11 For a Russian view, see Viktor Petrov, 'The Town on the Sungar', in Michael Glenny and Norman Stone (eds), *The Other Russia. The Experience of Exile* (London: Faber & Faber, 1990). For an illuminating shift of perspective to the Chinese side, see Carter, *Creating a Chinese Harbin*.

12 Bakich, 'Russian Emigres', pp. 86–96.

13 See Laurie Manchester, 'How Statelessness Can Force Refugees to Redefine Their Ethnicity: What Can Be Learned from Russian Emigrés Dispersed to Six Continents in the Inter-War Period', *Immigrants & Minorities*, 34, 1 (2016), pp. 70–91.

14 Victoria Romanova, 'The Harbin Jewish Spiritual Community and the Japanese Occupation Regime (1931–1945)', *Bulletin Igud Sin/ Association of Former Residents of China/English supplement*, 56, 399 (August–September 2009).

15 Interview with Sam Moshinsky, in Antonia Finnane, *Far from Where? Jewish Journeys from Shanghai to Australia* (Melbourne: Melbourne University Press, 1999), p. 108.

16 See John Stephan, *The Russian Fascists* (London: Hamish Hamilton, 1978).

17 Between 1931 and 1935, Harbin's Jewish community declined from thirteen thousand to five thousand. B. Bresler, 'Harbin's Jewish Community 1898–1958: Politics, Prosperity and Adversity', in J. Goldstein (ed.), *The Jews of China*, vol. 2 (Armonk, NY: M. E. Sharpe, 2000), p. 209.

18 The Japanese in Manchuria remained quite favourably disposed to the (generally well-off) Russian Jewish community, 'although taking into their hands part of the property of some of its members'. Smirnov, *Rossiiskie emigranty*, p. 88. See Chapter 12 in this volume.

19 Smirnov, *Rossiiskie emigranty*, p. 88.

20 Rana Mitter, *The Manchurian Myth: Nationalism, Resistance, and Collaboration in Modern China* (Berkeley, CA: University of California Press, 2000), pp. 80, 88; Smirnov, *Rossiiskie emigranty*, pp. 80–4.

21 Mara Moustafine, *Secrets and Spies: The Harbin Files* (Sydney: Vintage Books, 2002), pp. 346, 352–3.

22 Smirnov, *Rossiiskie emigranty*, pp. 125–6.

23 Galina Kuchina, *Memoirs of Galina* (Melbourne: Brolga Publishing, 2016), pp. 54, 56–7; and see Smirnov, *Rossiiskie emigranty*, p. 206.

24 Fitzpatrick, *White Russians*, pp. 124–9.

25 G. M. Sidorov, 'Vospominaniia skripacha: Muzykal'nyi Kharbin', in E. P. Taskina (comp.), *Russkii Kharbin* (Moscow: Izd. MGU, 1988), pp. 141, 144.

Statelessness and its (sometime) benefits 149

26 O. S. Koreneva, 'Operetta', in Taskina, *Russkii Kharbin*, pp. 182–3.

27 V. P. Volegov, 'Russkii ippodrom', in Taskina, *Russkii Kharbin*, p. 225; Carter, *Creation of Chinese Harbin*, pp. 167–8.

28 Lenore Lamont Zisserman, *Mitya's Harbin* (Bothell, WA: Book Publishers Network, 2016), p. 188; Smirnov, *Rossiiskie emigranty*, p. 154.

29 L. Mel'nikova, 'Odna iz poslednikh', in *Istoriia russkikh v Avstralii*, 4 vols. *K 80-letiiu russkikh obshchin v Avstralii (1923–2003)*, vol. 1 (Sydney: Avstraliada, 2004), p. 96.

30 L. Mel'nikova, 'Vot i Avstraliia ... A kak k nei privyknut'?', in *Istoriia russkikh v Avstralii*, vol. 1, p. 208.

31 Fitzpatrick, *White Russians*, pp. 86–7.

32 See the decree of the Soviet government on 15 December 1921, 'On Deprivation of Russian Citizenship', which removed this citizenship from all Russian emigrants and refugees and ordered that their property be confiscated. Smirnov, *Rossiiskie emigranty*, p. 13.

33 Fitzpatrick, *White Russians*, p. 80.

34 Bakich, 'Russian Emigres', pp. 86–96.

35 On the establishment and functioning of BREM (Biuro po delam rossiiskikh emigrantov v Man'chzhurskoi imperii), see E. E. Aurilene, *Rossiiskaia diaspora v Kitae, 1920–1950 gg. Monografiia* (Khabarovsky: chastnaia kollektsiia, 2008), pp. 50–5, 69–71; Mara Moustafine, 'Russians from China: Migrations and Identity', *Cosmopolitan Civil Societies Journal*, 5, 2 (2013), p. 151.

36 Aurilene, *Rossiiskaia diaspora*, p. 63.

37 Moustafine, *Secrets*, pp. 341–2; Smirnov, *Rossiiskie emigranty*, pp. 88, 91.

38 Aurilene, *Rossiiskaia diaspora*, pp. 50–2; quotation from p. 65.

39 Ibid., pp. 52–4; on Matkovsky and his status as Soviet spy, see also Fitzpatrick, *White Russians*, pp. 92–9.

40 Smirnov, *Rossiiskie emigranty*, p. 91; Aurilene, *Rossiiskaia diaspora*, p. 65.

41 Thomas David DuBois, 'Inauthentic Sovereignty: Law and Legal Institutions in Manchukuo', *Journal of Asian Studies*, 69, 3 (2010), p. 762.

42 On the ambiguities of Manchukuo's status, see Ryan Mitchell, 'Manchukuo's Contested Sovereignty: Legal Activism, Rights Consciousness and Civil Resistance in a "Puppet State"', *Asian Journal of Law and Society*, 3 (2016), pp. 351–76; and DuBois, 'Inauthentic Sovereignty'.

43 Aurilene, *Rossiiskaia diaspora*, p. 65.

44 Finnane, *Far from Where?*, p. 108.

150   *Refugees and the stateless in Asia*

45 Robert Bickers, 'Settlers and Diplomats: The End of British Hegemony in the International Settlement, 1937–1945', in Christian Henriot and Wen-hsin Yeh (eds), *In the Shadows of the Rising Sun* (Cambridge: Cambridge University Press, 2004), pp. 247–9; Finnane, *Far from Where?*, pp. 112–13.
46 For an example, see Fitzpatrick, *White Russians*, p. 133.
47 Moustafine, *Secrets*, pp. 94, 96–7, 258.
48 Ibid., pp. 98–112, 203–6.
49 Ibid., pp. 344, 354.
50 Aurilene, *Rossiiskaia diaspora*, p. 63.
51 See Fitzpatrick, *White Russians*, pp. 91–2, 130–1.
52 BREM archive, Khabarovsk: personal file on Vladimir Davidovich Trakhtenberg (this file includes agents' reports).
53 BREM Archive, Khabarovsky: personal file on Kazimir Kazimorovich Savitsky; interview by Katja Heath, Sydney, 20 September 2019, with Igor Savitsky and his wife Alla.
54 See questions raised in the Australian Passport Office about immigrants with Soviet passports, cited Fitzpatrick, *White Russians*, pp. 126–7, 130–1, 137–8, 228.
55 Young-Bruehl, *Hannah Arendt*, p. 157.
56 Siegelberg, *Statelessness*, p. 186, says that Hannah Arendt was able to depart for the United States in 1941 only 'through the securing of a Nansen passport and a US emergency visa'.

10

'I have been a refugee all my life': refugees in China in the era of the Second World War – evidence from UNHCR individual case files

Peter Gatrell

> What [does] protection mean to the individual, as a day-to-day matter – just where, in detail and in practice, his de facto statelessness hits him, and how it is overcome by conventions and by individual interventions? [It is necessary to] show exactly the connection between the principle and the daily life (Hersch Lauterpacht).[1]

This chapter is part of an ongoing project which examines the perspectives of refugees in the third quarter of the twentieth century as they negotiated the consequences of displacement and engaged with the international refugee regime. It draws upon extensive and hitherto untapped source material to gauge the aspirations and ambitions of refugees and where appropriate (as anthropologist João Biehl puts it), 'to restore context and meaning to the lived experience of suffering'.[2] This is not quite what Hersch Lauterpacht meant (see above), but the material that follows does have a lot to say about 'daily life' and the search by individual refugees for 'protection' and a resolution of their statelessness.

In the 1950s and 1960s, thousands of refugees approached the office of the United Nations High Commissioner for Refugees (UNHCR) mainly to request assistance in resettling in Western Europe, North or South America, or Australia. Here I concentrate, with a few exceptions, on Russian refugees who were living in China and Hong Kong. Specifically, I consider the experiences and aspirations of refugees against the backdrop of conflict and other upheavals and in the context of an emerging post-war refugee regime.[3] These applications form part of around twenty-five thousand individual case files that UNHCR deemed worth preserving to

152   *Refugees and the stateless in Asia*

guide its deliberations over refugees' eligibility for its protection in accordance with its original mandate in 1951.[4]

When writing to UNHCR, Russian refugees reflected on their experiences in pre-1949 China.[5] Many of them had reached an advanced age, but others were relatively young, having been born in China to parents who fled during the Russian Civil War or who had settled there before the First World War. Following the formation of the People's Republic of China in 1949, many of them made desperate appeals to leave and to live the rest of their lives in relative comfort.

The international refugee regime imposed specific requirements on refugees. To be eligible for recognition, the individual had to demonstrate a well-founded fear of persecution as per the UN 1951 Refugee Convention or to convince the High Commissioner that they deserved his protection and assistance. Having agreed to recognise a refugee as coming within its mandate, UNHCR then enlisted the help of voluntary agencies to arrange transport and resettlement to a third country where refugees hoped to find a new home.

It was thus incumbent on refugees to tell a convincing story and to provide adequate corroborating evidence of their predicament. They were required to recall momentous events rather than 'to forget more efficiently', as Hannah Arendt put it; they had no choice but to speak about their past.[6] One must bear in mind that refugees were 'in the midst of the story they are telling, and uncertainty and liminality, rather than progression and conclusion, are the order of the day'.[7] Although the individual case file served a legal-administrative purpose, it often included a singular narrative, usually described as a 'social history' or an 'autobiography'. Most extant accounts in the confidential case files are relatively brief, but nevertheless revealing. They testified to complicated odysseys in search of a place of safety and the need to circumvent obstacles, drawing upon what support and resources were available. There are plenty of stories of resourcefulness and resilience in the face of political upheaval and military conflict. It should also be emphasised that those who put pen to paper did so in situations of considerable constraint, reflecting not only the circumstances of their displacement and sometimes confinement, but also their encounter with UNHCR officials, where refugees played for high stakes.

'*I have been a refugee all my life*'   153

Given the tumultuous history of twentieth-century Russia, some case files were generated when someone enquired as to the whereabouts of a friend or relative. In March 1970, Soviet citizen Vladimir G. wrote to the ICRC from Gorlovka (Horlivka) in Ukraine to ask for help in tracing his relatives 'living in China at the time of his repatriation'. He was born in 1918 in Harbin, where his father had found work on the Chinese Far Eastern Railway before the Russian Revolution. In 1936, Vladimir moved to Shanghai to live 'an independent life'. In August 1947 he decided to move to the Soviet Union, one of the first Russian refugees to 'return' to the 'homeland'. Now, he was anxious to contact his younger brother and sister, born in Harbin in 1924 and 1928 respectively, and to enquire whether their father had made his way to Australia. His letter reached UNHCR's office in Hong Kong. He enclosed a photo of his sister and described his enquiry as his 'last hope'. Unfortunately, his hopes were dashed.[8]

Elderly Russian refugees who had spent most of their adult life in China explored the possibility of living their remaining days in a third country. In 1962, Sergei G. asked to be resettled in an old people's home in Australia. He was born in Birsk, Ufa, in 1888, and spent the years 1911–18 in Ekaterinburg before moving to Irkutsk. He had lived in Harbin since 1920 and had been employed by a Swedish company. He seems to have made a reasonable life for himself but, approaching the age of seventy-five, he had clearly had enough of China.[9] Likewise, seventy-six-year-old Vladimir K. wrote from Harbin in May 1960 with a 'humble request ... I and my wife lived last winter very heavily as it was need to stand in queues for provisions during the cold time and we are fear that the next winter we shall not be strength for it [*sic*] ... Hoping you will pardon my request and assuring you in advance of my gratitude, and allow me to await your favourable reply ... Your obedient servant, V. K. (Professor).' They were subsequently resettled in Belgium.[10] In other instances, the death of a spouse acted as the trigger to seek resettlement, such as in the case of Ida I., who was born in Smolensk in 1892 and who fled to Shanghai with her husband after the Russian Civil War. His death in 1952 convinced her to seek resettlement.[11]

Another case concerned Alexander P. (born in Ferghana in 1894), his wife (Julia, née Chang Yu-Lin, a Chinese national, born in 1914), and their son and two daughters. The case file was

154 *Refugees and the stateless in Asia*

voluminous. In a brief autobiography, he explained that he was Greek Orthodox, that his father was a post office employee, that he attended secondary school until 1910 followed by commercial school: 'I am a trained import-export clerk and also a language teacher. I have some experience in the fur trade. I am now a professor at the East China Pedagogical University in Shanghai.' He was stateless. In a letter written in 1963 and addressed to the Intergovernmental Committee for European Migration (ICEM) in Hong Kong and translated for the file, Alexander asked why they were deemed ineligible:

> Many Shanghai refugees have received a circular letter dated 6 February 1963, from you [regarding] Russian and Jewish refugees, offering them to leave Shanghai in the nearest future to Hong Kong. Jewish refugees can arrive in Hong Kong without destination visa and they can wait there for further proceeding [after] 3–4 months. We have been registered with your Office and World Council of Churches in Hong Kong for resettlement to abroad for the past nine years [*sic*]. I have asked the permission from the World Council of Churches in Hong Kong, whether I could come and wait in Hong Kong for my destination visa, but unfortunately they did not agree with my petition.

Mention was made of their possible resettlement in the Netherlands from Shanghai (Switzerland and Belgium had already rejected them), but the Dutch had reservations because of 'the family being an uneconomic unit'. An elder daughter married a Chinese national and they intended to remain in China. There was also 'a young spastic [*sic*] child [Antonia, b. 1950] who has since died'. UNHCR's Special Representative, Hong Kong described the children as 'mixed blood' and wrote to the World Council of Churches (WCC) to say 'you will no doubt agree with me that Latin America is the appropriate ground to explore visa opportunities due to the mixed composition of this family'. The case continued into 1967, when they were provisionally accepted under private sponsorship for Australia. But it suggested that a mixed marriage, the age of the parents, and their disabled child counted against this family.[12]

Even more complicated was the case of Viktor L., who wrote from Shanghai in November 1968 to Mrs S. J. Sims, UNHCR's Resettlement Officer in Geneva. In broken English, he wrote as follows [I have not corrected the spelling and grammar]:

'*I have been a refugee all my life*' 155

> Madam, I the undersigned Viktor D. L., a Russian refugee, take the liberty to request you to help me in my very precarious present situation. The matter is that I am awaiting for nearly 16 years to be resettled abroad and up till now no result has yet materialised. In 1966 I have been accepted by the Hong Kong Offices of the U.N. High Commissioner as eligible for resettlement to some country where I coud [*sic*] start a hardworking and healthy existence. All my letters remained unanswered and I do not [know] what to think. Please interfere on my regard and save a still young man, absolutely sound and capable to do any kind of hard work and aspiring only to lead a peceful [*sic*] life.

He went on to explain: 'If I have had in my youth certain mistakes, they have been dearly paid for and it is impossible to imagine that real humanitarian organisations have the intention to sentence me without appeal to total defection and perpetual misery.' Viktor was currently in a 'camp for displaced persons', his punishment for having been 'led into quarrels and fights with Chinese'. Further details emerged. He also enclosed a one-page 'autobiography' for the WCC, describing himself as 'a stateless Russian of Orthodox faith' who was born in China in 1928 and moved to Harbin with his parents in 1932 (this must have been just after the Japanese invasion of Manchuria and the formal establishment of the puppet state of Manchukuo in March 1932). Two years later, the family moved to Shanghai, where he remained during the Japanese occupation. In 1943, fifteen-year-old Viktor found work in a cargo freight company. In 1946 he was jailed for seven years for armed robbery but was released by the Chinese communist officials in 1949. History repeated itself in 1961, when he was sentenced to five years in prison for theft of government property, before being released in 1965. The WCC was unable to help because of his criminal past. The file includes another, typewritten letter from Viktor in which he wrote in vague terms about his 'past activities', and explained that he has no friends, that he knows nothing of the fate of his father, and that his mother died in the USSR in 1964, one of the large number of Russians who opted to return, presumably during the Japanese occupation. He promised not to 'indulge in drink or any hooligan behaviour'. The WCC noted that 'he was sentenced in 1960 to five years for fornication', but like much else in the file, Viktor's life remains shrouded in mystery. The file ended with his

156   *Refugees and the stateless in Asia*

prospective resettlement as a 'handicapped refugee' in Australia, presumably because Mrs Sims exerted some leverage and maybe because he made a great deal of his Orthodox faith.[13]

Many refugees navigated political turmoil and personal tragedy as best they could, knowing that it was important to explain their predicament as the result of events beyond their control. One lengthy case file from 1967 concerned Helen N., born in Smolensk in 1904 to Greek Orthodox parents. She wrote on behalf of her daughter Galina, who was born in Harbin in 1932, and Galina's children. Helen's signed typewritten statement provided a few details:

> In 1921, during the Revolution in Russia, I ran away from Smolensk to Sakalian [*sic*] where I lived until 1929.[14] From here I went to Harbin, where I got married to Fedor N. In 1932 [presumably following the Japanese invasion of Manchuria] we left Harbin for Shanghai. My husband died in the year 1938. I put my daughter in an orphanage, where I worked as a servant. Afterwards I got a job in a hospital to look after sick people. To support myself and my daughter I worked in my spare time in many families' houses, as a cook and as a housekeeper. Then after that I passed to live on my daughter. I ran to Macau, together with my daughter and granddaughters in 1958. *I have been a refugee all my life* [my emphasis].[15]

To add to her tribulations, Helen now had chronic tuberculosis. Galina had to cope with her own tragedy. She had married a 'stateless' man, Edward Zenkovitch, in Shanghai in 1953, but he died in a car accident in Brazil in 1959, leaving her to bring up their two young daughters by herself. But she was a survivor. She worked as a hairdresser and theatre usher. Rather than resettle from Macau to Switzerland as per arrangements made on their behalf in 1963, Galina planned to move to Mozambique. WCC suggested that this was 'rather a risky undertaking', not least because they spoke no Portuguese. However, Galina explained that she now had a new partner João S., 'who is helping me to bring up my children and mother', and who was a native speaker. She already had two more children with him. Unfortunately, the file contains no information about their ultimate destination.[16] Their condensed accounts – compressed to meet the bureaucratic expectations of the refugee regime – illustrate something of the characteristics of the Russian community in Harbin (such as the opportunities for marriage with other

'*I have been a refugee all my life*'   157

Russians) and point to the responsibilities that mother and daughter shouldered when things took an unexpected turn. In today's parlance, they would be described as resilient, but this over-used term scarcely begins to capture the enormity of their loss and their capacity to overcome tragedy and hardship, including a determination to make a new life in sub-Saharan Africa where they could count on joining other white settlers.

Other requests for resettlement began with convoluted stories of flight to China in the wake of revolution and civil war. Maria N., born in 1897, wrote from Shanghai in 1967 to request help in relocating to Switzerland, 'on account of my advanced age and failing health'. She recounts growing up in Orenburg where she attended a girls' gymnasium 'and graduated with a gold medal'. In 1919, she married an actor by the name of Konstantin and together they travelled around European Russia and Siberia with his theatre troupe. After they separated in 1923, she continued to pursue a theatrical career in the Far East, eventually settling in Shanghai as 'a Russian immigrant', where she taught English to the children of Russian refugees. UNHCR's Legal Division queried her eligibility because she held a 'Soviet citizen passport', issued in 1946, but its Hong Kong Representative pointed out that these passports were effectively acquired 'under duress'; in 1946, the Chinese authorities agreed with Soviet consular representatives that all 'White Russians' in China were required to register for Soviet citizenship or else be considered as local residents who must apply for Chinese citizenship. Most such refugees had given up these passports when they arrived in Hong Kong in exchange for a UNHCR certificate of travel, but Maria N. was still living in Shanghai. The officer on the spot concluded that, 'unless investigation brings to light information of a derogatory nature, a registered refugee in possession of such a passport is considered to be within our mandate'.[17] It was a reminder that refugees could tell their stories but also had to furnish or be furnished with the right documentation, and that not all refugees were therefore 'stateless' (see the chapter by Sheila Fitzpatrick).

The first generation of Russian refugees understandably alluded to their life in pre-revolutionary Russia and the ordeal of exile, but their testimony also disclosed unending upheaval. Nikolai G., a stateless refugee seaman, began a lengthy correspondence with UNHCR in 1958. He was born in Russia in 1896 'into a family who

158 *Refugees and the stateless in Asia*

were always connected with the Imperial Russian Government'. He served in the Russian army during the First World War and then with the White army. He made much of his anti-communism: 'When the Communists won the Civil War, I had the choice of either staying in Russia or becoming a Political Refugee. As the former was repugnant to me and would doubtless have resulted in my death because of my family and personal record I became a Political Refugee.' Having fled to Japan, the Japanese authorities immediately sent him to Korea, but in 1923 he was able to move to Shanghai, where he registered with the Russian Emigrants' Committee and Relief Association and joined the Shanghai International Special Police. Having survived the war and occupation he became a guard with the US Military Police but was made redundant at the end of 1946. He then joined a shipping company in the expectation that after a period at sea, he would re-join his wife in Shanghai. Unfortunately for him, Shanghai fell to the Chinese communist forces in 1949: 'As my record as an anti-Communist was well known in Shanghai, I knew that it was worth my life [*sic*] to return there. Consequently, I once again became a Political Refugee.' He went on:

> For seven years I was never permitted even to put my foot on shore in any country. The whole of this time I kept my wife, mother-in-law, brother-in-law, and other relatives in China. After being bled of over $20,000 I have succeeded in arranging the escape of my wife, mother-in-law, brother-in-law from Communist China.

They settled in the Netherlands, 'but I am still regarded as an untouchable Stateless Person'. He ended his letter, 'All I want is somewhere to settle with my wife and not to have to spend the rest of my days on board a ship going from one place to another harried by immigration officials.' His letters are remarkable not only because of this unending odyssey but because he complained that a great deal was being done for Hungarian refugees and not enough for Russians: 'could not something be done for me who has twice escaped from communist controlled areas because of my political beliefs?' It took three more years for him to gain admission to Holland and join his family. Nikolai had been exposed to two revolutions and made a reasonable life in exile only to be forced to spend years alone and in limbo, before being able to settle permanently in the West as he approached retirement age.[18]

'I have been a refugee all my life'   159

The question of resettlement became particularly difficult in cases where refugees had a criminal conviction, as in the case of Russian refugee Evgenii K. The story combined tragedy and melo-drama. Evgenii was born in Harbin in 1923. The dossier indicates that he engaged in illegal currency transactions in 1947 that ended in murder. According to Anthony Clabon, UNHCR-ICEM Special Representative in Hong Kong:

> He was engaged in one deal with this man in 1947 as with his for-estry work he was seldom in Harbin. His partner brought a Jewish merchant to his house late one night for a currency exchange (deal-ing in gold roubles and US dollars against Chinese currency). He (K.) stood watch outside and when he returned the Jew was dead still clutching a revolver. In fight K. helped dispose of the corpse by dumping in the river at Harbin, accepted a bribe to keep quiet about the affair and nothing more was heard for eight months. His erstwhile partner while engaged in some other criminal activity was caught by the police, shot and killed. His accomplice on that occa-sion named K. when questioned as implicated in the earlier murder.

Evgenii served ten years in jail from 1948 until his release in 1958, when he married Russian-born Lydia K. and moved to Hong Kong in the hope of settling in New Zealand. However, the authori-ties withdrew their offer and cancelled the family's entry permits. Clabon wanted to help, on the grounds that Evgenii was an unwit-ting bystander, not a hardened criminal: 'I believe his story told can-didly and without evasion and am quite impressed with both him and wife in comparison with others with whom we have to deal'. Clabon added that Lydia's eighty-six-year-old mother should also be considered: 'The old lady is very well for her age and the K. cou-ple particularly ask she stay with them on resettlement with their providing maintenance when self-supporting.' Evgenii and Lydia expected to be self-supporting by working as a tractor driver in a lumber camp and a dressmaker respectively. But no country was willing to accept them on account of his criminal record. The file indicates the readiness of UNHCR's local representative to speak up on Evgenii's behalf in the face of intransigence on the part of immigration authorities.[19]

There were other cases of criminal activity. In 1964, UNHCR came across Russian refugee George T., who was described as 'an

160 *Refugees and the stateless in Asia*

interesting case'. He was born in Harbin but moved to Shanghai in 1941 together with his mother, brother, and sister. According to UNHCR's office in Hong Kong, he 'began his advancement in the world as a criminal since he was a schoolboy', stealing vessels and plate from the Russian Cathedral Church in Shanghai: 'he was very enthusiastic about detective stories and imagined himself as Shanghai Al Capone and was a teddy boy [with] a big connection with Shanghai Chinese vagabonds and robbers'. His life of crime included pickpocketing and black-market transactions. He used an alias to avoid detection. After one large robbery, 'he called Police Headquarters teasing them and informing that he is still in town and he is a GHOST, they will never catch him'. With the help of a lump sum from his mother, who had moved to San Francisco, he was able to arrange for illegal entry to Macao. Three years later, he once again came to the attention of UNHCR, having tried to forge official documents attempting to assist two Russian refugees in Shanghai to gain admission to Macao. He was acquitted because of a lack of evidence that he intended to use the material in his possession to carry out this forgery. He hoped to be resettled in Brazil or Australia, but UNHCR suggested that he be resettled in Europe as a 'special case with a view to eventual rehabilitation'.[20]

Another voluminous file concerned Vladimir T., born in Russia in 1901 to a diplomatic family. The family left Russia in 1919. Vladimir lived a peripatetic life for the next two decades. He attended university in the United Kingdom, but things started to go wrong after he moved to France. He joined the Foreign Legion 'in a moment of despair' and was wounded and then discharged. He was deported in quick succession from France, Switzerland, and Italy before arriving in Shanghai in 1935. According to one sympathetic summary, 'as a language teacher and translator he was in touch with nationals of many countries'. Vladimir then fell foul of the Chinese authorities and spent several years in prison for 'political crimes'. In June 1965, he sought the help of the World Council of Churches in arranging for his resettlement. The WCC indicated that 'he comes from a good family, has had a first-class education, speaks several languages, and has visited many countries during his varied life'. WCC's resettlement officer in Geneva noted: 'he sounds like a broken man making a last plea'. But he added, 'According to Shanghai arrivals who know him Vladimir was a "rogue". Always very gay and charming,

'I have been a refugee all my life'   161

educated and coming from a noble family. He never seems to have earned a living by hard work but by petty swindling.' He explained to the WCC that he had a daughter living in Belgium but had not been in touch with her since he divorced her mother. In a final plea, he wrote that 'there are rest homes in Belgium as well as Holland or Denmark, countries where I have an absolutely clean record'. UNHCR eventually secured his resettlement in Ireland, where the Irish Red Cross found him a rest home in Dublin. He arrived in February 1969 but died less than two years later.[21]

From time to time, stories emerged of criminal activity in Shanghai in which the case files disclosed a mixture of antisemitism and character assassination. A case in point is the fascinating file concerning the family of elderly Romanian-Jewish refugee Leivi Itsokovitch I. It is not clear precisely when he arrived in Shanghai. Leivi contacted the United Nations in September 1952 to request emergency relief. Unfortunately for him, a report in February 1951 from Lorenzo Lo, a former IRO welfare officer in Shanghai, had already placed on record a wholly negative assessment of Leivi's character:

> In pre-war days he was known to be an associate of pimps and criminals. He has come to the attention of the police on numerous occasions in connection with thefts perpetrated in his houses, the victims of these crimes having invariably been his lodgers. Due to the nature of these crimes and the undoubtedly clear [clever?] method adopted by him in disposing of the stolen property, the police were unable to 'pin' these offences on anyone in particular, though I. himself was strongly suspected to be the perpetrator of these offences ... I. is a slippery, miserly and most obnoxious character and is known to be a criminal. Unfortunately, however, he has always been able to have an alibi ready and thus evade all police efforts to bring him to justice for his crimes. This person is a bad type ...

Equally vicious was the antisemitic letter from the Director of IRO's Shanghai Office to UNHCR in October 1952, which described Leivi as 'a typical element ... [who] is in the habit of withholding facts about his financial position and often tells ANYTHING BUT the truth' and who claimed IRO rations 'which were intended for destitute persons'. The Central Jewish Committee (representing HIAS in Shanghai) flatly contradicted Leivi's account of his financial hardship and launched a blistering attack on his character:

162   *Refugees and the stateless in Asia*

The case of the I. family is one of the most difficult and hopeless on our lists. Mr Leivi I., who is nearly 70 years old today and who is himself suffering from many serious ailments, has committed the fatal error of marrying and acquiring progeny at any age when normal persons are seriously planning for the hereafter. The results of his action have been disastrous: the two elder children are riddled with disease, the girl is tubercular, the boy Itska is a complete cripple unable to move, his legs having degenerated into useless appendices [*sic*]. As far as their migration or resettlement plans are concerned, there is this to consider: the marital bliss of which I. himself writes to the UNRO of July 11th is a gross exaggeration. According to his own statement in front of the undersigned on August 25th, he is certain that should the whole family be approved for resettlement in Sweden as TB patients, his wife as a Chinese citizen would never be permitted to leave. The youngest child, who has not been entered into Mrs I.'s Soviet passport [*sic*] he also does not intend taking with him. According to Mr I.'s opinion his wife would have no objections to the rest of the family, i.e. Mr I., his daughter Sarra and son Itska, leaving China. We doubt this very much, however, as with the departure of Mr I., his wife's only source of income would cease. At present the whole family are living together in unbelievable squalor.

In short, no one had a good word to say about Leivi I. The extensive comments on his character would not have endeared him to any immigration office, and an online search suggests that he remained in China.[22]

The files stretch into the 1960s and even into the 1970s. One file concerned Alexei Eliseevich S., born in 1894 in Mikhailovka, Nikolsk-Ussurskii District, Russia. According to the employment history that he completed in December 1962, Alexei enlisted in the Russian army in 1915 and then joined Kolchak's anti-Bolshevik forces during the Russian Civil War. At some point he moved to Harbin, where he met Anna Semenovna, who became his wife. (This was her second marriage.) She described other upheavals in her life and her scattered family [uncorrected text]:

In 1920 I married Grigori Iosifovich M. in Vladivostok and was living on full responsibility of my husband 6 August 1921 give birth to my 1st daughter Ludmila, she is at present in USA. 25th January 1926 gave birth to my 2nd daughter, Alla, she at present in Hong Kong. 28th February 1930 my husband died and I with my two children crossed the border to Harbin. At that time in Harbin, I met my

'I have been a refugee all my life' 163

relatives: my mother and my brother, both died [dead]. I was supported by the brother of my husband who also died and his family is now in Chile.

Alexei had run a small business making margarine, but his firm was liquidated in 1944 and he and Anna were now living on a small rental income. She ended her letter:

> I am a healthy and normal person and do not have any physical defects. I shall soon be sixty years old and therefore there is very little hope for my resettlement, as a worker. Please send me to a Home for the Aged.

There were various options. Alexei mentioned having a nephew in Australia. UNHCR's office in Hong Kong arranged for them both to be resettled in the United Kingdom, although they eventually moved to the United States.[23]

There are also indications of remarkable survival and determination not to buckle under extreme pressure. Consider the lengthy case file concerning forty-nine-year-old Pavel G., a refugee of Russian origin who came to the attention of UNHCR in 1966–67, at which point he was living in a camp for displaced persons in Shanghai. He was born in Manchuria to a Cossack family originally from Taganrog, his father having moved to the Far East to work for the Chinese Eastern Railway. He had various jobs, including as a chauffeur, a lumberjack, and a factory guard. In 1942, he found work as a ticket inspector. Having studied Japanese, he was enlisted as an interpreter by the Japanese occupation forces. After the war he again had several different jobs, including as an attendant in a Shanghai hospital and selling second-hand goods. In 1952, the Chinese government charged him in connection with collaboration with the Japanese and sentenced to two years for 'counter-revolutionary activities' (his words). His wartime activities put him on a WCC and UNHCR blacklist, and he asked for 'clemency' and 'magnanimity'. By 1966 he had been living in and out of a refugee camp for twelve years, apart from another spell in jail for (as he puts it) 'breaking socialist rules'. He complained that nothing was being done to help him. His first letter, in April 1966, began:

> Sir, I am appealing and asking for <u>Mercy</u> from you now, after that all my former efforts to get resettlement had been in vain. This is

164   *Refugees and the stateless in Asia*

my last hope and if this will be still without success, then I am sunk and lost forever. SOS! I am a stateless [*sic*] of Russian origin. Some people who are hostile against me, for reasons of <u>revenge</u>, have poisoned the mind against me by the organisations in Hong Kong who are concerned with the resettlement of displaced persons and now I have no way out from the abyss in which I am in. Once more, SOS. (original emphasis)

He accused UNHCR in Hong Kong and the WCC of blaming each other for not helping him to find a sponsor and to resettle in Australia. He knew no one there. He ended this letter by saying 'I am appealing to you <u>for justice and humanitarianism</u> ... and for moral support and encouragement which I <u>need</u> very badly. <u>I pray for salvation</u>' (original emphasis). In other letters he repeated his request for resettlement, 'somewhere on this globe'. In one of his letters, he said, 'I paid fully and dearly for my past mistakes and now I would deserve the benevolence of the kind-hearted world and not to be sentenced to stay in this camp for the rest of my life.' In subsequent letters he complains of being 'completely ignored'. He again rebutted the charges against him, adding that some of his fellow workers on the Shanghai tramway had levelled 'disgusting' accusations against him, which he believed was motivated by his having denounced them for taking bribes. Eventually, following a series of eye tests and other medical investigations that revealed two old bullet wounds, Pavel was resettled in Belgium. His physical ailments evidently came to his rescue.[24]

Resettlement presented fresh challenges. The K. family, presumably Soviet refugees living in New South Wales, were a case in point. A handwritten letter from Stefan K. in May 1958, addressed to the IRO, Geneva [*sic*], explained that he, his wife, and four children arrived in Australia in January 1950. The family worked as market gardeners, and he also worked a night shift in a factory:

After very hard job, was everything very nice in garden. In November 1956 came big hail storm and ruined everything in the garden and killed 70 chicks and ducks, they did not have time to find shelter. I started again and after everything was nice, in February 1957 when there came another hail storm and ruined in second time everything, plus my health. Working till to March 1957, but just for nothing.

'I have been a refugee all my life'   165

His letter went on to explain that he looked for a job but without success, and that they had to sell their valuables to find enough money for food and to travel to look for work. He fell ill and was hospitalised. Although he received sickness benefit, he was unable to pay the rent on their apartment. He ends, 'Dear Sir! Please help me, don't let me out. I working very much; I am very poor, and very unlucky'. Constance Moffit, International Social Services, Sydney, reported to her headquarters in Geneva in 1958 that social services in Sydney knew of the family: 'It seemed that every possible agency or resource that could be involved in this case, was already involved in it'. The Family Welfare Bureau took the view that the family had suffered a series of misfortunes but that 'the personalities of the parents made it extremely hard for anyone to work with them in a really helpful way. Their underlying anxieties made it difficult for them to sustain any relationship with a social worker for long, and these anxieties drove them to all sorts of impulsive actions'. They were eventually provided with emergency accommodation.[25]

The Russian diaspora sometimes contributed a sense of urgency. One such example emerged in 1966, when several Russian families wrote from Argentina to Felix Schnyder on behalf of Russian Old Believers living in Hong Kong: Matveev Samoila S., his son Markell, and his widowed daughter Maria. An office memo observed that 'they belong to the same sect and the families who are already in Argentina state that they are good and obedient people', so there should be no problem in resettling them in Argentina. The original letter was headed *proshenie*, the Russian word for a request, petition, or 'humble address'. Each family signed it in turn. Their endorsement relied upon indirect knowledge, the assumption that religious faith leant sufficient weight to claiming assistance on behalf of others. Unfortunately, no record has survived of the outcome.[26]

As these illustrative examples demonstrate, the case files were filled with emotional testimony. Refugees often adopted a tone of desperation and self-pity, and expressed a sense of hopelessness, albeit inflected in some instances with a recognition that their patience in the face of suffering was a Christian virtue.

I began by speaking of suffering and victimisation. Clearly, refugees suffered profound upheaval in their lives and that they hoped that their suffering could be alleviated in their final years when economic insecurity loomed. But the evidence presented here suggests

166   *Refugees and the stateless in Asia*

that refugees were capable of seizing opportunities in adulthood and that they managed to make a life for themselves in a strange land. Sometimes this involved dubious and even criminal behaviour. In all cases there was inevitably a high degree of self-centredness: how could it be otherwise, when the regime required refugees to speak of their own predicament?

To judge from these case studies, refugees did not compare their circumstances to the lives they might have lived in Russia, although there was an implicit counterfactual and a presumption that life in China was preferable to living in the Soviet Union, at least until 1949. Thousands of elderly Russians nevertheless held on until the UN campaign for World Refugee Year, a decade later, launched a publicity drive that drew attention to their decrepitude, acknowledged the need to make amends for having abandoned them, and arranged their resettlement.

Some Russian refugees, like the aforementioned Pavel G., demanded 'justice'; others pinned their hopes on charitable assistance, having come to the end of their tether. In sum, although their statelessness might be resolved by resettlement and sometimes repatriation, there are lots of threads and loose ends in the case files. Faced with tantalising fragments and gaps, it is often difficult for the historian to ascertain the outcome of their letters and petitions (see the chapter by Joy Damousi). The philosopher Sarah Fine aptly notes that 'Any attempt to engage with refugee and other migrant voices must acknowledge that the result is inevitably a selective, incomplete, partial representation, and forms just one contribution to a wider discussion and set of narratives.'[27] Yet, as Edward Said once said, 'fragmentary forms of expression' have been the common currency of the situation in which refugees found themselves.[28] This does not diminish the resonance and power of the stories that these individuals told in constrained circumstances.

Notes

1 Hersch Lauterpacht to Paul Weis, 26 February 1951, Paul Weis Papers, Bodleian Social Sciences Library, University of Oxford, PW/WR/PUBL/9. Lauterpacht (1897–1960) was a distinguished international lawyer whose life and career are illuminated in Philippe Sands,

East-West Street: On the Origins of Genocide and Crimes Against Humanity (London: Weidenfeld and Nicolson, 2017).

2 João Biehl, *Vita: Life in a Zone of Social Abandonment* (Berkeley, CA: University of California Press, 2013), p. 42; Peter Gatrell, 'Raw Material: UNHCR's Individual Case Files as a Historical Source, 1951–1975', *History Workshop Journal*, 92 (2021), pp. 226–41.

3 On the concept and practices of a refugee regime, see Claudena M. Skran, *Refugees in Inter-War Europe: The Emergence of a Regime* (Oxford: Clarendon Press, 1995); Emma Haddad, *The Refugee in International Society: Between Sovereigns* (Cambridge: Cambridge University Press, 2008). Both authors specify differences between the interwar and post-war refugee regime, noting inter alia the focus of the League of Nations on group definitions.

4 Gil Loescher, *The UNHCR and World Politics: A Perilous Path* (Oxford: Oxford University Press, 2001), p. 45.

5 John Hope Simpson, *The Refugee Problem: Report of a Survey* (Oxford: Oxford University Press, 1939), pp. 78–80, 495–513; Olga Bakich, 'Charbin: "Russland jenseits der Grenzen" in Fernost', in Karl Schlögel (ed.), *Der grosse Exodus: die russische Emigration und ihre Zentren 1917 bis 1941* (Munich: C. H. Beck, 1994), pp. 304–28; Marcia R. Ristaino, 'Shanghai: Russische Flüchtlinge im "gelben Babylon"', in Schlögel (ed.), *Der grosse Exodus*, pp. 329–45.

6 Hannah Arendt, 'We Refugees' (1943), in Jerome Kohn and Ron H. Feldman (eds), *The Jewish Writings* (New York: Schocken Books, 2007), pp. 264–74 (p. 265).

7 Marita Eastmond, 'Stories as Lived Experience: Narratives in Forced Migration Research', *Journal of Refugee Studies*, 20, 2 (2007), pp. 248–64 (quotation on p. 251).

8 UNHCR Records and Archives, Geneva, Fonds UNHCR 17, Records Relating to Protection, Sub-fonds 1, Confidential Individual Case Files, IC1053. For background, see George C. Guins, 'Russians in Manchuria', *Russian Review*, 2, 2 (1943), pp. 81–7. On the repatriation of Russian refugees, see Laurie Manchester, 'Repatriation to a Totalitarian Homeland: The Ambiguous Alterity of Russian Repatriates from China to the USSR', *Diaspora: A Journal of Transnational Studies*, 16, 3 (2007), pp. 353–88; Nataliia N. Ablazhei, *S vostoka na vostok: rossiiskaia emigratsiia v Kitae* (Novosibirsk: Izd. SO RAN, 2007), pp. 196–241; Bruce Adams, 'Re-Emigration from Western China to the USSR, 1954–1962', in Cynthia J. Buckley and Blair A. Ruble (eds), *Migration, Homeland and Belonging in Eurasia* (Washington, DC: Woodrow Wilson Center Press, 2008), pp. 183–201.

168 *Refugees and the stateless in Asia*

9 IC885. He was finally resettled thanks to the WCC, which organised his passage via Hong Kong.

10 IC4463. Kenneth Summers, UNHCR Special Representative, Hong Kong, to J. B. Woodward, 11 March 1960.

11 IC278. Eventually she was resettled in Switzerland. The World Refugee Year in 1959–60 helped resettle refugees who were living in China. See Peter Gatrell, *Free World? The Campaign to Save the World's Refugees* (Cambridge: Cambridge University Press, 2011), pp. 69–72.

12 IC10454. An online search indicates that Julia was living in Australia in 1984, so the family did eventually resettle.

13 IC5542, emphasis mine.

14 The Northern part of Sakhalin had been occupied by Japan but was returned to the Soviet Union in 1925. Presumably, Helen was talking about the Southern half that remained under Japanese jurisdiction.

15 IC8706.

16 IC8706.

17 IC8705. Maria N. was eventually resettled in the United Kingdom, where she died in 1975.

18 IC1223.

19 IC3486.

20 IC14607.

21 IC13985. In addition to office correspondence, the file includes a feature by Geoffrey Murray, 'He Lost His Ticket to Paradise!', *Ecumenical Press Service*, 24 April 1969.

22 IC2739.

23 IC12266. The file suggests that they had separated and were applying for separate visas, but an online search reveals that they both moved to Oregon, presumably to join Ludmila. Anna died in 1984, Alexei in 1994.

24 IC1219. Following a series of eye tests and other medical investigations that revealed two old bullet wounds, Pavel G. was eventually resettled in Belgium.

25 IC3462.

26 IC12277.

27 Sarah Fine, 'II – Refugees, Safety, and a Decent Human Life', *Proceedings of the Aristotelian Society*, 119, 1 (2019), pp. 25–52 (p. 32).

28 Edward Said, with Jean Mohr, *After the Last Sky: Palestinian Lives* (London: Faber, 1986), p. 6.

Section II.II

Refugees and the stateless in Shanghai and beyond

11

'A right to the city': New Villages for the Commoners, the Nantao Safe Zone, and humanitarian internationalism in Shanghai, 1932–40

Qian Zhu

In 1937, when the Japanese launched all-out war against China, Shanghai's refugee zones, which some called 'paradise for refugees', were widely documented and photographed by the world press and by major Chinese bilingual magazines and newspapers. The largest refugee zone that housed 250,000 to 300,000 Chinese refugees was Shanghai's Nantao or Nanshi refugee zone, including the old Chinese city and its suburbs South of the French Concession. Later known as 'the Jacquinot Zone', after the French Jesuit priest Robert Jacquinot de Besange who founded it, it was referred to favourably in the Geneva Convention of 1949 as the Shanghai Model of wartime neutral zones. The Nantao refugee zone was seen by the Chinese Nationalist government as a successful measure to protect Chinese non-combatants and to bring them 'back to peace and almost normalcy'.[1] While wartime refugees from nearby regions flooded into shelters in Shanghai's foreign concessions, many others presented a humanitarian crisis of major dimensions, as 'they were living on the streets, short of clothes and food'. The refugees were also seen as the 'other' in the city, as 'bandits', 'special agents', and a 'floating population' that 'worsened the sanitation and order of Shanghai'.[2] Even though Father Jacquinot was the founder of the Nantao refugee zone, the Nationalist government claimed that it was 'under the control of our territorial governance'. Under these circumstances, the International Relief Committee of China 'took over control of the area and started to solve problems of food, light, water sanitation, etc., for the welfare of the thousands of refugees'.[3]

'A right to the city'   171

Scholars have adopted three perspectives on refugee relief work in Shanghai in the 1930s. First, most of the historical research has concentrated on the founder of Nantao, Father Robert Jacquinot de Besange (known in China as 饶家驹, Rao, Jiaju). Jacquinot's leadership and the formation of the Nantao refugee zone added an important element to the history of war refugees and to the general narrative of the war against Japan, which has a tendency to overlook civilians.[4] Secondly, studies of the Jacquinot zone and the formation of wartime safe zones have focused on Jacquinot's humanitarianism within the framing of the Geneva Convention of 1949.[5] Thirdly, scholars have focused on Shanghai's grassroot charity organisations that worked with Father Jacquinot and his associations from 1937 to 1940.[6]

Research on the Nantao refugee zone attributes the success of setting up a safe zone in Shanghai to Jacquinot's personal charisma, his established reputation, and his remarkable administrative capacities, as well as his skill in negotiations with the Chinese and Japanese governments. This chapter highlights three facets of the history of what we call hereafter the 'Nantao Safe Zone'. First, the Nationalist government's mega housing project for the poor known as the New Villages for the Commoners (NVC) provided the principles and practices of the Nantao Safe Zone with respect to population control, civil education, and labour recruitment, essential for the reorganisation and regulation of the everyday life of refugees. While the Nantao Safe Zone was considered by the Nationalist state as 'Chinese territory', the demilitarisation of the area prioritised the Chinese government's effort to 'restore the peace'. Secondly, the formation of the Nantao Safe Zone reflected the collaborative efforts of Shanghai grassroots and international Christian charity organisations after the Chiang Kai-shek Nationalist resistance army retreated to the wartime capital of Chongqing. Operating under the framework of humanitarian internationalism, the autonomous and self-governing Nantao Safe Zone made it possible for the stateless to maintain formal Chinese sovereignty and to restore security and order. Thirdly, refugees knew that they were viewed as dangerous and potential criminals. Consequently, they accepted a structured approach to everyday life, showing that they were disciplined citizens. In the Safe Zone, refugees weathered the storm of war, and some of them continued their revolutionary political work.

172 *Refugees and the stateless in Asia*

Although the majority of the refugees in the Nantao Safe Zone were Chinese citizens, the retreat of the Nationalist army made them stateless people under the authority of the international relief zone administration. That is, the refugees in Nantao were perceived by both the Chinese and Japanese states, in the language of Hannah Arendt, as outlaws.[7] The Nationalist forces had no other choice than to accept the existence of a relief zone administration, responsible for relief work of this floating population. The Nantao Safe Zone fit into the global phenomenon of camps that emerged during the interwar crisis of statelessness.[8] But by the 1930s, this part of Shanghai 'was the only "country" the world had to offer the stateless'.[9]

From New Villages for the Commoners to 'A District of Safety for the non-Combatants'

The outbreak of war in 1937 realised the fears of the Chinese and the international community about Japanese imperialist ambitions in China. Already in 1932, as many as ten thousand to twenty thousand civilians lost their lives in the Zhabei District next to the International Settlement during combat that became known as 'the Shanghai incident'.

This incident was the topic of several meetings of the Shanghai Municipal Council (SMC). One proposal recommended establishing a neutral zone in the Chinese-administered areas of Zhabei and Hongkou, to be policed by forces other than Chinese or Japanese troops. This proposal was rejected by both the Chinese and Japanese members of the council. The foreign settlements in Shanghai did not base their legitimacy or decisions to use force on any specific treaty provision. Their basis for supporting any action was to provide protection for their nationals in Shanghai, at a time when the Chinese authorities would not or could not provide it. The British and American council members were worried about the number of Chinese refugees entering the International Settlement. They were not disposed to offer food or support, because they believed that to do so would attract more refugees. Refugees from Zhabei were trying to enter the International Settlement by water, but the Shanghai Volunteer Corps and Municipal Police blocked off all entry points

'A right to the city' 173

from Suzhou creek. It became filled with boats of refugees with nowhere to go. The SMC responded that a refugee camp be established at Minghang, outside the International Settlement. The first proposal was to house all the refugees, but then the plans were altered to house only Chinese ratepayers from the affected areas.[10]

Combat ended with the signing of the 1932 Shanghai Truce Agreement, which established a neutral zone specifically for Chinese civilians. NVCs in Zhabei, managed by the Shanghai Preparation Committee of the Commoners' Residential Houses, housed war refugees from Jiangsu and Zhejiang provinces and non-Chinese refugees who were residents of the International Settlement.[11]

In July 1937, when Japanese troops engaged in manoeuvres near Marco Polo Bridge in Hebei Province near Beijing, Chiang Kai-shek reached the conclusion that war was inevitable. Both sides resolved to fight. From the first aerial bombing in the battle of Shanghai on the morning of 14 August to 23 August 1937, the suffering inflicted upon the Zhabei, Pudong, and Nantao areas of Shanghai was catastrophic. Having no safe areas to turn to, the panic-stricken refugees, miserable and destitute, entered the foreign concessions. In addition to taking in and providing services for their own people in the bombed-out areas, the authorities in the International Settlement and French Concession had to deal with countless others.

One Chinese report in September 1937 estimated that there were fifty thousand refugees in the foreign settlements, an area only thirteen square miles.[12] The number of refugees peaked in November 1937, with 142 camps accommodating 91,815 refugees and counting 36,645 living in the streets and alleys.[13] The French Concession had in December forty camps, housing 25,900.[14] On the grounds of Aurora University (now Fudan University), there were 2,300 refugees living in shed housing.[15] Jiaotong University provided shelter for another large refugee camp, housing 17,000. The native Bankers' Guild School on Rue Luzon housed some 4,500 refugees.[16]

The SMC had a difficult time responding to the refugee crisis. Its policy was not to get involved in refugee work, but to leave it to the International Red Cross, the other international organisations, and the senior Chinese relief organisations. When the SMC did respond, it was in defence of order and the safety and property of the International Settlement. There was also much concern about the potential rise in crime, looting, and rice riots as a result of the

174 *Refugees and the stateless in Asia*

massive influx of destitute people. The possible spread of infectious disease led to a campaign to inoculate those in the camps against smallpox and cholera.[17]

Once the numbers of destitute refugees in the International Settlement overwhelmed the available resources, the Settlement authorities blocked all points of entry and established a rigid policy of registration to help control the flow of newcomers. The council exerted pressure on the various relief organisations to speed up the repatriation of Chinese refugees back to their former homes.[18]

The Chinese response was to continue with the repatriation work and relief programs. With so many competing national, international, and local organisations responding to the crisis, there were political battles over influence and resources. In October, the Greater Shanghai City Government put an Emergency Refugee Relief Committee in charge of overseeing refugee work. Associations of residents originating in particular cities, such as Canton, Ningbo, and Changzhou, continued their work of raising funds, supplying their camps, and repatriating their fellow citizens.[19]

In this phase of the war, Zhabei and parts of Hongkou were reduced to rubble. On 26 October, when Chinese troops retreated from Zhabei, Father Jacquinot and the international, national, and local refugee organisations proposed a neutral zone. The basic concept of a neutral zone would be considered again by the foreign powers as a basis for yet another truce agreement, meant to end hostilities in 1937. Another concern was that the Chinese forces would not be able to resist Japanese forces, making densely populated Nantao a new and horrific battlefield. As president of the Shanghai International Committee of the Red Cross and the head of its Refugee Committee, Father Jacquinot negotiated separately with the invading Japanese commander General Matsui Iwane and the Shanghai Mayor, Yu Hongjun, who was in charge of the large Chinese-administered sectors of the city. Both sides refused to sign a formal agreement on 'a neutral zone'. The Chinese side recognised the existence of Nantao as 'a relief camp', but claimed territorial sovereignty of the area, promising demilitarisation of the area, yet maintaining the Chinese-administered police force.[20] The Japanese side responded favourably to acknowledging Nantao 'as the residential district for the civilians' and agreed there would be 'no military operations in the district'.[21]

'A right to the city' 175

This wartime measure was a new framework for civilians. As Jacquinot wrote:

> this district in Nantao, a place of safety for the civilian populations, is not a 'neutral zone', for it is neither neutral nor a zone; it is not rightly called a demilitarized region; it is certainly not arranged for the French interests nor to protect Church property in Nantao ... It is purely and simply what it is called: a district of safety for the non-combatants. It has been possible because both the Japanese and the Chinese are desirous, for humanitarian reasons, to protect the non-combatants.[22]

'Paradise for refugees': peace and order

For the Chinese Nationalists, the opening of the Nantao Safe Zone was the continuation of their policy of providing NVCs to solve the overwhelming refugee crisis that arose after the outbreak of total war against Japan. It was an example of the collaboration of international and local charity organisations supported by the French Concession and Japan.[23] Upon the opening of the Nantao Safe Zone on 9 November 1937, the China-Foreign Charity and Relief Association (CFCRA)[24] Headquarters released a directive to highlight Chinese authority over the zone and the humanitarian and benevolent nature of relief work. At the opening ceremony, the four flags of the Shanghai International Committee of the Red Cross in China were flown. The Chinese map of Nantao was released indicating the boundaries and the main roads within the Safe Zone.[25] The directive showed that the zone was under China's jurisdiction, enforced by the presence of Chinese police 'with pistols and batons'. The CFCRA was granted the right of inspection and management of the zone.[26]

Upon the establishment of the Nantao Safe Zone, Jacquinot served as vice president of the Shanghai International Committee of the Red Cross and head of its Refugee Committee. His intention was to provide a protected safe zone for 250,000 Chinese and other refugees. In the international press in Shanghai, it was called 'the Jacquinot Zone' or the Shanghai Safe Zone. A new committee called the Nantao Supervisory Committee, headed by Jacquinot, became responsible for managing the 'safe zone'. It was

176 *Refugees and the stateless in Asia*

multinational in character: members included three Frenchmen, two Englishmen, one Norwegian, and one American, who were in charge of finance and communications with the SMC and the Chamber of Commerce.[27] The members who represented the Euro-American elites in Shanghai ensured that Jacquinot would have strong backing when he approached Chinese and Japanese authorities and foreign powers. More importantly, they helped in fund-raising by allocating multinational donations to the Safe Zone. The multinational executive committee also persuaded the Chinese state that Nantao could be self-sufficient and self-governed while bringing order to the floating population and protecting civilians.

By 1938, the Nantao Safe Zone served 'more than 300,000 people' as 'a fair-size city'. While temples, schools, churches, and public facilities were used as shelters, the 1932 Zhabei NVC was renovated. It provided camp-like shelters for wounded soldiers, and for international and Chinese refugees at the Northwestern corner of Nantao, bordering the French Concession.[28]

The Refugee Committee set itself up as the municipal council for a borough 'chopped out of an occupied city'.[29] Its responsibilities included feeding more than a hundred thousand refugees every day, and providing water and electricity. A local reporter noted that 'the Zone was self-governing, with its own "town council"'. The Supervisory Committee divided its budget into four categories: food, clothing, hospital and medical, and miscellaneous. The Shanghai Police Bureau organised the Safe Zone police force. To comply with Chinese authorities, the Supervisory committee created a criminal court, which operated 'Under the Protection of Heaven's Mercy', as a notice inscribed on the city temple put it.[30]

The Nantao Safe Zone was divided into nine districts according to the main eight roads on the Chinese map, the structure of which followed the Zhabei NVC. Each district was led by Chinese staff who worked in the NVC and were elected by the district refugees. These elected district officials presided over eleven sections, also staffed by Chinese section heads. The Chinese leaders had responsibility for housing, food, water, discipline, sanitation, medical care, education, repatriation, bookkeeping, registration, and inventory work. To help staff carry out these important responsibilities, the Safe Zone administration provided training in management skills and techniques, especially for the men and women who served as

'A right to the city'   177

section heads. In total, these elected district leaders cared for 104 refugee facilities in public buildings, schools, temples, and churches situated in Nantao. The International Red Cross Committee and the Salvation Army provided essential help managing food and clothing donations. An old house was turned into a hospital, staffed by the Convent of the Sacred Heart.[31]

As in the NVC, the Safe Zone established a school, divided into appropriate age-level classes. In addition to the regular program in reading, writing, and basic mathematics, the school followed the labour training program in the new villages. Instruction included practical training in weaving, basic medical services, logistics, sanitation, group games, and musical activities. The Chinese officials who had worked in the NVC believed that learning these skills might enable the refugees to put these lessons to good use once the Zone closed and the refugees returned to their homes.

In 1938 and 1939, education in the Safe Zone became mandatory for all the Nantao refugees. The Shanghai Municipal government stated that 'able-bodied workers must go through the training in order to fulfill their labor obligation or military service when receiving welfare relief. ... Those who refuse to comply, will lose their refugee status and be repatriated.'[32] Patriotic education for the Chinese refugees was carried out by group activities. Children eating together were told 'not to forget their hatred of the Japanese invaders'. Women were enjoined to 'weave clothes for the resistance soldiers in the frontline'. Guided by a woman teacher, children were 'singing loudly a song for national salvation to expel "the evil ghosts and spirits [of the Japanese]"'.[33]

Everyone was urged to cultivate good family sanitation habits, to save money and resources, to foster the virtues of harmony within their families and with their neighbours, and to develop the capacity to entertain others, speak publicly, and appreciate art. Moreover, everyone was instructed to study the civic virtues of orderliness and self-discipline in public life. The civic virtues prepared the villagers to participate in a variety of organised 'collective activities', such as 'Soccer Team for the Commoners', and 'Discussion Meeting of Women and Family'. Communal activities reinforced everyone's role as 'a good member of the community'.[34]

Large-scale collective activities were organised to nurture community pride and honour and to foster the civic virtue of 'being a

178　　　　*Refugees and the stateless in Asia*

lawful member of the Zone', the key (they were told) to harmony. Positive, progressive, and healthy communal events were essential to cultivating citizens as the future leaders of the nation. In September 1939, the Refugee Summer Olympic Games were organised in the Safe Zone to celebrate the disciplined, cooperative, and healthy life of the refugees.[35] Led by Chinese staff leaders, these events showed that the young refugees formed a collective, a new vanguard to lead the nation. They subjected themselves to rigorous self-discipline and embodied a new type of masculinity. The rest of the nation had only to follow, and the future would be theirs.

The White Russians, the Chinese revolutionaries, and the trade unions

By 1937, there were more than twenty-five thousand anti-Bolshevik White Russians living in Shanghai, the largest European group in the city. Only Russian-built Harbin in Manchuria, and Paris, had larger Russian émigré populations. While the Russian community of Paris combined well-off refugees with the remnants of the Tsar's armies, Shanghai's émigré community came from Russia's East, where, with Japanese military support, the Whites had held the Far Eastern Maritime Province as late as 1922 during the Russian Civil War. After the Bolshevik victory, they fled East and South, inhabiting Harbin and later Shanghai.[36]

Upon the opening of the Nantao Safe Zone, a steady stream of refugees that had previously sought shelter and safety in the International Settlement went through the French Concession to the new Safe Zone. The Chinese civil administration and its Chinese police force supervised the zone and patrolled its narrow streets. Chinese police carried no arms other than service revolvers and items like batons, needed for community policing. An additional level of security was organised by engaging a small unit of White Russians with military training to support and help train Chinese police.[37] An inspector from the French police worked with these Russian police. The Russian police unit was responsible for handling bandits, opium dens, and gambling dens operating in the Safe Zone. They also checked entry permits to the Zone. Possessing both entrance passes and mobility, the Russian policemen appeared to be superior to the Chinese in the Safe Zone.[38]

Some refugees in the Safe Zone worked in the arts and had joined various National Salvation Societies. Others worked with the Salvation Army. Operating together in the Safe Zone were politically diverse groups such as the Chinese Communist Party (CCP), the Nationalist Party, and the Three Peoples' Principles Youth Leagues. All were active in the Safe Zone and associated with the presiding umbrella body, the Shanghai International Rescue Society. According to a later account, the Communists operated as an underground party, but in the Safe Zone, the estimated thirty members organised a Party Branch and focused on recruiting 390 new party members.[39] The CCP youth were active in refugee schools spreading news and propaganda and recruiting. Later on, when refugee repatriation programs resumed and Shanghai conditions stabilised, this Party branch supplied 1,200 young cadre volunteer soldiers to the New Fourth Army in South Anhui, and some were sent to serve in the Yan'an Base Area from 1938 to 1941.[40] Fifty underground CCP members in Nantao went to the factories in Shanghai to organise workers. Some of them later became Shanghai CCP party branch leaders in the 1940s, such as Cao Diqiu, who was appointed mayor of Shanghai in 1955.[41]

By the end of 1938, the Shanghai municipal government urged the Nantao district officials to recruit refugee workers because 'they are fed too well and become idle; their spirit is waning and decadent with bad habits'.[42] The unproductive refugees were considered 'potential troublemakers' who were engaged in opium smuggling, gambling, and the alcohol trade.

To maintain 'peace and order', the Safe Zone enacted a set of labour regulations, under which 'all able refugees must fulfill their military or labor duty'.[43] Labour duty was mandatory for the Nantao residents to maintain their refugee status and to receive relief welfare and protection. Three larger districts established four refugee factories to recruit refugee workers to produce goods needed for self-sufficiency.[44] Meanwhile, some overseas Chinese refugees in Nantao, who had migrated from Southeast Asia to Shanghai, organised 'trade unions' to represent plumbers and mechanics in high demand for work for the Japanese in the Safe Zone.[45]

180   *Refugees and the stateless in Asia*

More importantly, 'The Livelihood Improvement Association', led by Maocheng Zhu, the chief architect of the Zhabei NVCs, along with ten overseas Chinese entrepreneurs from Southeast Asia, proposed to build six 'One Two Eight Refugee Factories', the name of which was to commemorate 'the January 28 Incident', the first time Shanghai was under direct Japanese attack. The proposal included six kinds of labour cooperatives: textiles, wood, glass, leather, straw weaving, and sewing. The refugee-organised trade unions in the nine districts responded positively to Zhu's proposal. Refugees quickly acquired skills and were put to work with raw materials and marketing provided by Zhu's association. The Livelihood Improvement Association (TLIA) supported the creation of labour cooperatives to 'improve and modernize non-industrial and semi-industrial manual labor through collective work'. In 1939, TLIA invested sixty thousand yuan that added to the donation of five thousand yuan from the Shanghai Christian Warzone Relief Association to the Nantao trade unions.[46] Training was provided by the trade unions. Two hundred refugees worked in the straw-weaving and sewing factories. Women refugees were trained and recruited by a French nun to work in a unit of the textile factory. By the end of 1939, the trade union also opened a towel factory and an embroidery factory, in which over one thousand women refugees were trained to work and manage the daily workload collectively. They later became shareholders of the cooperative.[47]

Conclusion

The establishment and managerial mechanisms of the Nantao Safe Zone in Shanghai were widely publicised and praised. Nanjing and Hankou adopted the Nantao model ahead of the advancing Japanese armies. Later, Canton, Hangzhou, Zhangzhou, Shenzhen, and Ouchang explored the idea of setting up a safe zone. They saw the Nantao Safe Zone as an example of international humanitarianism, which saved many lives through effective fundraising and protection.[48] Father Jacquinot and the committee provided various kinds of refugee assistance to the three hundred thousand refugees in the Zone. Monetary support for the Nantao Safe Zone came from a variety of sources. Besides the donations from the local and

'A right to the city'   181

overseas Chinese charity groups, the Shanghai municipal government gave fifty thousand yuan. Even the Japanese military leadership got involved in the funding, providing ten thousand yen, in pursuit of its own agenda.[49]

The Nantao Safe Zone reflected many features of international humanitarianism. Like his fellow missionaries who practiced humanitarian service through faith since the seventeenth century, Jacquinot had served as a spiritual advisor and parish priest and had earned a favourable reputation among the local Chinese. He also developed excellent connections within the foreign communities during his long career. More importantly, he was perceived by the Chinese and Japanese governments as neutral and 'trustworthy', without any political agenda. In contrast, the Chinese government prioritised its authority over the land and the people. Its financial support was there to underwrite state legitimacy, alongside acts such as the placement of national flags in the Safe Zone, the publication of a regional map, and the use of the Chinese language to name the Safe Zone. Chinese humanitarianism was a weapon in the defence of the nation. Its goal was to halt Japanese aggression and to restore order and social control among refugee populations.

For the Chinese government, Nantao, where the Zhabei New Villages for the Commoners were located, was a model of how to regulate and allocate resources for the refugees. Doing so legitimated their claim to authority over the Safe Zone. By the same token, Japanese humanitarianism underscored their colonial strategy of finding ways to defeat the local Chinese resistance. Japan needed to find competent leaders who were not Chinese to help them deal effectively with the uprooted civilian population. Jacquinot was ideal for this role.

International humanitarianism was a field of constant contestation. Although Jacquinot's story has been recently rediscovered in China, the Nantao Safe Zone's story is unknown. After all, the Safe Zone project entailed collaboration with the enemy, the Japanese, and with a French priest with strong connections to foreign powers. When Jacquinot visited Japan for a week in 1938, his 'diplomatic' negotiations with both sides and humanitarian work were criticised by Agnes Smedley, an American journalist who was working in China and was sympathetic to the Chinese communist cause. Historian Marcia Ristaino records how Smedley thought the war

182 *Refugees and the stateless in Asia*

was a godsend to missionary institutions, which were in a position to offer refuge to the Chinese. She did not believe Jacquinot's sole purpose was to rescue war refugees; rather, she viewed the Safe Zone as a 'reservoir of labor' for foreign factories and for the Japanese war machine.[50] Equally suspect was the Chinese state's involvement in the practices of controlling the floating population of migrant workers, refugees, or stateless foreigners, potential threats to 'peace and order'. The Nantao Safe Zone was instituted to provide a structure for urban governance. For the Japanese state, the Safe Zone was a way to present the virtues of Japanese protection in the fight against opium smuggling.[51] The refugee repatriation programmes were also carried out by Japanese troops to 'maintain the peace and order of humanitarian work', through which, in 1938, one hundred thousand Chinese refugees, White Russians, and international charity workers were sent to Japanese occupied areas.[52] When the Nantao Safe Zone was closed in June 1940, the Japanese immediately occupied the area and declared it 'under Japanese supervision'.[53]

Yet it was precisely the contested ideas and practices of international humanitarianism by the warring states and non-state international and local organisations that allowed the Nantao Safe Zone to become a dynamic space for refugees – and the stateless – to act on their specific interests. My story of the stateless – the White Russians, the progressive political groups and the capitalist-minded entrepreneurs – complicates our understanding of the formation and practice of international humanitarianism.

In her articles written in the 1940s and then in *The Origins of Totalitarianism*, published in 1951, Hannah Arendt concluded that the experience of the modern stateless proved that rights derive only from membership in a nation. Arendt articulated the tension between the aspiration to make all human beings the bearers of rights and the fact that in reality rights depend on citizenship in particular states. The political organisation of humanity into discrete sovereignties with full control over membership meant that anyone without political status was effectively devoid of rights. The only meaningful right would be a 'right to have rights', or a right to belong that could ensure a place in some political community.

Arendt's discussion of the stateless provides a framework to understand the history of safe zones, refugee camps, and refugees and their relationship with the receiving states. Refugee or nanmin

'A right to the city'

(难, in Chinese; it means people in crisis) was a political identity or status for a homeless individual who may at a future date reassert his or her right to belong. The Nantao Safe Zone in Shanghai can be seen as an embryonic form of this political community, in which everyone with a refugee status ultimately could obtain 'a right' to belong to Nantao. But to do so, they had to obey the rules and participate in the regulated collective refugee life, so as to maintain their membership in the community and sustain their refugee status. Maintaining a right, that is, refugee status, had a price. The rules of refugee life had to be followed.

Having secured refugee status, their rights were in fact the rights to the Zone, the place. I borrow Henri Lefebvre's notion of 'the right to the city' that 'manifests itself as a "superior" form of rights: the right to freedom, to individualization in socialization, to habitat and to inhabit'.[54] A 'right to the city' is a claim for the right to develop an individual's creativity in an urban context. Within the international framework of the Nantao Safe Zone under the joint supervision of Father Jacquinot and his benefactors, the Chinese authorities, and the Japanese authorities, Chinese refugees were obligated to work and contribute to the community in a particular place. Chinese authorities saw them as good Chinese citizens, who in a defined zone, a safe-haven, found respite from the pressures of war. The stateless refugees secured a place of relative autonomy in the Safe Zone. The revolutionary refugees in the Zone were able to continue their political mobilisations, maintaining their political commitments. Under the framework of humanitarian internationalism, refugees had rights that went beyond mere protection. However, the right to live in the Safe Zone depended upon Japanese toleration of their status. Their right to the city was a right to live in a liminal space, at a very special wartime moment. In that space, they could dream not only of peace, but also of having rights of their own.

Notes

1 'Paradise for Refugees (难民之乐园, nanminzhileyuan)', *Zhanshi Huakan*, 3, 19 (1938), p. 13.
2 Ibid., p. 14.

184 *Refugees and the stateless in Asia*

3 Ibid.

4 Marcia R. Ristaino, *The Jacquinot Safe Zone: Wartime Refugees in Shanghai* (Stanford, CA: Stanford University Press, 2008).

5 Su Zhiliang (ed.), *Rao Jiaju and Wartime Civilian Protection* (Guilin: Guangxi Normal University Press, 2015).

6 Ibid.

7 Hannah Arendt, *The Origins of Totalitarianism* (New York: Schocken Books, 1968), p. 283.

8 See Aidan Forth, *Barbed-Wire Imperialism: Britain's Empire of Camps, 1876–1903* (Oakland, CA: University of California Press, 2017).

9 Arendt, *The Origins of Totalitarianism*, p. 284.

10 Ristaino, *Safe Zone*, pp. 36–9.

11 *Jianzhu*, 1932.

12 *SMC Report*, 1937, p. 31.

13 Ibid.

14 *SMC Report*, 1938, p. 26.

15 Ibid.

16 Ibid.

17 'Cold and Hunger: Nantao 100,000 Refugees', *Shen Bao*, 20 October 1937, p. 52.

18 Ibid.

19 SMC Report, 1937, p. 112.

20 *Shen Bao*, 5 November 1937, p. 4.

21 La Zone Jacquinot de Changhai 1937–1939, Shanghai Municipal Archives, no. U38-2-1189.

22 'China at War', *China Weekly Review*, special supplement (December 1937), p. 8.

23 'A Variety of National Salvation Movements', 上海国际救济会年报, 1937.

24 The China–Foreign Charity and Relief Association was the international refugee relief organisation funded by the Nationalist government.

25 'Regional Map of Nanshi Refugee Zone' (nanshi nanmin quyutu, 南市难民区域图), *Jiuzai huikan*, 14, 11 (November/December 1938), Shanghai Nanyang Charity and Relief Association, p. 111.

26 Hang Seng, 'Report of Nantao Relief Camp', *Relief Association Monthly, The China–Foreign Charity and Relief Association*, 14, 11 (November and December 1937), p. 11.

27 *Story of the Jacquinot Zone*, p. 23.

28 Wang, Zhongxi, 'Shanghai International Refugee Shelter', *Zhandou Huabao*, 10 (1937), p. 4.

29 'Report on the Nantao Relief Campus', *Shen Bao*, 6 December 1937, p. 5.

'A right to the city'   185

30 Ibid.
31 'Nantao Refugee Zone: Planning the Nine Districts', *Shenzhou Daily*, 28 November 1938, p. 3.
32 'Refugees Must Pay Their Labor Duty and Military Service'. *Chinese Red Cross Monthly*, 9 (1938), p. 30.
33 'Life in the Nantao Relief Camp', *Zhandou Huabao*, 10 (1937), p. 4.
34 'Refugee Life in Nantao', *Shen Bao*, 29 May 1938.
35 'Shanghai Refugee Summer Olympic Games', *Shen Bao*, 25 September 1938, pp. 5–7.
36 'To Treat the Russian Refugees', *Guoji Gongbao* (1937), pp. 6–7. See also Chapter 9 in this book.
37 Ibid., p. 7.
38 'Nantao Refugee Area Formally Declared Open', *The North-China Daily News*, 10 November 1937, p. 5.
39 *Xinmin Wanbao*, 18 June 2005, pp. 8–10.
40 Ibid.
41 Yan Zhai, *Study of Refugee Relief by the Underground CCP in Shanghai in the Early War of Resistance*, Master's Thesis, 2010, pp. 35–6.
42 'Refugees Must Fulfill Their Labor Duty', *Chinese Red Cross Monthly*, 42 (1938), p. 29.
43 Ibid., pp. 29–30.
44 'Four Refugee Factories in Preparation', *Chinese Red Cross Monthly*, 35 (1938), pp. 26–7.
45 'The Self-Organized Trade Union in the Nantao Refugee Zone", *Chinese Red Cross Monthly*, 1, 8 (1939), p. 3.
46 'The Livelihood Improvement Association Preparing to Build "One Two Eight" Refugee Factories in Nantao', *International Trade News*, 4, 1 (February 1939), pp. 51–2.
47 Ibid.
48 Ristaino, *Safe Zone*, p. 81.
49 Ibid., p. 76.
50 Ristaino, *Safe Zone*, p. 99.
51 *SMC Report*, 1938, p. 117.
52 *Damei Wanbao*, 17 December 1938, p. 5.
53 'Father Jacquinot Will Return to Shanghai', *Shen Bao* (1940), p. 7.
54 Henri Lefebvre, *Writings on Cities* (Oxford: Wiley-Blackwell, 1996), p. 174.

12

Chinese Nationalists, Japanese occupiers, and the European Jewish refugees in Shanghai, 1938–41

Gao Bei

'[U]nder the current situation, even though it is anticipated to be dangerous, we still have to use the Jews. Just as the dish of *fugu*, although it is delicious, it will take your life if you don't know how to prepare it.' So said Captain Inuzuka Koreshige of the Japanese Naval Landing Party in occupied Shanghai in his report to a meeting of the Committee on the Muslim and Jewish Problem on 18 January 1939. The captain also called on the Japanese government to conduct comprehensive research on the Jewish refugees in the city to help determine Japan's policy toward them.[1]

Between 1938 and 1941, the Japanese Foreign Ministry's records show that 19,451 European Jewish refugees arrived in Shanghai.[2] The story of the wartime 'Shanghai Jews' is not just about the escape of twenty thousand Jewish refugees to East Asia during the Holocaust. It demonstrates how the 'Jewish issue' complicated the relationships between China, Japan, Germany, and the United States before and during the Second World War. It also shows that the Holocaust had complex repercussions that extended well beyond Europe.

When stateless European Jewish refugees began to arrive in Shanghai in the summer of 1938, China was at a critical moment in its war against Japan. Officials in both the Chinese and Japanese governments seemed to genuinely believe in the Jews' important economic and political influence in the West, especially in the United States. Therefore, both the Chinese Nationalist government and the Japanese occupation authorities thought very carefully about the Shanghai Jews and how they could be used to win international financial and diplomatic support in their war against one another.

Chinese Nationalists, Japanese occupiers 187

In the late 1930s, Shanghai, an open port since the Opium War of 1842, was a sanctuary of last resort for desperate European Jews. Its unique status as a city under foreign domination and the chaos created by the war made it possible for stateless Jewish refugees to enter it without permits, visas, or other papers. Before the first European Jewish refugees arrived in 1938, Shanghai was under the control of fourteen different countries and divided into four separate administrative units: the 'Chinese City', the French Concession, the International Settlement, and Hongkou, the Eastern side of the International Settlement, which was exclusively governed by the Japanese after August 1937.[3] Chiang Kai-shek's government managed passport control in the city until the outbreak of full-scale conflict between Japan and China in July 1937. However, after the Japanese won the Battle of Shanghai and the Nationalists retreated from the city in late 1937, the new Japanese puppet regime there, the Weixin Zhengfu or Reformed Government of the Republic of China, did not resume passport control.[4]

The Chinese authorities' absence from the city created a false impression that the Chinese government had little to do with the Jewish refugees. In fact, the Nationalist wartime government in Chongqing at the time not only had a carefully considered Jewish policy but was also deeply involved with the European Jewish refugees. The Jewish refugee issue, insofar as it affected the Japanese occupiers, directly and indirectly complicated China's relationships with Germany, Japan, and the United States from the late 1930s to the early 1940s.

Before the European Jews escaped to Shanghai, from the late 1920s to early 1937, China and Germany were *de facto* allies. In 1921, shortly after the end of the First World War, the two countries, which had fought on opposite sides during the war, reestablished diplomatic relations. Sun Yat-sen, the founding father of the Republic of China and the Chinese Nationalist Party, sought to use German military and economic resources for China's reconstruction and development.[5] Recently defeated Germany, which had lost its assets and privileges in East Asia, was willing to deal with China on an equal basis.[6] For their part, the Germans coveted China's massive market and strategic materials for its post-war recovery.[7]

The Chinese Nationalists and Germans cooperated closely until the early stage of the Sino–Japanese conflict. Two important events

188   *Refugees and the stateless in Asia*

changed the Sino–German relationship: after Germany signed the Anti-Comintern Pact with Japan in November 1936 and the Japanese began its full-scale invasion of China in July 1937, the Chinese Nationalists were no longer important strategic partners to Germany. The Germans apparently decided that the Japanese would provide a more effective check to the Soviet army in East Asia. Japan also began to pressure Germany to withdraw its military aid to the Chinese Nationalist government.[8] China was then fighting the Japanese alone and was forced to look elsewhere for both military and financial support. The Nationalist government did not have many options and was determined to explore any possible source of funds. The Chinese Nationalists, like their Japanese counterparts, attempted to wring capital from European and American Jewish communities, which they believed to have supported the Shanghai Jews, for their war against Japan.

In fact, important Chinese leaders had been well aware of the Jews and the so-called Jewish issue. Sun Yat-sen himself was a supporter of Zionism. In the early 1920s, Sun Yat-sen promoted nationalism in order to reunify and modernize China. He believed that nationalism 'held a nation together and enabled it to survive', and had allowed the Jews to survive for two thousand years without their own state.[9] On 24 April 1920, Sun Yat-sen wrote Nissim Elias Benjamin Ezra, the founder of the Shanghai Zionist Association, to express his sympathy for the Zionist movement. He reassured Ezra that 'all lovers of Democracy cannot help but support wholeheartedly and welcome with enthusiasm the movement to restore your wonderful and historic nation, which has contributed so much to the civilization of the world and which rightfully deserve [*sic*] an honorable place in the family of nations'.[10] Sun Yat-sen regularly cited the Zionists as role models for the Chinese and their own nationalist movement.[11] Although Sun Yat-sen died in 1925, officials in the Nationalist Party and government continued to support Zionism.

In the spring of 1939, Sun Ke, Sun Yat-sen's only son and president of the Nationalist government's Legislative Yuan, proposed a plan to settle Jewish refugees in Southwestern China.[12] Sun Ke pointed out that the idea was consistent with Sun Yat-sen's teachings that China should help and ally with minor powers and peoples. In addition, the plan would help bring China substantial

Chinese Nationalists, Japanese occupiers   189

benefits. For example, it might help to attract international Jewish capital, favourably impress the British and US governments, and help China secure the major powers' support in its war against Japan.[13] But, because China at the time was still nominally an ally of Germany, the Chinese were also concerned about Berlin's reaction to their plan. China could not afford to make Germany another enemy. According to a Foreign Ministry memorandum, in mid-March 1939, when the Chinese government began assessing the Jewish settlement plan, a secretary from the German embassy visited the ministry. The Foreign Ministry seemed to be particularly cautious about Germany's Jewish policy. The memorandum reads:

> We have to take into account Germany's Jewish policy under the current international situation. It might increase Germany's animosity against us if we suddenly allow Jews to settle [in China.] Recently, Kangpei, a secretary from the German embassy came to the ministry to show dissent toward the proposed settlement plan. [The secretary] Contended that although it was inappropriate for the German government to protest [against it], the Chinese government should consider the plan carefully since Jews always hated Germany. This demonstrates that the Germans are taking this matter very seriously.[14]

In the months following March 1939, the Ministries of Interior, Foreign Affairs, Military Affairs, Finance, and Transportation of the Executive Yuan studied Sun Ke's plan. The ministries established specific guidelines to regulate the entry of Jewish refugees. At their meetings, almost all the ministries raised concerns about the refugees' nationality. The officials believed that this would affect China's future control over them. For example, if the refugees were from a country that exercised consular jurisdiction in China, they were entitled to extraterritoriality. Therefore, the final draft of the Nationalist government's settlement plan comprised specific articles distinguishing between the treatment of 'Jews with nationality' and 'Jews without nationality'.[15] In July 1939, the Chinese government officially adopted 'General Principles Governing the Working of the Plan for the Immigration of Jews into China'. The document made it clear that 'Jews with foreign nationality will be treated exactly as all other foreigners are treated in this country'.[16] For Jews without nationality, 'the Chinese government would order its diplomats

190 *Refugees and the stateless in Asia*

abroad to grant special passports or visas to assist them in entering China'.[17]

In 1939, as the Nationalist government's records show, the Chinese officials in general seemed to believe that 'Jews who had fled [Europe] because of the persecution of German and Italian governments, except for a few (such as White Russian Jews) were stateless, all maintained their originally nationalities.'[18] Therefore, at first, the goal of China's Jewish settlement plan was to assist 'stateless' Jews, or non-German and Austrian Jews. Eventually, after the Chinese officials learned that American Jewish leaders were actively involved in the settlement plan and pledged to convince the US government to support China financially, they abandoned their concerns about Germany. The Nationalist government wanted to avoid aggravating its already troubled relations with Germany, but China's highest priority during this period was to win international assistance in defeating the Japanese.

Although the Chinese settlement plan initially aimed to help 'stateless' Jews, a German Jewish businessman in Shanghai, Jakob Berglas, and a politically active American Jewish dentist, Maurice William, both proposed to the Nationalist and American governments plans to help relocate European, especially German, Jews to China. The possible involvement of American Jewish financial power made Maurice William's plan especially appealing to the Chinese officials.

After conducting a field trip to interior China, Jakob Berglas proposed to the Nationalists that they permit a hundred thousand Jewish emigrants to settle in the Southwestern Yunnan Province, which had a small population and plenty of uncultivated land. He also asked the Chinese government to provide protection for the Jews and offer them employment opportunities. Most important, Berglas emphasised that each Jewish immigrant should before his or her arrival in China pay a fee of £50. So eventually, a total of £5,000,000 would be brought into the country. Berglas believed that the Jewish immigrants would constitute 'a valuable asset for the reconstruction and industrial development of China'.[19]

Berglas's plan immediately received the support of Long Yun, governor and warlord of Yunnan Province. The province couldn't afford to bring immigrants there to help cultivate its resources. The governor understood that many European Jewish refugees had

Chinese Nationalists, Japanese occupiers   191

recently arrived in Shanghai, and that they were 'more talented and wealthy than ordinary people'. He asked the central government's permission to use the Jewish refugees to cultivate the province since 'it could kill two birds with one stone' if he would 'be able to relocate those homeless people to Yunnan and use them to farm the land'.[20] Nevertheless, both the governor and Berglas seemed to have neglected one important weakness of this plan: its impracticality. As the secretary general of the Nationalist Central Political Council pointed out, based on a survey that specified the occupations of the refugees, only 1.74 per cent of them engaged in farming and forestry.[21]

Maurice William also enthusiastically communicated with the Chinese government about the possibility of transplanting German Jews to China. During the Sino–Japanese War, William was secretary of the American Bureau of Medical Aid to China and a member of the United Council for Civilian Relief in China, along with former President Herbert Hoover and Albert Einstein. In fact, as early as 1934, William and Einstein had come up with the idea of finding a home in China for German Jews. The two corresponded between 1934 and 1935 concerning this Jewish resettlement plan. William told Einstein that he had 'made a special study of this important problem' and had 'discussed it in great detail with the Chinese Minister [ambassador] at Washington'. William then concluded that China was 'the one great hope for Hitler's victims'.[22] Einstein replied in a letter of February 1934 that he considered William's plan 'very hopeful and rational and its realization must be pursued energetically'.[23] However, there is no record to show whether William ever discussed this plan officially with the Chinese government or, if so, how the Chinese government reacted.

In 1939, after William learned that the Nationalists themselves were planning to establish a settlement for Jewish refugees, he immediately contacted the Chinese ambassador to the United States. William emphasised to the ambassador that Chinese and Jews were both victims of aggressive wars and should cooperate and provide one another with aid. He also stressed that American Jews were capable of providing China with financial and political help in its war against Japan. William promised that 'the American Jewish people and others interested in the refugee problem will raise significant sums of money to finance' the settlement plan.[24]

192 *Refugees and the stateless in Asia*

William also wrote prominent Chinese officials individually and received encouraging responses. For instance, Sun Ke 'heartily' supported William's plan, and affirmed that he was 'more confident of our ultimate victory [over Japan] today than at any other time'. Sun Ke also maintained that he 'always felt that the power and influence of world Jewry especially in financial and governmental circles should be enlisted to support our cause'.[25]

Eventually, in August 1939, the Chinese government officially invited William to come to China to investigate the possibility of settling Jews who were expelled from Germany.[26] The opportunity to obtain financial support from the United States obviously brought new hope to China in its war effort. From then on, Chinese officials no longer worried about the refugees' German nationality.

However, no record exists to prove that William actually visited China. In addition, neither the Sun Ke plan, the Jakob Berglas plan, nor the Maurice William plan were discussed or pursued further at the governmental level. It seems that the lack of support, especially financial aid, from the American government was one important reason for the failure of these Jewish settlement plans. Beginning in 1939, the Roosevelt administration distanced itself from efforts to rescue European Jews. The American government restricted its quota of Jewish immigrants to the United States, and public opinion opposed providing further help to European Jews.[27] The American government's more hands-off attitude toward the plight of the Jews may have been behind in its unwillingness to support the Chinese Nationalists' Jewish settlement plans. As a result, the Chinese officials may have had to abandon the plans because of the lack of international, American in particular, financial and political support.

Although the Nationalist government's settlement plans failed, the experience of the Jewish refugees in Shanghai sheds new light on our understanding of Chinese politics and diplomacy during the Second World War. The Nationalist government was hampered both by corruption and incompetence during the Sino–Japanese conflict. However, its Jewish settlement plans demonstrate that the Chinese Nationalists were determined not only to fight the invading Japanese, but also to exhaust every available resource to win.

It is also important to note that from 1938 to 1940, Chinese diplomats in Europe issued visas to refugees who wished to go to China, although the majority of them entered Shanghai without

Chinese Nationalists, Japanese occupiers 193

visas. According to the Shanghai survivors, these Chinese visas served as proof of intention to leave Nazi-controlled territories during the time of forced migration.[28] Those who were unable to obtain foreign entry visas to leave their countries risked being put into concentration camps.[29] Nationalist diplomats in European cities, such as Vienna, Paris, and Hamburg, and the legation in Sweden all issued Jewish refugees visas to Shanghai.[30] Feng Shan Ho, the Chinese Consul General in Vienna, who was one of only two Chinese named 'Righteous Among the Nations' by Yad Vashem, Israel's Holocaust Martyrs' and Heroes' Remembrance Authority, testified in his memoirs that the Chinese Consulate General in Vienna received an order from the Foreign Ministry to 'be generous to Jews who wished to come to China and not to reject [their requests for visas]'.[31] He referred to the Foreign Ministry's instruction as the 'liberal visa policy'.[32]

Meanwhile, after the Japanese forces drove the Chinese Nationalists out of Shanghai in late 1937, Japan became a major power controlling the city along with twelve Western countries. Japan and Germany signed the Anti-Comintern Pact in 1936 and became allies, but the pragmatic Japanese did not approve of Germany's unfolding plan to persecute the European Jews under their control.

From the late 1920s to the early 1930s, through a series of violent actions in Manchuria and at home, the Japanese military assumed control over Japan's foreign policy.[33] The military's prominent influence in Japan's foreign policy decision-making made it possible for navy captain Inuzuka Koreshige in Shanghai and army colonel Yasue Norihiro in Manchuria, the country's 'Jewish problem experts', to turn their beliefs into official policy. The two men were either individually or jointly responsible for making Japan's Jewish policy in 1938 and 1939. Inuzuka and Yasue attempted to use the international connections of Jewish refugees, the United States in particular, to help bring Jewish investment into Japanese-occupied China and to improve Japan's relationship with the United States.

Inuzuka's and Yasue's policies ultimately helped persecuted Jews who had come to Shanghai to survive the Nazi menace; however, the experts did not attempt to rescue Jews for humanitarian or ethical reasons, as their supporters claimed after the end of the Second World War.[34] Like many of their contemporaries, Inuzuka Koreshige

194 *Refugees and the stateless in Asia*

and Yasue Norihiro first learned of and became interested in Jewish affairs during the Siberian Expedition in the early 1920s because of abundant exposure to antisemitic works published there.[35] Inuzuka and Yasue not only authored many antisemitic volumes in the 1920s and 1930s under different pseudonyms,[36] but also conducted research on what they saw as 'Jewish power' in the late 1930s. Their findings convinced them that Japan should take advantage of the refugees, rather than eliminate them.

In Shanghai, at the Third Department, or intelligence branch, of the Naval General Staff, Captain Inuzuka was responsible for three different newsletters on Jewish issues that were circulated around 1938: *Jewish Information*, *Secret Jewish Information*, and *Top Secret Jewish Information*. From early 1938 to late 1939, the Third Department published nearly one hundred issues of these newsletters. Naval intelligence focused its research on Jewish political and financial power in the United States and the European Jewish refugees in Shanghai.[37]

In Manchuria, the Research Department of the South Manchurian Railway Company (SMR) contributed greatly to Colonel Yasue's investigation of Jewish matters. Chinese historian Xie Xueshi refers to the SMR as 'the biggest intelligence network in East Asia' during the Second World War.[38] Based on the request of Colonel Yasue, the Research Department composed approximately fifty reports and issued a periodical on Jewish-related matters from 1938 to 1943. The investigation centred on the social, political, and economic influence of Jews in European countries and the United States, although many of the reports exaggerated or fundamentally misunderstood the role that Jews played in those countries.[39]

The information collected by the intelligence agencies helped confirm Inuzuka's and Yasue's belief that Jews, American Jews in particular, were financially and politically powerful in the Western world. The two seemed certain that the Jewish refugees under their control would be able to contribute to Japan's final victory in its 'holy war' in Asia. Further, Inuzuka's and Yasue's extensive research on the Jews shows that the military experts had a well-prepared long-term plan for harnessing the influence of the European Jewish refugees.

Captain Inuzuka Koreshige controlled the fate of the Jewish refugees in Shanghai. Inuzuka believed that the tens of thousands of European Jews under the Japanese Navy's control in the city were hostages and that Japan could use the refugees as a bargaining chip with world Jewish leaders.[40] At the same time, the captain warned the Japanese government that the Jews were different from other peoples, and therefore Japan should not treat them the same as other foreigners. Inuzuka also insisted that the Japanese government always keep the Jews under its thumb. Exploiting the Jews, he argued, would be like eating the delicious, but potentially poisonous, blowfish. If prepared properly, it could bring Japan great benefits. However, if it were done improperly, the risk would be very high; Japan might even be used by the Jews.[41] The Japanese experts' antisemitic ideas were unique and pragmatic, and they focused almost exclusively on manipulating the Jews; eliminating them didn't seem to be a pressing concern, at least at this point.

Colonel Yasue Norihiro of the Kwantung Army was deeply involved with the Jewish community in Manchuria, which at the time was home to another prominent Jewish settlement in China. Russian Jews had established themselves there since the late nineteenth century.[42] After Manchuria fell to the Japanese in 1932, Yasue tried to use his 'kind' treatment of the Manchurian Jews to impress and to obtain capital from their wealthy co-religionists in Shanghai and the United States. The colonel enthusiastically supported the Kwantung Army's plan to introduce foreign, especially American, wealth to develop Manchuria. The Japanese Army always regarded the Soviet Union as its most immediate potential enemy and prepared for war with the Russians in Manchuria.[43] At the same time, the army needed additional funds to carry out its expanding offensive against the Chinese. As a result, Yasue promised the Jewish community in Manchuria safety in exchange for their cooperation.[44]

In July 1938, the army made it very clear in 'The Army's Hopes Regarding Current Foreign Policies' that Japan's diplomatic efforts toward the United States should concentrate on 'persuading the United States at the very least to retain a neutral attitude, if possible to adopt a pro-Japanese attitude, and especially to strengthen friendly economic relations'. This document also pointed out that such diplomatic efforts should include conducting 'appropriate propaganda' to 'correct' the American view of Japan, promoting trade with the United States, and importing American capital.[45] Along with Yasue Norihiro, many Kwantung Army General Staff

196 *Refugees and the stateless in Asia*

officers supported and promoted the plan to use the Jews and their connections in the United States to attract American investment and to ease tensions with the Americans.[46]

In October 1938, before Japan established its official policy toward the Jewish refugees, Yasue underscored that 'Japan does not, and does not necessarily have to, adopt Germany's and Italy's antisemitic policies toward the Jews. It should instead follow its national policy of *Hakkō Ichiu*, cooperation and harmony among peoples, and embrace the Jews'.[47] Although Yasue repeatedly emphasised that Japan should 'embrace' the Jewish refugees, there was a significant precondition for this: Jews should contribute their financial power to Manchuria's economic development, so that the Japanese army could be well prepared to confront the Russians.

Yasue seems to have presented his theory of 'embracing the Jews' to Itagaki Seishirō, the army minister, former staff officer of the Kwantung Army and the colonel's friend and classmate from the military academy, before the Five Ministers' Conference on 6 December.[48] Itagaki then introduced Yasue's draft policy to the conference.[49] The Five Ministers' Conference determined the 'Outlines of the Jewish Policies' on 6 December 1938, as Japan's first official policy toward European Jewish refugees. The next day, foreign minister Arita Hachirō sent the 'Outlines' to the Japanese ambassadors to Germany, the United States, and Manchukuo, as well as to the Japanese consuls in China. The foreign minister explained to his diplomats in those countries that since maintaining a good relationship with Germany and Italy was at the core of Japan's foreign policy, Japan should basically 'avoid actively embracing' the Jews who were banished by allied countries. Those such as investors and technicians, who could be used by Japan, should be exceptions. Nevertheless, it would contradict Japan's advocacy of 'racial equality' if it openly persecuted the Jews as its allies had done. Arita emphasised that Japan, under a 'state of emergency', needed 'the introduction of foreign capital' in order to pursue economic construction as well as its war aims. At the same time, the foreign minister warned that Japan had to 'avoid worsening' its relations with the United States.[50]

Japan's first official Jewish policy thus guaranteed that the Japanese would not persecute Jews. Nevertheless, the lives of the Jewish refugees were still in constant danger if they did not comply

Chinese Nationalists, Japanese occupiers   197

with Japan's requests or would not cooperate with the military. In fact, there is ample evidence in the Japanese record that shows that the Jewish experts regularly threatened the safety of the refugees if they would not collaborate with the Japanese.

For instance, Captain Inuzuka in Shanghai regularly alerted his government to be cautious with the Jews. On 12 October 1938, the captain spoke to the Committee on the Muslim and Jewish Problem. Inuzuka emphasised to the committee that the Shanghai Jews were concerned about Japan's Jewish policy and were eager to approach the occupation authorities. He considered it a perfect moment for Japan to take advantage of them. However, he also cautioned the committee that the last thing Japan should do was to be too 'friendly' to the Jews. Instead, Japan should completely subjugate the Jews and always 'keep our hands around their throats'. On the other hand, Inuzuka tried to persuade his audience that Tokyo should not expel the Jews, since Jewish economic power in China, Shanghai in particular, could definitely benefit Japan. The captain wanted the central government to establish 'practical measures' to enable Japan to exploit the Jews.[51]

Colonel Yasue, Inuzuka's counterpart in Manchuria, was even more blatant. Before the Second Far Eastern Jewish Conference in Manchuria in December 1938, the colonel assembled all the Jewish leaders and delivered a speech in a private capacity. In his speech, Yasue pointed out that he expected the Jewish leaders to display their leadership prudently and properly since the current international situation was getting 'complicated'. 'If [the principles of] your leadership contradict Japan's ... holy ideals', he warned, 'it will definitely cause sorrow for your fellow Jews'. Therefore, Yasue insisted that the guiding principles of the Jewish leaders would directly affect the destiny of the Jews in East Asia. As a result, at the conference, the Jewish leaders were forced to pledge their support and collaboration in establishing Japan's new order in East Asia.[52]

After securing the cooperation of the Jewish communities, in July 1939, the two military experts proposed to the Japanese government that it establish a settlement for European Jewish refugees in Shanghai.[53] Captain Inuzuka and Colonel Yasue believed that in providing Jews a 'safe refuge', the Japanese government could use this opportunity to (1) favourably change American public opinion toward Japan, (2) make Jewish loans and investment more easily

198 *Refugees and the stateless in Asia*

accessible, (3) increase the sympathy of American and European Jews for Japan, and (4) obtain the absolute cooperation of the East Asian Jews with Japan.[54]

Nevertheless, because Japan's Jewish policy of 1938 and 1939 reflected the strategic needs of the military, the development of the war naturally and eventually affected the policy itself. After Japan signed the Tripartite Pact with Germany and Italy in September 1940, pro-German factions in both the military and the government acquired strength. Before the conclusion of the Tripartite Pact, although there was disagreement over Inuzuka and Yasue's Jewish policy, many Japanese officials, both military and civilian, not only tolerated it, but also joined the Jewish experts in attempting to use the Shanghai Jews to attract American capital and improve Japan's relationship with the United States. However, at this point, a direct conflict with the United States seemed to be unavoidable, and Japan's efforts to maintain a good relationship with the Americans became meaningless. The general mood in the Japanese government was that the alliance with the Germans was of the utmost importance and that Japan should not oppose Germany's Jewish policy as the experts had done. Captain Inuzuka and Colonel Yasue were soon removed from their positions in China, and the Japanese government decided to change its policy toward the Jewish refugees.[55] On 10 October, foreign minister Matsuoka Yōsuke cabled Japanese diplomats and ordered them to implement new regulations concerning 'refugees' who applied for visas to Japan. Now 'foreigners' who were also 'refugees' must hold on arrival not only travel tickets to their final destination countries but also at least 25 yen per person per day in order to stay in Japan during the transit period, the period during which they waited for an entry visa to a different country.[56] Japan's policy was still considerably different from Germany's 'final solution', and it aimed to prevent the arrival of Jewish refugees on its soil.

Unlike the military Jewish experts, Sugihara Chiune, Japan's acting consul in Kaunas, Lithuania, acted against his government's policy and issued visas that saved Jewish lives. After Japan signed the Tripartite Pact in 1940, the Tokyo government decided to transport more than one thousand Polish Jews, who were seeking temporary refuge in Japan, to Shanghai.[57] These refugees all received Japanese transit visas in the summer of 1940 from Sugihara Chiune. In that

Chinese Nationalists, Japanese occupiers 199

summer, Sugihara granted 2,132 transit visas to Polish Jews who did not qualify to receive them. This was more than one-third of the total number of transit visas that Japanese diplomats in Europe granted at the time.[58] However, the foreign minister soon discovered this and repeatedly ordered Sugihara not to grant transit visas to Jewish refugees unless they held destination visas to other countries and possessed enough travel money for their stay during the transit period in Japan.[59] Sugihara, however, kept issuing visas to every Jew who applied until he was forced by the Soviets to close his consulate in the fall of 1940.[60] Sugihara Chiune, as historian Pamela Sakamoto contends, was an 'extraordinary diplomat', since 'many Japanese diplomats issued visas that saved Jews, but only a few like Sugihara saved Jews by issuing visas'.[61] He was also honoured as 'Righteous Among the Nations' by Yad Vashem.

The few scholars who have written about the Japanese and the Jewish refugee community in Shanghai all contend that Japan adopted a different Jewish policy from that of their German allies.[62] However, they neglect Germany's influence over Japan's Jewish policymaking at the time the two nations negotiated and concluded the Tripartite Pact. These scholars also argue that after Pearl Harbor, the Japanese realised that the Jews were useless to them and decided to put them into a ghetto in Shanghai. In fact, Pearl Harbor was not the cause; what befell the Jewish refugees following Pearl Harbor resulted, ultimately, from the signing of the Tripartite Pact more than a year earlier. Japan's alliance with Germany ended all possibilities for the country to improve its relationship with the United States. The Japanese did not have a chance to use the Jews under their control to ease the tensions between the two countries or to help attract American capital. Consequently, the Jewish refugees in Shanghai lost their value to Japan.

When the European Jewish refugees fled to Shanghai, China and Japan were both seeking resources to help them defeat each other at the peak of the Sino–Japanese struggle. Both the Chinese Nationalist government and the Japanese occupation authorities formulated detailed plans to use the Shanghai Jews to attract international aid financially and politically. It appears that the Chinese Nationalists never intended to retaliate physically against the refugees if they failed to help execute the plans. The Nationalists simply put their strategies aside without repercussions for the refugees

200 *Refugees and the stateless in Asia*

when the expected assistance from the Jewish community around the world did not become available. In contrast, the Japanese record shows that the military Jewish experts considered the refugees to be hostages and regularly threatened their safety in exchange for the Jewish communities' cooperation.

However, indirectly, Yasue Norohiro and Inuzuka Koreshige's plans to exploit the Jews helped these stateless refugees to preserve their safe-haven in Shanghai, thereby avoiding the genocide unfolding in Europe. The refugees had escaped to China from the late 1930s to early 1940s because it was the only place that the stateless could go without a visa. They chose Shanghai because they had no other option. Consequently, the Shanghai Jews, both those with and without papers, survived, while so many of their families trapped in Europe perished in the Holocaust.

Notes

1 The Diplomatic Record Office of the Ministry of Foreign Affairs of Japan, Japan Center for Asian Historical Records (hereafter JACAR), http://www.jacar.go.jp. Accessed 19 May 2022. B04013210300, 0215–0235 (0228). 'Summary of Captain Inuzuka's Report at [a meeting of] the Committee on the Muslim and Jewish Problem: Personal Opinions on Current Situation of and Measures Taken toward the Jewish Refugees in Shanghai', 18 January 1939.

2 Archives of the Japanese Ministry of Foreign Affairs, 1868–1945, S series, microfilms (hereafter AJMFA). Secret, no. 1592, Yangshupu Police Station, 18 May 1943. Takahashi Takeji, Police Chief of the Yangshupu Police Station of the Japanese Consulate General in Shanghai and Police Inspector of the Ministry of the Greater East Asia, to Consul General in Shanghai, Yano Seiki. 'Concerning the Actual Conditions of the Jewish Refugees in Shanghai in the Past Three Years', S9460-3, 2587-2588.

3 Gao Bei, *Shanghai Sanctuary: Chinese and Japanese Policy toward European Jewish Refugees during World War II* (Oxford: Oxford University Press, 2013), p. 5.

4 JACAR, B04013210300, 0230. 'Summary of Captain Inuzuka's Report', 18 January 1939.

5 Guo Hengyu, 'Sun Zhongshan yu Deguo' [Sun Yat-sen and Germany], *Guoshiguan guankan* [*Journal of the Academia Historica*], 23 (1997), p. 83; Gao, p. 35.

Chinese Nationalists, Japanese occupiers 201

6 William C. Kirby, *Germany and Republican China* (Stanford, CA: Stanford University Press, 1984), pp. 253–4.

7 Guo, 'Sun Zhongshan yu Deguo', p. 83.

8 'Germany Colluded with Japan: Germany Recognized "Manchukuo"', 20 February 1938, p. 191; 'Germany Decided Not to Accept Military Trainees from China and Japan during the Conflict', 3 March 1938, p. 233; 'Germany Withdrew Its Military Advisors in China', 21 May 1938, p. 484; 'German and Italian Leaders Met in Roma and Decided to Strengthen Their Cooperation with Japan; Hitler Secretly Imposed an Arms Embargo on China', 3 May 1938, p. 442; 'Germany Recalled Ambassador Oskar P. Trautmann', 26 June 1938, p. 598, all in Zhu Huisen, Lai Min, and He Zhilin (eds), *Zhonghua Minguo shishi jiyao chugao: 1938* [First Edition of the Records of Historical Events of the Republic of China, 1938] (Taipei: Guo shi guan, 1989); Gao, *Shanghai Sanctuary*, pp. 35–6.

9 Audrey Wells, *The Political Thought of Sun Yat-sen: Development and Impact* (Basingstoke: Palgrave Macmillan, 2001), p. 72.

10 Copy provided by Zack Rothbart of the National Library of Israel, Jerusalem.

11 Sun Yat-sen and Zhang Qiyun, *Guo fu quan shu* [The Complete Works of the Founding Father] (Taipei: Guo fang yan jiu yuan, 1960), p. 198; Sun Yat-sen, translated by Frank W. Price, *The Principle of Nationalism* (Taipei: Chinese Cultural Service, 1953), pp. 20–3; Gao, pp. 14–15.

12 Academia Historica (the National Archives of Taiwan), Foreign Ministry Documents, 611.21/172–1/3046 (hereafter FMD). 'The Executive Yuan to the Ministry of Foreign Affairs Concerning the Establishment of a Jewish Settlement in Southwest China and the Drafting of Overseas Propaganda', 14 March 1939. Also see 'President of the Legislative Yuan Sun Ke's Proposal Concerning "the Establishment of a Settlement in Southwestern China to Accommodate Destitute and Homeless Jewish People"', 2 March 1939. Shao Minghuang (ed.), 'Kangzhan shiqi guomin zhengfu rongliu Youtairen jihua dangan yizu' [Collection of Documents Concerning the Nationalist Government's Plan to Accommodate Jews during the Sino–Japanese War], *Jindai Zhongguo* [Modern China], 147 (25 February 2002), pp. 168, 170–1.

13 Ibid.

14 FMD, 'From the Secretariat of the Executive Yuan to the Foreign Ministry: Opinions of the Ministries of Interior, Foreign Affairs, Military Affairs, Finance and Transportation Concerning the Settlement of Jewish Refugees', 15 March 1939.

15 Academia Historica, Executive Yuan Documents, 271.12/1/62/1330 (hereafter EYD). 'Minute of the 408th Meeting of the Executive Yuan',

202 *Refugees and the stateless in Asia*

4 April 1939. Also see 'Drafted Memorandum Submitted to the Highest National Defense Council: Opinions of the Executive Yuan concerning the Jewish Settlement Plan', 20 April 1939, in Shao, 'Collection of Documents', pp. 171–5.

16 EYD, Wei Tao-ming to Jakob Berglas, 26 July 1939.

17 EYD, 271.12/1/62/1330. 'Minute of the 408th Meeting of the Executive Yuan', 4 April 1939. Also see 'Drafted Memorandum Submitted to the Highest National Defense Council: Opinions of the Executive Yuan Concerning the Jewish Settlement Plan', 20 April 1939, in Shao, 'Collection of Documents', pp. 171–5.

18 See, for example, FMD, 'Opinions of the Secretariat of the Executive Yuan [on the Jewish Settlement Plan]', No. 871, 22 March 1939; EYD, 'The Foreign Ministry to the Secretariat of the Executive Yuan Concerning Governor Long Yun's Proposal to Use Jewish Refugees to Cultivate Yunnan', 4 July 1939.

19 FMD, 'Jakob Berglas to H. H. Kung', 6 June 1939. Attachment, 'Plan for the Immigration of Central European Immigrants into China'.

20 FMD, 'Governor Long Yun's Proposal to Use Jewish Refugees to Cultivate Yunnan, Forwarded by the Secretariat of the Highest National Defense Council to the Ministry of Foreign Affairs', 27 June 1939.

21 'Secretary-General Zhu Jiahua to President Chiang Kai-shek: Comments on Advantages and Disadvantages of German Jew Berglas's "Plan for the Immigration of Central European Jews into China" Forwarded by the Chinese League of Nations Union', 22 June 1939, in Shao, 'Collection of Documents', pp. 181–3.

22 The Maurice William Archives (hereafter MWA), UCLA, the Center for Chinese Studies, http://www.international.ucla.edu/china/WilliamMauriceArchive. Accessed 19 May 2022. A7.001, Maurice William to Albert Einstein, 30 January 1934.

23 MWA, A7.002, Albert Einstein to Maurice William, 13 February 1934.

24 EYD, 'Text of a Telegraphic Message from the Ministry of Foreign Affairs, Chungking, May 6, 1939', attached to Hu Shi to Maurice William, 18 May 1939. FMD, Maurice William to Hu Shi, 31 May 1939.

25 EYD, Sun Fo [Sun Ke] to Maurice William, 15 August 1939.

26 EYD, Wei Tao-ming to Maurice William, 9 August 1939.

27 David S. Wyman, *Paper Walls: America and the Refugee Crisis 1938–1941* (New York: Pantheon Books, 1968, 1985), pp. 210–11; Richard Breitman and Alan M. Kraut, *American Refugee Policy and European Jewry, 1933–1945* (Bloomington, IN: Indiana University Press, 1987), pp. 232, 8–9; Gao, p. 49.

Chinese Nationalists, Japanese occupiers   203

28 See Vivian Jeanette Kaplan, *Ten Green Bottles: The True Story of One Family's Journey from War-Torn Austria to the Ghetto of Shanghai* (New York: St. Martin's Press, 2002), p. 93; Berl Falbaum, *Shanghai Remembered: Stories of Jews Who Escaped to Shanghai from Nazi Europe* (Royal Oak, MI: Momentum Books, 2005), pp. 85, 98; Sidney B. Kurtz, *Marcel Singer: The Gentle Butcher of Hongkew* (Philadelphia, PA: Xlibris Corporation, 2003), pp. 20–3.

29 Sigmund Tobias, *Strange Haven: A Jewish Childhood in Wartime Shanghai* (Urbana, IL: University of Illinois Press, 1999), pp. 3–4; James R. Ross, *Escape to Shanghai: A Jewish Community in China* (New York: Free Press, 1994), p. 18; Gao, *Shanghai Sanctuary*, p. 50.

30 This information is based on the author's private visa collection provided by the Shanghai survivors with whom she corresponded from 2004 to 2006. The author also obtained copies of visas from the collections of the United States Holocaust Memorial Museum (USHMM), catalog no. 2005.24, 'Lubinski Family Papers, USHMM: Gift of Susan Herlinger', and USHMM's Photo Archives, 'Schenker Citizenship Document'.

31 He Fengshan, *Waijiao shengya sishi nian* [Forty Years of My Diplomatic Life] (Hong Kong: Zhongwen daxue chubanshe, 1990), pp. 75–6.

32 Ibid.

33 Gao, *Shanghai Sanctuary*, pp. 64–8.

34 For a discussion of how the Japanese, especially the military officers, saved and protected the Jewish refugees in China during the Second World War, see Uesugi Chitoshi, *Yudaya nanmin to hakkō ichiu* [The Jewish Refugees and Hakkō Ichiu] (Tokyo: Tendensha, 2002); Inuzuka Kiyoko, *Yudaya mondai to Nihon no kōsaku* [The Jewish Problem and Japanese Maneuvering] (Tokyo: Nihon Kōgyō Shinbunsha, 1982); and Yasue Hiroo, *Dairen tokumu kikan to maboroshi no Yudaya kokka* [The Dairen Intelligence Agency and the Phantom Jewish State] (Tokyo: Yahata Shoten, 1989); Gao, *Shanghai Sanctuary*, p. 30.

35 David Goodman and Masanori Miyazawa, *Jews in the Japanese Mind: The History and Uses of a Cultural Stereotype* (New York: Free Press, 1995), p. 77; Yasue Hiroo, Dairen tokumu kikan, pp. 34–5; Gao, *Shanghai Sanctuary*, p. 20.

36 Yasue published *Yudaya minzoku no sekai shihai?* [The Jewish Control of the World?] under his real name in 1933. Yasue Norihiro, *Yudaya minzoku no sekai shihai?* [The Jewish Control of the World?] (Tokyo: Kokon Shoin, 1933). Inuzuka published *Yudayajin no inbō to kokusai supai* [The Plot of the Jews and International Spies] in 1938 and *Yudaya mondai to Nihon* [The Jewish Problem and Japan] in 1939 under the pseudonym Utsunomiya Kiyō. Inuzuka Koreshige, *Yudayajin no inbō*

204   *Refugees and the stateless in Asia*

to kokusai supai [The Plot of the Jews and International Spies] (Tokyo: Naikaku Jōhōbu, 1938); Utsunomiya Kiyō [Inuzuka Koreshige], *Yudaya mondai to Nihon* [The Jewish Problem and Japan] (Tokyo: Naigai shobō, 1939); Gao, *Shanghai Sanctuary*, pp. 21–2.

37 AJMFA, 'Summary of the Jewish Refugee Issue in Shanghai', *Top Secret Jewish Information*, 5, 27 January 1939. S9460-3, 960–93.

38 Xie Xueshi, *Ge shi yi si: ping Man tie diao cha bu* [Thoughts Left by the Last Generation: Reviewing the Research Department of the South Manchurian Railway Company] (Beijing: Renmin chubanshe, 2003), p. 288.

39 Gao, *Shanghai Sanctuary*, pp. 24–5. Also see John Young, *The Research Activities of the South Manchurian Railway Company, 1907–1945: A History and Bibliography* (New York: East Asian Institute, Columbia University, 1966), pp. 585–9; Xie Xueshi, *Ge shi yi si: ping Man tie diao cha bu* [Thoughts Left by the Last Generation: Reviewing the Research Department of the South Manchurian Railway Company] (Beijing: Renmin chubanshe, 2003), p. 617; Ajia Keizai Kenkyūjo Tosho Shiryōbu (ed.), *Kyū shokuminchi kankei kikan kankōbutsu sōgō mokuroku* [General Catalogue of the Publications of the Organizations Related to Former Colonies] (Tokyo: Ajia Keizai Kenkyūjo, 1973–79), pp. 565–7.

40 JACAR: B04013207700, 0252–0254. 'Jewish Refugee Issue in Shanghai', 1 November 1939.

41 JACAR, B04013210300, 0230. 'Summary of Captain Inuzuka's report', 18 January 1939.

42 See Zhang Tiejiang, *Jiekai Haerbin Youtairen lishi zhimi = Reveal Enigmas of the Jewish History of Harbin* (Harbin: Heilongjiang renmin chubanshe, 2005), and Marvin Tokayer and Mary Swartz, *The Fugu Plan: The Untold Story of the Japanese and the Jews during World War II* (New York: Paddington Press, 1979).

43 Fujiwara Akira, 'Nihon rikugun to taibei senryaku' [The Japanese Army and Its Strategies toward the United States], in Hosoya Chihiro, Saitō Makoto, Imai Seiichi, and Rōyama Michio (eds), *Nichi-Bei kankei-shi- kaisen ni itaru 10 nen (1931–41nen)* [The History of Japanese–American Relations: 10 Years to the Outbreak of the [Pacific] War (1931–41)], vol. 2 (Tokyo: Tokyo Daigaku Shuppankai, 1971), pp. 75–6.

44 AJMFA, Foreign Minister Konoe Fumimaro to consular offices in China and Manchukuo, 'Colonel Yasue's Speech at the Meeting of the Committee on the Muslim and Jewish Problem', 13 October 1938. S9460–3, 750–66.

Chinese Nationalists, Japanese occupiers 205

45 JACAR, B02030539300, 0448–0454. 'The Army's Hopes Regarding Current Foreign Policies', 3 July 1938.

46 Ishiwara Kanji and Tsunoda Jun, *Ishiwara Kanji shiryō: Kokubō ron-saku hen* [Historical Materials on Ishiwara Kanji: Theories of the National Defense] (Tokyo: Hara Shobō, 1967), p. 292; Gao, *Shanghai Sanctuary*, p. 73.

47 See the rare collection held by Liaoning sheng dangan guan [The Archives of the Liaoning Province] (ed.), *Man tie mi dang: Man tie yu qin Hua Ri jun* [Secret Documents from the South Manchurian Railway Company: The South Manchurian Railway Company and the Japanese Invading Army] (Guilin: Guangxi shifan daxue chubanshe, 1999), vol. 18, pp. 303–8.

48 Inuzuka Kiyoko, *Yudaya mondai to Nihon no kōsaku*, p. 77; Yasue Hiroo, *Dairen tokumu kikan*, p. 109.

49 JACAR: B04013208300, 0282, 'Opinions Concerning the Treatment of Jewish Refugees', Consul General Miura in Shanghai to Foreign Minister Arita Hachirō, 18 April 1940.

50 JACAR: B04013205700, 0068–0072. Foreign Minister Arita Hachirō to Japanese ambassadors to Germany, the United States, and Manchukuo, and consulates in China concerning Jewish refugees, 7 December 1938.

51 AJMFA, Foreign Minister Konoe Fumimaro to consular offices in China and Manchukuo, 'Colonel Yasue's Speech at the Meeting of the Committee on the Muslim and Jewish Problem', 13 October 1938. S9460-3, 750–66.

52 JACAR: B04013210700, 0046–0047. Yasue Norihiro, 'Report on the Second Far Eastern Jewish Conference (Part Two)', 30 December 1938.

53 AJMFA, 'Joint Report of Investigation on the Jewish Issue in Shanghai', 7 July 1939. S9460-3, 1268–74.

54 AJMFA, 'Supplement to the Joint Report of Investigation on the Jewish Issue in Shanghai – Opinions of the Parties Concerned', July 1939. S9460, 1339–67.

55 AJMFA, Foreign Minister Nomura to Consul General Miura in Shanghai, 13 January 1940. S9460-3, 1686. 'Dairen Jewish Community Holds Banquet in Honor of Colonel Yasue', *Israel's Messenger*, 24 January 1941, p. 2; 'Reasons for Proposing the [New] Basic Policy toward Jews and Proposals for a [New] Basic Jewish Policy', 14 November 1940. S9460-3, 2357–61. Gao, pp. 102–3, 107–8, 111–12.

56 JACAR: B04013209400, 0099–0100. AJMFA Foreign Minister Matsuoka Yōsuke to the Japanese consular offices overseas, 10 October 1940.

57 AJMFA, No. 55876, Consul General Horiuchi in Shanghai to Foreign Minister Toyoda, 13 August 1941. S9460-3, 2497–2498. JACAR:

206 *Refugees and the stateless in Asia*

B04013209700. 0323–0324. Foreign Minister Toyoda to Consul General Horiuchi in Shanghai, 20 August 1941.

58 AJMFA, Acting Consul General Sugihara Chiune in Prague to Foreign Minister Matsuoka, 5 February 1941. S9460-3, 2410; for the list of 2,132 people to whom he issued visas, see Sugihara to Foreign Minister Matsuoka, 28 February 1941, USHMMIA, 'Exhibitions Division: Records Relating to Developing the "Flight and Rescue" Exhibition, 1998–1999', boxes 9–10, and Pamela Rotner Sakamoto, *Japanese Diplomats and Jewish Refugees: A World War II Dilemma* (Westport, CT: Praeger, 1998), p. 163.

59 JACAR: B04013208900, 0235. Foreign Minister Matsuoka to Consul Sugihara in Kaunas, 16 August 1940. JACAR: B04013208800, 0198. Consul Sugihara in Kaunas to Foreign Minister Matsuoka, 1 August 1940. The date of this cable is a mistake since Sugihara was responding to Matsuoka's telegram of 16 August 1940. Also, Sugihara's telegram of 24 August 1940 to Matsuoka was numbered 66, and this cable was numbered 67. Therefore, this cable must have been sent after 24 August 1940, not 1 August 1940.

60 AJMFA, Acting Consul General Sugihara in Prague to Foreign Minister Matsuoka, 5 February 1941. S9460-3, 2410; Sugihara to Foreign Minister Matsuoka, 28 February 1941. USHMMIA, boxes 9–10.

61 Sakamoto, p. 4.

62 See David Kranzler, *Japanese, Nazis and Jews: The Jewish Refugee Community of Shanghai, 1938–1945* (New York: Yeshiva University Press, 1976); Marcia Ristaino, *Port of Last Resort: The Diaspora Communities of Shanghai* (Stanford, CA: Stanford University Press, 2001); and Sakamoto, *Japanese Diplomats and Jewish Refugees*.

13

Statelessness, national sovereignty, and German and Austrian refugees in China during and after the treaty port era

Sara Halpern

> Naturally, most of the refugees desire that their home status as refugees be forgotten. They want to be treated on the basis of nationals with equal opportunities.[1]

A report of the American Jewish Joint Distribution Committee (JDC, the Joint) written in October 1945 drew attention to the fate of fifteen thousand Central European Jewish refugees stranded in Shanghai.[2] Nazi violence, especially in 1938, compelled them to flee as refugees to protect their dignity and their lives. They already had lost their citizenship and political rights (*Reichsbürger*) through the 1935 Nuremberg Laws. The Reich Citizenship Law demoted them to national subjects (*Staatsangehöriger*). 'The Law for Protection of German Blood and Honor' and its first supplemental decree defined Jews as a separate 'race'.[3] Ostracised, thousands of Jews fled their homes in Germany, Austria, and Czechoslovakia with the letter 'J'– stamped passports in hand. The 'J' was made mandatory in October 1938. These passports enabled over seventeen thousand adults and children to cross borders to various European ports to take ships to Shanghai. Other refugees took the Trans-Siberian Railway to Vladivostok and sailed to Shanghai via Japan. For many arrivals, entering Shanghai was not difficult, since Japanese authorities, who had replaced Chinese Nationalists as the effective power in control of the city, had removed border checks. Nevertheless, passports were necessary for obtaining local identity cards, employment, and housing.

On 25 November 1941, the Nazis promulgated what is known as the Eleventh Decree. As a supplement to the 1935 Nuremberg Laws, this new decree stripped German, Austrian, and Czech Jews

208   *Refugees and the stateless in Asia*

residing outside of the Reich of their status as *Staatsangehöriger*. This measure was explicitly designed to be a 'solution' to the 'Jewish Question', banishing Jews, including those who had emigrated, from the German nation.[4] Nearly two weeks later, the Japanese attacked Pearl Harbor and occupied all of Shanghai.

The Eleventh Decree turned a diaspora of over 250,000 Central European Jews stateless overnight. In Shanghai, the full impact of this development was not felt until September 1945 when the Allies dismantled the Nazi legal and diplomatic systems. After twenty-eight months in a 'designated area' instituted by the Japanese military, the Jewish refugees in Shanghai found themselves in a void as stateless persons at the end of the Second World War. Shanghai was now fully governed by the Nationalist government of the Republic of China (ROC); the port city was no longer shared between China and foreign powers. The Jewish refugees turned to the Shanghai office of the JDC to negotiate with the new authorities over their legal status. They feared that their freedom since Japan's surrender was under threat again.

The post-war atmosphere in Shanghai further complicated Jewish refugees' position for two reasons. First, Chinese perceptions of Jews differed from those of Europeans and Americans. In the late 1930s, a number of prominent Chinese Nationalists spoke out in favour of assistance to Jews, particularly those without citizenship. With support from several American Jews, they explored different settlement plans, which failed to materialise due to financial and diplomatic obstacles. However, after the war, their attitude changed. The Nationalists expressed reluctance to exempt Jews from their national reunification plans, which included encouraging the emigration of foreigners, particularly if they were destitute and unemployed. Their perception of Jewish refugees shifted from being victims of the territorial based nation-state system to being foreigners, who had enjoyed privileges during the treaty port era (1842–1943), characterised by foreign imperialism. This about-face unnerved the Jewish refugees.

Secondly, the Japanese takeover of Chinese administration in parts of Shanghai, including border checks, briefly opened the door to unimpeded migration into those areas from 1938 to mid-1939. Overlooked by the Japanese military authorities, the breach in control enabled thousands of Jews from Europe to enter Shanghai as

German and Austrian refugees in China   209

a port of refuge. Now, as the JDC report noted in October 1945, they were stateless with nowhere to go under a different regime. Immigration policies around the world remained severely restricted. Jewish refugees had to depend on the goodwill of the Nationalist government to be able to remain and emigrate to their desired destinations in their own time. It was particularly important to keep their options open as they had very little appetite to return to Europe and wanted a fresh start in the United States, Australia, or elsewhere.

These interrelated threads raise an important question about the meaning of statelessness in the study of the German-speaking refugee diaspora, which spanned the globe by 1940. Their statelessness was a result of state-sponsored mass denationalisation on the basis of 'race'.[5] The case of Shanghai, as a point of transit, fit well the analysis of Hannah Arendt, a German Jewish refugee herself, in her essay titled 'The Stateless People', published in *Contemporary Jewish Record* in April 1945.[6] Arendt called stateless people 'the saddest ... and the clearest sign of disintegration of European national states'. From her position in New York, she developed her ideas while observing how the growing number of stateless Jews were trapped in Central-Eastern Europe at the end of the war. Like European states, the ROC tied nationality and citizenship to either *jus sanguine* or *jus soli*.[7] Without an international legal framework for managing and protecting the stateless in a global regime of identity papers, Arendt contends, stateless people represent an anomaly.[8] Conversely, she insisted on the advantages of statelessness as an act of disassociation from former nationalities they had lost and chose not to reclaim. Repatriation was meaningless for many survivors of the war. Facing these difficulties, as we will see, Shanghai's Jewish refugees developed a strategy of buying time to secure recognition as friendly rather than enemy aliens, with rights to stay in China temporarily while they sought homes elsewhere.

Indeed, to extend their stay in China until they could emigrate of their own will, Shanghai's Jewish refugees had to depend on continued goodwill from the Nationalist government. Their advocates in the JDC Shanghai office and the Intergovernmental Committee for Refugees (IGCR) had to facilitate and maintain Chinese tolerance of the refugees' presence amid rising anti-foreigner public sentiment. Stranded in a recovering metropolis, the question of economic utility mattered as well. In the post-treaty port era, these

210   *Refugees and the stateless in Asia*

refugees competed for jobs and housing with Chinese people. Being foreign, destitute, and stateless made these non-Chinese more vulnerable under the Nationalist regime than they were during the treaty-port era.

This chapter considers how the problem of statelessness shaped the 'political life' of Shanghai's Jewish refugees and the JDC representing them. They had to develop an effective response to the attitudes and policies of Chinese authorities after the end of the war. They had to act without an international legal framework dealing with the stateless. That became available nine years later through the 1954 Geneva Convention on the Status of the Stateless. But in 1945, the meaning of the term 'statelessness' was fluid worldwide. Under these circumstances, members of the Jewish community still in Shanghai and the JDC as their diplomatic voice fashioned a position to deal with the immediate problem. They argued that they should be permitted to live temporarily in China as refugees. In China, as elsewhere, the presence of the stateless sharpened the question of 'who has the right to have rights'.

German and Austrian Jews in China the late treaty port era

When the Nuremberg Laws passed in 1935, many German Jews continued to believe that the Nazi dictatorship could not last much longer. They were proven wrong in 1938. The physical violence against Jews during *Anschluss* (Germany's annexation of Austria) in March and then the pogroms that spread across Germany and Austria in November were turning points. The Gestapo arrested upward of twenty-six thousand Jewish men and sent them to the Sachsenhausen, Buchenwald, and Dachau camps. Imprisoned men could be released on the condition that families could produce documents showing that they would leave within six weeks' time. Family members rushed to embassies and consulates to line up for a visa anywhere to get their relatives out of camps. A rumor spread rapidly: right now, one did not need an entry visa for Shanghai and no one questioned why.

The rumor was partly true. The Battle of Shanghai between Chinese and Japanese forces from August to November 1937 ended with Japan's occupation of the Chinese-controlled sections of the

German and Austrian refugees in China 211

city. This enabled them to take over administrative powers including border control. The ROC government required visas from all foreigners, but granted them to those with extraterritorial rights out of courtesy. Everyone else, including earlier waves of Jewish emigrants from Germany, had to apply for permission to enter Shanghai. But by 1938, neither the Japanese, nor the Chinese, nor the British-led Shanghai Municipal Council (SMC) operated border checks. For the British, staying neutral in the Sino–Japanese conflict came first.[9]

Jewish emigrants from Germany, Austria, and Czechoslovakia joined an already-existing German-speaking Jewish refugee community. They vastly outnumbered the Baghdadi Jewish population of one thousand and Russian (Ashkenazi) population of around six thousand. Though small in size compared to the British population of fifty thousand and over three million Chinese residents, the influx of German-speaking Jews did not go unnoticed. Western consular officials, including German residents, complained about it, fearing that the enlarged Jewish presence would harm their economic interests and the business of the medical profession.[10] Local Jewish communities feared that the needs of the impoverished arrivals would outstrip their resources. The newly created Committee for the Assistance of European Jewish Refugees in Shanghai (CAEJR) quickly contacted the JDC headquarters in New York and other Jewish relief organisations in Europe to send additional funds to feed and shelter the newcomers.

The Japanese faced a set of difficult choices. They controlled areas once under Chinese authority, including parts of Hongkou, where many refugees found lodging with cheap rent and where the Jewish relief committee had set up refugee camps. While the SMC debated policies to block Jewish immigration to the International Settlement, Japan walked a fine line between not provoking anger from its military ally Germany and upsetting diplomatic and financial ties with the United States and world Jewry. Japan also maintained its commitment to racial equality, further complicating her diplomatic stance.[11]

The pressure from other consular officials and from the resident Japanese community mounted as more and more Jewish refugees arrived in the spring of 1939 and sought local employment and housing. By June 1939, a plan to stop Jewish immigration to Shanghai went to Tokyo; it was approved, and applauded

212   *Refugees and the stateless in Asia*

by Germany.[12] Soon, the SMC and the French restricted entry of Jews into their respective areas, the International Settlement and the French Concession. They exempted those with applications for entry permits for relatives of Jewish refugees already in Shanghai, those with an employment contract, or those who could pay US$400.[13]

Several Nationalists saw a golden opportunity to offer succor to Jewish refugees seeking to leave Europe. Drawing on misguided antisemitic tropes of Jews as wealthy and politically powerful, these sympathetic bureaucrats considered the possibility of utilising the presence of Jewish emigrants in their efforts to secure financial support from the United States and Britain in their fight against Japan.[14]

The president of the Legislative Yuan, Sun Ke, saw a chance to help Jews, including those from Germany, find a new home and for China to benefit from their 'strong financial background and many talents' in its state-building projects. He envisioned a Jewish colony as a means of offering 'these people ... without a country [who had] for more than 2600 years ... moved about homeless' a place free from 'oppression'. Sun-Ke viewed Jews as people 'who have absolutely no way of returning' to anywhere they'd been forced to leave due to persecution. He turned to his ministries for comments and approval.[15]

Sun-Ke encountered a mix of support and skepticism from his ministerial colleagues. Kong Xianghxi was the vice president of the Executive Yuan and the Minister of Finance. He believed that Jews 'who are citizens of some state maintain their rights and duties as citizens of their original country'. He insisted that these Jewish citizens should follow procedures for entry into China like other citizens. Aware of the situation in Nazi Germany, he suggested waiving taxes on the property of Jewish refugees from Germany, since these people had been 'oppressed'.[16]

Kong Xianghxi considered Jews 'without citizenship' to be under 'special circumstances'. While Sun Yat-sen argued that China must always maintain its humanitarian principles, Kong Xianghxi reasoned that given the 'complex' situation of the Jewish diaspora, conditions should be set for their settlement with support from the League of Nations. First, Jews without citizenship should seek documentation confirming their statelessness from the League of Nations and get passports and visas from overseas Chinese consulates. Unlike Jews with citizenship, the stateless Jews would have to

German and Austrian refugees in China 213

follow Chinese laws and court orders. This entry was also conditioned on them promising not to 'engage in any political activity or disseminate any ideology or criticize or oppose Sun Yat-sen's Three Principles of the People, namely nationalism, democracy, and livelihood'. Upon arriving in China, Jews should not live among the Chinese until they received Chinese citizenship. Once they became citizens, they could live anywhere they wished. The government would work with the League of Nations to discuss ways Jews with skills relating to economic development could be employed, and other ways to help the destitute.[17]

For Kong Xianghxi, careful management of this particular group of stateless foreigners was a necessary step towards maintaining Chinese self-determination in areas outside of the treaty ports. He also considered China's international standing as a modern state. China's views on statelessness aligned with much of the international community. The 1929 Nationality Act was the most important reform for naturalisation and citizenship since ROC's founding in 1912. Specifically, Article 3 laid out the following conditions for naturalising foreigners without citizenship: uninterrupted residency in China for five years; being over twenty years old; being of good character; having 'sufficient property or skills and abilities to enable him (or her) to make an independent living'.[18] Under Sun Ke's plan, the Jewish refugees would no longer be stateless after five years as they would already fit other requirements.

Such an idea had its limits, in particular the notion of sociocultural interactions between the traditional Chinese society and foreigners. The Ministries of the Interior and Foreign Affairs (MOFA) offered the strongest opinions on what should be done, pressing for a settlement near international ports or near Burma, a British colony, rather than in the interior.[19] Even if the stateless Jews obtained Chinese citizenship, the Ministry of Interior urged that Jews remain in the 'open settlement areas'.[20] The MOFA took a judicial approach by suggesting that only the stateless Jews should live within the settlements; there Chinese laws would apply.

Naturalising Jews posed too much of a diplomatic risk. For example, the Chinese worried about possible diplomatic intervention from Germany, should the Chinese accept Jewish refugees from there. Although Germany had lost its extraterritorial rights in 1919, its diplomatic ties meant that Germany's views mattered. This

214   *Refugees and the stateless in Asia*

meant that accepting German Jews' right to asylum was a controversial step. Given that Germany had recalled its ambassador a year before, German views could not simply be ignored.[21] Through the framework of the 1929 Nationality Act, both ministries concluded that a small and remote settlement of stateless Jews would be good for China's economic development.[22]

At the same time, the secretary general of the Central Political Council, Zhu Jiahua, noted that 'If we require Jews to change to [Chinese] nationality, they must abandon their German nationality first. Germany might not be willing to allow ... Jews to give up their German nationality in order to emigrate to China.'[23] As early as July 1933, Germany had stripped German nationality from over sixteen thousand naturalised Eastern European Jews. Given the political, economic, social, emotional, and cultural significance of nationality and the history of Jewish campaigns for citizenship throughout Europe, Jewish citizens would not consider voluntary denaturalisation.

Sun Ke's and other resettlement plans failed to materialise as the war against Japan intensified and drained resources. After the German invasion of Poland in 1939, the issue of Jewish statelessness took on even greater urgency.

In this context, Chinese politics played a role in Jewish survival in China. Military and diplomatic entanglements with Germany, Japan, Britain, and the United States tested China's ability to act as a humanitarian agent with its resettlement plans. Like their partners, the Nationalists participated in the international regime of border management through passports and a shared negative attitude toward statelessness. Their beliefs about Jewish power and their need for cash to support their war against Japan further complicated their relationship with the Nazi regime. To walk the line, as Gao Bei has shown, the Chinese Nationalists maintained a 'liberal visa policy' as they reviewed various resettlement plans in hopes of meeting their eventual goal of soliciting necessary financial support from the United States, Britain, and their Jews in their war effort. The Chinese consular officers throughout Europe 'faithfully obeyed the order and granted Jewish refugees visas to Shanghai' until all escape routes from Europe closed in the summer of 1941.[24] Granting visas to Jewish citizens meant that they would become someone else's problem in Shanghai and other treaty ports. Unbeknownst to the Nationalists, this situation would reverse itself after the war.

German and Austrian refugees in China 215

Defining Jews as foreigners in the post-treaty port era

The Nationalists in the treaty port era made little distinction between the refugee and the foreigner when it came to Shanghai's Jewish population.[25] To the Nationalists in the post-treaty port era, refugees meant millions of displaced Chinese within China who needed assistance returning to their homes there or in Southeast Asia; foreigners meant everyone else. Thus, the Jewish refugees in Shanghai found themselves treated as *foreigners*, and no longer as refugees. Though stateless at this point, the Jews remained first and foremost foreigners in China.

The United Nations Relief and Rehabilitation Administration (UNRRA) and the IGCR – charged with refugee management – could insist on the right of asylum for Shanghai's Jewish refugees. Enforcing such a claim, however, would require violating China's sovereignty. As Arendt noted, the refugees' right of asylum violated the sovereignty each national state guaranteed to other states. The ROC was a member of UNRRA but not of IGCR. Created after the Évian Conference, the US and British-led IGCR elected not to invite countries at war, which included China and Japan.[26] Now in the post-war moment, the IGCR had to consider how best to approach the Nationalist government to assist Shanghai's Jewish refugees.

In October 1945, the JDC was alarmed by antisemitic headlines in the Chinese press. Everyone, though, was unprepared for a new decree published in the press two months later.

The Promulgation ordered internment and deportations of 'Germans, former Austrians, and German Jews'. In the inclusion of 'German Jews', the Promulgation suggested that the Jewish refugees should leave on the basis of their former German nationality. Despite having been persecuted by the Nazis and forced into a 'ghetto' in Shanghai for twenty-eight months by the Japanese, they did not have the same standing as the Chinese as victims of the war. They were not victims; they were foreigners.

Manny Siegel of the JDC was already worried about the possibility of discrimination against Shanghai's Jewish refugees. By October 1945, he cabled the IGCR for assistance in lobbying on behalf of German Jews to be recognised as 'friendly', and not 'enemy'.[27] Having already dealt with the expulsion of German Jewish refugees from France and Belgium, for example, the director of the IGCR,

216   *Refugees and the stateless in Asia*

H. M. Emerson, was hardly surprised to hear from Siegel about this matter.[28]

With China's status as a non-IGCR member and difficulties in Western Europe on his mind, Emerson considered the question of Jewish refugees' legal status in China. In his correspondence with the Chinese embassy in London, Emerson explained the IGCR's purpose and concerns with stateless 'European refugees' in Shanghai. By choosing the term 'stateless' rather than 'ex-enemy nationals', Emerson was acknowledging the true legal reality of the Jewish refugees in Shanghai. To be stateless, Emerson warned, meant that these people would not be able to hold assets, to cross borders, and to help strengthen the Chinese economy, rights that Chinese nationals already enjoyed. Emerson enquired how the ROC viewed the 'European refugees' and expressed his hope that they would be recognised as 'friendly nationals', not 'ex-enemy nationals'. He also reminded them that Jews were the first victims of Nazi persecution. At the same time, he acknowledged the importance of respecting China's national sovereignty.[29]

On 8 November 1945, the Chinese embassy replied. Indirectly ignoring Emerson's concerns, they stressed the importance of respecting national sovereignty. They asked to be given the same freedom as Britain enjoyed in the way it treated refugees. The reference to Britain was a reminder of how the British had exploited their extraterritorial rights to flout Chinese laws.[30] Upon reading this reply, Emerson knew he had to send someone to China.

The next month, the Promulgation of 27 November 1945 appeared in German and English language newspapers in Shanghai; it spelled out that

> Germans, former Austrians and German Jews in recovered and free China who did not commit any of the offenses [such as collaboration with the Japanese] shall be repatriated unless the Ministries of the Interior and Foreign Affairs sanction their further stay in China.[31]

In addition, such persons could ask their employers and the city for permission to remain longer. Otherwise, lacking legal protection, these groups were to be interned or deported.[32] The decree appeared to be the first step toward direct expulsion of foreigners from China.[33] This mirrored what Emerson had already seen in Europe, namely the expulsion of German Jews after the war.

German and Austrian refugees in China   217

The Promulgation confused and angered the Jewish refugees and put them in a vulnerable position. They rejected being categorised with Germans and 'former Austrians' slated for internment and deportations. As the editor wrote in *Die Neue Zeit*, a German-language Jewish paper in Shanghai, no one wanted to believe that 'the democratic minded and hospitable Chinese people, a people that until recently had been itself a victim of ruthless agression [*sic*] would consent to any measures discriminating against other victims of cruel persecution'.[34] For Shanghai's German Jews, a pragmatic approach was their only option. They worked for time and clarification of their position.[35]

An interview with the head of the Shanghai Office of the Ministry of Foreign Affairs, Chen Kuo-lien, in the *Shanghai Herald*, then republished in the *Shanghai Echo*, aggravated the situation. Chen Kuo-lien claimed that Jews 'were smuggled' into Shanghai when the 'National government was not in a situation to exert [its] sovereignty rights in the city'. He added that while his government intended to be lenient toward the 'unfortunate Jews', it expected them to repatriate now that Nazi Germany was defeated.[36]

The best way forward was to buy time. Moses Beckelman, Assistant Director of IGCR, and later director-general of the JDC, arrived in Shanghai on 17 January 1946. On the same day, the Jewish refugees published a petition. They first urged the ROC government to accept the Allies' policy in Europe 'that Jewish and other bona fide refugees from Axis countries be regarded as friendly, liberated peoples – to be distinguished from Axis nationals who maintained allegiance to Axis states'. Secondly, they asked the Nationalists to uphold Article 10(3) of the United Nations constitution: 'Promoting and encouraging respect for human rights and for fundamental freedoms for all without distinction as to race, sex, language, or religion'. Finally, the refugees asked not to be forcibly repatriated and to be left free to explore emigration possibilities. Alluding to their statelessness, they reminded readers that they 'have no great sovereign power to represent our cause and to guarantee our rights'.[37] Stateless people, they argued, should have the right to have rights, including protection from forced internment and deportation.

When Beckelman arrived in Hongkou, the Jewish refugees crowded around him to update him on their affairs. They demanded IGCR's protection until they could sort out their emigration plans.

218   *Refugees and the stateless in Asia*

Next, Beckelman met with the local bureaucrats, including Chen Kuo-lien, who merely reiterated his prior statements. In conversations with other officials in the MOFA Shanghai office and the Shanghai Municipal Government, Beckelman realised that none of the authorities had specific instructions from the state on how to proceed. They repeated the importance of Chinese national reunification and belonging and suggested that they meant to be 'generous' in their interpretation of the Promulgation.[38] In his update to his boss, Emerson, Beckelman reflected on current geopolitics and how the Nationalist government was attempting to repatriate their Overseas Chinese to Southeast Asia, where Britain, France, and the United States held colonies. He surmised that the 'German Jews' were being used as a 'bargaining chip' somehow. Beckelman saw no other motives for the Promulgation's inclusion of 'German Jews'; the local authorities clearly differentiated the Jewish refugees from other Europeans in private.[39]

Beckelman heard of other incidents of discrimination where the Promulgation was invoked. For example, the new director of the JDC Shanghai office, Charles H. Jordan, accused the city housing authorities of abusing the Promulgation's classification of Jewish refugees as 'ex-enemy nationals' to refuse Jewish claims to live in properties confiscated by the Japanese. These allegations were somewhat tempered by the fact that a number of other foreigners, not just those labeled 'ex-enemy nationals', faced this difficulty as well.[40] Some refugees also struggled to find employment because Chinese employers did not want to hire 'ex-enemy aliens'. Facing this type of discrimination convinced the Jewish refugees that they had, in Jordan's words, 'lost their status'.[41] These issues compelled Beckelman to fly to Chongqing to meet with the MOFA in early February 1946.[42]

Upon his arrival, he found that the MOFA had other ideas. While reassuring him that Jewish refugees would not be harmed or interned, the MOFA said that it expected them not to seek permanent residency in China or seek financial support for survival, specifically from public funds. The MOFA 'regretted' instigating 'false fears' but insisted that, instead of their issuing a public apology, the IGCR would make a public statement of agreement.[43]

This proposal infuriated Beckelman. Privately, he felt the IGCR had been disrespected. The Promulgation had been planned and

German and Austrian refugees in China 219

publicised by the Chinese government. They must have known it would cause harm, or at the very least, incite fear among the Jewish refugees. Recognising the MOFA's unwillingness to compromise for fear of tarnishing its global public image, Beckelman ultimately conceded in the interest of the refugees. Together, the MOFA and Beckelman drafted a statement that appeared in Shanghai papers and the *New York Times*.[44]

These same MOFA officials agreed to recognise Shanghai's Jewish refugees as '*bona fide* refugees' rather than ex-enemy nationals, and introduced a process for Jews to stay in China. In their translated notarised letter to Beckelman after their meeting, the MOFA outlined expectations for 'German and Austrian refugees'. In the Promulgation, 'German Jews' meant 'Jews of German and Austrian citizenship'. With all the German and Austrian Jews in Shanghai being stateless, they would be considered as 'refugees'. The MOFA outlined various options for these stateless people to remain in China, including legal protections allowing refugees to be employed and to rent housing, and the right to apply for Chinese nationality after five years of continuous residency.[45] In March 1946, the Chinese National Relief and Rehabilitation Administration (CNRRA) published an announcement in the newspapers that offered the right to work, to rent housing, and to hold assets to 'all refugees from Germany and Austria who have been registered with UNRRA', thereby making their remaining in China in the short term a bit more secure.[46] The pragmatism of the Joint and its diplomacy had bought the time the refugees needed to find a home elsewhere.

Conclusion

This chapter demonstrates the accuracy of Hannah Arendt's 1945 essay on the stateless when applied to the plight of German and Austrian Jews in China at the end of the Second World War. They too faced what Arendt took to be the central question: 'how can the refugee be made deportable again?' And they too discovered that 'the whole point of giving refugees legal status is to make them deportable'.[47]

Moreover, we have seen that China's post-war attitude and behavior was very similar to those of European countries previously

220 *Refugees and the stateless in Asia*

under occupation. Statelessness and refugeedom went hand-in-hand because there had yet been a clear internationally agreed legal framework. The presence of stateless Jewish refugees from ex-enemy countries presented the ROC government with the challenge of answering the question 'who has the right to have rights?' Obtaining a right to housing and to work under CNRRA's authority signified a victory for this group of stateless people in China; the White Russian community in Shanghai did not have such a privilege, if only because China and the Soviet Union were allies. White Russian foreigners had to go as well.

In the immediate aftermath of the war, the Nationalists focused first and foremost on their own grievances, especially the loss of Chinese sovereignty over its own territory. This concern eclipsed Chinese sympathy for Jews and their oppression in Europe. Instead, Jewish refugees were painted as foreigners, and their statelessness positioned them as easy targets for abuse.

More broadly, this chapter highlights the importance of focusing on the period 1945–54, that is, prior to the adoption of the 1954 Convention Relating to the Status of Stateless People. While work has been done in the European context, the Shanghai case reflects the globality of statelessness and decolonisation and discloses the degree to which perceptions of victimhood shaped different national discourses about refugees and their rights. Shanghai in 1946 showed how long would be the struggle, in Arendt's words, 'somehow or other', to restore to the stateless 'the inalienable rights of man'.[48]

Notes

1 Henrietta Buchman to Hyman Kaplan, letter, 8 October 1945, JDC Archives (AJJDCA), New York Office Collection (NYO) 1933–1944, Folder 464, File 1067.
2 Ibid.
3 'Gesetz Über Den Widerruf von Einbürgerungen Und Die Uberfennung Der Deutschen Staatsangehörigkeit, Vom 14. Juli 1933', *ÖNB-ALEX – Deutsches Reichsgesetzblatt Teil I 1867–1945*, https://alex.onb.ac.at/cgi-content/alex?aid=dra&datum=1933&page=605&size=45. Accessed 30 June 2023.

German and Austrian refugees in China   221

4 See §3(2) of The Eleventh Decree. 'Elfte Verordnung zum Reichsbürgergegesetz, vom 25 November 1941', *ÖNB-ALEX – Deutsches Reichsgesetzblatt Teil I 1867–1945*, https://alex.onb.ac.at/cgi-content/alex?aid=dra&datum=1941&page=750&size=45. Accessed 29 May 2023.

5 On denaturalisation, see Martin Dean, 'The Development and Implementation of Nazi Denaturalization and Confiscation Policy up to the Eleventh Decree to the Reich Citizenship Law', *Holocaust and Genocide Studies*, 20, 2 (2002), pp. 218–24.

6 Hannah Arendt, 'The Stateless People', *Contemporary Jewish Record*, 8, 2 (April 1945), pp. 137–53.

7 Hungdah Chiu, *Nationality and International Law in Chinese Perspective*, Occasional Papers/Reprints Series in Contemporary Asian Studies, 3, 98 (1990) (Baltimore, MD: School of Law, University of Maryland, 1990), p. 8.

8 Arendt, 'The Stateless People', p. 149.

9 Avraham Altman and Irene Eber, 'Flight to Shanghai, 1938–1940: The Larger Setting', *Yad Vashem Studies*, 28 (2000), pp. 61–3.

10 Steve Hochstadt, 'Japanese and Jews in Shanghai', *Modern Judaism – A Journal of Jewish Ideas and Experience*, 42, 3 (7 October 2022), pp. 215.

11 Hochstadt, 'Japanese and Jews', pp. 213–14.

12 See Altman and Eber, 'Flight to Shanghai', pp. 58–60.

13 Hochstadt, 'Japanese and Jews', p. 217.

14 Gao Bei, 'The Chinese Nationalist Government's Policy toward European Jewish Refugees during World War II', *Modern China*, 37, 2 (March 2011), pp. 210–29, and Chapter 11 in this volume.

15 'Document 26: 1. Official Dispatch of the National Defense Supreme Council to the National Government's Civil Affairs Office (March 7, 1939)', in Irene Eber (ed.), *Jewish Refugees in Shanghai 1933–1947: A Selection of Documents*, Archiv Jüdischer Geschichte Und Kultur, Band 3 (Göttingen: Vandenhoeck & Ruprecht, 2018), pp. 123–5.

16 'Document 26: 3. A Statement from Kong Xiangxi to the Nationalist Government (April 22, 1939)', in Eber (ed.), *Jewish Refugees*, p. 132.

17 'Document 26: 3. A Statement from Kong Xiangxi to the Nationalist Government (April 22, 1939)', in Eber (ed.), *Jewish Refugees*, pp. 127–9.

18 Chiu, *Nationality*, pp. 16–17.

19 Eber (ed.), *Jewish Refugees*, pp. 131–2.

20 'Document 26: 3. A Statement from Kong Xiangxi to the Nationalist Government (April 22, 1939)', in Eber (ed.), *Jewish Refugees*, p. 129.

222   *Refugees and the stateless in Asia*

21 Arendt, 'The Stateless People', p. 139. Gao Bei, 'The Chinese Nationalist Government', p. 208.

22 'Document 26: 3. A Statement from Kong Xiangxi to the Nationalist Government (April 22, 1939)', in Eber (ed.), *Jewish Refugees*, pp. 130–1.

23 Quoted in Gao Bei, 'The Chinese Nationalist Government', p. 213.

24 Bei, 'The Chinese Nationalist Government', p. 227.

25 Note the distinction between the refugee and the foreigner in Arendt, 'The Stateless People', p. 139.

26 See 'Confidential Memo to an American Delegate', confidential memo, undated, Franklin D. Roosevelt Library and Archives (FDRLA), Myron C. Taylor Papers, Box 3, Folder 'September 1938–December 1938 and undated'. On China's exclusion, see Tommie Sjöberg, *The Powers and the Persecuted: The Refugee Problem and the Intergovernmental Committee on Refugees (IGCR), 1938–1947* (Lund: Lund University Press, 1991), pp. 143–5.

27 Josselyn to Department of State, cable, 12 October 1945, AJJDCA, NYO 1933–1944, Folder 464, 1097; Manuel Siegel to Moses A. Leavitt, letter, 4 November 1945, AJJDCA, NYO 1933–1944, Folder 464, Files 1138-1139; JOINTDISCO to JOINTFUND, cable, 17 October 1945, AJJDCA 1933–1944, Folder 464, File 1062.

28 David Fraser and Frank Caestecker, 'Jews or Germans? Nationality Legislation and the Restoration of Liberal Democracy in Western Europe after the Holocaust', *American Society for Legal History*, 11, 2 (May 2013), pp. 391–422.

29 H. M. Emerson to His Excellency, letter, 26 October 1945, Archives Unbound (AU), National Archives and Records Administration (NARA), Records of the Intergovernmental Committee on Refugees, 1938–47, Intergovernmental Committee, Folder 1 of 4. MS Intergovernmental Committee on Refugees. National Archives (United States). Cited from Archives Unbound, link.gale.com/apps/doc/SC5100421131/GDSC ?u=wash13709&sid=bookmark-GDSC&xid=7b86c489&pg=39. Accessed 26 November 2024.

30 Wellington Koo to H. M. Emerson, letter, 8 November 1945, United States Holocaust Memorial Museum Archives (USHMMA), RG-68.066M, Selected Records from the American Jewish Joint Distribution Committee (AJJDC) Archives, Jerusalem, Reel 46, GIII/ L24/430/745.

31 'China Acts Against Germans', *North China Daily News*, 17 December 1945, United Nations Archives (UNA), UNRRA, S-0528-0035/ S1121/118. See also Williams, Clarke, Trevithick, and Soorma to Fred K. Hoehler, 7 December 1945, UNA, UNRRA, S-0520-0203/S1253/139.

German and Austrian refugees in China 223

32 US Consulate Shanghai to JDC New York Headquarters, cable, 19 December 1945, AJJDCA, NYO 1933–1944, Folder 464, File 1010.

33 Donald G. Gillin and Charles Etter, 'Staying On: Japanese Soldiers and Civilians in China, 1945–1949', *Journal of Asian Studies*, 42, 3 (May 1983), pp. 497–518.

34 Heinz Ganther, 'Open Questions', *Die Neue Zeit*, 18 December 1945, in AJJDCA, NYO 1933–1944, Folder 464, File 1011–12.

35 Alvin I. Fine to the World Jewish Congress, letter, 20 December 1945, American Jewish Archives (AJA), World Jewish Congress Collection (WJCC), Box H88, Folder 7; Alvin I. Fine, note, undated, UNA, UNRRA, S-0528-, 0035/S1121/118.

36 'Unsere Neue Situation [Our New Situation]', *Shanghai Echo*, 1, 1 (30 December 1945), p. 2.

37 'PETITION: an das Ministerium des Aeusseren in China [Petition: To the Ministry of Foreign Affairs in China]', *Shanghai Journal, Die Neue Zeit*, 12 (17 January 1946), p. 1.

38 Moses Beckelman to Hungerford B. Howard, letter, n.d., AJJDCA, NYO 1933–1944, Folder 465, Files 1373–1374; Moses Beckelman to H. M. Emerson, letter, 27 March 1946, USHMMA, RG-68.066M, AJJDC Archives, Reel 46, GIII/L24/430/743; Moses Beckelman to H. M. Emerson, letter, 27 January 1946, AJJDCA, NYO 1933–1944, Folder 465, File 1372.

39 Moses Beckelman to H. M. Emerson, letter, 27 January 1946, JDCA, NYO 1933–1944, Folder 465, File 1372. See Oyen, 'The Right of Return', pp. 546–71.

40 Moses Beckelman to Hungerford B. Howard, letter, n.d., JDCA, NYO 1933–1944, Folder 465, Files 1373–1374.

41 Charles H. Jordan to Moses A. Leavitt, report, 21 January 1946, JDCA, NYO 1933–1944, Folder 465, Files 1362–1366.

42 Moses Beckelman to H. M. Emerson, letter, 27 March 1946, USHMMA, RG-68.066M, AJJDC Archives, Reel 46, GIII/L24/430/743.

43 Ibid.

44 Ibid. 'Shanghai Relaxes Refugee Control: China Said to Extend Shelter Privileges to Bona Fide Exiles from Europe Leniency is Promised Japanese Instituted Ghetto', *New York Times*, 9 March 1946, p. 7.

45 Ministry of Foreign Affairs to Intergovernmental Committee for Refugees, letter, 8 March 1946, USHMMA, RG-68.066M, AJJDC Archives, Reel 46, GIII/L24/430/731–732.

46 Division of Administrative Services, Communications Branch, cable, 28 February 1946, UNA, UNRRA, S-0520-202/S1253/134.

47 Arendt, 'The Stateless People', pp. 149, 152.

48 Ibid., p. 153.

14

A moveable feast: the Mir Yeshiva from Vilna to Shanghai and beyond

Jay Winter

This chapter is a commentary on this photograph (Figure 14.1). It shows the members of a Yeshiva,[1] a Jewish academy of higher education, where unmarried men come together for the intensive study of the rabbinic commentaries on the Torah collectively known as the Talmud.[2] Their sole focus is on the text of the Talmud, its interpretation, and its consequences for Jewish law and practice. Students start in a Yeshiva in their teens and live together until they marry. Not all Yeshivot were or are residential. Those who teach in them are usually married, and their families and other staff form part of a unique community of learning with a shared way of life.

What is unusual about this photograph is that it shows all the members of one such Yeshiva in Shanghai in 1942. The word 'Yeshiva' means 'sitting down' in Hebrew. The study of the Talmud is difficult and time-consuming. Old and young learn the Talmud together, some moving rhythmically while perched over their bookstands.

What we see is the only East European religious academy of its kind to survive the Holocaust intact. Individuals from other Yeshivot in Eastern Europe made it through the fire, but only the Mir Yeshiva survived as a collective. They were joined by isolated members of other Yeshivot, but the majority of these students and rabbis had been together for years. Looking out at us from this photograph, they might well have thought that they were the last Yeshiva, the last collective survivors of an entire world of Talmud study centred on Lithuania and Poland. In fact, many individuals and groups of Yeshiva students found ways to escape the Holocaust. The Mir was

Figure 14.1 Students and teachers of the exiled Mir Yeshiva studying in the Sanctuary of the Beth Aharon Synagogue, Museum Road, Shanghai. 1942. Courtesy of Rabbi Jacob Ederman. United States Holocaust Memorial Museum, photo no. 40211.

the only Yeshiva to live through the Second World War and to survive as a collective.

The Mir had been one of the most celebrated Yeshivot in Eastern Europe. Founded in the early nineteenth century in what is now Byelorussia, the Mir Yeshiva quickly developed a reputation as a centre of Torah scholarship. Strictly Orthodox, and imbued with a tendency to view the modern world of nationalism, socialism, and Zionism as corrupt, the Yeshiva's leaders offered an alternative, one drawn from traditional Jewish practices and texts. While rejecting secular teachings, they privileged learning of religious texts as a way of life, and formed a recognised part of the Jewish world in the late-nineteenth-century and early-twentieth-century Pale of settlement.

Mir was celebrated internationally as a major centre of Jewish scholarship among what were termed the Lithuanian Yeshivot.[3] There were other Yeshivot known as centres of scholarship – Slobodka and Telz in Lithuania, Velozhin and Klesk in Byelorussia. They were rigorous schools of law, privileging erudition and legal reasoning on a dazzling variety of topics and themes touching on every facet of Jewish life.

226   *Refugees and the stateless in Asia*

The Mir Yeshiva was at the heart of this transnational world of Jewish scholarship. In the early twentieth century, the leadership of the Yeshiva resolved an earlier dispute as to whether to continue solely to study Torah and Talmud or to adopt the perspective of what was called the 'Mussar movement', which emphasised the study of ethics and introspection as a way of building character and a moral outlook. The advocates of 'Mussar' won the argument, and their views spread quickly to other Yeshivot.[4] This approach began in the Slabodka Yeshiva in Lithuania and spread from there to Mir.

Remarkably, this community found a way to continue its collective life throughout the Second World War. How did they do it?

From war to war

During the First World War, and to escape the fighting, the Yeshiva moved to Poltava, near Kharkov in the East of Ukraine. In 1921, at the end of the Russian civil war, the Yeshiva returned to Mir, one hundred kilometres Southwest of Minsk, capital of the Byelorussian Soviet Socialist Republic. Mir now was within the borders of the new Polish Republic, and entered what observers termed the 'golden years' of the Yeshiva's mission. Students came to Mir from all over the world. By 1939, there were approximately five hundred men of various ages affiliated to the Yeshiva.

After years of study, more than a few members of this tightly bound community ran Yeshivot of their own. Former members of the Mir Yeshiva had a unique *cachet* in the orthodox Jewish world. Most students were in their twenties or thirties and intended to leave the Yeshiva, to marry and to raise families. The only women living in these tight communities were the wives and children of the rabbis in charge of the Yeshiva and attendant staff. Together they formed a large and vigorous collective, fully conscious of its singularity.

We can appreciate the special atmosphere of Torah scholarship at Mir from the letters sent home to Alsace in 1938 by a young French rabbinical student, Ernest Gugenheim. From his early years, Gugenheim stood out as talented. Failing to obtain a visa to go to Palestine, he was sent to study at the Mir Yeshiva, the jewel in the crown of the Lithuanian school of advanced Torah and Talmudic

A moveable feast 227

scholarship. He went home in 1939, joined the French army, and spent the war in a German prisoner of war camp. After the war, he rose to the rank of Chief Rabbi of Paris.

Lithuanian in this context meant in the vicinity of the capital city of Kovno or of Vilna, part of Poland from 1918 to 1939. This city was a culturally rich cosmopolitan world. Polish poet Czeslaw Milosz wrote movingly of his native town.[5] So did Romain Gary, born Roman Kacew, in Vilna in 1914.[6]

Virtually all of the great Yeshivot were not in Vilna. They were located in a wide arc stretching from what is now Eastern Poland to Belarus, but a number of its most distinguished leaders and teachers lived in and around Vilna and Kovno. One such eminent rabbi was Chaim Ozer Grodzinsky, who from 1887 served as *Dayan* or religious judge in Vilnius. He was also a founder of the ultra-Orthodox anti-Zionist group *Agudat Israel*, and co-founder and head of the *Va'ad Hayeshivot*, the Yeshiva Council, based in Vilna, which provided financial support for Yeshivot throughout Lithuania, Poland, and beyond. We will hear more about him in a moment.

What were known as the Lithuanian Yeshivot were defined not by where they were based but by their approach. They emphasised law and legal interpretation as the foundation of Jewish life and tradition.[7] Further to the South, a second school of Yeshivot emerged. What were called 'Hassidic' Yeshivot also were Talmudic academies, but they focused as well on Kabbalah and the mystical tradition. Hassidic Yeshivot shared many features of the Lithuanian Yeshivot. Flourishing among poor communities in Galicia, in present-day Ukraine, the Hassidim found in the telling of tales and in popular culture the spirit and essence of orthodox Jewish life. It would be too sharp a distinction to describe the Lithuanian world as focusing solely on reason, law, and logic and to separate it from the Hassidic world of emotion, joy, and mysticism, but such a contrast has more than a grain of truth in it. Many Hassidic rabbis were charismatic, and some of their followers endowed their venerated *rebbis* (rabbis in Yiddish) with magical powers. The authority of Lithuanian rabbis was legendary too, but it arose less from charisma and more from decades of study of the sacred texts.

Both the Lithuanian and the Galician Yeshivot relied on charity to pay their upkeep. Financial aid from abroad was an important way these Yeshivot survived. By the early twentieth century, prosperous North Americans, many of whom did not live Orthodox Jewish lives, generously supported their brethren in Eastern Europe and in Palestine.

The life of a Yeshiva student was bounded by the collective. To study the Torah and the Talmudic commentaries was the business of groups of men, young and old, living together and working together to master a vast field of Jewish learning. In the 1930s, there were between two hundred and three hundred students in the Mir Yeshiva, perhaps 150 of whom were neither Polish nor Lithuanian, like Gugenheim. Their rabbis were formidable figures, held in very high esteem. Their Talmudic judgments were final, and only a few followed in Grodzinsky's footsteps as revered judges of community and personal affairs. Just below the head of the Yeshiva were spiritual advisors (*Mashgichim*), administrators, and teachers, who dealt with discipline and the organisation of domestic life and were important carriers of the message that Yeshivot were unique centres of learning and living.[8]

The regime of work in the Mir Yeshiva was demanding, normally entailing at least nine hours of study a day. Here is Ernest Gugenheim's daily schedule:

8am: Morning prayers
9:15am: Breakfast
10am–1pm: First study period
1pm–3pm: Group study with the rabbi
3pm–5pm: Afternoon prayer and lunch
5pm–8pm: Second study period, in pairs or larger groups (Havruta)
8pm–9pm: Dinner
9pm: Study of Mussar or ethics
10pm: Evening prayers[9]

Learning laced with fervour was the signature of the Lithuanian yeshivot. When Gugenheim first joined in prayers, and heard the members of the Yeshiva intoning the Jewish credo, 'Shema Yisrael', he thought the shouts of his brethren would bring the roof down. Here is how he tried to convey to his French family the emotional atmosphere of the Mir Yeshiva:

A moveable feast   229

Imagine a room half the size of the Bibliothèque Saint-Geneviève during its great days. There is constant movement; heads bow and move with particular force; desks, movable, dance; different languages circulate; there are cries, chants, fragments of words. It is impossible to resist this magnetic enthusiasm that captures you. This is the atmosphere of my world here; it is but one room and at the same time it encompasses the whole world; this is the Mir Yeshiva, where truth reigns.[10]

This account may be that of an outsider prone to exaggeration, but it gives us a sense of the collective. There is a kind of asceticism in this world, one in which the belief that man was created in order to study Torah was expressed in such a way as to reduce the rest of life to an appendage. Secular study was non-existent. And yet the Mir Yeshiva gestured towards the world at large by requiring students to end their long days of study with meditation on questions of ethics and honourable behaviour in all facets of daily life.

There was, Gugenheim wrote his parents, no discussion of Zionism, since they were there to study Torah and only Torah.[11] Here Ernest was touching on an issue which divided these ultra-Orthodox communities. Most rejected Zionism, as reducing to secular politics a divine project of the return of the Jewish people to what they saw as their land. This view was not shared by everyone, and many welcomed the idea of studying Torah in Palestine, then under British mandate. That was Gugenheim's initial plan, frustrated by his failure to obtain a visa.

Gugenheim's letters home captured elements of Mir life. Torah was at the heart of this world, and entering into it meant joining a collective. Here were educated and vigorous young men together, not only well versed in Torah but also aware of contemporary affairs. The Americans (and not only the Americans) among them rejoiced when they learned that on 22 June 1938, the African American boxing champion Joe Louis had knocked out the German champion Max Schmeling in the first round.[12] Gugenheim adopted other Lithuanian preferences. He wrote home that he preferred the Lithuanian approach to scholarly authority to the Hassidic tendency at times to venerate their 'Rebbes' even more than they worshipped God himself.[13]

Gugenheim left the Mir Yeshiva after eight months, just before the Munich conference of 1938. He bore the traces of his time there

230 *Refugees and the stateless in Asia*

for the rest of his life. Mobilised into the French army in 1940, he was captured and served as a prisoner of war for five years. He then embarked on a life of teaching Torah and Talmud in France, bringing to his students the spirit of learning he found in Mir. As Chief Rabbi of Paris, he adopted a strict and conservative stance in his judgments, especially with respect to liberal Jewry, a movement he detested. In the conclusion, we shall return to his post-war views, and those of people like him, who survived the war. For the moment, what mattered most was the fierceness of the ties he developed to the Mir Yeshiva before the war.[14]

The beginning of the end

The coming of war on 1 September 1939 completely undermined the position of the Mir Yeshiva in Poland. Mir had been under Polish rule between 1921 and 1939. The Soviets entered Mir only on 17 September 1939, but well before that date, everyone saw how precarious was the position of Yeshivot in this region. The leaders of the Yeshiva feared Soviet repression no less than they feared Nazi antisemitism, and consequently decided to move to Vilna, in still independent Lithuania, where Grodzinsky's *Va'ad ha yeshivot* was based.

Their move came too late to make a difference. On 10 October, the Vilna region was transferred by Soviet authorities from Poland to Lithuania. Six days later, on 16 October, the Mir Yeshiva arrived in Vilna. Eight months later, on 15 June 1940, Soviet troops occupied Lithuania. On 3 August 1940, Lithuania became a constituent part of the USSR. By then, the students of the Mir Yeshiva were scattered in a number of different sites, though they still formed a single Yeshiva.[15] By then, there were roughly 2,400 Yeshiva students and 170 rabbis seeking refuge In Lithuania.[16] All were dependent on financial support from Lithuania and the *Va'ad hayeshivot*.[17]

The responsibility borne by the rabbinical council in Vilna, headed by Reb Chaim Ozer Grodzinsky, was immense. The authority of Reb Chaim Ozer, as he was called, extended beyond religious questions to include virtually all aspects of ultra-Orthodox Jewish life.[18] Since 1923, he was elected head of Council of Great Torah Sages, and in the following year he was instrumental in the

A moveable feast   231

establishment of the Yeshiva Schools Council to fund traditional Jewish education as a whole in the region of Poland and Lithuania.

Grodzinsky was not a Zionist, but looked favourably on Jewish settlement in Palestine. His viewpoint was pragmatic. He believed that it was possible to create a balance between religious and secular life. In Lithuania as in Poland, religious courts worked alongside secular courts, each with its own domain.[19] As chief religious judge in Lithuania, his views carried particular authority. He was the embodiment of the doctrine of *Da'at Torah*, according to which Torah sages pronounced on many public issues and not just on religious questions.[20] He not only decided disputes over Talmudic controversies but also distributed the funds necessary for the survival of all the Yeshivot in Vilna and its environs. When he spoke, especially on issues of the interpretation of the law, most of his fellow Jews obeyed. His anti-Zionism was contested, but when he offered an interpretation of the Talmud, or spoke on vital issues of Jewish life, he commanded authority.

The choice

In normal times, when the great rabbis spoke, their edicts were law for the faithful. But 1940 was not normal times. Everyone knew they were perched on the edge of a volcano. How could they survive in Lithuania, occupied by one enemy, Stalin, who had signed a treaty with their other enemy, Hitler? Everyone mulled over the possibility of seeking a way out. Here is the point at which Reb Haim Ozer Grodzinsky issued a rare public proclamation. With his authority as head of the council of Yeshivot, he instructed the Yeshiva world not to flee but to stay put. The Hebrew phrase of his writ was even clearer: 'sit down and do nothing'.[21] This is a classic rabbinical language and not an original statement on his part.

Why did he issue this ruling?[22] One explanation is that he was seventy-seven years old, terminally ill, and limited in his ability to master a rapidly changing situation; in unstable time, the best advice, he decided, was to wait and see. Another explanation relates to Grodzinsky's own actions twenty-five years earlier during the Great War. Then he fled Vilna, and on his return, was criticised for having abandoned his flock. He regretted having done so.[23] A third

232 *Refugees and the stateless in Asia*

explanation is that Grodzinsky misjudged the situation and wanted to keep the Yeshiva world in Lithuania intact in order to rebuild traditional Jewish life after Hitler's eventual defeat.[24] In one meeting of heads of Yeshivot, he urged them 'not to panic, that every place is dangerous and that Lithuania might remain calm ... being neither black nor red, but pink'.[25]

Grodzinsky's view was shared by many. It is possible that he believed that some form of Divine intervention would lift the threat facing the Jewish people, just as had happened in the past. Similar sentiments were expressed daily by observant Jews (not just the Orthodox) in their prayers. Grodzinsky was in touch with Jewish leaders all over the world, but he and almost everyone else over-estimated fatally the extent to which money and political contacts could stop the Nazi tsunami that was building up in occupied Poland from overwhelming his flock.

A fourth explanation is more persuasive. Many rabbis had pored over the Talmud, without success, to find clear guidance over the question as to whether a rabbi should stay with his congregation, even if both are in mortal danger. Without a clear lead from the Torah, Grodzinsky told his fellow Jews to do nothing. He cited the Babylonian Talmud to support the view that 'abstention from the performance of an uncertain precept' was the right choice.[26] But forbidding Yeshiva students from leaving Vilna meant that those in danger had only to accept their fate, come what may. On this matter, there was doubt and dissent.[27] Grodzinsky thought the United States was a safe-haven, but that option was available only to the fortunate few with visas. In his last months – Grodzinsky died on 9 August 1940 – he faded away, crushed by the unbearable weight of his responsibilities, his fear for his people, and his own infirmity.[28]

Most of those who lived under Grodzinsky's authority heard him and obeyed.[29] He had spoken publicly, in a *Kol Korai*, or a public proclamation intended to be heard by all. Unfortunately, they paid with their lives for their loyalty. Others rejected Grodzinsky's proclamation, and among them, the most prominent were the men of the Mir Yeshiva.

One of those who decided to go against Grodzinsky's instruction was Eliezer (Laizer) Portnoy of the Mir Yeshiva.[30] He told of a tongue-lashing he received from Rabbi Aaron Kutler, of the Slutsk Yeshiva and later founder of the Lakewood Yeshiva – now the

A *moveable feast*   233

largest Yeshiva in America, whose offspring and students have great authority. He was a devout follower of Grodzinsky. Who was he, Portnoy, to go against the word of the leader of all the Yeshivot of Lithuania? What kind of a Jew was he? Was he a 'putrifier of Israel', an enemy of the faith? These words stung; Portnoy recalled that the days following this dressing down were the worst he had known. And yet he did not change his mind. None of the Mir Yeshiva students did.[31]

Why did they reject Grodzinsky's ruling? There was only one way to flee – to the East. But that meant approaching Soviet authorities for a transit visa either to try to reach Odessa, the Black Sea, and Palestine, or to reach Vladivostok and escape by sea to a safe-haven, preferably in Canada or in the United States. The path to Palestine was made more difficult when Italy entered the war on 10 June 1940. The eastern option was then slightly less daunting to the Mir Yeshiva than any other one.

But that still left the key difficulty in place. The fundamental reason Grodzinsky and others rejected this flight option was that it forced Orthodox Jews to turn to Soviet authorities for travel documents. Was this not, Grodzinsky's supporters held, a suicidal step? Thousands of those who did so in the 1930s wound up in the Gulag or dead. Why would anyone risk that?[32]

The answer of the Mir Yeshiva (and some Zionists in Vilna)[33] was that staying put was suicide, and that even the most dangerous path was better than inaction. With Soviet rule established in Vilna, the Joint Distribution Committee closed its offices, and the council of Yeshivot stopped providing financial support for the thousands of refugees flooding into the city. Following Grodzinsky's edict appeared more and more to be an act of madness.

And yet rejecting the edict was itself a considerable risk. Given the recent history of Stalin's purges, and his hostility to Orthodox Judaism, who could doubt that trusting Soviet authorities was more dangerous than trusting rabbinic authorities?[34] And yet the overwhelming majority of the Mir Yeshiva, despite hesitations and doubts, rejected Grodzinsky's instruction.

Initially, the head of the Mir Yeshiva, Reb Eliezer Judah Finkel, and the *Mashgiach*, Reb Yehezkel Levenstein, both accepted Grodzinsky's view. But they reconsidered their views when they saw that the majority of their community was determined to leave

234   *Refugees and the stateless in Asia*

Lithuania. Historian Marc Shapiro terms this a student revolt, an extremely rare moment when established authority gave way to youth. Some men in the Yeshiva, in particular Reb Leib Malin, were in their thirties, and had their own views on what to do.[35] Malin had the courage to act independently of his *Rosh yeshiva* and of other rabbinical authorities.[36] Some Yeshiva students were determined to stay in Lithuania, or for one reason or another, could not apply for an exit visa. But relatively quickly, the whole Yeshiva decided to find the documents they needed to escape. Reb Malin and others formed a committee of five to realise this plan, contacting Jewish supporters in New York to provide the funding.

Once they took the decision to go, there were numerous obstacles in their path to freedom. All were overcome through a combination of extraordinary acts of benevolence, lightning-fast fundraising in the United States, and more than a measure of astonishing good fortune. Reb Malin called this predestination or a miracle;[37] others would say that sheer good luck counts.

First, in July 1940, a Dutch-born woman stranded in Kaunas, Pessla Lewin, approached the Dutch Embassy in Riga to ask for a visa to enter Dutch islands off the coast of South America, including Surinam and Curaçao. She got it. Her husband, Dr Isaac Lewin, approached the Dutch representative of the Philips Electronics company and acting Dutch consul in Kaunas, Jan Zwartendijk, to ask if he could issue a visa like the one his wife had received. He agreed. Two Yeshiva students, Nathan Gutwirth and Chaim Nussbaum, heard the story, and they too received visas from Zwartendijk for travel to the Dutch island of Curaçao.[38] The lifeline was open. The Dutch consul also agreed to leave out of the visa document the fact that final permission to enter the island remained at the discretion of the Governor. With these Dutch visas in hand, the next step was to obtain a transit visa to Japan from Vladivostok. Here Chiuni Sugihara, Japanese consul in Kaunas, and a spy, obliged, and from late July until early September 1940, he signed over 1,500 visas for Jews.[39] The paperwork surrounding this effort was substantial; to expedite matters, Mir Yeshiva students helped him process the applications.[40]

Finally, the Mir applicants entered the lion's den of the Soviet bureaucracy, and to their great surprise, found that they could indeed obtain visas and train tickets to travel from Vilna to Vladivostok

A *moveable feast*

for a considerable sum of foreign currency. What had opened the door to escape was Soviet appetite for American dollars. The cost of transit visas and train tickets for the Mir Yeshiva was $80,000, or in today's dollars, $1,700,000. The cash was raised immediately through Orthodox networks in the United States. Many fundraisers even broke the sabbath to obtain these funds, on the grounds of *Pikuach Nefesh*, the principle that all laws may be broken in order to save lives. The money was wired to Intourist, the Soviet travel agent, in Vilna and Moscow, and the passage to freedom began.[41]

Additional financial help for both orthodox and secular Jews determined to leave Vilna was provided by a Zionist emissary in Vilna, Zorach Warhaftig, head of the committee to help save Polish Jewry. With British approval, he set up an 'Aliya (immigration) office' and helped smooth the path out of Vilna for hundreds of Jews. His belief was that they had to seize any chance to escape.[42] He also distributed financial support to them and throughout their unlikely voyage to Palestine or elsewhere.[43] He was part of the group that made the escape of the Mir Yeshiva possible.

There are a number of accounts of the unlikely first-class rail voyage of roughly three hundred Mir Yeshiva students, teachers, and wives, who traveled in groups of fifty from the Baltic to the Pacific. One man who did not join them was the head of the Yeshiva, Reb Eliezer Yehudah Finkel. He travelled South to Odessa and then took a ship to Palestine. His aim was to reestablish the Mir Yeshiva there. His *Mashgiach*, or second in command, Reb Yehezkel Levenstein, was critical of this decision; to him, what mattered most was that the Yeshiva remained together.[44]

Finkel's son-in-law and heir apparent, Chaim Leib Shmuelevitz, himself a distinguished Talmudic scholar, was on the train and took over as leader of the Yeshiva from this point on. The Mir contingent arrived in Vladivostok in December 1940. Then they travelled to Japan and were welcomed by a community of Jews and sympathisers in Kobe. They stayed in Japan beyond the limit of their short-term visas, renewed on numerous occasions. One young traveller, Chaya Leah Walkin, remembers her time in Japan as filled with Japanese generosity and kindness.[45] These refugees had no intention of heading towards Curaçao, but most were unable to break through the obstacles to obtain a visa to the United States.

236   *Refugees and the stateless in Asia*

While in Japan, the men of the Mir Yeshiva and other refugees, like Chaya Leah Walkin's family, benefited from financial support provided to them by the *Vaad Ha'hatzalah*, the American group that worked tirelessly to support and save the lives of ultra-Orthodox rabbis, Torah scholars, and their students. This targeted funding enabled many to survive and to rebuild their lives as Torah Jews.[46] Their sense of living as one led Malin and others even to turn down twenty-one visas to enter the United States they received in September 1941 in Japan. The Yeshiva was indivisible.[47]

By August 1941, the Japanese decided that these stateless people would be relocated to Shanghai, then under Japanese control. There were already twenty thousand Jewish refugees living in the city. Once again, we need to appreciate the good fortune of the Mir Yeshiva to arrive by ship in Shanghai in September–October 1941, just months before the Japanese attack on Pearl Harbor. Escaping from one occupied city, Vilna, to another, Shanghai, ensured their survival.[48]

There was one more piece of good luck from which the Mir Yeshiva benefited on arrival in Shanghai. A Sephardi Jew, Silas Hardoon, was a shady but very successful businessman. He amassed a fortune in real estate in Shanghai, married a Buddhist, and moved away from his Jewish roots, but he then tried to return to them in his latter days. He built a very large synagogue in Shanghai, Beit Aharon, in memory of his father. He died in 1931, so never saw the synagogue. The building was on Museum Road in the International Settlement, and remained empty and unused, shunned by the Jewish community of the city, until the Mir Yeshiva came and moved right in.[49]

Two months later, Pearl Harbor was bombed. For refugees, the vital foreign funding that supported the Jewish refugees was no longer secure. The Sephardi elite of rich Jewish families in Shanghai were compromised by their British passports, and the Joint Distribution Committee, as an American charity, could no longer openly provide vital funding for Jewish refugees.

The Mir Yeshiva was fortunate, though, in that they had in the *Vaad Ha'Hatzalah* their own separate fundraisers in North America, able to channel to them and them alone funding for their upkeep and their scholarship. To some, it was outrageous that the men of the Mir Yeshiva, who didn't have to work for a living, were better

A moveable feast 237

funded and better fed than were the children of assimilated Jews in Shanghai.[50] To others, there was the question as to whether the funds raised by Orthodox communities worldwide for the Mir and other Yeshivot should be shared with the whole Jewish community in Shanghai. The special efforts of Orthodox Jews in North America to rescue rabbis and rabbinical students arose out of an order of priorities not shared by other Jewish groups. To secular Jews, saving rabbis mattered, but no more than saving other Jewish lives. The Joint helped everyone, not just members of Yeshivot. The Joint spent approximately four times as much as the *Vaad Ha'hatzalah* in supporting the refugees who lived in Shanghai.[51] The per capita support given by the Joint to Yeshiva students and non-Yeshiva students was identical. Why should three hundred Yeshiva students be treated any differently than the eight thousand men, women and children who were fed daily by the Joint?

Even within the ultra-Orthodox world, there were quarrels. Some members of the Lubavitcher Hassidic movement stated that they were excluded from receiving funds from the *Vaad Ha'hatzalah*. Some secular Jews accepted the Yeshiva students as embodiments of Jewish tradition; others felt that all Jewish life had the same value, and no one group should be singled out for special treatment.[52] These Jewish refugees, like all refugees, brought their divisions, dislikes, and ideological quarrels with them into exile.[53]

There were times when these 'Shanghailanders' transcended such conflicts. In 1943, representatives of all Jewish communities in Shanghai agreed to construct a Jewish cemetery on Baikal Road in Hongkew. A Polish Jewish contracting group carried out the job.[54]

Torah study in Shanghai antedated the arrival of the Mir Yeshiva. There was both a Sephardi community and an Ashkenazi community, including a Lubavitcher Yeshiva led by Rabbi Meir Ashkenazi, who had come to Shanghai in the 1920s and served as Chief Rabbi of the city's Jewish population. It was Ashkenazi who directed the Mir scholars and students to reside in Beit Aharon on arrival in Shanghai. There was also a small group of refugees from Lublin, who formed their own Yeshiva, separate from the Mir.[55] Rabbi Shmuel David Walkin, Chaya Leah's father and the descendant of distinguished rabbis in Pinsk, led another house of study, and helped look after and feed the young men of the Mir Yeshiva as well. These close-knit circles provided a kind of family life for many

238 *Refugees and the stateless in Asia*

who had lost everything, except the Torah and their ties to fund-raisers abroad. To literary scholar Vera Schwarcz, this communitarian effort, encapsulated in the Yiddish word 'Ahdut', or unity, was the key to their survival.[56] At the core of this collective life was a *Jüdische Gemeinde*, or the Jewish Community of Central European Jews. It had an office on East Seward Road and helped settle disputes, find lawyers, and run youth associations and cemeteries.[57]

The students of the Mir Yeshiva had seen poverty, deprivation, and death in Poland and Lithuania, but what they saw in Shanghai was even more disturbing. Abraham Wainhaus recalled: 'I will never forget the first morning I went out and saw the bodies of dead children left out because they had died of starvation or had frozen overnight'.[58] Every day, in plain sight was evidence of the inhuman conditions under which four million Chinese residents and refugees lived in the city. The Mir Yeshiva returned to their studies. Their contact with the Chinese of Shanghai, like that of many other Jewish refugees, was minimal or non-existent.[59] Survivors recalled acts of kindness and generosity between Jewish refugees and their Chinese neighbours, but the pressure of hunger and overcrowding was unremitting.

The Mir Yeshiva was fortunate to have access to Shanghai's printing industry. To study Talmud, the Yeshiva students had to find ways to reproduce individual pages so that everyone studied it at the same time. In Kobe, they had received from New York several hundred copies of one tractate of the Talmud, *Kiddushin*. Now that war had been declared, foreign supply was impossible. Remarkably, they managed to print in Shanghai their own copies of over a hundred texts and commentaries, including almost all of the 2,600 pages of the Talmud.[60]

Most members of the Mir Yeshiva had to abandon Beit Aharon as their residence when all stateless Jews were forced to reside in a ghetto, or a restricted area for stateless refugees, starting on 18 May 1943. During this period, there was considerable friction between some Japanese officials and these stateless Jews. One official, Kanoh Ghoya, was a petty tyrant known for his brutality.[61]

This was a ghetto without barbed wire, and while overcrowding was severe, many people found ways to carry on working or studying outside of the ghetto. Some of the students of the Mir Yeshiva rejected the housing offered to them in a Salvation Army building.

A moveable feast

They even marched to the Russian Jewish administrators handling housing, and tore up the office. The *bochrim*, or militant young men of the Yeshiva, initially got what they wanted.[62] They used passes to leave their residence in the ghetto and continue their studies by day in Beit Aharon. A year later, they lost that privilege, and moved first to a smaller synagogue, Ohel Moshe, today part of the Shanghai Jewish Refugee Museum, and then to hotels.

At the end of the war, the Mir Yeshiva community waited until ship passage became available so that they could restart their lives. No one wanted to go back to Poland, Byelorussia, or Lithuania. There were two choices open to them. First, their Rosh Yeshiva, Reb Yehuda Finkel, had opened a Yeshiva in Jerusalem in 1944. His son was *Mashgiach*. Roughly half of the Yeshiva left Shanghai for Jerusalem. The other half went to New York, where they were welcomed by Rev Avraham Kalmanowitz, the indefatigable fundraiser of the *Vaad Ha'hatzala*, who had worked hard to pay the Intourist fees for the Mir's passage across European Russia and Siberia. He opened the American branch of the Mir Yeshiva in Brooklyn; others restarted their lives in Lakewood, New Jersey, already a major centre of Jewish learning, or elsewhere in the United States. These Yeshivot are flourishing today, and Mir Jerusalem, with over eight thousand students, is the largest Yeshiva in the world.

Exile in Asia

One way to understand the work of the Mir Yeshiva in Shanghai is to see it as the product of people who had no idea if any of the world they had left behind in Europe, their families, their parents, their friends, still existed. In a way, they acted as if they were the last people left of the entire world of Lithuanian Jewry. They knew Torah study went on in New York, in Jerusalem, and elsewhere, but even so, they had to do whatever it took to keep the study of Torah and Talmud alive. Given their structure of beliefs, we can understand why they felt that on them, and on Jews like them, the fate of the world rested. And over time, they came to know that their world, the world from which they came, had been completely destroyed.

240 *Refugees and the stateless in Asia*

The generosity of Jews all over the world financed their journey across Europe and Asia, and kept them alive while in Shanghai. The Mir Yeshiva was fortunate enough to be treated as a privileged elite who *deserved* better conditions than other Jews. Unsurprisingly, resentments and conflicts followed. In particular, Laura Margolis, the Joint Distribution Committee's agent in Shanghai, was exasperated by the outlook of these men.[63] Was there an element of selfishness, indeed of arrogance, in their comportment? Yes, some of these students of Torah felt that their survival mattered more than that of those who had wandered into the wilderness of modernity and assimilation.[64]

It is important not to turn refugees into saints or heroes. Their mission had flaws as well as strengths. But by preserving their life as a collective, the Mir Yeshiva emerged from the war as a living archive, a well-spring of thought and inspiration for those who sought one. The Nazis did destroy the world in which the Mir Yeshiva had been born and flourished. But they did not blot out Torah Judaism, or the Orthodox Jewish way of life. The pre-existing Yeshivas in Israel, Britain, and America kept alive the tradition of Yeshiva training, though it vanished from most of Poland, Lithuania, and Byelorussia. Still, the survival of the Mir Yeshiva was a remarkable act of defiance by a determined collective who survived against the odds.[65]

The comparative history of survival

Most of the Jewish population of Eastern Europe caught between Hitler and Stalin in 1939–41 were doomed. Those who survived did so for many reasons, best summarised under the headings of luck, money, and location. The first mattered the most, but location was a critical matter too. The decision of the Soviets to deport to Central Asia Polish Jews under their rule was crucial in keeping most of them alive; we can attribute that act to military necessity rather than humanitarian sentiment.

The odyssey of the Mir Yeshiva indeed reflected all three. Vilna was a free city for a time; money from Jewish organisations arrived, enabling the refugees seeking an escape route to take advantage of acts of diplomatic generosity. But the survival of one single

A moveable feast 241

Yeshiva, when all others in Poland and Lithuania perished in the war, depended on an act of defiance and disobedience. When high rabbinical authority said stay put, the Mir Yeshiva refused to do so and survived.

What the Mir Yeshiva did was to help ensure that what they took to be the essence of Jewish life – Torah study and the observance of Jewish laws and practice – would outlast the Nazis. Theirs was an act of resistance not unlike other efforts of secular Jews to keep their form of Jewishness alive. In Vilna and in Warsaw, secular and observant Jews managed to save Jewish manuscripts, books, and artefacts in ingenious ways. [66] These precious documents were retrieved after the war. In a way, the Mir Yeshiva was a living, breathing archive, a branch of a tree that could be replanted and grow again.

Here may be a subject relevant to many other explorations of survival of refugees and the stateless in extremis. Many of those who broke out of the trap chose daring, sometimes radically new, alternatives. In these terrible times, continuing in the old ways, following tradition, respecting authority without question, endangered those who did so. Those who took risks stood a better chance of survival than those who did not. A Lithuanian Yeshiva is an unlikely place to find iconoclasm, but in turning away from Grodzinsky's ruling, the Mir Yeshiva saved their own skins and helped keep alive the tradition to which he had dedicated his own life.

One last word on the post-Holocaust history of the Mir Yeshiva. As we have noted, the Mir Yeshiva was reborn twice, in Jerusalem and in Brooklyn. And yet this story of survival and growth masks a hidden history of loss. The Nazis destroyed the vibrant world of Yiddish and Orthodox Jewish life in Eastern Europe.

It was impossible after 1945 to reconstruct this *habitus*, the socially constructed and transmitted web of habits, tastes, skills, sounds, and dispositions. Reconstruction does not mean replication. All refugees know the truth inherent in this statement.

Haim Soloveitchik is an American scholar and rabbi in a distinguished line reaching back to the founders of the Lithuania Yeshivot. In 1994, he published an article about a shift in Orthodox Jewish life since 1945. He detected a new rigidity, a new literalism in Orthodox Jewish thinking moving away from respecting long-established practices to insisting on a strict, formalistic reading of the law. Text trumped practice, or rather the term 'text' lost its

242   *Refugees and the stateless in Asia*

meaning as a site of enquiry and became a matter of uncritical reading. The significance of 'how things were done' lost its authority when not documented in legal texts. Turning away from considering the business of daily life to construct a strict interpretation of Talmudic law constitutes a narrowing of perspectives, a reproduction of what is called the 'strict constructionist' school of American constitutional law. In both cases, fundamentalism is just around the corner.

To Soloveitchik, this development reflected the arrival of thousands of newcomers to ultra-Orthodox life, those whose zealotry is one of the signs of their new-found loyalties.[67] The old world of the Mir had space for 'how things were done'; after 1945, that space tended to disappear in the construction of rabbinic law in the new world of the Mir.

Refugeedom is a place defined by where we once were, and where we can no longer be.[68] To arrive *somewhere* else under constraint is to be forced to reconstruct *something* else than we once had and knew. As Soloveitchik concluded, what mattered was that 'the Holocaust, among other things, wrote finis to a culture'. No matter where the survivors made their homes, they revived what they could, but many were well aware of what they had lost or left behind.

Notes

1 The Hebrew plural is 'Yeshivot'.
2 Thanks are due to Saul Stampfer, Sam Spinner, Harvey Mendelsohn, and David Safier for comments and advice.
3 Shaul Stampfer, *Lithuanian Yeshivas of the Nineteenth Century: Creating a Tradition of Learning*, trans. Lindsey Taylor-Guthartz (Oxford: Littman Library of Jewish Civilization, 2012).
4 Immanuel Etkes, *Rabbi Israel Salanter and the Musar Movement* (Philadelphia, PA: Jewish Publication Society, 1993); Moshe J. Gerstel, 'The Musar Practices of Rabbi Yisrael Salanter', *Torah U-Madda Journal*, 17 (2016–17), pp. 218–34; Mark Steiner, 'Rabbi Israel Salanter as a Jewish Philosopher', *Torah u-Madda Journal*, 9 (2000), pp. 42–57, and Ben-Tsion Klibansky. *The Golden Age of the Lithuanian Yeshivas* (Bloomington, IL: Indiana University Press, 2022), pp. 163ff.

A moveable feast 243

5 Czeslaw Milosz, *Native Realm: A Search for Self-Definition*, trans. Catherine S. Leach (Garden City, NY: Doubleday & Co., 1968).

6 Romain Gary, *La promesse de l'aube* (Paris: Gallimard, 1960).

7 Israel Klausner, *Vilnah, Yerushalayim de-Lita: dorot aharonim, 1881–1939* (Tel Aviv: Bet Lohame ha-geta'ot, 1983; Henri Minczeles, *Vilna, Wilno, Vilnius: la Jérusalem de Lituanie* (Paris: La Découverte, 1993).

8 On *Mashgichim*, see Ben-Tsion Klibansky, *The Golden Age*, ch. 4 and epilogue.

9 Ernest Gugenheim, letter of 11 January 1938, in Gugenheim, *Lettres de Mir ... d'un monde de Tora effacé par la Shoah* (Paris: Biblieurope, 2006), p. 30.

10 Gugenheim, letter, 12 January 1938, in Gugenheim, *Lettres*, p. 33.

11 Gugenheim, letter, 17 January 1938, p. 39.

12 Gugenheim, letter, 29 June 1938, p. 103.

13 Gugenheim, letter, 14 August 1938, p. 123.

14 On the students (*bachurim*) of the Lithuanian Yeshivot, see Klibansky, *The Golden Age*, ch. 5.

15 Ibid., pp. 293–4.

16 Yitzhak Arad, 'Concentration of Refugees in Vilna on the Eve of the Holocaust', *Yad Vashem Studies*, 9 (1973), pp. 201–14.

17 On the refugees in Lithuania, see Simonas Strelcovas, *Antrojo pasaulinio karo pabėgėliai Lietuvoje 1939–1940 metais (Refugees of the Second World War in Lithuania in 1939–1940)*, PhD, Vytautas Magnus University, 2007, pp. 21–6.

18 On Grodzinski, see Klibansky, *The Golden Age*, pp. 183–4.

19 Alexander Kaye, *The Invention of Jewish Theocracy: The Struggle for Legal Authority in Modern Israel* (Oxford: Oxford University Press, 2022), ch. 1.

20 Jacob Katz, 'Da'at Torah: The Unqualified Authority Claimed for Halakhists', *Jewish History*, 9, 1 (1997), pp. 41–50; and Lawrence Kaplan, '*Daas Torah*: A Modern Conception of Religious Authority', in Moshe Sokol (ed.), *Rabbinical Authority and Personal Autonomy* (Northvale, NJ: Jason Aronson, 1992), pp. 1–60.

21 The phrase in Hebrew is 'shev ve'al ta'ase', which literally means sit down and do nothing.

22 Joe Bobker, 'To Flee or to Stay', *Hakirah*, 9 (2010), pp. 95–118.

23 Klibansky, *The Golden Age*, p. 279.

24 Bobker, 'To Flee or to Stay', p. 97, n. 44.

25 Ibid., p. 98.

26 Babylonian Talmud, *Eruvim*, 100a.

27 Yecheskel Leitner, *Operation: Torah Rescue* (Jerusalem: Feldheim Publishers, 1987), p. 44.

244   *Refugees and the stateless in Asia*

28 Yosef Friedlander, 'The Day Vilna Died', *Tradition*, 37, 2 (2003), pp. 88–92.

29 Marc B. Shapiro, 'The Mir Yeshiva and Its Shanghai Sojourn', in Kathryn Hellerstein and Song Lihong (eds), *China and Ashkenazi Jewry: Transcultural Encounters* (Berlin: de Gruyter Oldenbourg, 2022), pp. 195–6.

30 Kowner, 'The Mir Yeshiva's Holocaust Experience: Ultra-Orthodox Perspectives on Japanese Wartime Attitudes towards Jewish Refugees', *Holocaust and Genocide Studies*, 36 (2022), pp. 295–314, at p. 298.

31 Shapiro, 'The Mir Yeshiva', p. 197, n. 4. Kotler later fled Vilna to the United States; his students who followed Reb Chaim Ozer's edict were killed. Marc Shapiro, 'The Incredible Story of Mir Yeshiva's Escape to Shanghai, 1', https://www.youtube.com/watch?v=9ufqrltePEM. Accessed 20 July 2022.

32 Rotem Kowner, 'The Mir Yeshiva's Holocaust Experience', p. 298.

33 Pinhas Hirschsprung, *The Vale of Tears*, trans. Vivian Felsen (Toronto, ON: The Azrieli Foundation, 2016). See also Samuel Iwry, *To Wear the Dust of War*, L. J. H. Kelley (ed.) (Basingstoke: Palgrave Macmillan, 2004), p. 52.

34 Klibansky, *The Golden Age*, p. 301.

35 Marc Shapiro, 'The Incredible Story of Mir Yeshiva's Escape to Shanghai, 2', https://www.youtube.com/watch?v=Jdybtwtou5k. Accessed 20 July 2022.

36 Klibansky, *The Golden Age*, pp. 281ff.

37 Elhanan Joseph Hertzman, *The Miracle of Rescue of the Mir Yeshiva* (Jerusalem: n.p., 1976), pp. 31, 44.

38 Other accounts name the two Yeshiva students as Ben Fischoff and Nathan Gutwirth, both from the Telshe Yeshiva. See Jan Brokken, *The Just: How Six Unlikely Heroes Saved Thousands of Jews from the Holocaust* (Minneapolis, MN: Scribe Publications, 2021); and Hillel Levine, *In Search of Sugihara: The Elusive Japanese Diplomat Who Risked his Life to Rescue 10,000 Jews from the Holocaust* (New York: Free Press, 1996).

39 Simonas Strelcovas, 'Chiune Sugihara ir Janas Zwartendijkas – Pasaulio tautų teisuoliai. Istorinės peripetijos tarp sovietinių struktūrų, žydų pabėgėlių ir jų gelbėtojų', *Genocidas ir rezistencija*, ii, 14 (2003), pp. 44–51.

40 Levine, *In Search of Sugihara*, ch. 4. Moshe Zupnik was among them.

41 Marc Shapiro estimates that each transit visa cost the equivalent of $3,300 in today's dollars. See 'The Incredible Story of Mir Yeshiva's Escape to Shanghai, 2'. https://www.youtube.com/watch?v=Jdybtwtou5k. Accessed 20 July 2022. The sum contributed by the

Vaad Ha'hatzala in the United States and Canada was estimated by Zuroff at $80,000 in 1940 prices. See Efraim Zuroff, 'Rescue Priority and Fund Raising as Issues during the Holocaust: A Case Study of the Relations between the Vaad Ha-Hatzala and the Joint, 1939–1941', *American Jewish History*, 68, 3 (March 1979), pp. 305–26, at p. 314.

42 Klibansky, *The Golden Age*, p. 299.

43 See Zorach Warhaftig, *Refugee and Survivor: Rescue Attempts during the Holocaust* (Jerusalem: Yad Vashem, 1988).

44 On Levenstein, see Klibansky, *The Golden Age*, p. 197.

45 Vera Schwarcz, *In the Crook of the Rock – Jewish Refuge in a World Gone Mad: The Chaya Leah Walkin Story* (Brighton, MA: Academic Studies, Press, 2018), ch. 3.

46 Iwry, *To Wear the Dust of War*, p. 77.

47 Dovi Safier and Yehuda Geberer, 'Leader of the Lions: The Story of Rav Leib Malin', *Mishpacha*, 14 September 2021, https://mishpacha.com/leader-of-the-lions-rav-leib-malin/. Accessed 20 July 2022.

48 Andrew Jakubowicz, 'Stopped in Flight: Shanghai and the Polish Jewish Refugees of 1941', *Holocaust studies*, 24, 3 (2018), pp. 287–304.

49 David Kranzler, *Japanese, Nazis and Jews: The Jewish Refugee Community of Shanghai, 1938–1945* (Hoboken, NJ: KTAV Publishing House, 1988), p. 431.

50 See Chapter 15 in this volume.

51 Zuroff, 'Rescue Priority', pp. 305–36, esp. 324–5.

52 Shapiro, 'The Incredible Story', 4, https://www.yotube.com/watch?v=RBJhWNM4o4w. Accessed 20 July 2022.

53 Zuroff, 'Rescue Priority', pp. 305–26.

54 Joseph R. Fiszman, 'The Quest for Status: Polish Jewish Refugees in Shanghai, 1941–1949', *Polish Review*, 43, 4 (1998), pp. 441–60.

55 Shapiro, 'The Incredible Story', 4.

56 Schwarcz, *In the Crook of the Rock*.

57 Iwry, *To Wear the Dust of War*, pp. 108–9.

58 Shapiro, 'The Mir Yeshiva', p. 204.

59 Dr Lotte Lustig Marcus, 'Contradicting Revisionist History', *Points East. The Sino-Judaic Institute*, 29, 1 (March 2014), pp. 2–3.

60 Kranzler, *Japanese, Nazis and Jews*, p. 434, and Ernest G. Heppner, *Shanghai Refuge: A Memoir of the World War II Jewish Ghetto* (Lincoln, NE: University of Nebraska Press, 1993).

61 Iwry, *To Wear the Dust of War*, pp. 120ff.

62 On SACRA, see Fiszman, 'The Quest for Status', pp. 441–60. On the 'riot', see Iwry, *To Wear the Dust of War*, p. 115.

63 Irene Eber (ed.), *Jewish Refugees in Shanghai: A Selection of Documents* (Göttingen: Vandenhoeck & Ruprecht, 2018), p. 260, Diane Perelsztejn,

246 *Refugees and the stateless in Asia*

'Survivre à Shanghai', ZTF – RTBF, and Zuroff, *The Response of Orthodox Jews*, p. 193.

64 Yecheskel Leitner, *The Escape of the Mirrer Yeshiva from War-Torn Poland to Shanghai, China* (Spring Valley, NY: Feldheim Publishers, 1987) even blames Jewish assimilation for the Holocaust. This hagiographic account does not even mention the difficult choices faced by Reb Chaim Ozer Grodzinsky and the Mir Yeshiva. To Leitner, history is the unfolding of the miraculous.

65 Schwarcz, *In the Crook of the Rock*, passim.

66 On Vilna, see Diane Perelsztejn, 'Le Brigade des papiers', RTF Belge, 1986; and David E. Fishman, *The Book Smugglers: Partisans, Poets, and the Race to Save Treasures from the Nazis* (Lebanon, NH: University Press of New England, 2017); on Warsaw, see Jay Winter, *War beyond Words* (Cambridge: Cambridge University Press, 2017), ch. 5.

67 Haim Soloveitchik, 'Rupture and Reconstruction: The Transformation of Contemporary Orthodoxy', *Tradition*, 28 (1994), pp. 64–130. On newcomers, see p. 74.

68 On the origins of the term, see John Hope Simpson, *The Refugee Problem: Report of a Survey* (London: Oxford University Press, 1939), p. 108.

15

Agents of empathy

Kolleen Guy

Everything depends on the individual human being, regardless of how small a number of like-minded people there is, and everything depends on each person, through action and not mere words, creatively making the meaning of life a reality in his or her own being.

Viktor Frankl[1]

Emotion, empathy, and political action

Statelessness is a form of social and political exclusion. It was inflicted on German Jews after 1935 and on Austrian Jews after *Anschluss* in 1938. In 1941, German and formerly Austrian Jews lost their right to nationality. That is, on racial grounds, they were cast out from the German nation. Having neither citizenship nor nationality, German Jews were stateless. With the spread of fascism and war across Europe, millions of other Jews would join them, stripped of citizenship or without standing with respect to the state and its power to protect its inhabitants.

Hannah Arendt, herself made stateless by the Nazis, took statelessness to be crippling to both the individual and the community. To Arendt, 'Statelessness described a condition of alienation and homelessness more fundamental than any legal category. To lose one's nationality automatically cast one out of the sphere of politics and out of the sphere of social and economic networks that make daily life possible.'[2] A survey of the displaced during the war in Shanghai and Singapore suggests that the stateless did *not* lose all elements of social or political agency. They refashioned a kind of

248 *Refugees and the stateless in Asia*

sociability with informal rights below the level of state sovereignty. We can see this as well after the war in the camps for displaced people, where the stateless exercised autonomy to retrieve and reconstruct forms of social and political rights.

In this chapter, I investigate the role of what I term 'agents of empathy' in assisting with this return to autonomy and freedom. Agents of empathy were individuals and groups whose intervention on behalf of the stateless ensured their survival. They were a mixed group of people – doctors, nurses, administrators, bankers, diplomats, businessmen, international civil servants, military men, clergymen, members of religious orders or sects, artists, writers, poets, teachers, spies, and more.

Here, I focus on the efforts of two relief workers in building community and cultivating a sense of social responsibility in two distinct refugee populations. The first is in Shanghai among a group of nearly twenty-two thousand European Jews. These were individuals on their own and families who escaped from Europe after 1938 to what was one of the few places in the world with no requirement to pay landing fees or to have entry visas. These were educated (but poor) Jewish refugees from Central and Eastern Europe who had made their way to what was often referred to as a 'port of last resort'. They found themselves under the care of the American Jewish Joint Distribution Committee (JDC) and its remarkable local agent Laura Margolis.

The second story I tell is of an equally diverse group of stateless Jewish people who made their way out of hiding or Nazi camps to the American occupied zone in Southern Germany. They found themselves ushered into camps, under the care and leadership of Samuel Zisman, who from 1945 to 1947 was the director of the United Nations Relief and Rehabilitation Administration (UNRRA) team in Bavaria. His job was to oversee the administration of displaced persons in the cams throughout his district. In this capacity, Zisman was tasked with moving the stateless to a permanent 'place' in the world, which at that time meant a state other than where they were, in Germany. Both Zisman and Margolis clearly saw that 'rehabilitation', in the international order, was a euphemism for resettlement.

The make-up of these refugee populations and their living conditions are well documented by historians. What is less frequently

Agents of empathy 249

interrogated is the role of agents of empathy, like Margolis and Zisman, in assisting those who survived the trauma of war and the indignity of displacement to reconstruct a sense of belonging in the world. Much like Joy Damousi in her work on Australian humanitarians in the twentieth century, I focus on the experience, views, and perspectives of those who worked on behalf of the stateless during the Second World War.[3] This was a period when the rights of the stateless – human rights – were being articulated and debated in centres of power. Yet, as this chapter will demonstrate, for those who advocated for the stateless, like Margolis and Zisman, human rights were not something easily accessed; indeed, no one knew precisely what 'rights' refugees had simply by virtue of being human beings. And yet agents of empathy were in a position to facilitate the practice of those rights among the refugees. Outside actors, agents of empathy from abroad, insisted upon the reality of such rights and exerted them on behalf of the refugee communities at the very same time as jurists elsewhere worked to codify them. What sets these 'agents of empathy' apart from the humanitarians described by Damousi and others is their willingness to construct 'emotional communities' in ways that allowed for, indeed required, critiques of power and injustice.[4] Agents of empathy not only felt anger at the injustice faced by the refugees, but they used that anger as a catalyst to action. Neutrality was unthinkable.

Defining agents of empathy

As Victor Frankl understood, individuals had to make meaning in their new lives through action connected to community, however small. Those who survived the war were in need of the repair that only collective action within a community can provide. Feelings created community. Being pragmatic or emotionless was an effective individual coping strategy for those traumatised by upheaval, war, and the humiliations of refugee life. A return to life required a space for the stateless to reimagine their personal and collective landscape as one where they could publicly experience and feel emotions both personally and collectively. Finding a shared emotional language for their collective experience was essential for traumatised people to not only tell their story, but also to galvanise their community

250   *Refugees and the stateless in Asia*

for political action. For refugees, this was a politics of everyday life where articulating and exerting demands for basic rights, whether it was for basic food or a passport, constituted the foundations of what would later be recognised in law as civil or human rights.

Agents of empathy provided a pathway to the renewal through the cultivation and structuring of positive relations among refugee communities. These were community makers who mirrored empathetic responses to those who had faced hatred and exclusion. Empathy was a pre-requisite to positive relations, defined as those that have the potential of invoking emotional connection within groups. How we relate in groups reinforces and reshapes the personal and collective landscape. For refugees, an environment that recognised both their humanity and their suffering and allowed for the public display of fairness, comfort, inclusion, and trust was essential to restoring a sense of belonging.[5] It was this fundamental belonging that was stripped by their very public exclusion by the state.

Refugees, as Peter Gatrell points out, were not simply 'the inescapable victims of war' but also agents of change.[6] These agents of change were not alone. Agents of empathy were pivotal in creating an environment where refugee emotions were channeled into a code of political action. They did so by first recognising the injustices suffered by the refugees, demonstrating what might be gained by expressing emotions rather than hiding them in the name of 'objectivity'. Empathy is the ability to stand with someone, feel what it is like to be in their shoes, and care enough to try to alleviate suffering. The word origins from the German *Einfühlung*, meaning *feeling into*. Agents of empathy were willing to go beyond *feeling with* (sympathy) the refugees to *feel into* (empathy) the suffering of others.

We need to acknowledge that acting on this empathetic response can and did go awry. Critics are right to point out that too much distress related to empathy, in certain circumstances, can drive ineffectual or even detrimental responses.[7] Too much empathy can be as problematic as too little. The case studies outlined below demonstrate that what turned the empathetic individual into an agent of change was the ability to foster structures and organisations that channeled emotive responses into positive relations. Positive relations included several key components: collaboration (whether in

Agents of empathy 251

a theatre or in the soup kitchen); social expressions of solidarity, brotherhood, sisterhood, love, intimacy, or spirituality (by providing support for such things as mourning rituals or privacy for couples); and shared encounters or experiences that went beyond the pragmatic to build emotional connection.

In this way, agents of empathy helped validate emotional bonding within communities. Traumatised individuals or groups tended to find it hard to trust outsiders, those who had not seen what they had seen. Agents of empathy showed them that they were heard, that they were seen, and through direct contact and conversation, they began to believe, despite all that they had suffered, that there was such a thing as humanity and that they were part of it. Agents of empathy had to earn the trust of refugees, but once earned, they pointed the way to recovery. Yet recovery did not mean redemption. The wounds were too deep for that. Agents of empathy did what they could. This meant enabling those who were deeply damaged to believe there was not only today, but also tomorrow, and that tomorrow did not resemble the horrific yesterdays they had known. It also meant, as we shall see, pushing against the enormous pressures to execute a speedy resettlement in the guise of 'rehabilitation'.[8]

Navigating and narrating politics

Both Margolis and Zisman's stories can be told in part because of their skill as deliberate narrators, collectors, and conservers of documents. Both left documentary reports as to the challenges they faced, and through these documents, the historian can reconstruct the story that each of them wanted to preserve. It is a story of obstacles and determination, of enemies – both within and outside the refugee community – and friends and allies too. And it is a story of the political dimension of the works of agents of empathy. These documents challenge Hannah Arendt's contention that empathy is the diametrical opposite of politics. Indeed, they offer a counter argument that empathy is the driving force of political organisation and humanitarian action. In this regard, Zisman and Margolis made deliberate choices about what they collected, preserved, and narrated. Preserved documents were aides de memoire and justifications in the future, for their sometimes unorthodox actions on

252 Refugees and the stateless in Asia

behalf of the refugees. They left these documents precisely because they understood that their actions on behalf and with the refugee communities that they served would be viewed as political. By selection of evidence and themes to be remembered or archived, they exerted their power to narrate their stories in ways that are both obvious and surreptitious.

Both pushed against the silences that are inherent in history. Intuitively, they seemed to understand that something is always left out while something else is recorded. They were correct. In history, power begins at the source. During the war years and the immediate aftermath, the power of historical production was overwhelmingly in the hands of state institutions that conducted the war and international institutions that sought to shape the aftermath. Margolis and Zisman worked with and within American state institutions, such as the US Army Airforce and the US State Department, as well as international non-governmental organisations (NGOs), such as the JDC and the United Nationals Relief and Rehabilitation Administration (UNRAA), with massive bureaucratic machinery that generated oceans of reports, correspondence, and visual records. Their voices, along with those of the *kleinen Leute* or the 'little people', were likely to drowned into silence in this sea of documentation.[9] As Michel Trouillot reminds us, silences enter the process of historical production at four crucial moments: 'the moment of fact creation (the making of sources); the moment of fact assembly (the making of archives); the moment of fact retrieval (the making of narratives); and the moment of retrospective significance (the making of history in the final instance)'.[10]

Zisman attempted to defy this silencing by assuring not only that the injustices perpetrated against Jewish refugees were documented, but also that these documents were assembled to form a more complete narrative. When he left UNRRA in 1947, he took with him hundreds of documents, many of them marked 'Classified', that he copied or collected, with or mostly without official permission. The papers consist of biographical materials, team records, drawings and maps, memoranda and reports, personal correspondence, photographs, and printed materials documenting Samuel Zisman's service as UNRRA director of District 5 in Bavaria from 1945 to 1947 and the administration of displaced persons camps in that district. What he chose to collect bears witness to the hard work of the UNRAA team and the ways in which those far removed from the refugees, distanced from the 'little people', as he calls them, were often, perhaps unwittingly, a part of the continued suffering of the long persecuted. His collection is an indictment of the failure of international organisations and, particularly, the Americans to see the both the unique experience of the Jews and their need to reconstruct their lives on their own terms.

Read together, these documents seethe with anger. Zisman is outraged that the army put Jews in communities based on nationality, not recognising that they were made stateless by the very people who might be sharing their camp. Going home was emptied of meaning when it meant returning to the scene of the crime, a vast landscape of terror turned into an immense cemetery. Repatriation meant going back to a place that proved to have never been a home for many in the first place. He was outraged at the urgency of the US Military authorities to move out refugees regardless of what type of hardship and injustice they might return to. He was outraged at the wanton destruction of buildings by American GIs that he is now expected to convert to housing for desperate, stateless women and children. One classified report entitled 'Anti-Semitism in the American Zone' is a stinging indictment of American prejudice. The report vividly documents how American military personnel treat the local German population with greater respect and consideration than the displaced Jews. The report contains data from a survey conducted among the same local population that captures German confusion at American vilification of Nazi antisemitism when, from their perspective, Americans held similar attitudes against 'blacks'.[11] The areas of American control under General Patton were notorious for the harsh treatment of the Jews.[12] Zisman found himself facing both the world that his parents had fled and the blindness of his own country.

By all accounts, this was not a wartime story that Zisman shared during his lifetime. Perhaps like his homosexuality, this truth remained largely in a closet until his death in March 1970. He left the documents for safekeeping with his friends Frank and Camille Rosengren. The Rosengrens were owners of one of the most preeminent independent booksellers in South Texas. The bookstore was a cultural landmark with a national reputation as a literary salon where authors, celebrities, politicians, and local residents flocked

254   *Refugees and the stateless in Asia*

for intellectual inspiration and distinctive left-leaning Texas politics. Camille Rosengren had worked as a curator at the Institute of Texan Cultures, served as vice president of the San Antonio Conservation Society, and was an active member Women for Peace in the Southwest.[13] It is unclear whether she intended to inventory and eventually donate the Zisman papers. When the Rosengrens closed the bookstore nineteen years later, they sent the papers to Zisman's nephew Paul Spreiregen, who was unaware of either the contents or the existence of the collection. He donated most of the papers to the United States Holocaust Museum and Memorial in Washington, DC in 1996.

The 'myth of the war experience', as George Mosse called it, or the myth of heroism and brotherhood of war, was replaced, in many ways, with the 'myth of liberation' and the 'good war' won by Americans.[14] This myth silenced the angry voices of men like Sam Zisman. As Robert Abzug has documented through hundreds of oral interviews with former American GIs like Zisman, many struggled in silence to give some order to the crematoria, mass graves, instruments of torture, gas chambers, and personal stories of suffering they encountered. What they encountered among fellow officers and soldiers was an underlying suspicion and outright denial of their eyewitness accounts that often enraged the GIs. 'This sometimes led to silence among the soldiers about the camps', writes Abzug, 'an extension of that isolation most combat veterans feel about describing the war to those who have not experienced battle'.[15]

Zisman's collection defies that silencing even as he allowed a certain mythology to surround his wartime service and his advocacy for stateless Jews in his sector of occupied Germany during his lifetime. The eulogy at his funeral invoked none of the anger and frustration that he demonstrates in his document collection. The presiding rabbi recited an apocryphal story, often repeated by prominent friends such as architect O'Neil Ford, that Zisman had extracted a promise from King Christian X of Denmark that any Jews in his camps would be welcomed as Danish citizens once they crossed the border.[16] There is no evidence, in the Zisman papers or elsewhere, to suggest that this story was true. Yet it captures a more complicated truth that is in the papers: Zisman understood that Jews flocked to his sector in the American zone and it was unusual in that his sector became a crossroads for children. They were not

Agents of empathy 255

so much 'displaced' but people 'without a place'. This story, much like his documents, attests that he and his team worked tirelessly, particularly on the part of children, to assure that Jews were treated with dignity and had choice about where they would call 'home'. What is missing from the eulogy is that this often put him at odds with both his fellow Americans who occupied his sector and the international organisation he represented. His papers and his life are a dialectic of remarks and silences that remind us of the complexity of navigating the politics of refugee resettlement.

Pathways to empathetic practice

Long before 1945, powerful international institutions were already engaged in constructing the narrative of the war years. As a central player in the political intrigue and bureaucratic rivalries surrounding the treatment of refugees, Laura Margolis is a major figure in this story. She played a prominent role in the work of the 'Joint' in Cuba, China, Spain, France, and Israel. Her personnel file, reports, and correspondence with the decision-makers in the New York are preserved in the JDC Archives. She was treated in many ways like an American diplomat. After her release from a Japanese prison camp and repatriation as part of a prisoner of war exchange, she provided reports to the US State Department and testified before Congress. Margolis was extensively interviewed later in her life by researchers at the USHMM and Yad Vashem. Margolis was anything but silent in the historical record.

Yet Margolis, like Zisman, was angry about the treatment of the stateless. It was this anger that fuelled her determination that the refugees in Shanghai, before and during Japanese occupation of the city, would be fed, housed, and treated with human dignity. While officially she was the representative in Shanghai of the Joint between 1941 and 1943, with the departure of representatives of the US State Department from the city in 1941, she became a de facto point of contact with the United States. Japanese officials acknowledged as much when they asked her to convey messages to the US Treasury Secretary.[17] Known for her effectiveness in dealing with the complexity of caring for European Jewish refugees in a city whose fate shifted with the war, Margolis was more than a social

256 *Refugees and the stateless in Asia*

worker or even, as she recalled, 'an arm of the US Consulate'.[18] For refugees she was a lifeline. 'There is not [a] doubt in my mind', wrote one refugee, 'that without the professionalism, the dedication, the persistence, and *chutzpa* – displayed by Laura Margolis, thousands of refugees would have slowly starved to death'.[19]

Chutzpa was a euphemism for subterfuge, for decisions that were at best unorthodox and at worst illegal. She was resourceful and pragmatic enough to understand that sometimes the best way to help those in need was to pursue actions outside of legal norms, particularly when the norms were enmeshed in an inefficient bureaucracy. It was this bureaucracy, and not the Japanese occupiers, that was the source of her greatest frustrations. Her anger is summarised in a report, written from memory for the Joint, about everything that had happened since Pearl Harbor, when she, as an American, became an enemy of the Japanese. Her determination to record her version of events resulted in parts of the report being written on toilet paper and concealed in the elastic waist of her underwear, when she boarded a Japanese ship in early September 1943 en route to freedom. The report was lengthy, detailed, and full of blunt disclosures about the immense difficulties the Joint had in feeding over eight thousand Jewish refugees and caring for more in hospitals and a maternity home in Shanghai. One statement she made in this report captures the core of her understanding of her mission. She wrote in her conclusion:

> We have in Shanghai, and have always had, a group of Jews who have no social consciousness and no feeling of responsibility towards the community. Shanghai itself is not a community. Added to this, we have a group of refugees who are underfed and undernourished and terribly discouraged. I doubt that fifty percent of the group will be material for rehabilitation if this war lasts another two years.[20]

Here was her aim: to generate a sense of social consciousness and of community responsibility in a population ground down by displacement, malnutrition, disease, and despair.

Margolis might have seemed an unlikely candidate to play such a critical role in the high-stakes survival of thousands of stateless refugees. She acknowledged as much in one of her most frequently cited quotes: 'If I had been a man, I would have joined the Navy to see the world, but since I was a woman, I joined the JDC.'[21] Yet, being a woman, and an attractive one at that, created opportunities. As Rebecca Kobrin noted, 'It was Margolis's appreciation of the subtle power her gender potentially offered in her unique situation that enabled her to succeed in her mission in Shanghai.'[22] Her 'deferential female diplomacy' was on display, for example, when she sat down to tea with Captain Inuzuka just hours after Pearl Harbor to discuss cordially the continued feeding of the thousands of refugees in her care. With literally hundreds of panicking refugees in the lobby, she marched up to Captain Inuzuka's penthouse suite in the Cathay Hotel in Shanghai to persuade the new head of the Japanese occupation to allow her to continue to raise funds in the name of the JDC. The dinner parties and social affairs where she circulated with the international elite, including Captain Inuzuka, in her specially ordered cocktail dresses paid off. She was indeed the one and only lifeline for tens of thousands of stateless people in Shanghai.

How had she found her way to such a position? Her pathway to service was part of a benevolent tradition learned at home and enhanced by her training in social work. Born in Constantinople in 1903 to a prominent Jewish family, Laura grew up speaking multiple languages – English, French, Spanish, German, Turkish, Greek, and Yiddish – a skill that would serve her well in a career that literally spanned the globe. Her father was a Zionist, who worked in Ottoman Turkey for a time, before returning to the United States. Her family settled in Ohio, where she pursued her education and, in many ways, came to internalise key American values about democracy, equality, and efficiency, as well as a belief in an open-door policy for immigrants. These were coupled with a strong Jewish identity that followed from her father's commitment to Jewish rescue. While it would take her a bit longer to embrace fully her father's Zionism, she showed a strong commitment to social justice and care for those in need within the community during her studies in social work first at Ohio State University and later, pursuing her Master's degree, at Western Reserve University.

It was the upheaval of the Jewish world in Europe that took Laura from serving local American Jewish communities to assisting stranded Jewish refugees first in Havana, and then in Shanghai. She was trained in the model of a 'progressive reformer' – moving away from charity distribution to serving communities through rationalised and systematic relief delivery. As a social worker, she

258   *Refugees and the stateless in Asia*

believed that justice came from the rational, systematic distribution of aid to the poor and a heavy dose of self-help. As a woman schooled in the teachings of Progressivism and in keeping with JDC practice, she pushed her communities to attend to their own needs, whether through organising schools or setting up elections for self-governance.[23]

Rehabilitation of the stateless, for her, was an emotional process as well as a political struggle. She learned this early on in her international engagement on behalf of the Joint in Havana. There she was called upon to put order to the chaos of refugee arrivals. The scale of the task was daunting. Amidst these challenges, she was faced with the predicament of hundreds of stateless Jews on the ill-fated MS *St. Louis*. The Jewish passengers' fate was caught up in the bitter feuds and corruption within the Cuban government. She saw clearly that international refugee aid was a political problem that required allies and solidarity. As she noted in a later interview, 'I insisted that this was nothing which I felt I should handle alone. It was more political than social.' The failure to find a port for the MS *St. Louis* passengers and their return journey to Europe left her both sad and determined. The lessons of this 'in-service training', as she called it, would serve her well in Shanghai.[24]

By the time that she met for tea in the Cathay Hotel with Captain Insasuka, she had years of practice navigating the social and the political challenges of refugee assistance. 'Margolis achieved things her male predecessors failed to do', writes one historian, 'because she knew how to gain support for her cause by negotiating and practicing diplomacy in non-traditional spaces'.[25] She also understood that prioritising refugee well-being also meant acting outside legal norms. Having secured a flow of funds through the benevolence of Insasuka, Margolis understood that this money had to be stretched to feed a maximum number of desperate people for as long as possible.

Purchasing coal to fuel the old Chinese kitchens used to feed the refugees was a massive drain on the resources at her disposal. Margolis was alerted that some new boilers had arrived in the French concession the day before Pearl Harbor. A Polish engineer among the refugees assured her that the boilers could be fitted to the needs of the communal kitchens. Enquiries about the possibility of purchasing the boilers stalled in a loop of bureaucracy; the

Agents of empathy 259

boilers were sequestered as property of a British company that now was on the list as belonging to 'enemy aliens'. Margolis knew that this was the moment when rules were made to be broken. Under the cover of darkness, she went with the engineer and a team of Chinese labourers and 'highjacked', as she later recalled in laughter, the two giant boilers. Her summary was unapologetic: 'And from that point on, we built a new kitchen that was really giving nutrition and we burned up the old kitchens.'[26] Brecht once said first comes food, then comes morality. Margolis proved herself an empathetic Brechtian, who managed to navigate a difficult and dangerous political landscape in order to feed thousands.

Anger and frustration at injustice and bureaucratic inefficiency often spurred Margolis and Zisman to act as agents of empathy. Empathy, however, also requires *feeling into* the suffering of others. While both Margolis and Zisman acted on behalf of the stateless and displaced people of many nationalities and faiths, they both demonstrate a particular sensitivity to the plight of the Jews during the war. Judaism was as central to Margolis's motivations as were her American progressive ideals.

For Zisman, his historical narrative once again produces a bundle of silences. As a gay man born in 1908, he no doubt learned that cloaking areas of life in silence was a matter of survival. Like Margolis, he was born into a family of Jewish immigrants. Zisman's family fled to Boston in the wake of the Kishinev pogroms. Evidence suggests that he and his two brothers and sister were raised within Jewish practice and tradition. Yet he was one of the millions of Jewish young men and women born in the United States who had the freedom *not* to choose a Jewish life. Unlike Margolis, it was a freedom that he appears to have exercised once he left Boston after his studies in architecture and urban planning at MIT.

By the time of his death in 1970 at the age of sixty-one in San Antonio, his extensive network of friends and colleagues who gathered for his funeral were surprised that a rabbi delivered the eulogy. Sam, they discovered, was Jewish. Even more surprising was the arrival of distant Jewish relatives who were distressed to discover that there would be no Jewish mourning rituals. These surviving family members, some with connections back to the 'old country', were quite vocal in expressing their outrage that his children (adopted from his deceased brother James) had had no religious

260 *Refugees and the stateless in Asia*

instruction. According to his partner, the rift between the Jewish world that he had left behind and the life that he had made was palpable at the funeral, distressing the children and leaving Sam's largely secular friends wondering 'what planet these people came from'.[27]

Zisman had become a fixture in elite social circles in South Texas in his post-war life and had largely erased both his Jewish and Russian roots. Stories circulated about his wartime military service and his work on the behalf of the Jews, including the story of his relationship to the King of Denmark. Yet the San Antonio community assumed that he was German. He was a well-regarded urban planning consultant and architect who worked alongside celebrated architects and architectural firms in Texas. His name is tied to prominent university campus designs and urban renewal projects in the state. As he made a name for himself in Texas, he was also called upon as visiting expert on city planning for the Department of Defense, studying city rebuilding in Germany with the German-born planner Hans Blumenfeld. He spoke German fluently. Pictures in the local newspapers show him dressed in *lederhosen* distributing pretzels at the popular annual fiesta event known as 'Night in Old San Antonio', where the diverse immigrant cultures of South Texas were celebrated. Generations of San Antonio children remembered him fondly as the German 'Pretzel Man'.[28]

What Sam the German 'Pretzel Man' did not speak of was the way that his wartime military service in Germany brought him face-to-face with the hatreds that had caused his parents to flee Europe. In many ways, he had been trying to distance himself from that life. His collection of documents, sitting in a trunk in his San Antonio home, revealed that of which he never spoke in his lifetime. Letters among his personal correspondence demonstrate, for example, that his advancement in the US Army Airforce was thwarted by antisemitism. He was identified as a Jew and, despite his talents in planning, organisation, and logistics, as well as languages, the military would not promote him. Why? In the words of a colleague who advocated on Zisman's behalf, 'outfits … would frankly not give much of a break to a Jew'.[29] How he came to possess these letters that were written on his behalf is unclear. This same collection of records, interestingly, provides no information about how he ended up working for UNRRA, let alone heading up an entire district.

Agents of empathy

261

What Zisman chose to document was the injury and injustice of antisemitism. He was well aware of a cumulative record of injustices in the American-occupied zone.

Zisman took particular pains to document injustice against children. Here, we can see the power of *feeling into* injustice as a catalyst for action. His documentation of a 1945 Hanukkah march by children is one of the more poignant examples. The was the first 'feast of lights and freedom' for many children. Some, born in camps, in hiding, sent away to live with gentiles, were celebrating this holiday for the first time. Others, of varying ages and nationalities, might as well have been celebrating for the first time, given all that they had been through. These were children who had survived six years in an adult world dedicated to their extermination. Persecution, war, hiding, arrest, camps, terror, starvation, disease, death all around them disfigured the lives of these 'unaccompanied children', to use the label employed by UNRRA. Zisman and his staff knew that 'unaccompanied' was a euphemism to hide the brutal truth of the murders and deaths of parents and siblings, neighbours and strangers, the imprisonment and abuse of these children in forced labour camps, the disorientation that left these children without families, homes, and countries. Few parents would be making their way to the Fohrenwald Jewish Displaced Person Camp in Wolfratshausen in Southern Germany for reunions with their children. According to Zisman's documents, no parents arrived for this first Hanukkah after liberation.

What Zisman documented at Wolfratshausen brought into question not only the meaning of liberation but also the shining, heroic portrayal of the liberators. Zisman's documents show that no one disputed the basic outline of events. The estimated 750 children and the small staff of UNRRA workers dedicated to their care carefully prepared the festivities, marking the Hannukah story. Central to it was the legend that in ancient times oil sufficient to keep a candle alight for one night lasted miraculously for eight nights. These illuminations showed children of all ages what freedom meant. It also was a story of hope in a time of darkness.[30]

In Wolfratshausen, Jewish refugees organised a torch-light procession through the camp carried out in 'the religious and traditional Character, without any political intention'. At approximately 6:30 p.m., 'due to the fact of the holy [sic] and highly risen spirit', this group of young refugees left the camp and moved 'quite unexpected [*sic*] and spontaneously [*sic*] in the direction to Wolfratshausen'.[31] The children sought to share their celebration with those in the centre of town and to arrive at 'Military Government headquarters to express to them their deep appreciation of the help the Military Government have given the camp and also for the freedom they enjoy, which resulted from their liberation by the American Army'.[32] The children were, according to testimony gathered by Zisman, 'in perfect order and excellent discipline', with torches lit and in high spirits.[33] Here were hundreds of children walking in freedom.

Freedom led them face-to-face with a side of the American Army of Occupation that would become all too familiar to the camp population and UNRRA employees in Southern Germany over the next two years. What they saw and Zisman worked to document was bigotry, brutality, and insensitivity to those who had suffered.

Consider how the US occupying forces reacted to this incident. What they saw were not children on their Hanukkah march, but a 'mob'. The Jewish children of the Wolfratshausen camp were met by two platoons of armed troops and a number of visibly annoyed officers. They feared that the 'mob' of Jewish children might agitate the local German population, who would interpret the Hanukkah march as a 'looting raid'.

The first inclination of the officers from the Military Government and Tactical Unit was to arrest the entire group and put on trial 'the leaders'. Perhaps overwhelmed by the sheer number of children and unable to establish their 'command structure', the officers decided against this and ordered the 3 UNRRA caregivers, who they felt 'to be a party to this, to report to Military Government the following morning at 9 o'clock a.m.'.[34] The children were hurried back inside the camp, behind the gates and guards that had come to define their short lives. Here was the moment where Zisman's work as an agent of empathy took on a new meaning. He confronted the officers who blocked the road to Wolfratshausen and demanded that they arrest and try him instead. Arresting Zisman would have caused an incident, a blot on the record of the occupiers' ability to keep the peace. Phone calls would have had to be made; superiors would have had to be consulted; and should the story get out, the press would have a field day. Everyone stood down. Zisman, however, was keeping a record.

Agents of empathy

For Zisman, a great deal happened that day. Agents of empathy act out of anger. Was this the moment that Zisman decided to start collecting documents? Was this for him what the injustice of the MS *St. Louis* was for Margolis? It is difficult to say. We know that neither Zisman nor Margolis deflected emotion or attempted neutrality. Ordinary people become extraordinary agents of empathy in moments like these when they stiffen their commitment to defend those too weak or too young to defend themselves. They break the law or defy authority, if the law or authority behaves in ways that are irrational or cruel. It was irrationality that Margolis faced when denied the purchase of a couple of boilers that would have languished in disuse rather than feed thousands. And cruelty was precisely what Zisman rightly highlighted in the confrontation between refugee children and the soldiers on the road to Wolfratshausen. Emotions were channeled into codes of action designed to help refugee communities not just survive, but also to assert their rights as human beings.

Conclusion

In her essay 'We Refugees', Hannah Arendt refers to two Jewish personae – the social parvenu, or upstart; and the social pariah, or outcast. Parvenus are those who have made it – court Jews, millionaires, philanthropists. Pariahs are people who do not want to become parvenus, people who reject fulfilling Jewish stereotypes and prefer to identify not only with the Jewish people but with humanity.[35]

Where do Zisman and Margolis fit in this Arendtian scenario? Margolis was an agent of the biggest Jewish philanthropic institution in the world. And yet she breaks with the conventions of that world and refuses to look away from the sins and peccadilloes of the mostly male, Jewish leaders in Shanghai whose egos seemed to her larger than their intelligence. I would argue that both Margolis and Zisman were double outsiders. They were Jews unwilling and unable to feign neutrality as others were excluded and persecuted. Zisman, as a gay man and a Jew, showed enormous courage in speaking out for the 'little people' when it mattered most. Margolis, a Jewish woman navigating in the high-stakes world of international relief, was equally an outsider. She was sometimes willing to play a role among Arendtian 'court Jews', but she was also unwilling to bow down before them and the big-shot donors and sponsors of Jewish relief philanthropy. She was, in many ways, a rebel against the Jewish 'establishment' at the same time as she carried out their mission to feed the Jewish refugees of Shanghai. The Jewish pariah, as Arendt wrote, rebelled against elites of the kind that controlled the states that created the stateless.

Both Margolis and Zisman were agents of empathy, but they converted empathy into action, even when it meant breaking the rules. Zisman stood up to a military bureaucracy that failed to recognise that Jewish displaced persons were far more in need of help than most others. Antisemitism merged with hidebound policy, leaving the occupation forces unable to see how important it was for children to be treated like children, and instead turned a Hanukkah celebration into a threat. Margolis broke the rules too. When a more efficient food delivery system was needed, she found a way around the rules (and the law) to create one. Theft was a better way of describing what she was prepared to do. In both cases, defiance of the rules worked. Pariahs, in Arendt's terms, are outlaws. Both Margolis and Zisman turned anger into defiance. Empathy drove their efforts, that rested on a willingness to *feel into* the suffering of their community. Doing so showed those they served that they, too, could break the bonds of passivity. For the victims of appalling persecution and violence, these were the first steps back to political life and the dignity it represented. Refugees old and young took those steps inspired by two unlikely agents of empathy, who showed them that they mattered, that they had rights, and that their future was theirs to create.

Notes

1 Viktor E. Frankl, Daniel Goleman, and Franz Vesely, *Yes to Life: In Spite of Everything* (Boston, MA: Beacon Press, 2020).

2 Mira L. Siegelberg, *Statelessness: A Modern History* (Cambridge, MA: Harvard University Press, 2020), p. 206.

3 Joy Damousi, *The Humanitarians: Child War Refugees and Australian Humanitarianism in a Transnational World, 1919–1975* (Cambridge: Cambridge University Press, 2022).

4 For more on emotions and community, see Ute Frevert, *Writing the History of Emotions: Concepts and Practices, Economies and Politics* (London: Bloomsbury, 2024).

5 Thanks are due to participants in the online workshop 'Emotions and Holocaust Studies' sponsored by Penn State University and the Center for Antisemitism Research (TU Berlin), held 13–14 September 2022.

6 Peter Gatrell, 'Refugees – What's Wrong with History?', *Journal of Refugee Studies*, 30, 2 (2016), p. 175.

7 Paul Bloom, *Against Empathy: The Case for Rational Compassion* (New York: Ecco, 2016).

8 For more on the limits of rehabilitation, see David Nasaw, *The Last Million: Europe's Displaced from World War II until the Cold War* (New York: Penguin Press, 2021).

9 Wolfgang Benz (ed.), *Das Exil Der Kleinen Leute: Alltagserfahrung Deutscher Juden in Der Emigration* (München: C. H. Beck, 1991).

10 Michel-Rolph Trouillot, *Silencing the Past: Power and the Production of History* (Boston, MA: Beacon Press, 1995), p. 26.

11 1998.A.0122. Samuel B. Zisman Papers, United States Holocaust Memorial Museum Archives, Washington, DC.

12 Robert H. Abzug, *Inside the Vicious Heart: Americans and the Liberation of Nazi Concentration Camps* (Oxford: Oxford University Press, 1987), p. 1.

13 Al Lowman, 'The Life and Death of a Bookstore', *The Southwestern Historical Quarterly*, 91, 2 (1987), pp. 173–84.

14 George L. Mosse, *Fallen Soldiers: Reshaping the Memory of the World Wars* (New York: Oxford University Press, 1990).

15 Abzug, *Inside the Vicious Heart*, p. 138.

16 Larry D. Martino, in discussion with the author, San Antonio, Texas, April 2009.

17 Rebecca Kobrin, 'American Jewish Internationalism, Laura Margolis and the Power of Female Diplomacy, 1941–1943', *Journal of Modern Jewish Studies*, 21, 2 (2022), pp. 234–52, https://doi.org/10.1080/14725886.2021.1984832.

18 USHMM Interview 127, pp. 12–20.

19 Ernest G. Heppner, *Shanghai Refuge: A Memoir of the World War II Jewish Ghetto*, (Lincoln, NE: University of Nebraska Press, 1995), 1st ed., Bison Books, p. 1.

20 JDC Archives, Records of the New York Office, 1933–1944, Folder 463, Margolis, 'Confidential Report Dec. 8 1941–September 1943'.

21 Kobrin, 'American Jewish Internationalism', p. 235.

22 Ibid.

23 Daniel J. Walkowitz, 'The Making of a Feminine Professional Identity: Social Workers in the 1920s', *The American Historical Review*, 95, 4 (October 1990), pp. 1051–75.

24 USHMM Interview Transcript, p. 4.

25 Kobrin, 'American Jewish internationalism', p. 235.

26 USHMM Interview Transcript, p. 10.

27 Larry D. Martino, in discussion with the author, San Antonio, Texas, April 2009.

28 Ibid.

29 Letter from Ascher to J. D. Millet, 7 February 1945, in USHMM, Zisman Papers, RG-19.047.03, UNRRA-related and personal correspondence, 1944–1950.

30 'The Wolfratshausen Incident', USHMM, Zisman Papers, RG-19.047.02 *07, Team 106, 1945 July–1946 August.

31 Memo 'For Mrs. Henshaw Director of Camp Fohrenwald', 1 December 1945 in USHMM, Zisman papers, RG-19.047.02 *07, Team 106, 1945 July–1946 August.

32 Memo 'Chanukah Festivities', in USHMM, Zisman Papers, RG-19.047.02 *07, Team 106, 1945 July–1946 August.

33 Memo 'For Mrs. Henshaw'.

34 Memo 'Chanukah Festivities'.

35 Hannah Arendt, *The Jewish Writings*, Jerome Kohn and Ron H. Feldman (eds) (New York: Schocken Books, 2007).

16

From Shanghai to Australia: Jewish emigrés in the period of the Second World War

Seumas Spark

At the Évian conference of July 1938, the Australian delegate T. W. White made a now infamous statement about Jewish migration to Australia. He declared that the government would help Jewish refugees escape from Nazism, but not at the risk of importing a 'racial problem': the help would be contingent on considerations of race.[1] At the time, White's words offered no surprise, for racist and exclusionary principles had underpinned Australian immigration policy for decades, but they were significant in confirming that antisemitism was a tenet of Australia's position. Jewish immigration to Australia was not welcome, but under certain circumstances, it would be tolerated.

The extent of Australian antisemitism, in both official circles and the community, was soon tested. The *Kristallnacht* pogrom of November 1938 marked the start of a decade-long period in which Nazism and its consequences forced thousands of Jewish refugees to Australia, often against the wishes of the Australian government and public. This migration had three main phases. The first involved around 7,385 Jewish refugees finding sanctuary in Australia before the Second World War.[2] The second phase came during the war, when more than 2,100 'enemy aliens', most of them Germans and Austrians of Jewish heritage, arrived in Australia from Britain, where they had been arrested on the basis of their nationality. Many of these aliens, all of whom were men, had fled Hitler, a fact that the British government knew and ultimately chose to disregard. In July 1940 they were deported on the HMT *Dunera* from Britain to Australia, where it was intended they be interned for the duration of

268   *Refugees and the stateless in Asia*

the war.[3] More 'enemy aliens' came to Australia on the HT *Queen Mary*, which in September 1940 brought 266 men, women, and children from Singapore to Sydney.[4] In common with the *Dunera* internees, most of the *Queen Mary* aliens were German and Austrian Jews. The third phase came in the post-war period, when in 1945 the Australian government instituted a scheme that allowed for Jewish survivors of the war to enter Australia provided they had close relatives in the country.[5] This scheme, which operated under the direction of Arthur Calwell, Minister for Immigration in the Labor government, eventually fell victim to entrenched antisemitism in the Australian community and ended in January 1947.[6] Some of Calwell's opponents were his colleagues in government.[7] Thereafter, Jewish immigration continued under the general rubric of Australian law, but with more administrative restrictions placed on entry, a measure designed to limit the number of Jewish wartime refugees arriving in the country. By December 1948, fifteen thousand landing permits had been issued to Jews since the end of the Second World War, and from 1945 to 1954, it is thought that around seventeen thousand Jews arrived in Australia.[8] Probably about two thousand of these immigrants came to Australia from Shanghai.[9]

The politics of this period in Australian migration history and Australian Jewish history has been well covered by scholars.[10] The chapter does not revisit that territory in an extended way. Rather, it dwells on two related topics. First, it uses a case study of one family, supported by other testimonies, to explore the post-war lives of *some* Jewish refugees who came to Melbourne from Shanghai. While there is a broad and impressive literature on the Shanghai emigrés, this scholarship reveals less about what followed their double exodus, to Shanghai then to Australia. How did they adapt to Australia? What of their past came with them? To what extent did their experiences of displacement and persecution define their Australian lives? While definitive answers to these questions await further qualitative and quantitative research, this chapter offers certain preliminary conclusions.

Second, the chapter considers the extent to which the timing and circumstances of arrival in Australia shaped the refugees' path to an Australian life. The scholar Andrew Markus has written that the question of Jewish migration to Australia was of less importance

From Shanghai to Australia 269

in the war years, insofar as it attracted less attention.[11] The lack of attention was to benefit the *Dunera* internees, who came to a country at war and were interned immediately, unlike pre- and post-war Jewish emigrés who were free to enter Australian society from the time of their arrival. Those emigrés were faced with decisions and choices that the *Dunera* and *Queen Mary* internees, initially at least, were denied. Tucked out of sight in rural internment camps, and unable to plan Australian lives, the *Dunera* and *Queen Mary* internees could hardly contravene social mores and sensibilities, which meant that Australian objections to their presence tended to the abstract; it was hard to put faces to this xenophobia. This situation, and the myriad distractions of the war, offered the internees a measure of anonymity that rendered their histories, as Jews and foreigners from enemy countries, less visible than those of other Jewish emigrés. The plight of the refugees from Shanghai, by contrast, was discussed extensively in newspapers, their lives subject to the gossip and prejudices of political and public opinion. The Shanghai emigrés who arrived in Australia by air rather than sea managed to avoid some unwelcome attention, but it remained that their presence in Australia was visible immediately.

This chapter suggests, somewhat counter-intuitively, that the timing and nature of the *Dunera* internees' arrival helped to ease their way into Australian society.[12] To be sure, they too suffered prejudice and antisemitism. But they also benefitted from an unforeseen situation in that they were interned in a country that came to need them at a time of national emergency. The vagaries of war combined to offer the *Dunera* internees an unexpected path into Australian society, and thus a means by which to escape the curse of displacement and statelessness. Other Jewish emigrés had to find this path themselves.

This contention leads to a related question. Does the smoother path taken by the *Dunera* internees explain the attention later afforded them in accounts of German and Austrian Jewish emigration to Australia? A stereotype holds that the *Dunera* boys, as they are now commonly known, were uniformly successful, their Australian lives a triumph of good citizenship and material achievement. As always, the limitations of the stereotype outweigh any truth it holds, but it shapes *Dunera* memory nonetheless. Tales of *Dunera* accomplishments overshadow other stories from this period in Australian Jewish migration history. For instance, the popular imagination sometimes has it that the economist Max Corden, an emigré from Breslau, and the music composer George Dreyfus, an emigré from Wuppertal, came to Australia on the *Dunera*.[13] Corden arrived in Australia with his parents and brother in January 1939, the Dreyfus family later that year.[14] *Dunera* has become a byword for Jewish success, the word itself an explanation.

This chapter uses the term 'emigrés', a noun commonly associated with 'political exile', with a caveat.[15] The *Dunera* internees and Shanghai refugees were emigrés in the broader sense, though not always for reasons of politics, or not that alone. For instance, many *Dunera* internees were religious exiles, others political and religious exiles, and some neither of these things, although all were the victims of nationalist politics in Germany and Britain. This chapter employs 'emigrés' in its more general sense, and because other nouns prompt even more caveats.

The story of Leopold and Herta Maehrischel

The Maehrischel (originally Mährischel/Mährischl) name comes from Brünn (Brno) in Moravia. At some point, probably in the second half of the nineteenth century, the name came South to Vienna.[16] Alfred Maehrischel was born in Vienna on 17 July 1885. His wife Helene was also Viennese-born, on 11 June 1891. Her parents had moved to Vienna from Romania. Together Alfred and Helene had three children: Leopold, born 18 June 1911; and twins Karl and Regina, born 14 November 1920.

Alfred and Poldi, as Leopold was known, were two of many Jews arrested in Vienna in March 1938 in the wake of the Anschluss. Alfred was soon released from custody after being recognised by a policeman friend, while Poldi was held for several days longer, during which time a gun was held to his head. He was released on the condition that he leave Austria immediately, an encouragement that he heeded.[17] Soon after, Poldi and his cousin Arnold sailed for Shanghai, a city for which travellers did not need a visa. Probably they left from Trieste, though that, and the date they sailed, is uncertain. Karl followed in October, departing Trieste for Shanghai on the *Conte Rosso*. Also on this ship was Herta Zauner, a milliner from

Salzburg and Poldi's girlfriend.[18] Her emigration was informed by love rather than circumstance, for she was not Jewish; for love, she made herself a refugee. Some members of her family were committed Nazis, and later were arraigned at the Nuremberg war crimes trials.[19]

When Alfred, Helene, and Regina arrived in Shanghai in February 1939, the Maehrischel family was together once more.[20] Despite his arrest after the Anschluss, Alfred had been reluctant to leave Vienna, reasoning that 'the Germans would not dare touch him as he was born in Austria and he had fought in the Austrian Army'.[21] Helene had convinced him to go.

Shanghai brought Poldi and Herta more liberty than the couple had enjoyed in Vienna, where Helene had disapproved of Poldi's courtship of a gentile.[22] The old world and its strictures were a long way from Shanghai. Poldi and Herta married in Shanghai on 14 May 1944.[23] Herta converted to Judaism from Catholicism, and together they determined that their daughter Jeannette, born in Shanghai on 17 March 1946, would be raised in the Jewish tradition, if not the religion.[24] In common with many German and Austrian Jews of his generation and middle-class milieu, Poldi's

Figure 16.1 The Maehrischel clothes shop in Vienna. Source: Jeannette Abrahams.

attachment to Judaism was, initially at least, more social and cultural than religious. Jeannette's twin sister, never named, died at eight hours old and is buried in the Jewish cemetery on Point Road, Shanghai.

Poldi and Herta lived on Yuyen Road in the International Settlement. Poldi had worked as a master tailor in Vienna, and his skills brought him work in Shanghai. At his workshop at 190 Peking Road he made custom suits for clients, including American diplomats and wealthy Chinese. Herta also worked, probably either as a milliner or a seamstress, at a fashion shop on Rue Cardinal Mercier in the French Quarter. Their employment financed a comfortable existence, more comfortable than that enjoyed by the rest of the family, who lived together on Tongshan Road in Hongkew. Poldi and Herta had enough money to employ an amah to care for Jeannette.[25]

When the war ended, Poldi and Herta saw no reason to leave Shanghai. They had not suffered the privations of the ghetto, their lives were stable, and they were grateful for safety, far from Europe. For them Shanghai was a place of good luck, a city of welcome and forgiveness.[26] Their determination to stay was undermined by the departure of friends and family to new homes in the United States and elsewhere, and by the advance of Mao's communist forces. Poldi and Herta considered Canada and Australia as destinations,

Figure 16.2 Poldi's business card, Shanghai. Source: Jeannette Abrahams.

From Shanghai to Australia 273

on the basis that both were liberal democracies a long way from their old world in Europe. They chose the latter because in February 1948, Ernest Marish, a paternal relative in Sydney, offered to sponsor them, thus meeting a condition of entry.[27]

By August that year, Poldi, Herta, and Jeanette were registered with the Shanghai branch of the International Refugee Organisation as 'bona-fide Displaced Persons' eligible for assistance.[28] Probably this assistance was with logistics rather than finances for in early November the Maehrischels flew to Australia, the tickets likely paid with their own money. Helene accompanied Poldi, Herta and Jeanette; Alfred had died in Shanghai on 27 November 1944.[29] Their first Australian stop was in Darwin, where they slept a night in an army barracks.[30] Next they flew to Sydney, where they arrived on 2 November 1948, then to Melbourne.[31] Melbourne attracted many Shanghai refugees, including couples with whom Poldi and Herta shared friendships and common experience; all had followed the same path from Vienna to Shanghai to Melbourne.[32] Tribalism came to be a defining characteristic of many of the Shanghai refugees who settled in Australia, and for some, that loyalty was traced to a common place of origin.

Poldi's siblings also settled in Australia. Karl and his wife Cecylia, a Russian Jew from Harbin whom he had met and married while in Shanghai, arrived in Sydney by aircraft on 6 February 1949.[33] In Australia, Cecylia became Sylvia in a nod to her new life, this name and spelling more familiar to Australians. Regina and her husband Wilhelm had arrived in Sydney two years earlier in January 1947, having travelled from Shanghai by sea on the *Hwa Lien*.[34] Initially, the three siblings and their spouses lived in Melbourne, though Karl and his family moved to Sydney in 1958 or 1959. Karl had business interests there, Sylvia her family. Members of the Gohshtand and Prosterman families, sponsored by Karl and Poldi respectively, had emigrated to Sydney in 1949.[35]

Why Regina and Wilhelm were the only members of the family to travel to Australia via sea is not clear. Possibly it was a matter of money. The American Jewish Joint Distribution Committee, commonly known as the Joint, paid the fares of the 306 Jewish refugees on board the *Hwa Lien*.[36] The experience of travelling by sea rather than via air was certainly slower and considerably more uncomfortable. The *Hwa Lien* was a converted ferry that had been

Figure 16.3 The Maehrischel family in Shanghai, c. 1941. Alfred and Helene (front) with their three children; Karl, Poldi, and Regina. Poldi is in the centre. Source: Jeannette Abrahams.

built in 1908 for relatively short journeys; modifications to the ship that allowed for longer voyages had not made it any more comfortable.[37] Dreadful living conditions prevailed on the twenty-eight-day voyage to Sydney. Food was scarce, and so too water, some of it not potable. Toilet, washing, and cooking facilities were grossly inadequate. An incident after the ship reached Cairns, in Northern Queensland, prompted passengers to open revolt.[38]

Jewish refugees from Shanghai who travelled by sea faced another problem particular to their mode of transport. Because they came to Australia in large groups, and slowly, with advance notice given of their arrival, their emigration generated more attention than for those who arrived by air.[39] This was certainly true for the refugees aboard the *Hwa Lien*, whose arrival in Sydney in January 1947 attracted 'a hostile reaction from the general Australian public' fed by 'negative and alarmist headlines in the press' and jibes from MPs and other public figures.[40] Reputable broadsheet newspapers such as the *Sydney Morning Herald* gave free voice to medieval anti-Jewish stereotypes. The newspaper's front page informed readers that

From Shanghai to Australia 275

the *Hwa Lien* had been searched for gold bullion and counterfeit money on arrival in Sydney; nothing was found.[41] The Melbourne *Age* saw a potential importation conspiracy, noting in another article that certain non-household items belonging to the passengers would fetch high prices in Sydney. The same article offered the blithe observation that the *Hwa Lien* passengers had been 'held up in the Far East' since being 'allowed to leave' Nazi Europe.[42] Less reputable publications offered worse.[43]

Any on board who may have thought to object to this welcome, or the conditions on ship, said little under instruction from Walter Brand, secretary of the Australian Jewish Welfare Society, who had accompanied the passengers from Cairns. Brand acted with the imprimatur of Arthur Calwell, Minister for Immigration.[44] Brand's long-held view was that any publicity about Jewish emigrés was a threat both to the position of these newcomers in Australian society, and to established Australian Jewry. The task of the Jewish emigré was to keep quiet, as Brand made clear.[45] By the time the *Hwa Lien* reached Sydney, there was little talk of the revolt at Cairns, or of conditions on board ship. Rather than speak openly of their fears, grievances, and hopes, the *Hwa Lien* refugees offered platitudes about Australia, if they said anything at all.[46]

Poldi and Herta knew well enough to keep quiet. Like so many refugees before and since, they opted for discretion, delineating between their home and public lives. At home they spoke German to Jeannette, and raised her in the Jewish tradition, as they had determined to do. In public they spoke English, having become reasonably fluent in Shanghai, and made no 'noise', as their daughter puts it.[47] This approach suited Poldi and Herta and, more importantly, they knew it would serve Jeannette, whom circumstance had dictated would grow up Australian. She was sent to St Leonard's Girls' College, a private Presbyterian school, to learn the 'Australian way'.[48] There and in the community she rarely experienced antisemitism, which she attributes to a tolerant and welcoming environment at St Leonards, and to her parents shielding her from prejudice, their selflessness a treasured gift. Poldi and Herta wanted her to feel free, to live without the burdens they had known, and they took this desire to extremes. One day in the late 1950s, a swastika appeared on the house of their Latvian neighbours. The Maehrischels knew the neighbours to be antisemitic, and suspected they painted the

276   *Refugees and the stateless in Asia*

swastika themselves, but Poldi and Herta did not stop Jeannette playing with their children. For their daughter, they would tolerate almost anything.

But there were limits. Poldi did not draw attention to his identity, but he was sure of it. He never sought to disguise that he was Jewish, or his Austrian heritage, which in the early post-war years in Australia was another potential source for abuse and exclusion. To Melbourne, he brought with him a stronger sense of the sacred than had animated him previously. After the death of his father, Poldi had started to attend synagogue in Shanghai, an experience that seems to have confirmed a sense of faith, though not necessarily a belief in the dictates of religion.[49] He observed few religious rules, including on food – the Maehrischel household was never kosher – and did not think of himself as a religious Jew, but he held fast to his idiosyncratic understanding of Jewish identity. Poldi was an early member of the Moorabbin Hebrew Congregation, an Orthodox synagogue founded in 1949 to cater for his and other Jewish families in the area.[50] A tallit bag he brought from Shanghai, which he always kept close, became a family heirloom. And, unlike many Austrian and German immigrants in Australia, he and Herta did not anglicise their names. Poldi would find his way in Australia as Leopold Maehrischel, Jew from Vienna via Shanghai.

In finding their way, Poldi and Herta benefitted from an act of altruism. Soon after their arrival in Melbourne, they met a builder named Leo Gallagher, who worked in and around Moorabbin. Knowing that the Maehrischels lacked sufficient capital to both buy a house and establish themselves in work, he sold them a home, on terms, and allowed them to use an empty factory until such time as they could pay him back the rent, that advance made on the basis of a small deposit and a large dose of trust. Home was at 318–320 South Road, Hampton East, the area a haven for Jewish emigré families. At the factory, in Melbourne's Jewish heartland of St Kilda, Poldi, Herta, and Helene manufactured women's wear, including blouses and dresses. Poldi designed and cut the garments, while Herta and Helene stitched and sewed.[51] This was not work to which master tailors were accustomed, but it paid. Poldi adjusted to his new reality, and in three years, he and Herta had cleared their debt to Gallagher. Their business, named Hobby Styles, occupied them for the rest of their working lives, and Gallagher became a

From Shanghai to Australia

dear friend. He introduced Poldi to Australian Rules football, and for thirty years the two mates went to Moorabbin football ground on Saturdays to watch St Kilda play.[52] The Maehrischel family has never forgotten Leo Gallagher's benevolence.

Poldi knew his good luck, first in escaping Vienna and then Shanghai, and in meeting Gallagher. But he saw no triumph in this. The fact of his survival, and his success in making a good living in Australia, did not conceal the hurt he felt. He was bruised by the war, says Jeannette, and harboured a deep sense of loss about what had been taken from him and his family. Antisemitism had denied him the life he wanted and believed was his: in Vienna, and possibly also in Shanghai, he could have expected to achieve greater prosperity than he did in Australia. His ambition was to thrive, not simply to exist. In the words of Jeannette, he wanted to be someone, but never felt that he was.[53] Poldi, Herta, Jeannette, and Helene became naturalised Australians in 1955.[54] Probably Poldi saw this as a prosaic development, a necessary step in his Australian life, rather than a moment of great significance or the symbolic endpoint of his life as a refugee. Poldi had no wish to escape his past.

Shanghai emigrés in Melbourne

Beginning in 1950, a group of Shanghai emigrés who settled in Melbourne met every Tuesday fortnight, a tradition they continued for about sixty years until there were too few people left to sustain the gatherings.[55] So loud was the chatter that the occasions came to be known as *Schreiabends* (boisterous evenings), the use of the German an indication of the language in which the high spirted events were conducted. There was no national bias to these gatherings, for the participants were of Austrian and German heritage in equal number.[56] Rather, they were united by their experience as Jewish refugees in Shanghai, and in making new lives in Melbourne, usually in near proximity to each other. Most eventually settled in and around St Kilda, Caulfield, and Bentleigh in Melbourne's Southeast. As the historian Antonia Finnane has written, 'they watched each other's families growing up, serving as aunts and uncles to children whom the Holocaust had largely deprived of extended families'.[57] Age was the main influence on the development and organisation

278   *Refugees and the stateless in Asia*

of the *Schreiabends*. Ilse Sherwin (née Suran), who arrived with her parents in Melbourne in September 1946 aged twenty, states that the gatherings were for her generation rather than that of her parents.[58] Ilse's parents Charlotte and Friedrich did not attend the *Schreiabends*, and nor did Poldi and Herta.

Georg and Margarete Prager, born in Berlin in 1904 and 1906 respectively, were other Shanghai emigrés who did not join the *Schreiabends*.[59] Georg had been arrested on Kristallnacht in November 1938 and then imprisoned in Sachsenhausen concentration camp for a short time. The next month he and Margarete, along with their baby son Lothar, had fled Berlin for Shanghai, where they endured a precarious existence in Hongkew; Georg and Margarete hawked items, including personal possessions, to survive.[60] They flew to Australia from Shanghai in November 1946, their tickets paid for by the Joint, and arrived in Melbourne the following month, on a Friday.[61] On the Monday, Georg, a printer by trade, started work at the *Australian Jewish News* in Carlton, the job arranged by the same cousin who sponsored the Prager family's emigration. Margarete's Melbourne life did not move so quickly, her nerves an initial impediment to her seeking employment. Moreover, she and Georg spoke very limited English, her husband only able to work because he joined a Jewish employer. Lothar, by this time eight years old, had learned some English in Shanghai. He started at Brighton Road State School in St Kilda, where he experienced antisemitic taunts, but otherwise was able to avoid such bigotry; the family deliberately kept to Jewish circles. After renting in shared accommodation, they settled in a small flat in St Kilda. In common with Poldi and Herta, Georg and Margarete spoke of their past, but at home, where others could not hear.[62]

Hans and Ursula Becher met as teenagers in Shanghai. Hans had left Austria as a seventeen-year-old in 1937, while Ursula, known as Uschi, had fled Berlin after Kristallnacht when she was 14.[63] They wed in Shanghai in 1947 in what they joked was a mixed marriage, their union between a German Jew and an Austrian Jew.[64] They arrived in Sydney by aircraft on 12 February 1949, then moved to Melbourne. Initially they lived in boarding houses, where antisemitism found open expression, before finding a flat to rent in Mitford Street, St Kilda.[65] In 1950 they chose to open a gift shop business in Brunswick, beyond Melbourne's Jewish heartland, exposing

From Shanghai to Australia 279

them to further bigotry, though their daughter Judy is unsure if this prejudice was informed specifically by antisemitism or general xenophobia.[66]

Hans and Uschi did embrace the *Schreiabends*, and took succour from the sense of familiarity and trust that these gatherings offered; they built on friendships forged in Shanghai. The Holocaust was discussed rarely. Uschi drew no parallels between her experience and those who had endured the Holocaust; she was adamant that she, and other Shanghai refugees, were not Holocaust survivors, a position on which the ex-Shanghai community in Melbourne was broadly agreed.[67] Religion was another instrument by which Hans and Uschi ordered their Australian lives. Most Shanghai emigrés who settled in Melbourne were liberal Jews, primarily from Germany and Austria, who worshipped at liberal synagogues: usually Temple Beth Israel in St Kilda, or the Southern Liberal Congregation, also known as Bentleigh progressive synagogue (now Etz Chayim). Together Hans and Uschi and their *Schreiabend* friends attended Bentleigh progressive, forging another ritual through which a supportive community was created.[68] In certain instances, these connections have crossed the generations. Some children of the *Schreiabend* collective grew up together and have stayed close, their relationships familial.[69]

Though the details of these histories differ, there are common threads to the stories of the Shanghai emigrés who settled in Melbourne. Their biographies are more communal than those of the *Dunera* internees.

The *Dunera* internees in Australian life

Dunera history is well represented in print and film.[70] For the purposes of this chapter, only brief details are necessary. During the voyage of the *Dunera* from Britain to Australia, the approximately 2,130 German and Austrian male enemy aliens aboard were treated with wanton cruelty by their British captors.[71] When the ship reached Australia, about 135 of the enemy aliens were disembarked at Melbourne on 3 September 1940 and transferred to internment camps at Tatura in the Goulburn Valley of Victoria. The others sailed to Sydney, then were taken seven hundred kilometres

280   *Refugees and the stateless in Asia*

West to Hay in the Riverina region of New South Wales. About four hundred of these men would later spend six weeks at Orange, in the New South Wales Central Tablelands.[72] In Australia, the treatment of the internees was considerably better than on board ship, and for most, their internment proved relatively benign.

By 1941, and probably earlier, the British and Australian governments were agreed that the internees should be released. Officials in both London and Canberra knew that they had visited an injustice on men who had committed no crime and posed no threat to the Allied cause. The first main avenue for release allowed for internees to return to Britain and join the British Army Pioneer Corps. Around four hundred internees took this option in 1941.[73]

Soon enough other options arose, including for release in Australia. Internees with specialist skills were freed to work in jobs of national importance. Georg Fröhlich and Hans Meyer, opticians from Berlin, left internment early in July 1941 to work at the Mt Stromlo observatory in Canberra, at the request of its director.[74] Ernst Reichelt, a Catholic engineer from Bohemia, was released later that month to assist in the manufacture of medical syringes, a field in which he had expertise.[75] Ernst Rodeck, a Jewish engineer and draughtsman from Vienna, was freed in March 1942 to work in aircraft production.[76] The definition of national importance was applied liberally, an indication that by 1941–42 the British and Australian governments wanted as few barriers as possible to the release of the *Dunera* internees. Ludwig Hirschfeld-Mack, a modernist who had taught colour theory at the Weimar Bauhaus, was released in April 1942 to teach art at Geelong Grammar, a private school in Victoria.[77] In the space of a few days, he went from enemy alien internee to teacher entrusted with the education of some of the most privileged children in the country. 'Hirsch' or 'Hirschy', as students knew him, was accepted quickly.[78] He spent a happy fifteen years at the school, revered by students and staff alike for his noble example in the ways of art and life.[79]

Even more remarkable and unlikely was the transformation of enemy alien internees into Australian soldiers. The bombing of Pearl Harbor on 7 December 1941 and the start of the Pacific War hastened a decision to allow *Dunera* (and *Queen Mary*) internees to join the Australian Army. As members of the 8th Employment Company, a unit that laboured on the home front, they did not

From Shanghai to Australia　　　281

carry weapons, nor were they permitted to serve beyond Australian territory, but they were Australian soldiers, allowed all the freedoms that came with the uniform.[80] Indeed, the uniform was taken as proof of loyalty and good intentions. The scholar Jon Stratton has written that, historically, Jews violated 'two major discourses of Australian population policy: race and nation'.[81] The King's uniform, however, hid those personal histories that might otherwise have fed prejudice. From April 1942, when the 8th was raised, a total of 564 *Dunera* internees joined the unit, with many serving three or four years.[82] Their military service made them eligible for funding under the Commonwealth Reconstruction Training Scheme when it launched in 1945.[83] The scheme paid for ex-servicemen and women to study at university, and many *Dunera* men from the 8th, alert to the possibilities, seized the opportunity. After all, they were Australian soldiers entitled to an Australian education.

For the 630 or so *Dunera* internees who chose to settle in Australia, timing and circumstance certainly eased their way.[84] Most were freed between late 1941 and mid-1942, when the country's attention was on Japanese forces massed to the near North.[85] Their release into Australian society, including into so exalted a national institution as the Australian Army, attracted little public comment. With the war so close, few Australians had time to object. The savage irony of German and Austrian men joining the Australian Army to fight a war against their homelands essentially passed unnoticed.

The fact that circumstance forced *Dunera* internees into Anglo-Celtic Australian society also offered another advantage. Whether an internee joined a civilian employer or the Australian Army, his public life tended to encourage engagement with Australian mores. The *8th Gazette*, a news sheet published by and for the men of the 8th Employment Company, included such content as tips for the Melbourne horse races.[86] For those who joined the civilian workforce, their freedom often relied on the continuing patronage of their employers, who acted as sponsors to secure their release from internment and as guarantors of their good behaviour. A life of detachment was not a ready option.

This public embrace of Australia came to be reflected in the personal lives of many *Dunera* internees. Of those who were Jewish, a majority had only fragile or distant ties to this heritage.[87] And where these ties existed, Australian life often made them weaker

282 *Refugees and the stateless in Asia*

still; perhaps the confidence engendered by a sense of belonging lessened the need to turn to the past for reassurance and guidance. Traditions weakened. The Australian historian Ken Inglis befriended many former *Dunera* internees during his studies at the University of Melbourne in the late 1940s, and subsequently during his academic career. All of the *Dunera* men he knew 'married out', their wives from non-Jewish families.[88] The Buchdahl brothers, Gerd and Hans, wed the Wann sisters, Nancy and Pamela, from a wealthy and long-established Protestant, rural Australian family.[89] The Buchdahls married into the Australian gentry.

Beyond a general preference for Melbourne, the city to which most were released, former *Dunera* internees tended not to congregate in particular Australian locations. They spread across the country, occupying a diverse range of jobs, including some that brought prominence. Fred Gruen became economic advisor to Prime Minister Gough Whitlam, Steven Strauss QC a judge of the Family Court.[90] And not until their Australian lives were made did *Dunera* men come together to exchange memories of their shared past. The first organised *Dunera* reunions took place in the 1960s, the gatherings a happy indulgence now that the former internees had time and security – now that they felt Australian.[91] For some of the Shanghai emigrés, gatherings had a different and more important function as a means by which to endure. Anecdotal evidence indicates that more Shanghai children than *Dunera* children speak German, and that the descendants of Shanghai emigrés tend to a more visceral connection with their German or Austrian, and Jewish, heritage.

An uncomfortable aspect of the *Dunera* story is that it can tend to triumphalism.[92] The cultural achievements and material success of some former *Dunera* internees, probably no more than fifty of the 2,130 men deported on the ship, has washed over the collective. Such versions of the *Dunera* story encourage the unedifying idea that a refugee's life and place in the social order can somehow be quantified by what they might 'contribute' to society – by what they give to Anglo-Celtic Australia. This lens serves only to obscure histories such as those of the Shanghai refugees, whose presence in post-war Australia has been less visible than that of the *Dunera* men and their descendants. Antonia Finnane has observed that the remarkable tale of Shanghai's Jewish refugees is continually discovered anew, the story coming and going with time.[93] The same cannot be said for the *Dunera* story.

The *Dunera* internees who settled in Australia were little different from other German and Austrian emigrés who came to the country in the late 1930s and 1940s. They too were exiles in need of sanctuary. They too sought niches in which to create an Australian life. In common with many of the Shanghai emigrés, they too maintained an awkward silence about the Holocaust.[94] *Dunera* men tended to reject comparisons between their experiences and those of Holocaust survivors.[95]

What the *Dunera* and Shanghai emigrés did not always share was equally fortunate circumstances. Bern Brent, who fled Berlin on a *Kindertransport* in December 1938, believes his internment and subsequent deportation on the *Dunera* to be among the greatest blessings of his life; the ship delivered him to a new country where, almost immediately, he had agency to fashion a new existence, unencumbered by his German and Jewish heritage.[96] For the Jewish emigrés from Shanghai who settled in Australia after the Second World War, the path away from statelessness was rarely that clear.

Acknowledgement

Thanks to Jeannette Abrahams, Judy Becher, Peter Kohn, Lothar Prager, and Ilse Sherwin for enlightening conversations, and to Suzanne Rutland for sharing so graciously her remarkable knowledge of Australian Jewish history.

Notes

1 Cited in Andrew Markus, 'Jewish Migration to Australia 1938–49', *Journal of Australian Studies*, 7, 13 (1983), p. 21.
2 The figure of 7,385 comes from Suzanne Rutland. Email from Suzanne Rutland, 21 May 2023.
3 Ken Inglis, Seumas Spark, and Jay Winter, with Carol Bunyan, *Dunera Lives: A Visual History* (Melbourne: Monash University Publishing, 2018), p. xvii.
4 Thanks to Carol Bunyan for the figure of 266.

5 Suzanne D. Rutland, 'Australian Responses to Jewish Refugee Migration Before and After World War II', *Australian Journal of Politics and History*, 31, 1 (1985), p. 42; Klaus Neumann, 'The Admission of European Refugees from East and South Asia in 1947: Antecedents of Australia's International Refugee Organization Mass Resettlement Scheme', *History Australia*, 12, 2 (2015), p. 72.

6 Markus, 'Jewish Migration', pp. 27–8.

7 Ibid., p. 24.

8 Ibid., p. 28. Thanks to Suzanne Rutland for information on Calwell's close family reunion scheme.

9 How many Jewish refugees came to Australia from Shanghai, and in the post-war period generally, is not clear. The issue of numbers is a vexed one. Thanks to Suzanne Rutland for these figures and related advice. Emails from Suzanne Rutland, 13 December 2022; 21 May 2023.

10 For example, see Markus, 'Jewish Migration', pp. 18–31; Neumann, 'The Admission of European Refugees from East and South Asia in 1947', pp. 62–79; Jayne Persian, '"The Dirty Vat": European Migration to Australia from Shanghai, 1946–47', *Australian Historical Studies*, 50, 1 (2019), pp. 21–40; Rutland, 'Australian Responses to Jewish Refugee Migration Before and After World War II', pp. 29–48; Suzanne Rutland, 'Postwar Anti-Jewish Refugee Hysteria: A Case of Racial or Religious Bigotry?', *Journal of Australian Studies*, 27, 77 (2003), pp. 69–79; Suzanne Rutland, '"Waiting Room Shanghai": Australian Reactions to the Plight of the Jews in Shanghai after the Second World War', *The Leo Baeck Institute Year Book*, 32, 1 (January 1987), pp. 407–33.

11 Markus, 'Jewish Migration', 24.

12 The argument might apply also to the men, women, and children deported to Australia on the *Queen Mary*, but the focus here is on the *Dunera* internees, the number of whom was much greater.

13 Inglis et al., *Dunera Lives: A Visual History*, p. xviii.

14 See Max Corden, *Lucky Boy in the Lucky Country: The Autobiography of Max Corden, Economist* (Cham: Palgrave Macmillan, 2017); George Dreyfus, *The Last Frivolous Book* (Sydney: Hale & Iremonger, 1984).

15 Lesley Brown (ed.), *The New Shorter Oxford English Dictionary*, vol. 1 (Oxford: Clarendon Press, 1993), p. 807.

16 Karl Maehrischel, *In Protective Custody* (Sydney: Sydney Jewish Museum, 2004), p. 4; interview with Jeannette Abrahams (née Maehrischel), Melbourne, 30 November–1 December 2022.

17 Maehrischel, *In Protective Custody*, pp. 8–9; Abrahams interview.

18 Ibid., pp. 9, 17, 27.

19 Abrahams interview.

20 Ibid.; Alfred Maehrischel Reisepass, Jeannette Abrahams private papers.

From Shanghai to Australia 285

21 Maehrischel, *In Protective Custody*, pp. 18–19.

22 Abrahams interview.

23 Maehrischel/Zauner marriage certificate, Jeannette Abrahams private papers.

24 Abrahams interview.

25 Ibid.

26 Ibidw.

27 Ernest Marish statutory declaration, 3 February 1948, Jeannette Abrahams private papers.

28 International Refugee Organisation document, 4 August 1948, Jeannette Abrahams private papers.

29 NAA, B78, 1955/MAEHRISCHEL H (Helene); Alfred Maehrischel death certificate, Jeannette Abrahams private papers.

30 Abrahams interview.

31 NAA,B78,1955/MAEHRISCHEL L; NAA,B78,1955/MAEHRISCHEL H (Herta).

32 Abrahams interview.

33 NAA, B78, 1955/MAEHRISCHEL K; NAA, B78, 1955/ MAEHRISCHEL C; Abrahams interview.

34 NAA, B78, 1956/BRAUN R; NAA, B78, 1956/BRAUN W.

35 NAA, A261, 1949/382; NAA, A261, 1949/383.

36 Rutland, 'Waiting Room Shanghai', p. 413.

37 Ibid., pp. 413–14.

38 Ibid., p. 414. See also *Sydney Morning Herald*, 21 January 1947, p. 5.

39 For instance, see the article 'Refugees Here from China' in the *Sydney Morning Herald*, 7 February 1949, p. 3. The article gives no more than a few bare facts about some Jewish refugees who arrived from Shanghai by air.

40 Rutland, 'Waiting Room Shanghai', p. 415.

41 *Sydney Morning Herald*, 29 January 1947, p. 1.

42 *The Age*, 30 January 1947, p. 8.

43 For example, see *Smith's Weekly*, 8 February 1947, p. 10; and 22 February 1947, p. 3.

44 Rutland, 'Waiting Room Shanghai', p. 415.

45 With regard to Jewish emigrés keeping quiet, see *Australian Jewish News*, 12 April 1946, p. 1 and 11 October 1946, p. 11; and *Sydney Morning Herald*, 16 September 1946, p. 1. See also Inglis et al., *A Visual History*, p. 137.

46 *Sydney Morning Herald*, 29 January 1947, p. 1.

47 Abrahams interview.

48 Ibid.

49 Ibid.

50 Email from Jeannette Abrahams, 19 May 2023.
51 Ibid.
52 Abrahams interview.
53 Ibidw.
54 NAA, A446, 1955/33398; NAA, A446, 1955/33450; NAA, A446, 1955/33555.
55 Antonia Finnane, *Far From Where? Jewish Journeys from Shanghai to Australia* (Melbourne: Melbourne University Press, 1999), p. 1.
56 Antonia Finnane, 'Every Second Tuesday for 58 Years', *Australian Jewish News*, 18 July 2008, p. 17.
57 Ibid, p. 17.
58 NAA, B78, 1952/SURAN F; interview with Ilse Sherwin (née Suran), Melbourne, 18 January 2023.
59 NAA, BP9/3, STATELESS PRAGER G; NAA, A435, 1950/4/1608.
60 Interview with Lothar Prager, conducted via Zoom, 7 December 2022.
61 NAA, BP9/3, Stateless Prager G.
62 Prager interview.
63 NAA, A12701, Becher H; interview with Judy Becher, conducted via Zoom, 9 December 2022.
64 Becher interview.
65 NAA, B78, 1954/Becher H; email from Judy Becher, 16 May 2023.
66 Finnane, *Far From Where?*, p. 210.
67 Becher interview.
68 Ibid.
69 Ibid.
70 Accounts include Benzion Patkin, *The Dunera Internees* (Sydney: Cassell Australia, 1979); Cyril Pearl, *The Dunera Scandal: Deported by Mistake* (Sydney: Angus and Robertson, 1983); 'The *Dunera* Boys' telemovie directed by Ben Lewin, Jethro Films, 1985; Inglis et al., *A Visual History*; and Ken Inglis, Bill Gammage, Seumas Spark, and Jay Winter, with Carol Bunyan, *Dunera Lives: Profiles* (Melbourne: Monash University Publishing, 2020).
71 Seumas Spark, 'The "*Dunera* Boys": History, Memory and the Holocaust', in Avril Alba and Jan Láníček (eds), *The Palgrave Handbook of Australia and the Holocaust* (Basingstoke: Palgrave Macmillan, 2025).
72 Ibid.
73 Ibid.
74 NAA, MP1103/1, E39535; NAA, MP1103/1, E40244; NAA, MP508/1, 255/721/41.
75 NAA, A816, 54/301/88; NAA, MP1103/1, E40419.

From Shanghai to Australia

76 NAA, A2908, P22, Part 7, Cablegram, December 1941; NAA, MP1103/1, E40454.
77 NAA, A2908, P22, Part 7, Cablegram, December 1941; NAA, MP1103/1, E39779.
78 Resi Schwarzbauer with Chris Bell, *Ludwig Hirschfeld-Mack: More Than a Bauhaus Artist* (Place of publication unknown: HistorySmiths, 2021), pp. 190, 194.
79 Inglis et al., *Profiles*, p. 206.
80 Inglis et al., *A Visual History*, p. 321.
81 Jon Stratton, 'The Colour of Jews: Jews, Race and the White Australia Policy', *Journal of Australian Studies*, 20 (1996), pp. 50–51, 52.
82 Spark, 'The "*Dunera* Boys"'.
83 Inglis et al., *Profiles*, p. 310.
84 Spark, 'The "*Dunera* Boys"'.
85 Inglis et al., *A Visual History*, p. 517.
86 Jewish Museum of Australia, 3322, *The 8th Gazette*, edition 1, 11 June 1943.
87 Inglis et al., *A Visual History*, p. xx; Spark, 'The "*Dunera* boys"'.
88 Personal knowledge.
89 Inglis et al., *A Visual History*, pp. 406–7.
90 Ibid., pp. 445, 448.
91 Ibid., pp. 454, 468.
92 For example, see Cyril Pearl, 'By Dunera: A Cargo of Talent', *Reader's Digest*, December 1973; Deborah Katz, 'The Dunera Boys', *Hamodia*, 11 May 2016.
93 Antonia Finnane, 'China's Schindler', *Australian Jewish News*, 18 July 2008, p. 17.
94 In this regard, see Finnane, *Far From Where?*, pp. 12–13.
95 Spark, 'The "*Dunera* Boys"'.
96 Inglis et al., *A Visual History*, p. 16.

Section II.III

The end of cosmopolitan Shanghai

17

The rise and fall of US military power in China

Zach Fredman

The presence of the US military in Shanghai reached its zenith after Japan's surrender ended the Second World War. The United States and Chiang Kai-shek's Republic of China (ROC) had become allies after Japan's 1941 attack on Pearl Harbor, and by V-J Day, approximately seventy thousand US military personnel were deployed in China. Another fifty-three thousand American Marines joined these troops in October 1945, hailed by Chinese crowds as liberators in formerly Japanese-occupied cities like Tianjin, Beijing, and Shanghai.[1] In addition to boots on the ground, the US military's logistical capacity in China enabled the rapid air and sealift of hundreds of thousands of Chinese Nationalist soldiers to parts of China now freed from Japanese control. On 8 September, General Albert Wedemeyer, commander of US forces in China and chief of staff to Chiang Kai-shek, endorsed Chiang's proposal for the creation of a massive five-to-ten-year American military mission in China comprising headquarters, ground, air, naval, and logistics groups working together to 'create modern [Chinese] military forces capable of coping with any situation that may confront China'.[2]

While Chiang, Wedemeyer, and the population of newly liberated cities like Shanghai might have held high hopes for Sino–American military cooperation, most American soldiers deployed to China before Japan's surrender wanted no part in Chiang's plans. Sino–American military-to-military relations among the men in the ranks had deteriorated to their lowest level of the war by August 1945, with violent confrontations a near daily occurrence.[3] And while US Army advisors had trained and equipped the better part of thirty-nine Chinese Army divisions during the war, they now questioned

The rise and fall of US military power in China   291

whether China was worthy of further American tutelage. Daily life in China had become a grind, with soldiers complaining endlessly about the unpalatable food provided by the Nationalist government and the pervasive, inescapable stench of human faeces – the side effect of night soil use and the lack of modern plumbing. Theft and price gouging made matters worse, becoming so acute by mid-1945 that General Claire Chennault, commander of US Army Air Forces in China, warned journalists in Chongqing that the average American soldier now believed 'that every Chinese he sees about him is a potential thief'.[4] A poem GIs circulated around the time of Japan's surrender summarised their feelings: 'I'm glad I came, but darned anxious to go, give it back to the "Chinks", I'M READY TO BLOW!'[5]

In contrast to residents of newly liberated cities on the Chinese coast, most Chinese who interacted with American soldiers during the war would have been happy to see the US military go. Chinese interpreters, hostel workers, and soldiers had long rankled at what they perceived as unequal treatment at the hands of US military personnel. Chinese civilians, though sometimes able to profit from economic opportunities brought by US forces, also viewed the US military as a source of physical danger due to its high rates of violent crime targeting civilians, accidental shootings, traffic collisions, and frequent vigilante justice exacted against alleged Chinese thieves. Displacement and inflation caused by the US military construction and spending added to civilian resentments, as did sexual relations between American servicemen and Chinese women, which sparked violent anti-American demonstrations in spring 1945.

The US forces who landed in Shanghai and other coastal cities were unaware of these tensions, as were local populations who had lived nearly eight years under Japanese occupation, but wartime patterns of mutually damaging Sino–American engagement continued, quickly poisoning ties. By examining the rise and fall of US military power in China during the Second World War and the Chinese Civil War, this chapter reveals how the US–ROC alliance transformed into an occupation that inadvertently undermined the US-allied Chinese Nationalist government.

We are clearly in a political world very different from that described in Hannah Arendt's *The Origins of Totalitarianism*. The state in China is remote from European or North American

292   *Refugees and the stateless in Asia*

equivalents. That is why statelessness took on different forms in Asia than it did in what we broadly term 'the West'.

This chapter shows that state sovereignty is a function of military power. The end of direct imperial domination in China still left the country dependent on foreign military aid. Tensions between GIs and the people they were sent to help took many forms. They provided the friction behind a shift from assistance to occupation, demonstrating how enduring were older patterns of Western domination and Chinese subordination in the period of the Second World War and beyond.

Before Pearl Harbor, as this chapter shows, the United States was a secondary player among many countries that deployed military forces in China. After the United States entered the war, the US military presence in China grew steadily, reaching the apex of its power after Japan's surrender, when Chiang Kai-shek proposed his peacetime plan to transform the entire Chinese military along American lines. Yet less than four years later, the Truman administration pulled the last American troops out of China and washed its hands of the Chinese Nationalists, who were soon driven from the mainland by Mao Zedong's Chinese People's Liberation Army.

Unlike most chapters in this collection, this chapter focuses on state power. Statelessness is not a term that applies to Americans in China during the 1940s, the great majority of whom were soldiers – the military arm of the US state. The Chinese Nationalist state, meanwhile, depended on US military power for its very survival, making the US military the central player in Sino–American relations throughout the decade.

The city of Shanghai, meanwhile, plays only a minor role in this story. Before the Second World War, US forces deployed in Shanghai, but they were also present in large numbers in other treaty port cities, including Tianjin and Beijing. Because Shanghai fell to the Japanese in November 1937, the city did not host US military personnel who joined the war effort against Japan. Nearly all the American troops who deployed to China during the Second World War served in the country's Southwest, particularly in Yunnan Province, which was home to the military airfields that connected China to India, and in the wartime capital city of Chongqing. US Army Air Force B-29s, based in the nearby city of Chengdu, bombed Japanese-occupied Shanghai several times in late 1944 and early 1945.[6] US

The rise and fall of US military power in China   293

forces returned to Shanghai after Japan's surrender, but the cities of Tianjin, Beijing, and Qingdao were more important to the US military's mission during this period, as Shanghai served largely as a shipping-out point for American military personnel departing for the United States after V-J Day. This chapter examines each of these three periods in turn and concludes with a brief discussion about the legacy of US military power in China.

The US military in China before the Second World War

By the time of Japan's attack on Pearl Harbor, the US military had operated in China for nearly ninety years, tasked with protecting American lives and property. From the beginning, Shanghai served as an important base of operations. In 1853, the USS *Susquehanna*, the flagship on Commodore Matthew Perry's expedition to Japan, sailed up the Yangtze River from its mouth at Shanghai. By the 1870s, warships from the US Asiatic Fleet frequently sailed between Shanghai and Hankou (Wuhan) along the Yangtze. The US Navy organised its Yangtze Patrol as part of the Asiatic Fleet in 1919. By the 1930s, the Yangtze Patrol included six modern gunboats plying the river between Shanghai and Chongqing. A smaller South China Patrol operated in waters further South. In tenser periods, such as Chiang Kai-shek's attempt to unify the country under his control during the 1926–27 Northern Expedition, US authorities could call upon more troops and naval vessels.[7] As Chiang's forces approached Shanghai in 1927, the US Asiatic Fleet anchored four cruisers and four destroyers near the city, while the 3rd Marine Brigade, consisting of 238 officers, 18 warrant officers, and 4,170 enlisted men, came ashore on 2 May to protect Americans in the Shanghai International Settlement. The Marine Corps' 4th Infantry Regiment, part of the force that landed in 1927, remained on garrison duty in Shanghai until November 1941, when it was withdrawn to the Philippines.[8]

The US Army and Marine Corps also stationed forces in Northern China and occasionally deployed more troops in shorter military interventions. Beginning in 1898, a small detachment of marines guarded the US Legation in Beijing, which came under siege during the Boxer Rebellion in 1900, with both Boxer rebels and Qing

294 *Refugees and the stateless in Asia*

government troops joining the attack on the foreign legations. An eight-nation alliance comprising forces from the United States, Germany, Japan, the British Empire, France, Russia, Italy, and Austria-Hungary launched a relief campaign that suppressed the rebellion in 1901. The US Army's 9th and 14th Infantry Regiments took part in the mission, but Japan, Russia, and the British Empire supplied more troops. The Boxer Protocol, signed after the rebellion ended in September 1901, specified a larger foreign troop presence in China, paving the way for marines to return to Beijing in 1905 and for the US Army's 15th Infantry Regiment to deploy at Tianjin in 1912. The 15th remained at Tianjin until 1938, with troop strength as high as 1,800 officers and enlisted men. When Japanese and ROC forces clashed in Shanghai in 1932, the Army's 31st Infantry Regiment guarded the International Settlement for nearly six months.[9] During the 1920s and 1930s, China sometimes hosted the largest US military presence on foreign soil in the world.[10] But the US was always a secondary military power in China before the Second World War compared to the British and Japanese.

The US state – like the French state Christian Henriot examines in this volume – stood squarely behind and above its citizens in China. The 1844 Treaty of Wangxia granted the US government extraterritorial rights in China, stipulating that American citizens – including military personnel – who committed any crime in China would be subject to trial and punishment only by US consular authorities or other public functionaries of the United States.[11] In 1906, the US government established a district court in China located in the Shanghai International Settlement: the United States Court for China, which operated until the US government rescinded its extraterritorial rights during the Second World War.[12] At the same time, treaties between the US and Chinese governments gave legal cover to the expansive US military presence around the country, including naval patrols and the garrisoning of troops at various treaty ports. While subject to US jurisdiction, American citizens in China could also rely on US military protection during periods of civil unrest. As Brooke Blower has shown, fortified US military outposts in nations like China, Nicaragua, and Cuba anchored American activities abroad long before the emergence of America's post-1945 network of overseas military bases.[13]

The rise and fall of US military power in China 295

From Chinese perspectives, the US military presence, like all foreign military deployments in China, was a humiliating violation of Chinese sovereignty. Chinese from across the political spectrum – including the Nationalists and communists – sought an end to extraterritorial military basing in China and aimed to extend full sovereignty over the treaty ports where foreigners lived outside the jurisdiction of Chinese law. Many Chinese civilians were killed or injured because of military engagements, accidents, or violent crimes involving American military personnel. In all cases, Chinese authorities had no recourse other than protesting to the US government or seeking compensation through Congressional investigation, a process that invariably dragged on for years. For example, in 1925, the Yangtze Patrol gunboat USS *Hart* caused a collision on the river that killed Li Yinting's son, daughter-in-law, and two grandchildren. A Navy investigation found the *Hart's* crew responsible for their deaths, but Congress did not approve Li's compensation claim until 1937, five years after Li himself had died. Criminal cases followed a similar pattern, with perpetrators rarely punished and compensation (if any) coming many years after the fact.[14]

Japan's 1937 invasion of China and the outbreak of war between Japan and the United States four years later brought the US military presence in China's treaty ports to an end. Men from the 15th Infantry Regiment came under fire in Tianjin in 1937 as the Japanese seized the city.[15] On 12 December, 1937, Japanese warplanes sank the USS *Panay*, a Yangtze Patrol gunboat anchored twenty miles upriver from Nanjing. Four Americans died in the attack, sparking a crisis in US–Japan relations that Japanese authorities defused by apologising and paying a $2.2 million indemnity.[16] By early 1938, the US State and War Departments concluded that it had become too dangerous to keep the 15th in Tianjin, leading to the unit's withdrawal to the United States on 2 March.[17] Gunships of the Yangtze and South China Patrols – with the exception of the USS *Tutuila*, marooned in Chongqing after the Japanese captured Hankou in October 1938, and the USS *Wake*, left in Shanghai as station ship – all departed Chinese waters for the Philippines by the end of November 1941, as did the Marine Corps' 4th Infantry Regiment.[18] After 7 December, remaining US forces in China were quickly taken prisoner, including the fourteen-man crew aboard the USS *Wake*

296   *Refugees and the stateless in Asia*

and nearly two hundred marines comprising the Legation Guard at Beijing and smaller detachments at Tianjin and Qinhuangdao.[19]

From alliance to occupation: the US military in China during the Second World War

As US forces returned to China after Pearl Harbor, both US and ROC officials sought a break with the treaty port era. Immediately after the United States entered the war, as Erez Manela has shown, American President Franklin Roosevelt wanted to elevate China into the ranks of the great powers. Roosevelt pushed relentlessly to upgrade China's international status despite opposition from Soviet Premier Joseph Stalin and British Prime Minister Winston Churchill, envisioning the country as one of four policemen responsible for post-war security alongside the Americans, British, and Soviets. Roosevelt's intense opposition to colonialism made support for China a central element of his plan to create a global post-war order based on self-determining nation states.[20] Chiang, meanwhile, sought to reorganise and reequip the Chinese military along American lines.[21] He also made the attainment of international racial equality a central war aim, setting his sights on pushing the Roosevelt administration to rescind its extraterritorial rights in China and end America's longstanding Chinese exclusion immigration policy.[22]

The US Army produced training material for China-bound personnel that adhered to Roosevelt's vision, but neither the War Department nor the senior Army commanders it sent to China were ready to treat Chinese as equals. The Army's *Pocket Guide to China* warned soldiers against racism and urged them to 'show the Chinese that Americans treat the Chinese as we treat any of our allies, and that we respect them as human beings on an equality [*sic*] with ourselves'.[23] Yet when being interviewed for the position of commander of US forces in China and chief of staff to Chiang Kai-shek, General Joseph Stilwell – a 15th Infantry veteran and former Army attaché with ten years' experience in China – told Secretary of War Henry Stimson that the key to success in China would be obtaining unrestricted US military command over China's armed forces. Stimson approved and offered Stilwell the job.[24]

The rise and fall of US military power in China 297

The pitfalls in the US government's contradictory approach to China became apparent to Chiang during the failed spring 1942 defence of Burma, the first mission Stilwell undertook after taking up his post. Stilwell arrived in Chongqing on 4 March, just days before the city of Rangoon fell to the Japanese, which threatened to cut off China's last remaining supply route, the Burma Road. Chiang convinced the British to allow Chinese troops to participate in Burma's defence. He reluctantly granted Stilwell command over a Chinese Expeditionary Force comprising his best remaining armies, hoping that Stilwell would protect his forces from British interference. Despite instructions from Chiang to use his troops for defensive purposes only, Stilwell ordered two divisions to launch a counterattack against the Japanese on 25 March, which predictably faltered due to the lack of adequate Allied airpower, artillery, and naval support. Stilwell refused to allow Chinese forces to retreat while they still had time and then abandoned the troops under his command and retreated to India with a small party of around eighty people. The Chinese Expeditionary Force split apart and withdrew through the jungle to India and China, with losses suffered during the retreat more than double those suffered in battle, totalling some thirty thousand casualties in all. Outraged at Stilwell's refusal to follow orders and arrogant attitude toward Chinese officers during the campaign, Chiang wrote in his diary on 16 June that Stilwell should be sent back to the United States and court-martialed.[25]

Stilwell's arrogance and disregard for Chinese authority fractured his relationship with Chiang, but with all supply routes to China now severed, Chiang concluded he had no choice but to continue working with Stilwell; US military power was his sole lifeline. Supplies to China now had to arrive by plane over 'The Hump', the US Army Air Force route over the Himalayas from Assam to Yunnan. US airpower also halted Japanese bombing attacks on Chinese cities, with American pilots first taking to the skies over Kunming on 20 December 1941 and shooting down six Japanese bombers.[26] Chiang and other senior military commanders now loathed Stilwell, but Chiang believed that if he could keep Stilwell in Chongqing and focused on the needs of the China Theater, it would strengthen ROC ties with the United States and lead to greater material support for China.[27]

298 *Refugees and the stateless in Asia*

US military training and liaison programs for Chinese armed forces, which began in late 1942, aligned with both countries' visions for a new era of Sino–American relations. ROC Foreign Minister Song Ziwen had proposed a thirty-division training program for Chinese forces in meetings with War Department officials before Pearl Harbor, so Chiang had no issue approving a 1942 proposal from Stilwell to train and equip one hundred thousand Chinese soldiers in India.[28] The US Army soon began another training program for Chinese forces in Yunnan as well as a liaison officer program to advise, assist with supply, and coordinate air support for Chinese troops in the field.[29] Neither China nor the United States had ever attempted such a massive foreign army-building program before, but military commanders from both countries saw this partnership as the central piece in their respective visions for China's future. The Americans wanted a reliable security partner capable of serving as Roosevelt's fourth policeman after the war ended, while the Chinese aimed to create a modern fighting force capable of defeating the Japanese and unifying the country. The military arm of the US state, just a few years before one secondary imperialist power among many in China, had risen to a position of unrivalled prestige.

But disputes over sovereignty still exacerbated Sino–American tensions across all levels of the alliance. The US government rescinded its extraterritorial rights in China in 1943 but insisted on another agreement that granted the US military exclusive jurisdiction over all American servicemen deployed to the country.[30] Immunity from Chinese law and lenient military policing facilitated widespread misconduct. Chinese authorities complained endlessly – and to no avail – over American troops' involvement in smuggling, traffic accidents, indiscriminate shootings, and violent crimes against Chinese civilians.[31] While the United States negotiated wartime jurisdiction agreements with Australia and Great Britain that allowed local police to arrest and detain American military personnel, US authorities refused to share policing duties with the Chinese, revealing their failure to live up to the *Pocket Guide to China*'s claims about treating the Chinese 'as we do any of our allies'.[32] This disparity contributed to resentments at the senior level, as Chinese officials continued to push for joint policing throughout the war. At the street level, Chinese police soon learned to avoid American soldiers altogether because some were beaten and even killed after

The rise and fall of US military power in China 299

intervening to halt property damage or assaults on civilians. Most of these crimes, meanwhile, went unpunished, as US military courts-martial seldom convicted GIs for crimes against Chinese unless American military police caught the offenders in the act.[33]

Military-to-military disputes also centred on the issues of sovereignty and authority. During the 1942 defence of Burma, Stilwell placed lower-ranking American officers in charge of higher-ranked Chinese counterparts, which added to resentments over Stilwell's other command failures in Burma.[34] Stilwell retained command over the Chinese forces that retreated to India, which became another source of frustration to the ROC government. While Chinese troops trained at US Army–run facilities in India, Stilwell and his deputies undermined Chiang's most senior generals by breaking up high-level Chinese command structures in order to ensure the US Army maintained control once Chinese troops went on the offensive in Burma.[35] After the second Burma campaign's successful conclusion in early 1945, US Army efforts to control smuggling by Chinese forces on the newly opened Ledo Road to Yunnan led to violent confrontations.[36] According to American officers, these disputes became more frequent after US and Chinese forces returned to China.[37]

Stilwell's frustrations with the Chinese Nationalists during the Burma Campaign led him to convince US Army Chief of Staff George Marshall to support his bid to gain unrestricted command over all Chinese armed forces, resulting in the worst US–ROC diplomatic crisis of the war. Based on Marshall's recommendation, Roosevelt wrote to Chiang on 7 July 1944, requesting that he place Stilwell in command.[38] Outraged and humiliated, Chiang felt compelled to go along and began working with White House envoy Patrick Hurley to reach a final agreement. But Stilwell's decision to publicly humiliate Chiang on 19 September – before the agreement was finalised – by handing him a blunt message from Roosevelt demanding that Stilwell immediately be given unrestricted command, convinced Chiang that Stilwell had to go.[39] Stilwell's continued presence, Chiang realised, would render him a mere figurehead in China, and on 24 September, he cabled Roosevelt and demanded his recall.[40] After an intense three weeks in which nearly all Chiang's advisors urged him to back down, Roosevelt accepted Chiang's request on 18 October and replaced him with General Albert Wedemeyer, who

300 *Refugees and the stateless in Asia*

established a much better working relationship with Chiang and quickly expanded training and liaison work.[41]

While high-level ties improved under Wedemeyer's tenure, Sino–American relations on the ground continued to deteriorate. US troop strength in China doubled in the first half of 1945, just as China's wartime inflation peaked.[42] Theft and prostitution targeting American military personnel increased sharply. Backed by an August 1944 judge advocate ruling that authorised the use of deadly force to protect US government property, American soldiers killed several suspected thieves over a two-month stretch at a single base in Yunnan beginning in May 1945.[43] Chinese civilians and officials alike regarded this as a blatant violation of Chinese sovereignty. US Army military police also acted without authorisation from Chinese authorities to search Chinese homes and businesses for stolen goods, leading to protests by Yunnan Governor Long Yun.[44] Meanwhile, resentment over sexual relations between American soldiers and Chinese women, which included widespread fears that Americans were snatching women off the streets and raping them, sparked violent anti-American demonstrations that targeted US military personnel in Chongqing.[45]

By the time of Japan's surrender, American troops had worn out their welcome in China, but Chiang and Wedemeyer believed that continued, large-scale US military support for the Chinese Nationalist government was imperative. Both men were pleased with the US Army's training and liaison programs in China and supported expanding them under the aegis of the massive peacetime American Military Mission in China, which Chiang outlined on 8 September. Chiang and Wedemeyer also feared that Mao Zedong's communists would exploit Japan's unexpected surrender, while the stunningly successful Soviet drive against Japanese forces in Manchuria set off alarm bells in Washington about Soviet expansionism. Within 48 hours of Japan's surrender, the US government ordered the Marine III Amphibious Corps to prepare for deployment to China. Once the Americans landed, they began a massive air and sealift of Chinese Nationalist military personnel from Southwest China to formerly Japanese-occupied parts of the country. The tremendous military capacity the United States had developed during the war would now be employed to ensure that Chiang retained control of the country.

The rise and fall of US military power in China 301

The US military returns to Shanghai and North China

Approximately fifty-three thousand American marines landed in China before the end of October as part of Operation Beleaguer. Officially, they were tasked with receiving Japan's surrender and repatriating Japanese forces.[46] Most deployed to Beijing, Tianjin, and Qingdao. While they had orders to avoid participation in any civil strife, their arrival in China signalled a limited intervention on behalf of the Chinese Nationalists, as they assisted Chiang's forces in seizing control of formerly Japanese occupied territories ahead of Mao's communists. As the marines helped Chiang retake control, President Harry S. Truman sent wartime Army Chief of Staff George Marshall to China on mission to mediate between the Nationalists and communists, seeking to unify the two parties under Chiang's leadership.[47] However, neither Chiang nor Mao placed much hope in Marshall, as each man was convinced that civil war was inevitable and that his own forces would eventually prevail.[48]

Sino–American relations quickly deteriorated along the same patterns that had emerged during the war. The Marines Corps' presence fuelled an epidemic of theft by Chinese civilian labourers and impoverished residents living near base areas, resulting in frequent shootings of suspected thieves, many of whom were just children. Price gouging and arguments over rickshaw fares led to fistfights. The US military insisted on retaining exclusive jurisdiction over its troops, contributing to rates of violent crime and vehicle accidents that exceeded wartime levels. And wherever US troops deployed, boomtown economies based on alcohol and military prostitution popped up practically overnight.[49] One military policeman responsible for enforcing curfew near a US base in Tianjin told his wife that all thirty or so of the bars or cafes catering to US forces in the area were actually brothels.[50] The Chinese press, particularly in Shanghai, which enjoyed a degree of greater degree of press freedom than any city under Nationalist control during the war, devoted substantial space to all of these issues. Residents of formerly Japanese occupied cities had greeted Americans as liberators in October 1945, but by summer 1946, resentment against the US military presence had become a central feature of civil war politics.[51] Many Chinese concluded that they had traded one occupation for another, while American frustrations with Chiang's government and

302   *Refugees and the stateless in Asia*

their contradictory mission in China led the Truman administration to quickly downgrade military advisory plans to a mere shadow of what Chiang had proposed in September 1945.

Without a common Japanese enemy, Mao Zedong's forces skilfully exploited resentment against the Americans and used it as a propaganda tool against Chiang's Nationalists. Beginning in June 1946, the Chinese Communist Party launched a press campaign to highlight misconduct by American personnel. At the same time, underground Party operatives took control of student government organisations at campuses around the country, including schools in Beijing, Tianjin, and Qingdao, where US forces were congregated. When two intoxicated marines raped a Peking University student on Christmas Eve 1946, the communists took the lead in popularising a protest campaign that swept across the country, with an estimated half million participants joining in demonstrations that stretched from Xinjiang to Taiwan. The protest campaign coincided with the failure of Marshall's mediation mission, resulting in a large-scale drawdown of US forces, though American military personnel who remained continued to commit high-profile crimes. The last US forces departed China on 25 May 1949, leaving from Qingdao, into which the People's Liberation Army marched unopposed a week later.[52]

Conclusion: China and America's rise to global power

The rise and fall of American military power in China paralleled America's rise to global power during the Second World War. When Chiang gained international recognition as China's leader following the 1927 Northern Expedition, the United States was a secondary player in China. Throughout the 1930s, Chiang prioritised military cooperation with Germany and the Soviet Union. The United States, in fact, provided little meaningful help to China before Pearl Harbor, and Chiang pinned his hopes on a Soviet declaration of war against Japan rather than American entry into the conflict between 1937 and 1941.[53] After Pearl Harbor and the Japanese conquest of Burma, however, US support became an existential issue for Chiang, as US airpower provided China's sole link to the outside world. US military aid, diplomatic support, and army-building programs

The rise and fall of US military power in China   303

shored up the Nationalist government throughout the conflict, and the disparity of power between the two allies grew larger each year. The United States emerged from the war at the apex of its power, while Nationalist China ended the conflict almost totally dependent on US military support and economic aid for its continued survival.

The rise and fall of American military power in China also paralleled the global transformation of empire from traditional colonialism to a postcolonial mode of wielding power. The historian Prasenjit Duara describes this new framework as the 'imperialism of nation-states', which emphasised political and military vassalage rather than formal colonial rule. The US–ROC alliance set patterns for America's Cold War–era alliance system, particularly in Asia, with its network of overseas military bases, which transformed local economic and social patterns; exercise of extraterritorial jurisdiction; and lopsided, clientelist relationships with subordinate security partners who relied on US military and economic aid to stay in power. It was in wartime China that this system first unfolded and came undone.

The US military failed in China in large part because it declined to break with treaty port–era patterns. The Roosevelt administration sought to elevate China to a great power during the Second World War, but the US forces that deployed to China during the 1940s treated the host country population as inferiors. Stilwell devoted his entire tenure in China to gaining unrestricted command over China's armed forces, seeking greater authority than any American general had over US forces. This behaviour would have been unthinkable in Great Britain, Australia, or the Soviet Union, but the War Department took it for granted that Stilwell's approach was key to US success in China. The exercise of US military jurisdiction in China, meanwhile, denied Chinese police the same rights granted to their counterparts in other allied countries, which contributed to violence against civilians and deadly accidents. The US government learned from this failure by instituting joint policing and negotiating status of forces agreements that allowed host country governments to exercise jurisdiction in certain cases – such as murder, robbery, and rape – during the Cold War. The Chinese recognised that US military power played a central role in defeating Japan. But the US military's disregard for Chinese sovereignty enabled the Chinese communists to articulate a persuasive case

304 *Refugees and the stateless in Asia*

that continued support for the US military presence by Chiang's Nationalist government prevented China from consigning foreign imperialism irrevocably to the past.

Notes

1 Personnel Strength – China Theater, January 1945 to January 146, Record Group [hereafter RG] 493, UD-UP 590, Box 11, Charts on Strength, National Archives and Records Administration [hereafter NARA], College Park, Maryland, USA; III Amphibious Corps War Diary, 1 October 1945 to 31 October 1945, *China Marine Scuttlebutt*, December 2003, 6.

2 Albert Wedemeyer to George Marshall, 8 September 1945, RG 493, UD-UP 590. Box 25, Military Advisory Group CT, NARA.

3 'Chinese-American Relations', 10 August 1945, RG 493, UD-UP 541, box 67, 000.5, Crimes folder from 22 July 1945, NARA.

4 Theodore White via press wireless, 7 April 1945, box 58, folder 8, Theodore White Papers, Harvard University Archives [hereafter HUA].

5 'Panorama of China', Earl M. Revell Collection, box 2, folder 15, US Army Center for Military History, Carlisle, PA [hereafter USACMH].

6 Toh Boon Kwan, '"The Effects of Our Bombing Effort": Allied Strategic Bombing of the Japanese Occupied Territories during World War II', *Air Power History*, 68, 3 (Autumn 2021), pp. 41–53.

7 Kemp Tolley, *Yangtze Patrol: The U.S. Navy in China* (Annapolis, MD: Naval Institute Press, 1984), pp. 2–41, 58; Zach Fredman, 'The Longer History of Imperial Incidents on the Yangtze', *Modern American History*, 3, 1 (March 2020), pp. 87–91.

8 Alfred Emile Cornebise, *The United States Army in China, 1900–1938: A History of the 9th, 14th, 15th, and 31st Regiments in the East* (Jefferson, NC: McFarland and Company, 2015), p. 69; Katherine K. Reist, 'State Department Soldiers: Warlords, Nationalists, and Intervention', in *Armed Diplomacy: Two Centuries of American Campaigning* (Fort Leavenworth, KS: Combat Institute Press, 2003), p. 110.

9 Cornebise, *The United States Army in China*, pp. 32–7, 39, 67–75, 181–92.

10 Zach Fredman, *The Tormented Alliance: American Servicemen and the Occupation of China, 1941–1949* (Chapel Hill, NC: University of North Carolina Press, 2022), p. 13.

The rise and fall of US military power in China   305

11 The Treaty of Wangxia, 18 May 1844, https://china.usc.edu/treaty
-wangxia-treaty-wang-hsia-%E6%9C%9B%E5%BB%88%E6%A2
%9D%E7%B4%84-may-18-1844. Accessed 20 July 2022.

12 See Eileen Scully, *Bargaining with the State from Afar: American
Citizenship in Treaty Port China* (New York: Columbia University
Press, 2001).

13 Brooke Blower, 'Nation of Outposts: Forts, Factories, Bases and the
Making of American Power', *Diplomatic History*, 41, 3 (2017), pp.
455–8.

14 On the Li case, see 'bei shanghai huaren changxu biao', 17 March 1937,
file no. 11-33-02-06-013, waijiao bu dang'an, Institute of Modern
History Archives [hereafter IMHA], Academia Sinica, Taipei. On crimi-
nal cases, see, for example, 'Report of Investigation on the Assault Made
Upon Proprietress of the Chicago Bar', 10 January 1929, US Congress,
House of Representatives, document no. 117, 4th Cong., 1st session, 4
March 1935, file no. 11-33-02-06-013, waijiao bu dang'an, IMHA.

15 Cornebise, *The United States Army in China*, pp. 100–1.

16 Fredman, 'The Longer History of Imperial Incidents on the Yangtze', p.
87.

17 Cornebise, *The United States Army in China*, p. 103.

18 Zhipu gang cheng Tang Yi dian, 18 October 1940, file no. 61-15-02080,
Chongqing Municipal Archives [hereafter CMA]; Jame M. Santelli, 'A
Brief History of the 4th Marines', *Marine Corps Historical Reference
Pamphlet* (Washington DC: Historical Division, US Marine Corps,
1970), p. 21; Aaron B. O'Connell, 'Defending American Imperial
Interests in Asia and the Caribbean, 1898–1941', in James C. Bradford
and John F. Bradford (eds), *America, Sea Power, and the World*
(Hoboken, NJ: Wiley Blackwell, 2023), p. 161.

19 Chester M. Biggs, *The U.S. Marines in North China* (Jefferson, NC:
McFarland and Company, 2010), p. 210.

20 Erez Manela, 'The Fourth Policeman: Franklin Roosevelt's Vision for
China's Global Role', in Wu Sihua Fangshang Lü and Yongle Lin (eds),
Kailuo xuanyan de yiyi yu yingxiang [The Significance and Impact of
the Cairo Declaration] (Taipei: Zheng da chu ban she, 2014), pp. 213–
21, 231–2.

21 Ch'i Hsi-sheng, *Jianbanuzhang de mengyou: Taiping yang zhanz-
heng shiqi de ZhongMei junshi hezuo guanxi 1941–1945* [Allies at
Loggerheads: Chinese–American Military Cooperation during the
Pacific War] (Beijing: Shehui kexue wenxian chu ban she, 2012), pp. 95,
173–5, 300–4, 646–7.

22 Meredith Oyen, *The Diplomacy of Migration: Transnational Lives and
the Making of U.S.–Chinese Relations during the Cold War* (Ithaca,

306 *Refugees and the stateless in Asia*

NY: Cornell University Press, 2016), pp. 13–68; Meiling Soong Chiang, 'First Lady of the East Speaks to West', *New York Times*, 19 April 1942.

23 US Army Service Forces, *A Pocket Guide to China* (Washington DC: War and Navy Departments, 1943), pp. 2–3.

24 Ch'i, *Jianbanuzhang de mengyou*, pp. 83–5.

25 Ibid., p. 249.

26 Daniel Ford, *Flying Tigers: Claire Chennault and His American Volunteers, 1941–1942* (New York: Smithsonian Books, 2007), pp. 100–7.

27 Ch'i, *Jianbanuzhang de mengyou*, pp. 192–7.

28 Charles Romanus and Riley Sunderland, *Stilwell's Mission to China* (Washington DC: Department of the Army, 1953), pp. 14, 25–7.

29 Eric Setzekorn, *The Rise and Fall of an Officer Corps: The Republic of China Military, 1942–1955* (Norman, OK: University of Oklahoma Press, 2018), pp. 11, 60–4.

30 George Atcheson to Wu Guozhen, 21 May 1943, file no. 53-10-19, pp. 60–68, CMA.

31 Fredman, *The Tormented Alliance*, pp. 124–31.

32 The agreements stipulated that American personnel who had been arrested or detained by Australian and British authorities would then be turned over to US custody. See United States of America (Visiting Forces) Act, 1942, 5&5 Geo. 6, c. 31, https://www.legislation.gov.uk/ukpga/1942/31/pdfs/ukpga_19420031_en.pdf. Accessed 20 July 2022; John McKerrow, 'Scenes from a Marriage of Necessity: Social Relations during the American Occupation of Australia, 1941–1945', PhD Dissertation, McMaster University, 2009, pp. 21–42, 265–324.

33 Fredman, *The Tormented Alliance*, p. 146.

34 Ch'i, *Jianbanuzhang de mengyou*, p. 185.

35 Zheng Dongguo cheng Jiang Jieshi dian, 18 August 1943, file no. 020-020300-0024-023, Academia Historica Archives, Taipei [hereafter AHA].

36 See, for example, 'Non-Compliance with Orders', 16 March 1945, RG 493, UD-UP 215, box 7, Barred or Restricted Places, NARA; 'Final Report: Black Market Smuggling by Chinese Troops', 22 March 1945, RG 493, UD-UP 185, box 10, 000.5 Crimes 1943, NARA; Boatner to Regional Office, Theater Provost Marshall IBT, APO 689, 10 April 1945, RG 493, UD-UP 215, box 1, 000.51 Smuggling, NARA.

37 Wedemeyer to Chiang, 5 August 1945, RG 493, UD-UP 590, box 15, Contact Liaison with the New First Army, NARA.

38 Ch'i, *Jianbanuzhang de mengyou*, pp. 541–4.

39 President Roosevelt to Generalissimo Chiang Kai-shek, 16 September 1944. *FRUS: 1944, China*, pp. 157–8.

The rise and fall of US military power in China   307

40 Ch'i, *Jianbanuzhang de mengyou*, pp. 595–604.
41 Albert Wedemeyer, *Wedemeyer Reports!* (New York: Henry Holt, 1958), pp. 278–82; Ch'i, *Jianbanuzhang de mengyou*, pp. 668–75.
42 Arthur Young, *China's Wartime Finance and Inflation* (Cambridge, MA: Harvard University Press, 1965), 265–68; 'Personnel Strength: China Theater', undated, RG 493, UD-UP 243, box 15, Black Book China no. 1, NARA.
43 'Attached Report on Theft of Building Material and Incidental Shooting', 21 August 1944, RG 492, UD-UP 419, box 244, Correspondence 1944, NARA; 'Incidents of Shooting Chinese', 19 June 1945, RG 493, UD-UP 306, box 663, Correspondence with Chinese Authorities June to September 1945, NARA.
44 Junshi weiyuan hui zhi waijiao bu dian, 2 March 1945, file no. 020-050201-0054-0049x to 0050x, AHA.
45 Zach Fredman, 'GIs and "Jeep Girls": Sex and American Soldiers in Wartime China', *Journal of Modern Chinese History*, 13, 1 (September 2019), pp. 76–101.
46 Henry I. Shaw, *United States Marines in North China, 1945–1948* (Washington DC: Historical Branch, G-3 Division Headquarters, US Marines Corps, 1968), p. 1.
47 On the Marshall Mission, see Daniel Kurtz-Phelan, *The China Mission: George Marshall's Unfinished War, 1945–1947* (New York: W. W. Norton, 2018).
48 Hans van de Ven, *China at War: Triumph and Tragedy in the Emergence of the New China* (Cambridge, MA: Harvard University Press, 2018), pp. 209–15; Harold Tanner, *The Battle for Manchuria and the Fate of China: Siping, 1946* (Bloomington, IN: University of Indiana Press, 2013), pp. 36–9, 50–1.
49 Fredman, *The Tormented Alliance*, pp. 163–95.
50 Carl Johnson to Marion Johnson, 6 January 1946, Carl Johnson Collection box 7, folder 7, Center for the Study of World War II and the Human Experience, Florida State University.
51 Matthew Johnson, 'Anti-Imperialism as Strategy: Masking the Edges of Foreign Entanglements in Civil War-Era China', in Barak Kushner and Serzod Muminov (eds), *Overcoming Empire in Post-Imperial East Asia: Repatriation, Redress, and Rebuilding* (London: Bloomsbury, 2019), pp. 123–31.
52 Fredman, *The Tormented Alliance*, pp. 188–93.
53 Ch'i, *Jianbanuzhang de mengyou*, pp. 12–15.

18

From paradise to hell: the downfall of French interests in China

Christian Henriot

Introduction

The war with Japan and the post-war period marked the tipping point beyond which France, as a power, lost its standing in China. While the war *per se* failed to have a serious impact on the life of the French community in the immediate years after 1937, two sets of events put France on the path towards its future as a post-imperial nation. In Europe, after the military defeat of French armies in 1940 and the establishment of the Vichy government under Pétain, the French state turned away from the legitimate Chinese authorities. On the one hand, it never formally recognised the collaborationist regimes in China, including the Wang Jingwei Reformed government. And yet, on the other hand, the Vichy government pursued a policy of active cooperation with the Japanese and the Chinese collaborationist authorities.[1] In China proper, the French suffered two major setbacks, first with the forced retrocession of their settlements, then with the March 1945 coup by the Japanese military. Yet French diplomats clung to a vision of the past that tarnished their vain attempts to retain fragments of their privileges.[2]

The victory of the Allied powers in 1944–45 failed to reestablish the status of France in China. The Chinese came out of the war squarely on the side of the victors, having sacrificed millions of lives during the war. And yet the Chinese state did not fully establish its sovereignty until 1949. The structure of the Chinese state both during and after the Second World War was very different from those examined in Hannah Arendt's work. The struggle to end imperial domination was long and intermittently bitter, but over time, the

From paradise to hell   309

French, like the British, had to accept the inevitable and relinquish their hold over Shanghai and other parts of China.

This chapter is based on French diplomatic archives. The reports, memos, and telegrams convey the vision that the diplomats had of their own role, of the French community, and of what they conceived as 'French interests' in China. They document in detail their proposals and actions, and show their persistence in using pre-war imperial notions in a different post-war setting.

While we can observe the rationale of their thinking and actions, it is more difficult to get a sense of how the French residents of whom they spoke experienced this period. We see them through the eyes of the diplomats.[3] The top French representatives, Henri Cosme, ambassador to China (1938–44), then Japan (1944–45), and Roland de Margerie, consul-general in Shanghai (1940–44), then ambassador/chargé d'affaires in China (1944–46), appear many times in this narrative. They played a special role, not just because of their responsibilities, but also because they were loyal servants of the Vichy regime.[4]

In this chapter, I follow a dual track. On the one hand, I examine how French diplomats sought to protect 'French interests' in China. What vision of 'France in China' did they have? How did they handle the successive setbacks that challenged France's position during and after the war? On the other hand, I analyse the impact of war on the French community. How did war nurture dissenting voices and inflect disputes among various segments of this population? How did the French population experience life in wartime and post-war China?

French privileges in China?

The French present an unusual case in this volume. Statelessness is not a term or a condition that applies to their experience in China in general or in Shanghai in particular. There were a few cases of citizens who lost their citizenship due to marriage – almost exclusively women – but this is a marginal situation. The most obvious fact was that the French state stood squarely behind the privileges enjoyed by its citizens and protégés in China. It was not French statelessness, but as Rana Mitter suggests above, the limits to Chinese sovereignty

310 *Refugees and the stateless in Asia*

that enabled the French community to enjoy a privileged existence in Shanghai and, as Qian Zhu shows above, to offer refuge to large numbers of refugees.

Throughout the long history of the French presence in the country, diplomats established themselves at the centre of power. During the war, they never lost their diplomatic status. It gave them leeway to pursue their actions, especially because they maintained privileged relations with both the Chinese and the Japanese in the occupied territories. Even after the March 1945 coup, they retained unofficially their capacity to act as representatives of France. The Vichy-appointed diplomats (and those who pledged their loyalty) sought a path of appeasement with the Japanese, even when it entailed losing important facets of their authority. Finally, in the aftermath of the Japanese defeat, the French in China lost much of their standing. All diplomatic pretensions notwithstanding, France simply did not merit the concern of Chinese officials.

The outbreak of the war in China in 1937 created uncertainty and potential dangers. Major cities came under assault by the Japanese army, deploying heavy artillery and airpower. The vast majority of the French community, however, stayed in China, mostly in French-administered enclaves and, if not, in foreign-administered areas in cities. Only Catholic missionaries were to be found in the countryside. The number of French residents in North China was estimated at 1,100 in 1943. In Shanghai, the number of French residents even increased marginally until 1942. In February 1942, the French Concession had 855,000 inhabitants, including 30,000 foreigners and, among them, 2,500 French. Most French residents were middle class (middle managers, employees, and shop owners). Another characteristic of the French population was its skewed socio-professional profile, with an over-representation of municipal employees and Catholic personnel. The number of administrators arose out of the structure of the French Concession itself.[5]

During the first phase of the war in China, the French community remained undisturbed. Things changed with the outbreak of war in Europe, with French military defeat and the establishment of the Vichy government. Military defeat weakened the position and prestige of France in China. The choice by the Vichy regime to collaborate with Nazi Germany and the nascent movement of resistance abroad by De Gaulle created tensions and divisions within

From paradise to hell 311

the French community.[6] The diplomats appointed before the beginning of the war remained in place and most shifted their allegiance to Vichy. Some even actively engaged in pursuing, harassing, and arresting the French citizens who sided with De Gaulle. The French diplomats cultivated friendly relations with the Japanese officials to protect the French community from the adverse effects of the Japanese occupation.[7] There was little worry among French diplomats before 1942, when the embargo imposed by the Allied powers and the poorly implemented command economy by the Wang Jingwei government caused increasing economic difficulties and galloping inflation.[8]

The takeover of the International Settlement by the Japanese in December 1941 signalled a new era that placed Westerners under increasing restrictions. Eventually all the nationals from enemy nations were interned in camps.[9] The French Concession remained free of Japanese occupation, but it became subject to unilateral action by the Japanese military or police. The French diplomats concluded a 'verbal agreement' on 8 December, which allowed the Japanese to station twenty-five constables, later increased to fifty with the possibility to add another 150 men.[10] The French government condoned the informal agreement that was formalised by an exchange of letters that stipulated the conditions under which the Japanese constables could operate. The agreement was kept secret.[11] These actions targeted Chinese who were suspected of involvement in anti-Japanese activities, but in other cases, even foreigners were arrested.[12] In fact, the Japanese did conduct operations repeatedly without the consent of the French police, which they labelled as 'misunderstandings'.[13] All in all, the room to counter Japanese demands was almost non-existent, but French diplomats chose to take the path of least resistance.

Dissent emerged early within the ranks of the French residents. The majority, as in the metropole, was politically passive. Viewed from Shanghai, the Vichy government was the legal government of France. Yet in Shanghai, a group of individuals emerged who opposed collaboration and became affiliated with Free France. French ambassador Cosme pursued an active policy to counter the activities and influence of those who disagreed with the Vichy regime. To ensure administrative discipline, he issued two consular ordonnances on 16 August 1940 and 2 July 1941 that prohibited

312   *Refugees and the stateless in Asia*

any 'dissident activity' within the French community. All the diplomatic personnel and the employees of the French Concession were required to take an oath of loyalty to the Vichy government. Cosme and *consul-général* de Margerie were relentless, and even had the leader of the Gaullist group, Roderick Egal, arrested and sent to Indochina to stand trial, in violation of all legal procedures.[14] According to Cosme, however, the Japanese takeover of the International Settlement had given him reason for these measures, because the French residents realised at that time that neutrality was a much safer course that protected them, their property, and their money. Supporting Free France jeopardised this neutrality. For Cosme, the French Concession was stable and fully behind the Vichy government.[15]

The collapse of French interests in two steps

The era of cordial relations with the Japanese ended abruptly with two Japanese decisions that challenged French interests in China directly. French diplomats lost ground when they received the Japanese demand that they give up all French leased territories and return them to the Wang Jingwei government. France had a string of tiny territories in China, but the jewel of its possessions was of course the French Concession in Shanghai. Tianjin was the second most important settlement in terms of presence and properties. All the other settlements, in Hankou, Canton, or Guangzhouwan were inconsequential territories with little French investment and hardly any French presence.[16]

The second time they lost power came as a complete surprise and left the diplomats not just powerless, but even almost irrelevant. In March 1945, Japan saw the French provisional government preparing for the restoration of the Republic, a change of regime that would make France an enemy nation. In the early hours of 10 March, the Japanese army took over French military installations and confiscated weapons and instruments of communication in all French settlements in China.

As early as 23 February 1943, the Vichy government announced its readiness to abolish extraterritorial rights and to restore the French concessions to China, not Japan.[17] In March 1943, the

Japanese made it known that they expected the Shanghai Municipal Council (SMC) to dissolve and to entrust all its operations, services, and properties to the Chinese municipality under collaborationist Chen Gongbo. The transfer of the prerogatives of the SMC to the Chinese raised little difficulty. On the one hand, the Japanese had already taken full control of the administration of the International Settlement and staffed its services with their own men. On the other hand, the SMC was truly an autonomous administrative entity that did not come under the control of any nation.[18] This autonomy had been at times a thorn in the foot of British diplomats when conflicts erupted. The May 30th movement was a case in point. The SMC was out of sync with the change of policy of Great Britain in China, which sought a middle course to accommodate Chinese nationalism.[19] French diplomacy never came to this realisation.

When the Japanese demanded the retrocession of the French Concession in Shanghai, the strategy of French diplomats was to delay as long as possible the actual transfer.[20] Cosme, in particular, emphasised the need for obstruction for several months.[21] Yet the diplomats soon realised that the Japanese and the Chinese were not prepared to wait.[22] The Wang Jingwei government itself made clear its demands to the French to return all their settlements, except Shanghai, by the end of April, and Shanghai by the end of July.[23] On 29 March, an agreement was reached on the restoration of administrative rights in the former Legation Quarter in Beijing. On 8 April, it was the turn of the French participation in the International Settlement in Xiamen, and on 18 May, another agreement was reached about the retrocession of the French settlements at Tianjin, Hankou, and Guangzhou (Shamian).[24]

In March 1943, the Minister of Foreign Affairs, Chu Minyi, met informally with the French ambassador to initiate negotiations for the restoration to China of the French Concession.[25] The Japanese government itself sent its ambassador to meet with Pierre Laval in Vichy to press for the speedy return of the concession.[26] The Laval government tried to change Japanese policy through direct discussions with the Japanese Ministry of Foreign Affairs in Tokyo. The Japanese government, however, was unrelenting.[27] On the ground, Cosme clung to the idea that he could delay the retrocession until the end of August.[28] He held meetings with the Japanese ambassador and Chu Minyi, but Chu refused categorically to postpone the date

314 *Refugees and the stateless in Asia*

of the retrocession.[29] Eventually, Cosme officially recused himself to avoid being party to the agreement signed with the Wang Jingwei government.[30] Robert de Boisséson and de Margerie conducted the actual negotiations.[31] By not getting involved and not signing any agreement, Cosme hoped to preserve a semblance of deniability were the Japanese to be defeated and the Chinese national government restored to power over China.

The final agreement was signed on 22 July, by which France accepted to return to Chinese authority the French Concession in Shanghai.[32] The details were spelled out in a separate document that aimed to protect the interests and privileges of French residents before the regime of extraterritoriality was abolished. They also preserved the contracts signed in favour of French public companies (water, electricity, tramway).[33]

In the months before the agreement was signed, French diplomats scrambled to salvage anything they considered as inherently part of 'French interests'. Their priority was to preserve as much as possible of the numerous and valuable properties that the municipal authorities owned in Shanghai and Tianjin.[34] In Tianjin, the French municipality owned and funded several institutions with a substantial number of properties. French diplomats artfully removed the most important ones from the list of properties that they transferred to the Chinese municipality. They used the French Centre (*Centre français*), a legal entity, to register all the properties under its name. In parallel, the consul issued a consular ordonnance to change the statutes of the French Centre to place it firmly under his control. Cosme boasted that France would maintain in Tianjin a façade 'that no other white nation possessed'.[35]

It was far more complex in Shanghai, where the French municipal council owned large tracts of land and many buildings. The intricate relationship between the consul general and the French municipality created a configuration by which the consul and his services were closely involved in the management of the French Concession. The consul general acted as the sole and exclusive administrator of a territory that came under French administration. Yet the French Concession as such was not French territory. Its municipality was not part of the French administrative apparatus. The contradiction between the extensive powers that the consul enjoyed and the actual status of the French Concession came to light when the

Japanese, then the Chinese, challenged the existence of the French Concession and the privileges that the French residents, especially those employed by the municipal administration, had enjoyed.

The basic strategy of the diplomats was to constitute a 'war treasury' that would cover the expenses that the French state was bound to assume after the return of the French Concession.[36] The Laval government fully supported this approach, which sought to reduce as much as possible the potential expenses that the French state would have to assume.[37] The rationale of the French diplomats was to keep as many properties as possible to preserve 'French influence' in China in the long term, which they thought could not be achieved without the physical presence embodied in land and buildings. The properties of the municipality were formally private property and, as such, could not legally be transferred to the French state. The French diplomats designed an elaborate scheme with the help of the missionaries to change the status of or sell properties before the time of the transfer. Between late March and mid-April 1943, the consul organised the exchange of properties between the French municipality and the Catholic missions that resulted in the creation of a consular domain of five hectares (valued at 20,000,000 francs), a French Centre with properties valued at 40,000,000 francs, and a domain under the Charity Fund (*Caisse des Oeuvres*) valued at 20,000,000 francs. Even the land and barracks of the French garrison, formerly owned by the French municipality, were donated to the French Centre.[38] The properties transferred to the French consulate represented a capital of 185,000,000 CRB. The CharityFund held capital of 875,000,000 CRB, and another 40,000,000 CRB were obtained from the sale of land and equipment. Cosme stated with pride that the French flag would still be flying over a magnificent consular domain that included the French Centre, the French *collège*, the French Club (*Cercle sportif*), various sports facilities, the Pasteur Institute, two former military barracks, and six houses.[39]

A critical issue was the future salaries of the French employees.[40] The French municipality had a limited amount of capital, whereas it employed four hundred French, six hundred Russians, about one thousand Vietnamese, and several thousand Chinese. The cost of repatriation was estimated at thirty million CRB, which would leave fifteen million CRB in the coffers of the municipality for a severance package of four months' salary for the municipal employees.[41] The

316   *Refugees and the stateless in Asia*

main difficulty they faced was that they could not send the French employees back to France. The war was raging in the Pacific, and all communications were suspended. From the start, both the Laval government and the diplomats in China agreed that discharged employees would be sent to Indochina.[42] Yet even in early 1944, when the governor general of Indochina offered to send a ship to Shanghai, the Ministry of Foreign Affairs declined out of concern for the safety of ship passage.[43] Most former employees needed to be supported financially for an indeterminate period there.

The terms for the re-employment of the former municipal employees were far better than the diplomats had expected. A special deal was negotiated, through a secret exchange of letters, by which the French employees would be maintained until repatriation to France became possible.[44] Many in fact were not very keen to work under Chinese administration and readily accepted the indemnity paid from the Charity Fund.[45] Nevertheless, even with this reserve fund and a salary from the Chinese municipality, the earnings of the French employees were eroded by inflation. The salary increases by the municipality failed to keep pace with inflation.[46] Those who remained on their jobs eventually turned to the consulate for help, arguing that the Chinese municipality was not compensating them for inflation at the same rate as they were compensating their Chinese employees. Eventually, the French consulate chose also to subsidise the French employees who applied for financial help.

When the municipalities were dissolved, all the funds realised were transferred to the consulates, making the diplomats the sole arbiters of how the money would be used. From the start, some employees believed that they were not fairly compensated and sued the consulate before the consular court.[47]

The Ministry of Foreign Affairs confirmed the status of the French settlements in China: they existed outside any form of authority of the French state. Therefore, the French state could not be held responsible, legally, or financially, for the obligations incurred by these municipalities.[48] There was a measure of hypocrisy in this legal argument as, from the start, French diplomats imposed their authority on the French municipality and put it under their jurisdiction. The municipalities, including in Shanghai, had always been under the authority of the consul. Formally, the diplomats admitted

From paradise to hell   317

no official link between the former French municipality and the Ministry of Foreign Affairs. In reality, the Ministry was well aware of the role these men and women had played and were intent on finding solutions to help them out of their predicament.[49]

From French rule to Chinese administration

The transfer of the French Concession to China represented a political and diplomatic victory for the Wang Jingwei government. The Chinese authorities spared no effort in publicising their successful negotiations.[50] In the eyes of the French diplomats, however, the retrocession was an act taken under duress, pending better days when – so they hoped – French interests would eventually be restored. This was delusional. It did not take account of the genuine expectations of the Chinese population and reflected the short-sightedness of French diplomacy.[51]

Ceremonies for the formal end of the French Concession took place on 30 July 1943.[52] The French Municipal Council had held its last meeting one hour earlier to read and sign the act of dissolution.[53] In the aftermath of the retrocession, the Chinese municipality was faithful to the terms of the informal agreement to which it had subscribed. In particular, it maintained in its ranks foreign employees – not just the French, but also Russians, Germans, and Japanese.

The Chinese authorities were intent on reducing the number of their French employees. They prepared a plan for laying off their employees. The dismissed employees and policemen would receive an indemnity of six months' salary. Eventually, the diplomats planned to have all the policemen, even those still in the service of the municipality, assigned to the BST.[54] Soon, however, these arrangements would become obsolete. In March 1945, the Japanese made the decision to disarm all French soldiers and police in China. The measure applied to all the French military units in Beijing, Tianjin, and Shanghai.

In Tianjin, Japanese marines encircled the French consulate and the Contal military barracks in the middle of the night and blocked all access with a cordon of marines and several tanks. It took only two days to strip the French military of all weapons and equipment.[55] The same process unfolded in Shanghai with the French

318   *Refugees and the stateless in Asia*

garrison and the French policemen still employed by the Chinese municipality.[56] The Japanese eventually forced the expulsion of all French soldiers of the *Bataillon Mixte d'Infanterie Coloniale de Chine* from their barracks in both Beijing (*Caserne Voyron*) and Tianjin (*Arsenal de l'Est*).[57] Within a month, the operation was complete and the French military presence was eliminated.[58] In Shanghai, de Margerie made a formal protest, but he could only acquiesce to the Japanese demands.[59] The French consul managed to find housing for 300 members of the French garrison (COC).[60] All contacts with other nationals were prohibited under the threat of being placed under police surveillance. Interaction with the Chinese population was expected to be limited strictly to everyday needs.[61]

The Wang Jingwei government gave instructions that French official representatives could no longer operate in Chinese territory. Diplomats lost their diplomatic status and had to turn in their equipment, especially the devices that allowed them to send and receive encrypted telegrams.[62] The Japanese recognised them as conduits and still trusted them with taking care of their constituencies, but only in an informal capacity. Their communications became subject to Chinese censorship.[63]

The change of policy by Japan toward French residents in China did not fundamentally change their living conditions and status. Various accounts of French consular agents indicated that the measures taken by the Japanese were friendly.[64] The French residents in North China benefited from conditions that allowed them to escape from serious interference from the Japanese military, as de Margerie wrote to the Japanese ambassador on 15 August 1945. He expressed his personal gratitude for the consideration shown by the Japanese authorities toward French citizens.[65]

The fate of the French population

The French indeed never became stateless, but they suffered a general downgrading, mostly due to economic difficulties, and after December 1941, they lived in nearly complete isolation from the homeland. On the scale of what other categories of population experienced during the same period – violence and famine for the Chinese, internment for the British, American, Dutch, and so on

From paradise to hell 319

– the French undoubtedly fared much better. Yet the role of the historian is not to measure and distribute grades on the scale of suffering. It is to observe and report on how the people they study experienced the war. The French community was exposed increasingly to the ravages of inflation, especially those who depended on a salary to support their families. The diplomats were extremely concerned not to see a French resident reduced to destitution, which would affect 'French prestige' in China.[66]

In May 1944, a substantial French community remained in Shanghai: five hundred soldiers and officers of the French garrison (COC), and their accompanying two hundred wives and children, 1,500 Vietnamese, 220 missionaries, and around two thousand other French residents. Except for 250 individuals who were unemployed, eight hundred residents had jobs in private companies, while two hundred worked in the various French official services. There were also 250 individuals – seven hundred with their families – who were former employees of the French municipality.[67] A group of one hundred persons depended entirely on the subsidies paid by the Charity Fund established by the consulate at a cost 2.5 million CRB per year. The former municipal employees were paid by the Chinese municipality, but their salaries failed to keep up with inflation. De Margerie decided to draw on the fund for repatriation to help those who were most in need.[68] Eventually, the consulate subsidised this segment of the French community at a cost of two million CRB per month. The cost of supporting the French families was expected to double in 1945 to keep up with inflation. At this rate, de Margerie foresaw the rapid exhaustion of the reserve fund created in 1943.[69] By that time, French diplomats were making decisions on their own, especially to keep their services afloat and to pay the salaries of the diplomatic and military staff in China. To make ends meet, de Margerie started to sell furniture and some old equipment of the embassy and encouraged consuls to make similar plans.[70]

In the course of 1944, the economic situation of French residents in Shanghai worsened considerably. In December, Guy Fain, who had taken over as Consul General, warned about the impending complications that inflation caused within the French community. He pointed out issues of discipline among the former soldiers and policemen, both French and Vietnamese. Almost all had fired their Chinese servants. Even the employees of the consulate had used up

320　　　　　*Refugees and the stateless in Asia*

the five-month advance that they had received on their salaries.[71] One can feel in the letters addressed to the French consul the growing anxieties of the French residents in Shanghai.[72] The former municipal employees were reduced to purchasing the bare minimum. The diplomatic staff also suffered from declining revenues.[73] Eighteen months after the retrocession, the fund set aside to help the former employees was running dry;[74] twenty thousand French residents depended entirely on the subsidies of the consulate.[75]

In April 1945, the consul sought the support of the French community to create a communal approach to the problems its members faced in daily life. He organised six groups – housing, former employees, food supply, French solidarity, youth/school/culture, health – that were expected to examine the problems French residents had and help find solutions.[76] The French Solidarity group sought to collect money from the residents who could afford to draw on their savings to share with their compatriots, in the name of 'national mutual help' (*entraide nationale*).[77] The association of former municipal employees saw this as a manoeuvre to circumvent the consulate's role and to undermine the associations with French residents. The executive committee of the association refused to send delegates to the *entraide nationale*, taken to be a tactic to divide the French community. In the same report, the association questioned the right of the consul to manage and control the resources that came from the former municipality, especially the fund created to ensure the payment of their salaries and subsidies.[78]

Earlier, former French municipal employees and policemen in the French Concession established an association (*Association amicale des anciens employés de la municipalité et de la police française*) to defend their interests. While only some of the municipal employees joined, all the members of the police did so.[79] The Vietnamese soldiers of the French police were not members, and we do not know whether this absence reflected a decision of the association or something due to the military status of these Vietnamese. In any case, the association took care not to get involved in the protests that ensued among the Vietnamese guards.[80] The association aimed at obtaining the adoption of a permanent system of weekly salary adjustments.[81] The association was marred by internal disputes that intensified over time. But the major problem was its relationship with the consul, whom it accused of exercising arbitrary power. The

From paradise to hell 321

consul became very reluctant even to meet the representatives of the association. In June 1945, he refused to receive the members of its executive committee.[82]

By the end of July 1945, French diplomats were left to fend for themselves. French residents, officials and civilians alike, felt abandoned. Communications had become more difficult or even impossible. The postal system was completely disrupted at the international level. Contact with families was lost, creating a sense of loneliness and uncertainty. Some residents remained without news from their relatives for years. An anonymous letter dated 9 August 1943 written by a Shanghai resident said that she had received only two letters in two years from 'Henry'. She had no news about France, even if there are signs in the letter indicating that she was relatively well-to-do. Only a few people like her had been allowed to keep their short-wave radios, which allowed them to tune in to different radio stations beyond China.[83] They were also eager to send news from France after the end of the German occupation.

In the absence of regular channels of communication, families in France turned to the Ministry of Foreign Affairs to convey messages to their relatives in China. It is unclear to what extent these messages were sent or received. In the archives, we find originals of messages sent to China, more rarely the replies from the recipients.[84] These messages were not sent directly as such, but they were transcribed and incorporated in official telegrams to the nearest diplomatic station in China. In terms of content, the messages betray the anxieties of the families and individuals on both sides and their pressing desire to send even the most minimal message. In their requests to the ministry, they most often emphasised the complete lack of news and hope to reassure their relatives about the wellbeing of their family in France. Some sent pictures to introduce their new husbands and children, which reveals how long the interruptions may have lasted.[85] The notes are often written on small pieces of paper, as if to make them as light as possible to be sent to China. Some messages included very specific information, especially if someone had died, but essentially, they usually summed it all up under 'we are all in good health'. Emerging from the war, these families wanted to convey that they were alive and in good shape.[86]

322   *Refugees and the stateless in Asia*

After the Japanese defeat: a slow reorganisation

The sudden Japanese capitulation after the double nuclear bombing of Hiroshima and Nagasaki took everyone in China by surprise. French diplomats had been starved of communications from their own ministry after the confiscation of their equipment by the Japanese. By and large, they were completely isolated. The centre of gravity of French diplomacy had moved to Chongqing in parallel with the collapse of the Vichy government and the formation of the Provisional Government under Charles de Gaulle. In April 1944, Zinovi Pechkoff, a general in the Free France movement, was sent to Chongqing as the delegate of the French Committee of National Liberation, then as ambassador in November.[87] For several months, however, the diplomats that served the Vichy government had very little interaction with the French ambassador in Chongqing.

With the news of the Japanese capitulation, French diplomats rushed to regain all that had been confiscated (equipment) or occupied (buildings) by the Japanese army. In Beijing, de Margerie officially asked the civil and military authorities to lift all restrictions on the movement of persons and to return all the communications devices, weapons, and ammunition seized in March 1945.[88] In Shanghai, Fain attempted to get back the seized weapons, but to no avail. He had lost contact since the spring with the Ministry of Foreign Affairs in Vichy and corresponded only with de Margerie in Beijing.[89] Yet the French officials competed with Americans seeking accommodation for troops in the buildings still controlled by the Japanese.[90] The official ceremonies of the Japanese capitulation took place in October 1945 in Beijing and Tianjin.[91] In November 1945, all the Japanese troops in North China – around 130,000 men – were relieved of their role in maintaining public order.[92]

One month after the Japanese surrender, the US liaison team in Beijing told de Margerie that they had been informed that his role as *chargé d'affaires* for France was coming to an end. The new Ministry of Foreign Affairs was about to send a new representative and to repatriate all other diplomatic personnel.[93] Although the new leadership of France's Chongqing embassy harboured reservations about the existing diplomats, it had to make do with reality. The French embassy in Chongqing sent instructions to all diplomatic

From paradise to hell 323

agents to stay in place until further notice and to wait for instructions and to inform it of any urgent needs.[94]

In a manuscript letter, probably written in September 1945, de Margerie stated that as soon as the Provisional Government had been established, he had sought to make contact to provide information on the situation in occupied China. He claimed to have sent reports continuously since 1943 on Shanghai to René Massigli, Jacques Meyrier, and others in Algiers.[95] On 22 August 1945, de Margerie finally managed to resume contact with the French embassy in Chongqing. In this document, he pleaded for himself, stating that he had 'found himself brutally exiled in 1940' and only longed to return to France as soon as possible after the 'four very tough years spent in Shanghai that left me worn out'.[96]

In January 1946, de Margerie, by then demoted to *conseiller d'ambassade*, wrote a lengthy report to the Minister of Foreign Affairs, Georges Bidault, to describe his action to 'defend French interests' between 20 June 1944, when he was appointed ambassador, to 11 September 1945, when he received instructions from Zinovi Pechkoff, the new ambassador. De Margerie expressed the regrets of the French diplomats who remained in China and were not able to take part in the liberation of France. Speaking for himself more than anything, he claimed that since 1940, French diplomats had laboured only to one end, the defence of 'our traditional interests'. He expressed his relief at receiving the instructions from Massigli, the *de facto* Minister of Foreign Affairs in the French provisional government, to 'maintain our positions as much and as long as possible', which he read as an endorsement of his own action.[97]

It is clear that this self-congratulatory report was meant to cover up de Margerie's unsavoury actions in his capacity as general consul in Shanghai in the service of Vichy. Whether he was a true believer or a faithful servant is hardly debatable. In a letter to the French consul in Shanghai, de Margerie referred to Kaufmann, the former president of the French Consular Court, as a 'deplorable element' who should never have been entrusted with this position before the war. Kaufmann was labelled 'a calamitous judge', who was only half responsible for his own misdeeds as 'a heavy heredity weighed on him'. Kaufmann was Jewish and had clashed repeatedly with de Margerie because of Kaufman's work for Free France. In the summer of 1945, de Margerie did not hesitate to put in writing his

324 *Refugees and the stateless in Asia*

antisemitic sentiments.[98] Yet he continued to serve in China well into 1946, and thereafter, as a faithful civil servant in key positions in the Ministry of Foreign Affairs. His outlook may help account for the unrealistic line that French diplomacy pursued in China after 1945.

To the end, the French authorities clung to preserving their material interests and influence in China. The change of French administration at home failed to alter the general course of French policy in Asia, always dominated by Indochina. Contrary to their British counterparts, they were blind to the new geostrategic reality, marked by the prestige the United States enjoyed in the immediate aftermath of the war. The French diplomats imagined that simply by dismissing the agreement signed between France (Vichy government) and China (the Wang Jingwei government), they could turn back the clock. Reality hit them hard when the Chinese government arrested several French policemen under the accusation of collaboration with the Japanese. They made the withdrawal of China's troops in the North of Indochina contingent on the complete renunciation by France of all her rights and interests in China.[99]

Conclusion

The end of the French presence in China during and after the war does not raise the same set of issues that other less protected populations suffered. Extraterritoriality, a shallow but real military presence, self-administered settlements, a small but active contingent of forty diplomats, and, above all, continuous cordial relations with the Japanese authorities shielded the French from the deprivation that other foreign nationals suffered, not to mention the suffering the Chinese population endured under Japanese occupation. The French never found themselves stateless. They were always part of France, even though the French Third Republic had collapsed. The French saw little of the war, except in Shanghai, yet they were under the protection of the foreign settlements. There was little incentive to leave China, especially after war started in France in 1939. The Japanese attack on Pearl Harbor and, in China, the occupation of the settlements under British administration should have been a wake-up call. Yet, on the one hand, the official association between

From paradise to hell 325

Vichy and Tokyo spared the French from the restrictive measures imposed by the Japanese army on other nationalities; on the other hand, the cessation of transportation under safe conditions simply left them stranded in China.

The ambivalent position of France and its official representatives in China was destroyed by the Japanese decision to force the retrocession of all extraterritorial rights and leased territories. The French presence in China faced its day of reckoning on 30 July 1943, when the French Concession in Shanghai was dissolved. Through legally dubious operations, French diplomats sought to salvage something from the political and diplomatic wreckage. Divided on their assessment of Japan's chances of coming out of the war victorious, they made contingency plans to hold onto anything that would preserve the future and leave France with an eminent domain and influence in China. Despite the circumstances, what is striking about these tactics was their short-sighted view of the shifting balance of power in China, regardless of the competition between Chongqing and Nanjing. Both were committed to bring to an end French – and all Western – dominance based on the nineteenth-century treaties.

From 1943 onward, the French met with increasing economic difficulties. The dependence of a large segment of this population on positions in the French municipalities or in companies tied to the French Concessions left them powerless when their jobs were transferred to the Chinese administrations. It was no more than an expedient for both the French and Chinese officials to find a middle ground pending the end of the war. But in March 1945, all such pretensions evaporated. The Chinese authorities summarily laid off all their French employees. The privileged economic status that the French had enjoyed thanks to higher salaries than their Chinese co-workers came to an end when inflation set in and rapidly exhausted their earnings. None fell into poverty, thanks to the resources that the diplomats had gathered, but there was a widespread sense of social downgrading, and few were looking forward to staying in Shanghai after 1945. Most left for good.

French diplomacy in China remained constant throughout the whole period. The diplomats served faithfully the Vichy regime to the end, then moved on to serve the government in exile that had fought to topple it. Although there was a turnover and eventually complete replacement of the diplomatic staff after 1945, one can

326   *Refugees and the stateless in Asia*

only see a high degree of continuity of French diplomatic action in China. Whether under the Vichy government or under the Provisional government, French diplomats clung to a backward-looking view of China and the French position therein. Their telegrams abound with expressions like the 'prestige of France' and the pervasive notion of 'French interests'. They were imbued with the idea of unparalleled achievements in the settlements under French administration, with the century-old French Concession in Shanghai the epitome of French influence and success in China. At no time did they see or consider that whatever the French had achieved, they had no legitimacy in the eyes of the Chinese political elites and population. The game was over.

Notes

1 On the international status of the Reformed Government under Wang Jingwei, see David Serfass, 'Le dilemme de Nankin. Tergiversations autour de la reconnaissance du gouvernement de collaboration chinois (1940–1945)', *Vingtième Siècle. Revue d'histoire*, 133, 1 (2017), pp. 99–111.
2 Telegram, de Margerie to Laval, 27 May 1944, FDA Nantes, Pékin 513PO/A, Box 261.
3 There is no general history of 'France in China', as we have for Great Britain, nor the depth of knowledge that Robert Bickers has produced in multiple volumes and papers. Bensacq-Texier's book on France is focused mostly on diplomats and adheres to an obsolete form of diplomatic history. See: Robert A. Bickers, *Britain in China: Community Culture and Colonialism, 1900–1949* (Manchester: Manchester University Press, 1999),
   Bickers, *Out of China: How the Chinese Ended the Era of Western Domination* (Cambridge, MA: Harvard University Press, 2017); and Nicole Bensacq-Tixier, *La France en Chine de Sun Yat-sen à Mao Zedong, 1918–1953* (Rennes: Presses universitaires de Rennes, 2019).
4 For a broad overview of French diplomatic history in modern China, see Bensacq-Tixier, *La France en Chine de Sun Yat-sen à Mao Zedong, 1918–1953*.
5 Cécile Armand and Christian Henriot, 'Paris in the Orient: A Spatial Micro-History of the French in Shanghai (1942)', *Urban History* (2020), pp. 17–19.
6 Bensacq-Tixier, *La France en Chine*, p. 288.

From paradise to hell 327

7 Ibid., p. 9.

8 Christian Henriot, 'Rice, Power and People: The Politics of Food Supply in Wartime Shanghai (1937–1945)', *Twentieth-Century China*, 26, 1 (2000), pp. 41–84.

9 Felicia Yap, 'Voices and Silences of Memory: Civilian Internees of the Japanese in British Asia during the Second World War', *Journal of British Studies*, 1, 4 (2011), pp. 917–40.

10 Telegram, Cosme to Ministry of Foreign Affairs, 24 March 1942, FDA, Courneuve, Vichy-Asie 3GMII, Box 144.

11 Telegram, Ministry of Foreign Affairs to Cosme and de Margerie, 25 March 1942; Telegram, de Margerie to Ministry of Foreign Affairs, 3 April 1942; Telegram, Cosme to Ministry of Foreign Affairs, 4 April 1942, FDA, Courneuve, Vichy-Asie 3GMII, Box 144.

12 Telegram, de Margerie to Ministry of Foreign Affairs, 5 March 1942; Telegram, Cosme to Ministry of Foreign Affairs, 20 March 1942; Telegram, de Margerie to Ministry of Foreign Affairs, 8 April 1942, FDA, Courneuve, Vichy-Asie 3GMII, Box 144.

13 O. Torog, Ministry of Foreign Affairs to French ambassador, 27 March 1942; Telegram, de Margerie to Ministry of Foreign Affairs, 3 May 1942, FDA, Courneuve, Vichy-Asie 3GMII, Box 144.

14 Claude Jaeck, 'Français libre de Shanghai: Roderick Egal, gaulliste de la première heure et incorruptible'. *Le Souvenir Français de Chine* (blog), 24 June 2010. http://souvenir-francais-asie.com/2010/06/24/roderick -egal-gaulliste-de-la-premiere-heure-et-incorruptible/. Accessed 20 July 2022.

15 Telegram, Cosme to Ministry of Foreign Affairs, 23 May 1942, FDA, Courneuve, Vichy-Asie 3GMII, Box 144.

16 Bensacq-Tixier, *La France en Chine*, p. 355.

17 This decision caused the Chinese government in Chongqing to sever all diplomatic relations with the Vichy Government, which finally opened the way for the De Gaulle organisation in London to initiate relations with Jiang Jieshi. Fabienne Mercier, '1940–1944: Quelle politique Chinoise pour L'Etat Français?', *Guerres Mondiales et Conflits Contemporains*, 172 (1993), pp. 125–36; Serfass, 'Le dilemme de Nankin', p. 109.

18 Isabella Jackson, *Shaping Modern Shanghai: Colonialism in China's Global City* (Cambridge: Cambridge University Press, 2018).

19 Nicholas R. Clifford, *Spoilt Children of Empire* (Ann Arbor, MI: University of Michigan Press, 1979); Bickers, *Britain in China*.

20 Christine Cornet, 'The Bumpy End of the French Concession and French Influence in Shanghai (1937–1946)', in Christian Henriot and Wen-hsin Yeh (eds), *In the Shadow of the Rising Sun: Shanghai under*

328   *Refugees and the stateless in Asia*

Japanese Occupation (Cambridge: Cambridge University Press, 2004), pp. 257–76, esp. p. 264.

21 Telegram, Cosme to Ministry of Foreign Affairs, 3 June 1943, FDA Courneuve, Vichy-Asie_3GMII, Box 141.

22 Telegram, Cosme to Rochat, 11 June 1943, FDA, Courneuve, Vichy-Asie 3GMII, Box 141.

23 Telegram, Cosme to Laval, 9 April 1943, FDA Nantes, Pékin 513PO/A, Box 261.

24 Statement by Dr Chu Min-yi, Minister of Foreign Affairs, on the signing of the agreement, 22 July 1943, FDA Nantes, Pékin 513PO/A, Box 261; Telegram, Cosme to Ministry of Foreign Affairs, 7 June 1943, FDA, Courneuve, Vichy-Asie 3GMII, Box 141.

25 Statement by Dr Chu Min-yi, Minister of Foreign Affairs, on the signing of the agreement, 22 July 1943, FDA Nantes, Pékin 513PO/A, Box 261.

26 Note, General Secretariat, 21 June 1943, FDA Courneuve, Vichy-Asie 3GMII, Box 141.

27 Mercier, '1940–1944: Quelle politique chinoise pour L'Etat français?'

28 Telegram, Cosme to Ministry of Foreign Affairs, 1 July 1943, FDA Courneuve, Vichy-Asie 3GMII, Box 141.

29 Telegram, Cosme to Ministry of Foreign Affairs, 9 July 1943, FDA Courneuve, Vichy-Asie 3GMII, Box 141.

30 Telegram, Cosme to Ministry of Foreign Affairs, 1 July 1943, FDA Courneuve, Vichy-Asie 3GMII, Box 141.

31 Telegram, Cosme to Ministry of Foreign Affairs, 23 July 1943, FDA, Courneuve, Vichy-Asie 3GMII, Box 141.

32 Statement (communiqué), Ministry of Foreign Affairs, 25 July 1943, FDA Courneuve, Vichy-Asie 3GMII, Box 141.

33 Telegram, Cosme to Ministry of Foreign Affairs, 23 July 1943, FDA Courneuve, Vichy-Asie 3GMII, Box 141.

34 Cosme to Ministry of Foreign Affairs, 2 April 1942, FDA Courneuve, Vichy-Asie 3GMII, Box 144.

35 Telegram, Cosme to Ministry of Foreign Affairs, 27 June 1943, FDA Courneuve, Vichy-Asie 3GMII, Box 141.

36 Telegram, Cosme to Ministry of Foreign Affairs, 12 June 1943, FDA, Courneuve, Vichy-Asie 3GMII, Box 141; Cosme to Ministry of Foreign Affairs, 17 April 1943; Cosme to Ministry of Foreign Affairs, 12 May 1943, FDA, Courneuve, Vichy-Asie 3GMII, Box 144.

37 Note, Direction politique, Ministry of Foreign Affairs, 21 June 1943, FDA Courneuve, Vichy-Asie 3GMII, Box 141 ; Réunion interministérielle, 28 June 1943, FDA, Courneuve, Vichy-Asie 3GMII, Box 144.

38 de Margerie to Ministry of Foreign Affairs, 29 March 1943, FDA, Courneuve, Vichy-Asie 3GMII, Box 144.

From paradise to hell 329

39 Telegram, Cosme to Ministry of Foreign Affairs, 23 July 1943, FDA, Courneuve, Vichy-Asie 3GMII, Box 141.

40 Telegram, French consul to French embassy, 30 March 1943, FDA Nantes, Pékin 513PO/A, Box 261.

41 Summary of telegrams of 12, 16, and 17 June 1943, FDA, Courneuve, Vichy-Asie 3GMII, Box 141.

42 Réunion interministérielle, 28 June 1943, FDA, Courneuve, Vichy-Asie 3GMII, Box 144.

43 Telegram, Lagarde, Ministry of Foreign Affairs to French ambassador in China, 29 January 1944, FDA Courneuve, Vichy-Asie 3GMII, Box 141.

44 Telegram, Cosme to Ministry of Foreign Affairs, 10 July 1943, FDA Courneuve, Vichy-Asie 3GMII, Box 141.

45 Telegram, de Margerie to Ministry of Foreign Affairs, 5 August 1943, FDA Courneuve, Vichy-Asie 3GMII, Box 141.

46 Telegram, French consul to French ambassador, 25 October 1944, FDA Nantes, Pékin 513PO/A, Box 261.

47 Telegram, Cosme to Ministry of Foreign Affairs, 19 June 1943, FDA Courneuve, Vichy-Asie 3GMII, Box 141.

48 Telegram, Direction politique, Ministry of Foreign Affairs to Cosme, 25 June 1943, FDA Courneuve, Vichy-Asie 3GMII, Box 141.

49 Telegram, de Margerie to French ambassador, 18 December 1943, FDA Courneuve, Vichy-Asie 3GMII, Box 141.

50 Statement by Dr Chu Min-yi, Minister of Foreign Affairs, on the signing of the agreement, 22 July 1943, FDA Nantes, Pékin 513PO/A, Box 261.

51 'Need for Eradication of Enemy Prestige Here Seen with Return of Settlement', *The Shanghai Evening Post*, 5 July 1943.

52 Cosme to Gougal, Hanoi, 30 Juillet 1943, FDA Nantes, Pékin 513PO/A, Box 261; Telegram, de Margerie to Ministry of Foreign Affairs, 30 July 1943, FDA Courneuve, Vichy-Asie 3GMII, Box 141.

53 Letter, anonymous, 9 August 1943, FDA, Courneuve, Vichy-Asie 3GMII, Box 144; 'Pour avis no. 232', Domei news agency, FDA, Courneuve, Vichy-Asie 3GMII, Box 144.

54 Memorandum. Réduction des effectifs français laissé à la disposition des autorités chinoises, 4 July 1944, FDA Nantes, Pékin 513PO/A, Box 261.

55 G. Cattand et al., Procès-verbal, 13 March 1945; 'Kojosho' 口上書 (Verbal note), Japanese general consulate in Tianjin, 10 March 1945, Japanese original and French translation, FDA Nantes, Pékin 513PO/A, Box 755.

56 Telegram from de Margerie to Nanjing French consulate, 29 March 1945, FDA Nantes, Pékin 513PO/A, Box 755.

330 *Refugees and the stateless in Asia*

57 Note, de Margerie, 27 March 1945, FDA Nantes, Pékin 513PO/A, Box 755.

58 Andurain, 'Entretien avec M. le lieutenant Sakamoto du Quartier-Général des troupes japonaises de la Chine du Nord', 26 March 1945; 'Conference du vendredi 30 mars à l'Etat-major japonais', compter rendu du colonel Yvon, 30 March 1945, Pékin 513PO/A, Box 755.

59 Letter, de Margerie to general Shinomura, 27 March 1945, FDA Nantes, Pékin 513PO/A, Box 755.

60 Telegram from French consulate, 18 April 1945, FDA Nantes, Pékin 513PO/A, Box 755.

61 Telegram, French embassy to all consulates, 10 March 1945, FDA Nantes, Pékin 513PO/A, Box 755.

62 Letter no. 1450, Huabei zhengwu weiyuanhui (華北政務委員會) to French embassy, Chinese original and French translation, 10 March 1945; 'Une déclaration de M. Wang Yin-tai sur la situation des Française en Chine du nord', *Journal de Pékin*, 11 March 1945, FDA Nantes, Pékin 513PO/A, Box 755.

63 Telegram, Consul in Nanjing to French embassy, 16 March 1945, FDA Nantes, Pékin 513PO/A, Box 755.

64 Phone call memo, Consul Crepin to French embassy, 2 May 1945, FDA Nantes, Pékin 513PO/A, Box 755.

65 Letter, [de Margerie] to General Kusumoto, Japanese ambassador, 15 August 1945, FDA Nantes, Pékin 513PO/A, Box 755.

66 Telegram, Cosme to Ministry of Foreign Affairs, 11 June 1944, FDA Courneuve, Vichy-Asie 3GMII, Box 141.

67 Telegram, de Margerie to Laval, 27 May 1944, FDA Nantes, Pékin 513PO/A, Box 261.

68 Telegram, de Margerie to Ministry of Foreign Affairs, 20 February 1944, FDA Courneuve, Vichy-Asie 3GMII, Box 141.

69 Telegram, de Margerie to Laval, 27 May 1944, FDA Nantes, Pékin 513PO/A, Box 261.

70 Telegram, de Margerie to Consul in Nanjing, 1 December 1944, FDA Nantes, Pékin 513PO/A, Box 755.

71 Telegram, Consul Fain to de Margerie, 16 December 1944; Letter, policemen (Descos, Guéroult, Béréziat, Osellame) to French consul, 9 November 1944, FDA Nantes, Pékin 513PO/A, Box 755.

72 Letter, Descos to French consul, 12 September 1944, FDA Nantes, Pékin 513PO/A, Box 261.

73 Telegram, de Margerie to French embassy in Tokyo, 24 November 1944, FDA Nantes, Pékin 513PO/A, Box 755.

74 Telegram, de Margerie to Ministry of Foreign Affairs, 16 December 1944; Telegram, de Margerie to Gougal Hanoi, 16 December 1944;

From paradise to hell   331

Telegram, de Margerie to Ministry of Foreign Affairs, 16 December 1944; Telegram, de Margerie to Fain, 16 December 1944, FDA Nantes, Pékin 513PO/A, Box 755.

75 Telegram, de Margerie to Ministry, of Foreign Affairs, 17 December 1944, FDA Nantes, Pékin 513PO/A, Box 755.

76 Bulletin d'information, Avis, 12 April 1945, 1–2, FDA Nantes, Pékin 513PO/A, Box 261.

77 Bulletin d'information, Avis, 10 May 1945, 3, FDA Nantes, Pékin 513PO/A, Box 261.

78 Association amicale des anciens employés de la municipalité et de la police française, Circulaire, April 1945, FDA Nantes, Pékin 513PO/A, Box 261.

79 Hand-written note on copy of Resignation letter, Laignelot to Amicale, undated [March 1945], FDA Nantes, Pékin 513PO/A, Box 261.

80 Circulaire no. 3, Association amicale des anciens employés de la municipalité et de la police française, June 1945, FDA Nantes, Pékin 513PO/A, Box 261; Séance du comité [Association amicale des anciens employés de la municipalité et de la police française], 7 June 1945, FDA Nantes, Pékin 513PO/A, Box 261.

81 Circulaire no. 3, Association amicale des anciens employés de la municipalité et de la police française, June 1945, FDA Nantes, Pékin 513PO/A, Box 261.

82 Letter, Comité de l'association to French consul, 19 juin 1945, FDA Nantes, Pékin 513PO/A, Box 261.

83 Letter, Mrs. Civet to Henry Civet, 9 August 1943, FDA, Courneuve, Vichy-Asie 3GMII, Box 144.

84 Letter, General Pechkoff to Minister of Foreign Affairs, 9 October 1944; Letter, Minister of Foreign Affairs to General Pechkoff, 21 November 1944 and 11 itemised messages; Letter, Minister of Foreign Affairs to General Pechkoff, 5 December 1944 and two itemised messages, FDA, Asie-Océanie 337, Box 119QO.

85 Letter, J. Tiart to F. Tiart, 22 November 1944; Letter, Soeur Ursule Marguerite de la Croix to Armand Pucheu, 26 November 1944, FDA, Asie-Océanie 337, Box 119QO.

86 Untitled document, 13 itemised messages, undated [1944] and 8 itemised messages, FDA, Asie-Océanie 337, Box 119QO.

87 Pechkoff was appointed by the French Committee of National Liberation (CFLN) under De Gaulle in April 1944. The CFLN became the Provisional Government of the French Republic that ruled the country from 3 June 1944 to 1946. On Pechkoff, see Yuichiro Miyashita, 'Pechkoff et le Japon, 1946–1949', *Relations Internationales*, 158, 2 (2014), pp. 59–74.

332   *Refugees and the stateless in Asia*

88 Letter, Japanese consul general Tanaka to French consul general in Tianjin, 16 August 1945, FDA Nantes, Pékin 513PO/A, Box 755.
89 Telegram, Fain to French embassy, 19 August 1944, FDA Nantes, Pékin 513PO/A, Box 755.
90 Telegram, French consul in Tianjin to French embassy, 29 September 1945, Pékin 513PO/A, Box 755.
91 Telegram, French consul in Tianjin to French embassy, 6 October 1945; Telegram, French consul in Tianjin to French embassy, 10 October 1945, Pékin 513PO/A, Box 755.
92 Telegram, French embassy in Chongqing to Ministry of Foreign Affairs, 16 November 1945, FDA Nantes, Pékin 513PO/A, Box 755.
93 Letter, Robert E. Wampler, Chief, Liaison Team to de Margerie, 11 September 1945, FDA Nantes, Pékin 513PO/A, Box 755.
94 Telegram, Pechkoff, French embassy in Chongqing to [de Margerie], 13 September 1945, FDA Nantes, Pékin 513PO/A, Box 755.
95 de Margerie, Letter, undated [September 1945], FDA Nantes, Pékin 513PO/A, Box 755.
96 Letter, de Margerie to Daridan, 22 August 1945; 'Personnel du consulat de France à Tientsin', 17 September 1945, FDA Nantes, Pékin 513PO/A, Box 755.
97 Letter, de Margerie to Georges Bidault, 20 January 1946, FDA Nantes, Pékin 513PO/A, Box 755.
98 [de Margerie] to Salade, French consul in Shanghai, 21 July 1945, FDA Nantes, Pékin 513PO/A, Box 755.
99 Bensacq-Tixier, *La France en Chine*, pp. 473–74; Marie-Claire Bergère, 'L'épuration à Shanghai (1945–1946) l'affaire Sarly et la fin de la concession française', *Vingtième Siècle. Revue d'histoire*, 3, 1 (1997), pp. 25–41.

19

Out of Shanghai

Robert Bickers

Mr Archer, an elderly man, sits in a small apartment in a high-rise building on a council housing estate in Hackney, East London, and talks about his past. The estate is being redeveloped, and this building is slated for demolition. As part of a set of activities designed to engage with, consult, and support the residents whose lives are being turned upside down, a varied programme of community projects has been developed, including some art initiatives coordinated by the Holly Street Public Art Trust. Mr Archer has volunteered more than once as a subject for those projects, and as a result, he and his flat become quite comprehensively documented, caught in different sets of photographs taken by an established documentary photographer, and by at least two visual artists, both at the onset of their careers. As Catherine Yass, one of these young artists, prepares a portrait of him, Charles Archer tells his story, which is caught on a short film being made for television about the process of artistic creation, and which will be shown on BBC television in December 1997.

This is not the only occasion during these projects when Mr Archer tells his story. In this one, there is a scene in which he and Yass page through a photograph album, and she uses the images to prompt him to talk:

> *Catherine Yass:* So who's this body builder in the photograph?
> *Charles Archer:* Oh that's me.
> *Catherine Yass:* It was you?
> *Charles Archer:* Yes.
> *Catherine Yass:* That's great.
> *Catherine Yass:* When was that taken?

334   *Refugees and the stateless in Asia*

Charles Archer: Oh that's quite a number of years ago in Shanghai. Just after the war.

Catherine Yass: Mm hmm.

Charles Archer: After 1945 or so, the Japanese, Communists came in and about a year after that, we were all put into camp, suspected as spies.

Catherine Yass: So how long were you actually imprisoned in Shanghai for?

Charles Archer: I was detained for about 10 years.

Catherine Yass: Oh was it, gosh.

Charles Archer: From my prison cell I could see the back yard of a garden and they were dragging all these young students, I would call them students, made them all kneel down and shot them through the head.

Catherine Yass: And you saw that happen? Oh wow.

Charles Archer: Actually.

Catherine Yass: Do you still think about that time a lot and does it, do you think it still affects you?

Charles Archer: Well you can't really forget a thing like that, all of a sudden. It drags on, playing in my mind.

As Archer describes the executions, the voice track is laid over a shot of him standing in front of his flat window, looking out, the atrocities, we are expected to infer, drag and drag on, playing and playing again in his mind.[1]

Another version of his story was captured early the following year by a newspaper journalist, Sally Vincent. 'Mr Archer is a bit of a mystery man', began a profile she composed, and here again Charles Percival Archer replayed his story, or a story: born in Hong Kong in 1914, orphaned at fifteen, he 'struggled along on his own'. He was 'up to something in Shanghai – he can't remember what' when he was conscripted into the British armed forces, but then was captured at sea by the Japanese and interned. After the war, the communists came to Shanghai and he was jailed again for ten years as a spy. In the accompanying portrait, one of a series of the residents of the Holly Street estate taken by the artist Tom Hunter, Archer sits alone in the same sparsely furnished sitting room, the photograph album just visible on the shelving unit behind him.[2] In these images of the room, we can see three photographs on display: Archer the bodybuilder, Archer in a black and white studio portrait

Out of Shanghai 335

in a smart suit, and a portrait of a woman, evidently taken at the same time.

There are more, more photographs and film, and more stories, transcribed in archives and newspapers. I have found them in Shanghai, London, and Washington DC. I heard another in Vancouver and one in Bristol as well. There is storytelling that undoubtedly took place but which I cannot retrieve. Mr Archer was a 'mystery', his story was 'strange', he himself stood out for his accent and his clipped and precise delivery, and his careful smart appearance, which gave him 'a sense of authority', thought Hunter, who recalled 'his formidable stance' and 'intense gaze'.[3] In Hackney, at the end of the twentieth century, Charles Archer lived a settled and respectable life; he was labelled one of a couple of 'elderly East Enders' by the documentary's scriptwriter; his portrait can be found in the Museum of London (twice); he was a prominent voice in the community consultation that saw the unplanned retention of one of the Holly Street estate's residential towers and its rehabilitation as a home exclusively for elderly residents. But hidden between the careful phrasing of his storytelling, and outside the frames of those photographs, lie the facts that for most of the first five decades of his life, at least, Charles Archer lived on the edge of society, and on the edge of statelessness.

Charles Archer was tried at least seven times in various jurisdictions, jailed at least three times, and held in custody on other occasions. He was a liar, a bigamist, a thief, a black marketeer, a suspected traitor, and an accessory – at least – to murder. Those are the crimes for which he was caught, or of which official suspicions were recorded. It is how state records tell his story. He was also a 'Eurasian', which displaced him in the eyes of many Britons from the heart of their society in China. But what makes Archer most interesting to me is his vulnerable position as a man of uncertain ancestry and social precarity, through whom I can explore a network of British subjects living and working in Hong Kong and Shanghai, and other cities in China, at the margins of citizenship in an era when the British state was in slow, raggedy retreat from its privileged position within China's borders.

Decolonisation spawned refugees in their millions, and these included hidden immigrants and 'repudiated' repatriates who moved to Western Europe as the European empires were battled

336 *Refugees and the stateless in Asia*

out of Africa and Asia or withdrew or reconstituted themselves in the aftermath of the Second World War.[4] Archer was one of these repatriates, although the prefix is redundant, for he had never been to Britain before he shipped there in 1956. In fact, we might simply say that he was patriated. These displaced men and women have, for various reasons, attracted far less attention from scholars, but studying them offers new insights into colonial power, the colonial experience, and the instabilities of wartime and the post-war world. In Shanghai, many of the British subjects amongst whom the European refugees who form the subject of most of the studies in this book found themselves led lives finely balanced between inclusion and exclusion in the British world, between acceptance and repudiation, between citizenship and statelessness.

I want to use Archer's story in three ways here. First, I want to explore the way some of his personal network amplifies this story of the ways a subset of China Britons scrambled to hold on to their status and recognition by the British state. Secondly, I want to look further at Archer's storytelling and the ways in which his assertion of respectability and inclusion lay at the heart of this. Thirdly, I will sketch further how his experience serves as a study of the end of British Shanghai. I will preface these with a sketch of Archer's background, his life, and the key developments against which this story unfolds.

Archer was indeed born in Hong Kong in early June 1914.[5] His precise parentage is unclear, but he was baptised at the colony's Roman Catholic Cathedral as the son of a black Barbadian, Charles Percival Archer, a ship's purser; and Angelina Salvador, whose address at the time of their marriage in 1910 is given as the city's Catholic orphanage.[6] It is thought that she had a Black American father, born in Georgia, and a Macanese mother. Young Archer himself was adopted. Archer senior died in 1925, shortly after which point his mother seems to have relocated to the Chinese capital, Peking, where she worked in cabarets (nightclubs). She died there in 1959. The couple had two older daughters, Ethel, born four years before their marriage, and Dorothy, born in 1912. Both lived all their lives in Hong Kong. By his own account, told to a police recruiter in 1941, Archer, after attending a respectable Catholic school in Hong Kong, spent four years in Manila from 1931 to 1935, first at high school, and then as a salesman. After returning to Hong Kong,

Out of Shanghai 337

he married a Macanese woman in 1936, who gave birth to their daughter later that year. Archer was jailed in Hong Kong for fraud in 1940, and by the British Supreme Court in Shanghai for theft in December 1941, just five days before the Japanese seized the city.

I do not know when Archer was released from this last jail sentence, but he probably served out his time, for the ordinary business of administration of the city largely continued much as it had before Pearl Harbor.[7] He certainly was interned by the Japanese, as most British subjects in occupied China were, in March 1943. Just before this, British and Chinese diplomats signed a new treaty that abolished extraterritoriality and all the related privileges and concessions enjoyed by individual British subjects and corporate interests. This made no difference to their situation in 1943, but when Archer was able to leave camp in September 1945, he emerged into a city in which the old British position was not going to be re-established. In October 1945, Archer married Natalia Andrevna Zaharovna, the Russian widow of a British subject, Bertie Hayton-Fleet, who had been interned in the same camp with her son, and in August 1947, he was arrested with an American marine, Thomas Malloy, on suspicion of the murder of a Chinese black-market bullion dealer, Yu Shengxiao. Tried separately, the American by a US military court, and Archer by the Shanghai District Court, both men were sentenced to life imprisonment, the American for murder, Archer for armed robbery leading to death. An appeal upheld the sentence, and he was the only British subject in jail in Shanghai when it fell to communist troops in May 1949 (Malloy was sent to a federal prison in the United States). Archer was released on parole in June 1956, and arrived in Hong Kong a month later, sailing on to join his wife Natalia in London, where he arrived in September 1956 (and was briefly, and as far as I know perhaps finally, detained on remand for theft there in November 1957). As he put it himself in 1997, Charlie Archer was certainly always 'up to something'.

It is all a long way from London's East End. Archer was born in a British colony, and lived and worked, and was incarcerated by British authorities there and in Shanghai. He was interned by the Japanese occupation authorities, and then tried and jailed under Guomindang rule, and held later on in jail in the People's Republic. Charlie Archer's story unfolded as British power in China unravelled. He was born just before the First World War, during which

338   *Refugees and the stateless in Asia*

conflict the British position, long dominant amongst the concert of foreign powers that had degraded China's sovereignty since the first British–Chinese war of 1839–42, was challenged by Japan. Japanese political demands for what would be a controlling role in China's state, mostly those associated with the 'Twenty-One Demands' made of China's republican government in January 1915, were largely rolled back, but its economic interests markedly developed while the European powers fought each other. British and French weakness in wartime saw secret pledges to transfer German assets in China to Japan after the war, and even while Japanese aggression sparked steady and growing Chinese nationalist opposition, the Japanese position grew in strength, confidence, and ambition. So did Chinese popular nationalism, which undergirded the revolutionary forces of the 1920s that brought to power the Guomindang, led by Chiang Kai-shek, which established in 1928 its National Government, based at Nanjing.

When Archer arrived in Shanghai on 12 March 1941, these double pressures had already altered and weakened the British position. Since 1927, Guomindang challenges had led to key elements of the British presence in China being seized, formally or implicitly surrendered, or reformed. A network of British-controlled concessions and settlements across prominent Chinese riverine and maritime cities had been shrunk, with just the British-dominated International Settlement at Shanghai, a smaller one at Xiamen, and the wholly British-controlled concession at Tianjin remaining. The Guomindang's National Government had re-established full or greater control over other areas, such as the Chinese Maritime Customs Service, long a British-dominated agency. At Shanghai, Chinese pressure had seen substantial changes to the ways in which the largely British-administered International Settlement operated.[8] But Chinese pressure had been significantly tempered after Japanese forces invaded and seized Manchuria in 1931 and fought a brief, bloody war around Shanghai in 1932. Chinese anti-imperialist nationalism had not dissipated, but after 1931 it was focused instead on the existential threat posed by Japan. The wider war that erupted after July 1937 left the International Settlement isolated as Japanese forces occupied East China, and its power was degraded or aggressively contested by the Japanese. The outbreak of the war in Europe would leave it more vulnerable and anxious yet.

Shanghai was a city made by refugees. Across almost the entire century of the foreign administration there, successive national, regional, or international crises had prompted the movement across its borders of people seeking shelter and security. This in turn had driven property development, especially for those who did not return, and those who opted to base themselves and their interests in its care. Chinese fled the Taiping civil war, the Boxer crisis, the revolution of 1911, and the civil wars of the 1920s. Others fled there too: Germans and Austrians had arrived from enemy-held colonies in the First World War, for China's neutrality until 1917 made the International Settlement a safe-haven for them, even if British dominated; Russians came after the revolution and civil war, while Korean and Indian revolutionaries based themselves there, and others too.[9] The Russians formed the single largest community, and for the British their experience was the most salutary. Shorn of their extraterritorial rights in 1924, and of their citizenship, the Russians came under Chinese jurisdiction, and Britons leapt on every injustice and indignity they spotted to exemplify what might happen if they lost their own privileges. After the fall of France in May 1940, and the German invasion of the Soviet Union in June 1941, and in the face of unrelenting Japanese pressure, this stark prospect of joining the White Russians in their position of stateless vulnerability loomed larger and larger in the British imagination, where there could be no worse fate.

The pressures faced by the British can be seen in Archer's activities in Shanghai. He presented himself at the headquarters of the settlement's Shanghai Municipal Police on 21 March 1941, and applied to join. Archer gave an ostensibly detailed but patchy and deceptive account of his life that skipped his various convictions and recent release from jail, and overlooked the fact that, according to a Special Branch report from Hong Kong, he had embarked for Shanghai boasting that he would there 'offer his services "in any capacity"' to a Japanese intelligence agent. In September, the same department noted that having volunteered for the British army, he had passed through the colony on his way to Singapore, adding, laconically, that before leaving Shanghai 'he managed to pass a worthless cheque on the British Consul'.[10] Resigning after four months' police service, Archer was in fact fleeing an inevitable arrest, for he had passed several such cheques, including one

340 *Refugees and the stateless in Asia*

that covered a farewell party he threw at a nightclub, and he was detained on arrival at Singapore and shipped back to Shanghai to stand trial, where he was jailed by the British Supreme Court on 2 December 1941. In normal times, British recruits for the SMP were secured through the Council's London-based agents, but the European war prevented this, and also saw army reservists leave to rejoin the colours, and other men resign to take families away from an increasingly tense violent city.[11] Under intense pressure from the Japanese authorities to increase the numbers of Japanese personnel at all levels in the force and the municipal administration, the SMP was keen to take on any European who could help plug the gaps, even an evident drifter like Archer. Additionally, a less distracted force would have found out quickly from Hong Kong that Archer had lied to them.

The British position had been evolving markedly even before this. Ten years earlier, British diplomats had negotiated a new treaty with China that would pave the way for the end of extraterritoriality and the eventual handover of the remaining concessions and settlements, and while the Japanese invasion had seen that initiative lapse, it was clear that this transition was inevitable. British interests had steadily been preparing themselves to adapt to a post-treaty world. British firms had entered into joint ventures with Chinese enterprises, tried to build relationships with Chinese politicians and business elites, and generally retreated from quasi-colonial practices and a mindset that would be less striking in a colony than in a recognised sovereign, independent state. In so doing they were, like British diplomats, quite prepared to jettison the institutions that had grown up across the treaty ports, and those who served them. But, nonetheless, Archer was sentenced by a British judge at the Supreme Court for China, Sir Alan Mossop, an imperial subject, a South African who sat, wigged and gowned, at the apex of the British legal system in China.[12] Despite this state of uncertainty and anxiety, Britons like Archer still enjoyed extraterritorial rights, and so it was Britons in the SMP who arrested him, while a Briton served as head of the Ward Road Gaol, the largest in Asia, to which he was sent on 2 December. Several hundred Britons still worked in the SMP and in other branches of the municipal council. British power, even honoured in the breach by the Japanese – for the moment – secured the neutrality of the settlement and its exclusion

Out of Shanghai 341

from direct Chinese administration. It remained, as a result, largely run on British lines, and its status made it a destination for refugees, and that also included Britons forced out of other cities in China by the Japanese.

I will now turn to members of Archer's family network and their position as British subjects. 'British', as a category, was capacious, but also capricious. Some Britons were more British than others.[13] They could lose their status, and a significant minority began to do so in the 1930s on these margins of empire, but they could also evade their British subjecthood when they needed to. Mr Archer's first wife was a Macanese, or, more precisely, Hong Kong-born to a Macanese father and Filipino-Macanese mother. She was, by virtue of her place of birth, a British subject. In the aftermath of the traumatic Japanese conquest of Hong Kong in December 1941, she and their daughter found safe-haven, as thousands of their fellow Hong Kong Macanese, did in the Portuguese colony across the Pearl River delta. Others lived on under Japanese rule in Hong Kong, but unlike white Britons – 'Europeans' in colonial parlance – they were not interned by the conquerors, unless they had fought with Hong Kong's volunteer defence forces. They were, in effect, able to choose to be British enough for the Japanese, or not. Ethel and Dorothy, Archer's sisters, also spoke Macanese, but stayed in Hong Kong and passed as Indians during the early occupation because of their appearance, even adopting saris to reinforce the deception and to receive ration cards for food supplies made available to British Indian subjects in the colony, who like, the Macanese, were set apart from white Britons by the Japanese.[14] After the war, destitute, Ethel applied for 'repatriation' to Barbados, her father's birth-place, seeking the assistance of the League of Coloured Peoples in London. As she could show no domicile there, this was refused. Adopting a different strategy, she married an elderly American in 1947, a cook on a transpacific liner and thereby secured the right to US citizenship. Despite thereafter presenting herself as an American, Ethel never left the British colony in which she was born and never tested her right to US citizenship.[15]

Archer's second wife had been born in 1898 in the Siberian city of Khabarovsk, close to the Chinese border. Natalia had been the third wife of a St Petersburg-born British subject, Bertie Hayton Fleet, whose father was a grain dealer and had become a high-ranking

342   *Refugees and the stateless in Asia*

member of the merchant elite in the Russian capital. The son worked first in Saint Petersburg, then for a gold mining company in Siberia. The First World War and the revolution and civil war in Russia found him moving to shelter under the British umbrella, even serving for a while as an assistant consul. By the early 1920s, Fleet was living in Harbin, operating a language school, a newspaper and related publishing operation, and other businesses. British officials did not trust him. He was 'a bad lot', suspected of being in the pay of the Soviets, and by them of being a British agent of some sort.[16] After the Japanese occupation of Manchuria and the creation of the Manchuko puppet state, Fleet found himself under greater and greater Japanese pressure, as did British interests generally, and in 1936 he relocated to the greater apparent security of Shanghai with Natalia. Pressure continued to be applied, and the British continued to distrust him. He died in February 1942, shortly after the Japanese occupation of the settlement. British officials eventually recorded his death, but obituaries only appeared in Shanghai's Russian press. It is not clear to me that Fleet ever spent any extended period of time in Britain. He lived off-shore. Some Russian women married to British men were able to stay out of the camps, falling back on their Russian status. This tactic could serve some of them well, allowing them to preserve assets and help support those in camp, but others, like Natalia, were interned. Even so, and even though duly interned as British subjects, other Britons would later voice criticism of the Russian women who entered the camps, seeing them as unnecessarily adding to the acute pressures on space and on supplies of all kinds.

These men and women were all legally British subjects, but circumstance and ethnicity actually placed them in a more fluid zone between secure subjecthood and exclusion. This could be advantageous in times of acute crisis and allowed them to adopt pragmatic strategies for survival. But, ultimately, they all needed the power and presence, acquiescence and tolerance, of the British state to be able to flourish, whether that was in Hong Kong, Macao (where the refugees were succoured by the British consul), Harbin, or Shanghai. The Fleet's son, a British official noted in December 1945, 'is rather a nere-do-well and is no doubt more Russian than British in outlook, but the fact remains that he is a British subject'.[17] I use the term 'tolerated' deliberately. While the British held onto

Out of Shanghai 343

the lineaments of power in China, officials largely discharged their duties to those in their charge, however distasteful they found them at times, but there was room for individual caprice, for refusing to recognise a claim for protection, and for the engendering of a state of anxiety amongst these almost-Britons. As a result, none of these men and women felt secure in their British legal status.

Let me now return to Archer the storyteller, for storytelling was vital to the business of keeping up British appearances. It is worth saying at the start that he did not always display anything remotely like common sense, and certainly acted by any measure stupidly and cruelly, and did so repeatedly. After all, he was quite frequently caught out, and caught. But there are some five modes of self-preservation and promotion in his stories: dissemblance, passivity, pliability, self-criticism, and finally, respectability.

Archer lied. Notably, he lied to the Shanghai police Special Branch interviewer in 1941, and then, in his storytelling in Hackney, he disassembled and omitted and he 'forgot'. But this was a quite deliberate forgetting. He was, recalled Tom Hunter, 'very clued in': he was in full possession of his faculties in old age. And I think we can assume safely that the petty crook also committed other offences in Hong Kong, Shanghai, and possibly in Manila. For the police, his omissions allowed him to present himself as a man with what was certainly a mediocre career but respectable enough to be a policeman in a time of need. For later interviewers, he presented himself as a victim of the Japanese, and of ill-founded communist suspicions. He was never suspected of being a spy, but he was certainly suspected of being a traitor.

He did not lie in court. Archer's approach to his pre-war court appearances was to plead guilty, and judges and magistrates noted his apparent regret for his actions, his relative youth (he was twenty-six when he was first jailed), and the possibility of full repentance and reform. Giving evidence immediately after the killing in 1947, Archer said he 'was astonished' to hear a shot being fired in the car he was driving, and later added that he was 'so frightened that he was at a loss what to do'. Fingered as an international drug smuggler whilst he was later in jail, he wrote to the press to protest 'the terrible grave injustice' of this 'ludicrous' suspicion. 'Someone', he concluded, 'is definitely set [on] keeping me permanently in jail'.[18]

344 *Refugees and the stateless in Asia*

The appearance of repentance in a (repeat) defendant is hardly unusual, but Archer often faced a double layered accusation when he was charged. He was routinely described quite pedantically as a 'Hong Kong born British subject' or words to that effect, not just as a 'British subject'. This was an obvious code that readers will have understood. It was rarely necessary to describe him more explicitly as a 'Eurasian'.[19] From the 1930s onwards, it had very slowly started to become less acceptable to use this term in this way as an explicit label for men and women of plural heritage. It was not just that Archer was accused of crime; he was also implicitly accused of being an inauthentic and undeserving Briton. The ambiguous and unstable position of Eurasians in British colonial Asia is well attested, even setting aside the consistently negative way in which they were represented in Anglophone culture. The law, and practice, was subject to change, and their ability to retain a hold on nationality, assuming that they secured it, could be challenging. The anxiety of his position, their position, was also on display when Natalia took out an advertisement in the *North China Daily News* in December 1947 to plead for contributions to pay for an appeal for her husband, a 'British subject', she noted; 'Help! Help!' it began.[20]

Passive and pliable in court, Archer proved a polite, grateful, and cooperative subject of consular business after he was jailed in 1947. A former SMP colleague, now working for the British consulate, observed the trial, the first of a British subject since the end of extraterritoriality. They continued observing thereafter. In compiling lists of British subjects held in Chinese jails after the establishment of the communist regime in October 1949, British officials routinely included his name, but noted that there were no grounds on which to make any representations for his release. He was a duly convicted criminal. Behind the scenes, they visited him periodically, and reports on these visits survive from 1949 and 1954, and Archer made himself useful, providing information on the prison regime, and on fellow prisoners. The end of extraterritoriality had found expression in the prison experience too. At the former Ward Road Gaol, now known as Tilanqiao jail, Chinese and non-Chinese inmates had formerly been subjected to different regimes, but after 1945 they were all subjected to the same regime, and the same sets of expectations.

Out of Shanghai

345

In stories that I cannot retrieve, which I know he will have told of himself, Archer possibly came as close as he ever did to telling his audience who he actually was. Republican China's penal philosophy was focused on rehabilitation, and therefore on reflection, but under the communist prison regime, self-criticism became the central strand of the convict's experience.[21] After May 1949, Archer reported that the daily routine included one hour each morning and afternoon of what he called 'conferences' (probably for the Chinese word *kaihui*, meetings) at which the inmates were

> allowed, even encouraged ... to discuss and critique the general policies of the New People's Government and especially ourselves. We also formed self-governing bodies, divided in groups ... each one of us (generally) has to write an article for the 'Wall-paper', posted upon the outside of each block, condemning and criticizing ourselves and our past lives, and praising communism.[22]

Accounts of prison routines in communist China are consistent on this score. Early after the establishment of the new regime, this type of activity was described as being 'encouraged', but it became the central defining feature of communist practice. The inmate was to be 'reformed' though labour, study, and 'guided' confession. Inmates wrote, and rewrote, their lives. They also had to voice these to their fellow prisoners, and were routinely criticised and rebuked by them for failing to properly confess in what were called 'struggle sessions'. They will also have duly accused others in turn, probably, in Archer's case, focusing on his US military co-accused, Thomas Malloy. In keeping with the anti-American campaigns of the Korean War period, accounts of the murder and trial published after the establishment of the communist state focus on claims of alleged US military complicity in shielding Malloy from justice.[23] In 1954, Archer was reported by the consular prison visitor to have said that the authorities had 'one or two points regarding his trial that they want to settle', but it was over eighteen months later that his sentence came to an end.[24]

The precise technical reason for Archer's release on parole is unclear, but presumably those points had finally been settled to the satisfaction of his interlocutors. Set free in June 1956, Archer crossed the border into Hong Kong a month later, where he was met by Red Cross officials and taken to hospital. As a 'distressed British

346   *Refugees and the stateless in Asia*

subject', he was promptly provided with a passage to join his wife, who had sailed for London in August 1951. News about Archer's release had first come through correspondence from Shanghai about jailed Roman Catholic priests, whom he had provided information about.[25] It is likely that he told his story more fully to the authorities in the colony, who eagerly sought any intelligence that they could glean from those crossing the border, especially about other foreign nationals in China's jails. On the passenger manifest, Archer's occupation was listed as 'merchant'. Unlike his sister Ethel, lack of domicile in the United Kingdom presented no obstacle to repatriation.

When Archer was jailed, there were some 4,400 British subjects living in Shanghai; by February 1950, the figure had halved. By June 1951, it had halved again, and other a third of those were deemed by the consul-general to be 'Eurasians without strong British roots'. By 1954, most businesses had surrendered their operations and assets to the city authorities or to Chinese firms. Foreign nationals with private property, such as Natalia, who owned two houses, found their hold on these usurped. Most were left with, and left with, nothing bar personal possessions.[26] By 1962, there were only forty-two British subjects in Shanghai, and half of those were regarded by the Chinese authorities as Chinese citizens: they were the Chinese widows of British men, for example, or adopted children of Chinese birth. The British had gone. Some of those most rooted to China had moved no further than Hong Kong, but most found their way further afield. By 1956, only three British firms remained in Shanghai, and all the elaborate infrastructure which had still been in place when Sir Alan Mossop jailed Charles Archer in 1941 had been swept into the history books and into the archive.

The British government had recognised the new state with indecent haste in January 1950, but the new People's Government had not acknowledged this. Relations were regularised to an extent in 1954, but it would be another 22 years before relations were officially normalised. While the British retained their consulate in Shanghai, it was not recognised as such – the consul-general was now a representative of the British chargé d'affaires in Beijing. The once powerful centre of British power which occupied an extensive site on Shanghai's riverfront Bund was now an irrelevance. In 1967, the remaining staff were withdrawn, and the consular complex, including the court where Archer had been tried in 1941,

Out of Shanghai

347

was thereafter taken over by the municipal government. Lodged in the eaves of the building were its archives, which would outlast the presence of British officials by some fifteen years before they were rediscovered and returned. In amongst them was a record of Archer's trial. The city that had been shaped by British power and British interests was now entirely shorn of the British.

All British subjects had cause for some anxiety in the face of China's drive to reclaim full sovereignty. Fundamentally, their interests depended on the continuation of the impairment of that sovereignty. The Japanese assault on China and the outbreak of the European war in September 1939 exacerbated their fears. But British subjects like Charles Archer and his relatives had even more cause, for their British status was always marginal and contingent. The state could and did surrender the very ground beneath their feet, and could and did remove its protection – even if, grudgingly, officials dutifully supported them as British subjects. I think for those in receipt of this support, this was something they never took for granted. They needed to prove themselves, again and again in words and in deeds – by any means possible – and show that they were deserving. Many of their strategies for doing so can be seen in Charles Archer's story.

In the twilight of his life – he died in 2002 – Mr Archer might have been a mystery man, but this mystery was visible only because he put himself forward into community affairs, and in front of the camera, and on film, all now on deposit in museum and gallery collections and in books (and plastered all over the internet). In this way, Charles Archer, elderly Eastender, secured acceptance and the anonymity of belonging – until I found him. So let me return to where I first encountered Charles Archer, in Tom Hunter's photograph when it was published in the *Guardian* newspaper in February 1998. In this spartan, tidy sitting room sits this smartly dressed and evidently self-respecting man, well groomed, contained, the pen in his shirt pocket a sign of his being prepared. The fact of his sitting for Hunter was itself a facet of his community-spiritedness, his readiness to help, and his willingness to put himself forward. Sally Vincent's text provides a contrast to the image as much as it did a gloss, in its presentation of a difficult life. It was not a life I then had any success in excavating, as the details were too vague – deliberately so, it now turns out – and I recall that I thought it then

Figure 19.1 Charles Archer, from *Holly Street Residents*. Photograph © Tom Hunter, 1998.

a piece of exaggerated storytelling. The omissions and elisions now seem symptomatic instead of Archer's state of latent insecurity, and his well-founded desire to obscure his past. So too, in a different way, was the manner in which the man offered himself so fully and transparently to the camera, and did so repeatedly.

Silently overlooking this scene is another of his claims to respectability and inclusion, in the form of the only photograph in Archer's room that was neither of Natalia nor himself. There on the back wall was a portrait of Queen Elizabeth II and the Duke of Edinburgh, one of a number taken in October 1960 by the photographer Anthony Buckley in preparation for a royal tour of India and Pakistan. Reports of Archer's conviction in 1947 appeared in the press in Shanghai on the same day, and often on the same page, as news of the wedding of then Princess Elizabeth and Philip Mountbatten. Hunter's photograph shows, I think, that in this way, too, finally, Charles Archer presented himself fully and lastingly as a worthy British subject (Figure 19.1).

Notes

1 'Date with an Artist', broadcast 3 December 1997, BBC Two, https://www.bbc.co.uk/schedules/p00fzl97/1997/12/03. Accessed 24 November 2024.

2 Tom Hunter and Sally Vincent, 'Heaven Up Here?', *Guardian Weekend*, 25 April 1998, pp. 43–4.

3 *East End News*, 15 November 1957, p. 2; transcript of filmed interview with Tom Hunter, 24 April 2019.

4 Elizabeth Buettner, *Europe after Empire: Decolonization, Society, and Culture* (Cambridge: Cambridge University Press, 2016).

5 This biographical sketch is drawn from extensive research for a longer form work in progress. I have written about the most notable of his trials, that at the British Supreme Court in Shanghai in 1941, and at the Shanghai District Court in 1947 in an essay on extraterritoriality: 'Legal Fictions: Extraterritoriality as an Instrument of British Power in China in the Long Nineteenth Century', in Brian Padair Farrell and Donna Brunero (eds), *The History of Empire in Asia: Volume II: The Long Nineteenth Century* (London: Bloomsbury, 2018), pp. 53–80.

6 Angelina's name has also been given as Angeline Mary Campbell-Moore.

7 For a report on the jail in 1942 which bears this out, see Shanghai Municipal Council, *Annual Report 1942* (Shanghai: 1943), pp. 40–3.

8 Isabella Jackson, *Shaping Modern Shanghai: Colonialism in China's Global City* (Cambridge: Cambridge University Press, 2017); Chihyun Chang, *Government, Imperialism and Nationalism in China: The Maritime Customs Service and Its Chinese Staff* (London: Routledge, 2013).

9 Marcia Reynders Ristaino, *Port of Last Resort: The Diaspora Communities of Shanghai* (Stanford, CA: Stanford University Press, 2001).

10 'Charles Percival Archer: Candidate for Shanghai Municipal Police', 25 March 1941: National Archives and Records Administration, Record Group 263, Records of the Shanghai Municipal Police Special Branch, file D8741; 'Quarterly summary of Japanese intelligence activities, First Quarter 1941', 15 April 1941; 'Monthly Report: August 1941', 11 September 1941: TNA, FO 371/27621.

11 Frederic Wakeman Jr, *The Shanghai Badlands: Wartime Terrorism and Urban Crime, 1937–1941* (New York: Cambridge University Press, 1996).

12 Alexander Thompson, *British Law and Governance in Treaty Port China 1842–1947: Consuls, Courts and Colonial Subjects* (Amsterdam: Amsterdam University Press, 2024).

13 Catherine Ladds, 'Eurasians in Treaty-Port China: Journeys across Racial and Imperial Frontiers', in Jacqueline Leckie, Angela McCarthy,

350 *Refugees and the stateless in Asia*

and Angela Wanhalla (eds), *Migrant Cross-Cultural Encounters in Asia and the Pacific* (New York: Routledge, 2017), pp. 19–35.

14 Catherine S. Chan, *The Macanese Diaspora in British Hong Kong: A Century of Transimperial Drifting* (Amsterdam: Amsterdam University Press, 2021); Colin Day and Richard Garrett (eds), John Pownall Reeves, *The Lone Flag: Memoir of the British Consul in Macao during World War II* (Hong Kong: Hong Kong University Press, 2014); Vivian Kong, *Multiracial Britishness: Global Networks in Hong Kong, 1910–45* (Cambridge: Cambridge University Press, 2023).

15 Hong Kong, Public Record office: HKRS41-4-1689, 'Ethae [*sic*] Archer – Request for Assistance for Repatriation to Barbados'; *South China Morning Post*, 7 January 1947, p. 2; 'Mystery Woman of Hong Kong', *Ebony* (February 1959), pp. 89–93.

16 W. Stark-Toller, 29 October 1929, minute on file 'Activities of Mr. Hayton Fleet, Editor of the Harbin "Observer"': TNA, FO 371/13958.

17 A. G. N. Ogden to L. H. Lamb, Shanghai No. 133, 19 December 1945: TNA, FO 371/53608.

18 'Statement of C. P. Archer in Connection with the Murder of One Chinese Named Yue Zang Siao on 1/8/47': Shanghai Municipal Archives, Q185-2-23884; *North China Daily News*, 10 August 1948, p. 5.

19 *China Mail*, 4 September 1947.

20 *North China Daily News*, 12 December 1947, p. 1.

21 In this paragraph I draw on Jan Kiely, *The Compelling Ideal: Thought Reform and the Prison in China, 1901–1956* (New Haven, CT: Yale University Press, 2014), ch. 7, pp. 255–96.

22 C. P. Archer to H. F. Gill, 23 November 1949: TNA, FO 369/4437.

23 'Yu Shengxiao de qizi yao ernü xiang Meiguo qiangdao baochou' ('Yu Shengxiao's wife wants their children to take revenge on the American bandits'), *Xinmin wanbao*, 6 November 1950, p. 2. Malloy spent longer in jail than Archer; he was in Leavenworth Federal Penitentiary in 1963, and it is not currently clear when he was released: email from SS, Archives Specialist, National Archives at Kansas City, 23 May 2023.

24 Consulate General, Shanghai to Chancery, British Embassy, Peking, 18 November 1954: TNA, FO 369/5138.

25 *Hong Kong Standard*, 27 July 1956, p. 1.

26 For more on this process, see the work of Jonathan J. Howlett, including his '"The British Boss Is Gone and Will Never Return": Communist Takeovers of British Companies in Shanghai (1949–1954)', *Modern Asian Studies*, 47, 6 (2013), pp. 1941–76; and his in-progress book manuscript 'Decolonisation at the Margins: Socialist Revolution and the Human Legacies of Semi-Colonialism in Shanghai, 1949–1976'.

Conclusion: statelessness in the global Second World War

Kolleen Guy and Jay Winter

Since she published *The Origins of Totalitarianism* in 1951, Hannah Arendt's work has served as a guide to the problem of statelessness. She knew of what she wrote. She was what Avishai Margolit terms a 'moral witness', someone who knew the suffering of the stateless from within.[1] She never claimed that she had written the last word on the subject. There is more to say, and this book was written in the hope of contributing to a conversation about statelessness from a global perspective.

One way forward is to shift the centre of gravity of the study of statelessness away from her focus on Europe and the transatlantic world to other continents. In different settings, we have followed the experience of refugees and the stateless in the Asian and Pacific theatre of operations in the period of the Second World War. The outcome of this research is to present statelessness as not one but many conditions. The ways people got into and out of statelessness varied with time, place, and circumstances. Different state and imperial forms confronted statelessness in different ways.

The city of Shanghai was the site of fierce fighting in 1932 and 1937, after which the Japanese army and navy controlled the Chinese administered city. A number of long-standing extraterritorial treaties had made Shanghai a place where Chinese authority was severely limited. The heart of the city remained in the hands of a British-dominated International Settlement and a French administration.

352   *Statelessness after Arendt*

For many reasons, Shanghai was one of the few places in the world where those fleeing persecution and violence could arrive without a visa. Consequently, Shanghai was able to offer a refuge to the stateless fleeing violence in Europe. Upwards of twenty thousand German, Austrian, and Polish Jews, all made stateless in the 1930s, found refuge there. They found there other stateless people, many Russians, as well as a large number of Chinese refugees fleeing the Japanese advance.

When the German and Austrian Jewish refugees arrived in Shanghai in the late 1930s, their statelessness did not bar them from working in it. After the war, they had to leave Shanghai and China. They were no longer seen by the Chinese authorities primarily as stateless refugees, fleeing persecution elsewhere, but as living representatives of European privilege in China. A small number of Europeans stayed to build the new China; they were the exceptions. Too many Chinese had bowed the knee before British grandees, French *hautes fonctionnaires*, and American soldiers before and during the war. The old order of European privilege had to go. The effort to eradicate the traces of imperial power in Shanghai had begun well before 1945. By then, it was time to reconstruct Chinese sovereignty in such a way as to exclude foreign stateless people. The sun had set on the complex network of extraterritorial institutions and practices that had diminished Chinese sovereignty at times to the vanishing point.

The welcome Chinese residents of Shanghai offered to European stateless people in the period 1938–41 is the subject of the state-sponsored Shanghai Jewish Refugees Museum in Hongkou. The city of Shanghai, say the organisers of the museum, served as a 'Noah's ark' for stateless Jews.[2] Everyone was welcome. That was true, at least for a time in 1938 and early 1939. Then in August 1939, restrictions were imposed on the numbers allowed to enter the city.[3] The flow of refugees into Shanghai continued, but at a very reduced level. The problem with the museum's narrative of Noah's ark concerns a later period. At the end of the Second World War, the earlier welcome to the stateless was withdrawn categorically. The Chinese state that left its doors ajar in the 1930s was not the same as the Chinese state that closed its doors, even before the victory of Mao and the Chinese communists in 1949. Building post-war China took precedence over providing a safe-haven for the stateless.

Conclusion 353

The weight of evidence in this book reinforces a multifaceted and changing history of statelessness. The men and women of Harbin, in Sheila Fitzpatrick's chapter, used statelessness to their advantage when they could. As Meredith Oyen and Gao Bei show, diplomats – Japanese, American, Chinese, British – treated the stateless like pawns on a chessboard. Laura Margolis, the agent in Shanghai of the American Jewish Joint Distribution Committee, exploited the diplomatic game masterfully, as Kolleen Guy documents. The rabbinical students in the Mir Yeshiva saw themselves as privileged carriers of the Talmudic tradition. Unlike Margolis, these stateless ultra-Orthodox Jews saw diplomacy as something Orthodox Jews did for other Orthodox Jews whatever the Christian world or the Joint thought of them. The survival of the Mir Yeshiva, told by Jay Winter, is a story of statelessness triumphant very different from that told by Hannah Arendt. In effect, moving to the Asian and Pacific sectors of the Second World War provides a complementary history to that of Arendt's Europe.

There were multiple ways men and women moved from political exclusion and a corresponding absence of rights to what might be termed urban citizenship, or in Qian Zhu's and Henri Lefebvre's words, 'the right to the city'. The history of Shanghai highlights vividly the way in which the pathway to full citizenship or to exclusion varied according to time, place, and context. Political conflict in China led its leaders 'not so much [to worry] that people might become stateless, but that the state itself might do so', in the words of Rana Mitter.

By moving the centre of gravity of our story to Asia and the Pacific, we see how statelessness operated in the British empire. Robert Bickers' chapter offers a very British story of the seedy side of empire. In Eva de Jong-Duldig's chapter, we follow her father, sculptor Karl Duldig. He was born in Poland, moved to Vienna, and then fled with his family first to Switzerland and then to Singapore in 1938. A year later, upon the outbreak of war, the family was categorised by the British authorities in control of Singapore as enemy aliens, even though Nazi Germany had stripped them of their German citizenship. Then came Dunkirk, and the fear of invasion of Britain and the collapse of the British empire, including Singapore. To British officials, these stateless 'enemy aliens'

354   *Statelessness after Arendt*

– including two-year-old Eva – were a security risk, and had to be interned, deported, and incarcerated in Australia.

Karl Duldig's story shows that one way the stateless became part of the political world was through military service. After Pearl Harbor, the Australian government decided to think again about the stateless. There was a labour shortage, especially in the agricultural sector. These stateless men, interned in Northern Victoria, were given the opportunity of leaving internment, and of putting on Australian army uniforms, albeit without the right to use weapons. They formed a labour battalion, a kind of French Foreign Legion without guns. Not yet Australian, they were stateless labourers wearing Australian slouch caps. Their unit was headed by the only non-white officer in the Australian army, a Maori, Colonel Edward Broughton. He was a man sensitive to the racial prejudice these men had faced and to the injustice done by their internment in Australia.[4]

What ended the saga of statelessness for the soldiers of the 8th Employment Company? The answer is the Japanese attack on Hawaii, which created a labour shortage in Australia. That is why they got out of internment. They harvested fruit. Once demobilised, they could apply for Australian citizenship. Their story is part of Seumas Spark's chapter in this volume.

In overpopulated Shanghai during the war, stateless European refugees had no such advantage in the local labour market. But they were not in any way as isolated as the stateless people in Hay or Tatura in rural Australia. In Shanghai, people of many different outlooks, languages, races, and ages were thrown together. They had to endure overcrowding, stifling heat, chronic disease, and hunger. They were formally free, very much in contrast to those behind Australian barbed wire. In China in 1943, stateless Jewish refugees had to move to a designated area, known as the Shanghai ghetto, but they were free to leave during the day, with Japanese police permission. This was a ghetto with no barbed wire. The crushing burden of daily survival constrained their world more than did the incarceration of the stateless prisoners held in Australia.

What we have seen in this book is evidence not only of extreme hardship, but also of the ways displaced people, thousands of miles away from Europe, came together to begin their escape from statelessness. They were active men and women, and despite obstacles of

Conclusion 355

many kinds, many still found ways to keep their collective identity alive.

This book documents their efforts at preserving their humanity and at forging a nascent, liminal kind of democracy. The interned German and Austrian prisoners in rural Australia drafted a constitution through which they operated a very limited kind of self-rule in the camp. They remained internees, deported from Britain, but they still ran their own lives. They had all the resources the free refugees in Shanghai struggled to find.

The Japanese controlled Shanghai but did not provide food, clothing, or shelter for the city's population. And yet the stateless refugees ran schools, newspapers, cafés, clubs, theatres, and sporting events, with the help of the local Jewish community and the Joint Distribution Committee. There in Shanghai was the only surviving and intact Lithuanian Yeshiva in the world, the Mir Yeshiva, still functioning, still living the traditions of the Torah. All these different groups of people were stateless. And yet, through their actions, they began to shape their own futures long before they had the chance to realise them.

One way to understand these collective activities is to describe them as pre-political; another way is to say that they helped refugees forge a bridge, fragile but palpable, between statelessness and freedom. Even in severely confined circumstances, stateless people showed what a political life could be. Their varied conversations about freedom begun in bondage prepared the way out.

The passage of the 1951 United Nations Convention on Refugees led three years later to a Convention on the status of stateless persons. This measure came into effect in 1960. It established 'that stateless persons have the same rights as citizens with respect to freedom of religion and education of their children'. As to the right of association, the right to employment and to housing, 'stateless persons are to enjoy, at a minimum, the same treatment as other non-nationals'.[5] As Peter Gatrell has shown, the bureaucracy set up to process claimants placed new obstacles on the pathway between statelessness and citizenship. He has shown that the stateless had to construct a story that made sense to the officials processing their cases. They needed to translate the tale of their lives into the categories of the International Refugee Organization, founded in 1946, and succeeded by the UN High Commission on Refugees in 1952.

356   *Statelessness after Arendt*

In many of the chapters of this book, we see that the construction of narratives is a necessary, though not sufficient, element in the escape from statelessness. Narratives matter; refugees who are not stateless adopt similar strategies to those who are. As Joy Damousi notes, family stories are essential parts of the tale of displacement refugees tell. Images and fragments of family displacement are critical to Peter Balakian's poems and to Mary Behrens's art. Those in search of rights and of a stable home form their own narratives, but they must do so in a political world that tells them how to tell the tale.

Statelessness is not a matter limited to history. It still exists today, primarily but not only in West and South Asia, in Africa and in Eastern Europe. The Office of the UN High Commission on Refugees estimates that in 2023, there were over ten million stateless people scattered across the world.[6] The Kurdish people are stateless; they have been so for a century. The Palestinians are a stateless people. So are the Rohingya people, expelled in 2017 from Myanmar. So are the Roma, scattered throughout Eastern Europe. According to the UN, there are approximately one million stateless people in West Africa.[7] The UN states that at least one-third, and probably more, are stateless children.[8] To understand the complexity of their predicament, we need to avoid a Eurocentric approach to the problem of statelessness and its earlier history.

One of the findings of this book is that many stateless men and women found a way to enter the political world before they shed their statelessness. Hannah Arendt never explicitly reached this conclusion, but in Chapter 1, Jay Winter uses some of her later work to construct this argument. We, like Arendt, have highlighted the role of narrative and performance in these transformational moments. Some of these narratives tell of the forming of collectives under very difficult circumstances and the framing of demands for the recognition of rights. Families tell stories that transmit across generations narratives of statelessness. By being sensitive to those images and expressions of statelessness preserved privately or in public archives, we can tell the story of this large population that lived precariously on or beyond the margins of nation states.

One way to capture the multiple faces of statelessness is to pause for a moment and consider a photograph, taken by Arthur Rothstein, working for UNRRA in Shanghai in 1946[9] (Figure 20.1). This book is (among other things) about families, many with children, living in

Figure 20.1 Stateless Jewish children in Shanghai, 1946. Arthur Rothstein. Source: Dr Ann Rothstein Segan, director of the Arthur Rothstein Legacy Project.

Singapore, Shanghai, Australia, and elsewhere in Asia, waiting for the moment when they could shed the clothes of the stateless. How many children with and without families in different parts of the world are still trying to do the same?

Notes

1 Avishai Margalit, *The Ethics of Memory* (Cambridge, MA: Harvard University Press, 2002).
2 http://www.shhkjrm.com/node2/n4/n6/index.html. Accessed 20 November 2024.
3 David Kranzler, 'Restrictions against German-Jewish Refugee Immigration to Shanghai in 1939', *Jewish Social Studies*, 36, 1 (1974), pp. 40–60.
4 Bill Gammage, Seumus Spark, Jay Winter, with Carol Bunyan, *Dunera Lives: Profiles* (Melbourne: Monash University Publishing, 2020), ch. 2.
5 https://www.unhcr.org/ibelong/wp-content/uploads/1954-Convention-relating-to-the-Status-of-Stateless-Persons_ENG.pdf. Accessed 20 November 2024.

6 https://www.unhcr.org/ibelong/statelessness-around-the-world/. Accessed 20 November 2024.
7 https://www.unhcr.org/news/stories/stateless-west-africa#:~:text=At%20least%20750%2C000%20people%20are,harrowing%2C%20and%20littered%20with%20obstacles. Accessed 20 November 2024.
8 United Nations Human Rights Commission, *Under the Radar and Under Protected: The Urgent Need to Address Stateless Children's Rights* (London: Plan Limited and UNHCR, 2012).
9 See Ann Rothstein Segan and Brodie Hefner, 'For the Benefit of Society: A Portrait of the Photographer Arthur Rothstein (1915–1985)', in Daniela Pscheiden and Daniella Spera (eds), *Die Wiener in China: Fluchtpunkt Shanghai* (Vienna: Jüdisches Museum Wien, 2020), pp. 106–21.

Index

Abzug, Robert 254
Africa 40, 157, 336, 340, 356
agents of empathy 248–51, 259,
    263–4
Agudat Israel 227
Albury 59
Aleppo 41
Alsace 226
American Bureau of Medical Aid
    to China 191
American Jewish Joint Distribution
    Committee 4, 112, 116–17,
    125, 207–11, 215–18,
    236–7, 240, 248, 252,
    255–8, 273, 353
American Military Mission in
    China 291, 300
Anatolia 39, 43
Andartes, Greek resistance fighters
    84
Anderson, Benedict 98
Anglo-Celtic Australian Society
    281
Anschluss 52, 54, 210, 247,
    270–1
Anti-Comintern Pact 188, 193
antisemitism 67, 138, 161, 230,
    253, 261, 264, 267, 269,
    277, 279
Archer, Charles Percival 333–48
Arendt, Hannah 2–3, 5, 12–16,
    18–22, 28–9, 31–2, 75,
    81–3, 88, 90–1, 97, 100,
    109, 119, 133–5, 145–6,
    152, 172, 182, 209, 215,

    219–20, 247, 252, 263–4,
    291, 308, 351, 353, 356
and Blücher, Heinrich 146
Burden of Our Times, The 18
on citizenship 18–19, 23, 28, 82,
    90–1, 133–6, 141
Human Condition, The 13, 18,
    20, 23–4, 29
Origins of Totalitarianism, The
    18, 20, 23–4, 182, 291, 351
'Stateless People, The' 209
on statelessness 2, 12–16, 18,
    23–4, 28–9, 32, 75, 81, 83,
    88, 91, 97, 100, 109, 119,
    133–4, 145–6, 172, 182,
    209, 219, 247, 351, 356
'We Refugees' 75, 81, 263
Argentina 123, 165
Aristotle 19
Arita Hachirō 196
Armenians 3, 17, 38–40, 42–4
Army, Japanese 69, 123, 195–6,
    310, 312, 322, 325, 352
Aroosian, Bedros 40
Arsenal de l'Est (Shanghai) 318
Ashkenazi, Reb Meyer 237
Asia 2–5, 12, 23–5, 28–9, 32, 69,
    97, 102, 108, 187–8, 194,
    197, 240, 292, 303, 324,
    336, 340, 344, 351, 353,
    356–7
Southeast Asia 69, 112–13, 116,
    119–20, 122, 179–80, 215,
    218
Assam 297

360 *Index*

assimilation 77, 88, 240
Athens 83
Augustine, of Hippo 14
Auschwitz, liberation of 97
Australia, Commonwealth of 53, 115, 282
  Australian Jewish News 278
  Australian Jewish Welfare Society 275
  Australian Jewry 61, 275
  Australian Military Forces 70, 280–1, 354
    8th Employment Company 70, 280–1, 354
    8th Gazette 281
  Australian Parliament 61, 67
  Darwin, Australia 69, 273
  Family Welfare Bureau 165
  Labor government 67, 268
  Labor Party 66–7, 268
  New Australians 88
  Rushworth 59
  Victoria 52, 59, 279, 280, 354
Austria 52, 123, 210, 219, 270–1, 278
Axis Powers 118, 143, 217

bacteriological warfare 104
Baer, Ilse 55
Baer, Wener 55
Baghdad, Jews 211
Balakian, Nafina 40
Balakian, Peter 3, 38–40, 356
Bali 53
Bangkok 53
Bank, Stephen 70
Bankers' Guild School 173
Bartrop, Paul 70
Bataan Death March 104
Bataillon Mixte d'Infanterie Coloniale de Chine 318
Bauhaus, Weimar 280
Bavaria 248
BBC 333
Becher, Hans 278
Becher, Ursula 278
Beckelman, Moses W. 116–17, 217–19

Beijing 96, 102, 104, 106, 173, 290, 292–4, 296, 301–2, 313, 317–18, 322, 346
  Imperial Palace 104
  Memorial Museum of the War of Resistance to Japan 102, 106
  Palace Museum 104
  Tiananmen Square 96, 109
Beit Aharon synagogue, Shanghai 238
Belgium 54, 153–4, 161, 164, 215
Bengal 32
Benhabib, Seyla 21, 31
Benjamin, Walter 20–1
Berglas, Jakob 190–2
Berlin 54, 189, 278, 280, 283
Bidault, Georges 323
Biehl, João 151
Black Sea 39, 44, 233
Blau, Hans 61
Blitz (1940) 104
Blower, Brooke 294
Blumenfeld, Hans 260
Bosphorus 40
Boxer rebellion 293, 294, 339
Brand, Walter 275
Brazil 137, 156, 160
Brecht, Bertolt 259
Brent, Bern 283
Breslau 270
Britain 1, 15, 18, 23, 54, 60, 69, 97, 100, 137, 212, 214, 216, 218, 240, 267, 270, 279–80, 298, 303, 313, 336, 342, 353, 355
  British Commonwealth 24
  British Consul, Shanghai 339, 342
  British Empire 24, 55, 69, 294, 353
  British Mining Company 54
  British nationality 57
  British North Borneo 120, 123
Broughton, Colonel Edward 70, 354
Brünn (Brno) 270
Brunswick 278

Index

361

Buchdahl, Gerd 282
Buchdahl, Hans 282
Buchenwald camp 210
Buckley, Anthony 348
Bulter, Judith 22
Bureau for the Affairs of Russian
Emigrants (BREM)
141–5
Burma 120, 122, 213, 297, 299,
302
Bush, George W. 22
Byelorussia 225–6, 239–40

Cairns 274–5
Cairo declaration 102
Calwell, Arthur 268, 275
camps, extermination 14
camps, internment 14, 16, 23, 53,
58, 60, 112, 269, 279
Canada 115, 123, 233, 272
Canberra 280
Mt Stromlo observatory 280
Canton 312
Cao Diqiu 179
Caserne Voyron 318
Caspé, Simon 138
Central British Fund for German
Jewry 69
Central Jewish Committee,
Shanghai 161
Central Political Council, Chinese
Nationalist 191, 214
Chaing Kai-shek 99–102, 171, 173,
187, 290, 292–3, 296–304,
338
and Nanjing regime 99
Changzhou 174
Charity Fund (*Caisse des Oeuvres*)
315–16, 319
Chen Gongbo 313
Chen Kuo-lien 115, 217–18
Chengdu 292
Chennault, General Claire 291
Chilinguirian, Hagop 40
China 1–5, 17, 53, 96–109,
112–27, 137, 140, 143–4,
151–8, 162, 166, 170–2,
175, 181, 186–200,

208–10, 212–16, 218–20,
255, 290–304, 308–10,
312–19, 321–6, 335–41,
343–7, 352–4
Chinese, overseas 113–14, 116–17,
119–23, 125–7, 179–81,
212, 218
Chinese Communist Party (CCP)
96–8, 101–2, 106, 109,
179, 302
Chinese Communists 98, 100,
121, 124, 139–40, 179,
295, 300–3, 352
Chinese Consul General in Vienna
193
Chinese Eastern Railway 135–6,
140, 143–5, 153, 163
Chinese Expeditionary Force 297
Chinese Maritime Customs Service
338
Chinese Ministries of Interior
and Foreign Affairs (MFA)
114, 189, 213, 217–19,
316
Chinese Ministry of Foreign Affairs
(MOFA) 116, 217, 316–17,
321–2, 324
Chinese National Relief
and Rehabilitation
Administration (CNRRA)
114–15, 117, 121, 219–20
Chinese nationalism 97–9, 101,
120, 137, 188, 213, 338
Chinese Nationalist government
101, 106, 170–1, 186,
188–92, 199, 208–9, 215,
218, 291, 303–4
Chinese Nationalists 96, 98–102,
106, 109, 119, 121–2,
126–7, 139, 171–2, 175,
187–8, 190–3, 199, 207–8,
210, 212, 214–15, 217,
220, 291–2, 295, 299,
301–2, 338
Chinese patriotic education 97,
177
Chinese People's Relief Association
126

362   *Index*

Chongqing 100, 102, 187, 218, 291–3, 295, 297, 300, 322–3, 325
Christian X of Denmark 254
Chu Minyi 313
Churchill, Sir Winston 23, 296
citizenship 2, 12, 16–19, 21, 23, 28, 71, 82, 90–1, 113–15, 121, 124, 127, 133, 135–6, 141–3, 145–6, 157, 182, 207, 209, 212–14, 219, 247, 269, 309, 335–6, 339, 341, 353–5
Citrin, Walter 125
civilians 46, 52, 77–8, 84, 172–6, 291, 295, 298–300, 303
Clabon, Anthony 159
Cold War 98, 100, 118, 127, 146, 303
Collison, William 122
Collonge Sous Salève 40
Colombo 54
Committee for the Assistance of European Jewish Refugees in Shanghai (CAEJR) 211
Committee on the Muslim and Jewish Problem, Japanese 186, 197
Commonwealth Reconstruction Training Scheme 281
Communism 24, 139, 146, 158, 345
Communists 98, 100, 121, 125, 139–40, 158, 179, 295, 300–3, 334, 352
Constantinople 39, 257
Conte Rosso, SS 270
Convent of the Sacred Heart, Shanghai 177
Corden, Max 270
Cosme, Henry 309, 311–15
Cossacks 140
Cuba 255, 258, 294
Cultural Revolution, Chinese 99, 100, 102, 111
Curaçao 234–5
Czechoslovakia 3, 207, 211

Dachau camp 210
Danglow, Rabbi Jacob 60
Davidoff, Leonore 84
de Boisséson, Robert 314
de Certeau, Michel 24
De Gaulle, Charles 310–11, 322
    Gaullist group in Shanghai 311
de Margerie, Roland 309, 312, 314, 318–19, 322–3
decolonisation 32, 113, 119, 127, 220, 335
DeGooyer, Stephanie 82
democracy 188, 213, 355
Denmark 31, 161, 254, 260
Die Neue Zeit 217
Dinesen, Isak 29
Dink, Hrant 38, 42
displaced person (DP) 17, 29, 33, 46, 113–14, 116, 118, 120–1, 123–4, 127, 135, 146, 155, 163–4, 252, 264, 273
Diyarbakir 40
Dove, Rita 39
Dreyfus, George 270
Duara, Pransenjit 303
Dublin 161
Duffy, Justice Gavan 68
Duldig, Dr Leo 54, 61, 69
Duldig, Irene Gutwirth, née 54, 69
Duldig, Karl 52, 54, 56, 58, 64, 353–4
Duldig, Slawa Horowitz 54
Duldig, Stefanie 54
Duncan, Ada Constance 61
Dunera, HMT 23, 67, 69–71, 268–70, 279–83
Dunkirk 23, 353
Dutch East Indies 120

East China Pedagogical University, Shanghai 154
Eber, John 56
Egal, Roderick 312
Egypt 138
Einstein, Albert 191
Eisfelder, Horst 121
Ellis Island 38, 40–1, 123

Index

363

Emergency Refugee Relief Committee 174
Emerson, H. M. 216, 218
empathy, agents of 247–51, 259, 263–4
Eurasians 58, 344, 346
Europe 3–6, 12–13, 15, 17, 24, 28, 32, 54–5, 59, 68, 71, 96–7, 102, 105, 111–12, 115, 146, 160, 192, 199–200, 208–9, 211, 214, 216–17, 224, 228, 240, 248, 258, 335, 338, 351
Evatt, Dr Herbert Vere 67
Évian Conference (1938) 268
Ezra, Nissim Elias Benjamin 188

Fain, Guy 319, 322
Far Eastern Maritime Province 178
fascism 24, 247
  fascist 68–9, 118, 120, 137–8, 142, 145
Feng Zikai 105
Figdor, Alfred 54, 61
Fine, Sarah 166
Fink (Funk), Professor George 63
Finkel, Reb Eliezer Yehudah 233, 235, 239
Finnane, Antonia 277, 282
Five Ministers' Conference, Japanese 196
Florina 77, 83–4
Ford, O'Neil 254
Forde, Frank, Australian Minister for the Army 67, 70
France 15, 20, 29, 98, 147, 160, 215, 218, 230, 255, 294, 308–12, 314, 316, 321–6, 339
Frankl, Victor 249
Free France 311
French Committee of National Liberation 322
French Concession, Shanghai 112, 143, 170, 173, 175–6, 178, 187, 212, 258, 310–15, 317, 320, 325–6
French Foreign Legion 160, 354

French Indochina 120, 122, 312, 316, 324
Fröhlich, Georg 280
Fudan University (Aurora University) 173
Fushun 105

Gallagher, Leo 276–7
Gao Jianfu 105
Gary, Romain 227
Geelong Grammar School 280
Geneva Convention (1949) 170–1
Geneva Convention on the Status of the Stateless (1954) 210
genocide 39, 200
  Armenian 3, 38–9
Germany 15, 17, 19, 47, 52–4, 56, 68, 85, 100, 115–16, 123–4, 133, 135, 186–90, 192–3, 196, 198–9, 208, 210–14, 217, 219, 248, 254, 260–2, 270, 279, 294, 302, 310, 353
Fohrenwald Jewish Displaced Person Camp (Wolfrathausen) 261
Gestapo 210
Ghoya, Kanoh 238
Gordon Highlander regiment 57
Gottlieb, Johannah 57
Gottlieb, Otto 54, 57, 63
Gottlieb, Ruth 57, 63
Goulburn Valley 70, 279
Gowrie, Lord Alexander Hore-Ruthven 61, 70
Great Leap Forward 127
Great Patriotic War 97, 100
Greco-Turkish War (1919–22) 39
Greece 40, 77, 79–80, 83–4, 86–7
  Civil War 78, 83
  Greek Orthodox Church 154, 156, 230
Grodzinsky, Reb Chaim Ozer 227–8, 230–3, 241
Gruen, Fred 282
Guardian 347
Gugenheim, Ernest 226, 228–9
Guomindang 337–8

364 *Index*

Gurs concentration camp 29
Gutwirth, Hendrik 54
Gutwirth, Irene 69
Gutwirth, Nathan 234

Hailar 144
Hakkō Ichiu 196
Hambro, Dr Edvard 127
Hamburg 53, 193
Hamlish, Tamara 104
Hangzhou 180
Hankou (Wuhan) 181, 293, 295, 312–13
Harbin 23, 133, 135–41, 143–5, 153, 155–6, 159–60, 162, 178, 273, 342, 353
Haw, Aw Boon 55–6
Hayden, Robert 39
Hayton-Fleet, Bertie 337
He Fengshan 193
Heaney, Seamus 39
Hebei Province 173
Heidegger, Martin 20
Heimatlosen 13
Hiroshima 322
Hirsch, Marianne 39, 81–3
Hirschfeld-Mack, Ludwig 280
Hitler, Adolf 22, 59, 67–8, 191, 231–2, 240, 267
Holly Street Estate (London) 334–5
  Holly Street Public Art Trust 333
Holocaust 77–8, 81, 104, 113, 187, 193, 200, 224, 241–2, 277, 279, 283
  Holocaust Martyrs' and Heroes' Remembrance Authority 193
Home Office, British 69–70
Homer 39
Hong Kong 122–3, 125–7, 151, 153–5, 157, 159–60, 162–5, 334–7, 339–46
Hongkou 112, 172, 174, 187, 211, 217, 352
Hoover, President Herbert 191
humanitarianism 164, 171, 181–2
Hunter, Tom 334–5, 343, 347–8
Huntley, Alfred 57

Hurley, Patrick 299
Hwa Lien 273–5

immigrants 116, 123, 190, 192, 257, 259, 268, 276, 335
immigration, post-war 79
imperialism 5, 24, 133, 208, 303–4
India 108, 292, 297–9, 348
Indianapolis 40
Indonesia 120, 123
Inglis, Ken 1, 282
Intergovernmental Committee for European Migration (ICEM) 154, 159
Intergovernmental Committee on Refugees (IGCR) 113, 115–16, 209, 215–18
International Committee of the Red Cross 173, 177
International Refugee Organisation 30, 273
International Relief Committee of China 170
International Social Services, Sydney 165
International Tracing Service 115
internees 52, 57–62, 66–71, 268–70, 279–83, 355
  Australian 53, 70
  German and Austrian 1, 23, 67
  Singapore 67, 70
internment 14–15, 23, 52, 55–7, 58, 60, 69–71, 143, 215, 217, 269, 279–81, 283, 318, 354
Iran 71
Ireland 161
  Irish Red Cross 161
Israel 115, 123, 125, 193, 233, 240, 255, 279
Istanbul 38, 39, 41–2
Itagaki Seishirō 196
Italians 55, 58, 112
Itsokovitch, Leivi I. 161
Iwane, General Matsui 174

Jackson, Michael 21

Index

Jacquinot de Besange, Father Robert 170–1, 174
Jacquinot Safe Zone 170–83
see also Shanghai, Nantao Safe Zone
Japan 4, 69, 97–103, 106, 109, 139, 181, 187–8, 193–9, 211, 214, 234–5, 295, 302, 308–9, 312, 318, 338
Attack on Pearl Harbor 69, 112, 199, 208, 236, 256–8, 280, 290, 292–3, 296, 298, 302, 324, 337, 354
Foreign Ministry of 186, 313
Invasion of Manchuria, 155–6
Japanese 5, 24, 52, 69, 100–2, 105–6, 111–12, 123, 137–44, 155
Navy 195
Occupation of Shanghai 52, 101, 138–9, 141–2, 155, 163, 186, 199, 255, 257, 291, 310–11, 324, 337, 342
Java 53
Jewish Refugee Relief Committee 211
Jews 2, 16, 21–2, 53, 67–8, 113, 115, 125, 133, 138, 141, 143, 186, 189–93, 195–200, 208, 212–13, 215–16, 220, 231–7, 239–41, 253–6, 259–60, 263–4, 268–70, 279, 281, 353
American 191, 194, 197, 208
Austrian and German 1, 114, 190–1, 207, 210–11, 214–19, 247, 268, 271, 352
European 32, 112–16, 187, 192–3, 195, 197, 208, 214, 238, 248
Russian-speaking 136, 142
Shanghailanders 186, 188, 197, 199
stateless 190, 209, 212–14, 238, 254, 258, 352
Jiangsu Province 173
Jiaotong University 173

Jones, Stanley W., Colonial Secretary 55
Jordan, Charles H. 218
Judaism 233, 240, 259, 271–2

Kahn, Michael 85
Kalmanowitz, Rev Avraham 239
Kan, Dr Nai-kuang 116
Kindertransport 283
Kinzer, Benjamin 117
Kishinev pogroms 260
Klesk 225
Klinkatsis, Fanni 84
Klinkatsis, Pandelis 78, 83
Klinkatsis, Sophia Damousi 84, 86–8
Klinkatsis, Victor 78–9, 86, 88
Kobe 235, 238
Kobrin, Rebecca 257
Kong Xianghxi 212–13
Korea 112, 142, 158, 339, 345
Korean War 125
Koreshige, Captain Inusuka 186, 193–4, 200, 258
Koselleck, Reinhard 20
Kristallnacht 54, 267, 278
Kristeva, Julia 22
Kutler, Reb Aaron 232
Kwantung Army 195–6

Lakewood, New Jersey 233, 239
Latin America 123, 154
Lauterpacht, Hersch 151
Laval, Pierre 313
Laval government 315–16
Layton, Major Julian 69–70
League of Coloured Peoples in London 341
League of Nations 133–4, 212–13
Convention on the International Status of Refugees 135–6
Lefebvre, Henri 183, 353
Legislative Yuan 188, 212
Levenstein, Reb Yehezkel 233, 235
Lewin, Dr Isaac 234
Lewin, Pessla 234
Li Yinting 295
Liang, Colonel M. C. 126

Index

Lithuania 141, 145, 198, 224–34, 238–41, 355
Livelihood Improvement Association, Shanghai 180
Liverpool 23
Lloyd, Rt. Hon. Lord 55
Lo, Lorenzo 161
Long Yun 190, 300
Louis, Joe 229
Lubavitcher Hassidic movement 237

Macao 160, 342
McCarthy, Mary 18
Macedonia 84
Maehrischel family (Mährischel/ Mährischl) 270–1, 273, 275–7
  Alfred 270
  Helene 270
  Karl and Regina 270
  Leopold 270, 273
Maier, Charles 5
Malaya 57, 120, 122
  Malayan Communist Party 122
  Malay Peninsula 52, 54
  Malayan Union 122
Malin, Reb Leib 234, 236
Manchukuo, 139, 141, 142–3, 146, 155, 196, 342
Manchuria 104, 135–6, 139–42, 144–5, 163, 178, 193–7, 300, 338, 342
Manela, Erez 296
Manila 336
Mao Zedong 96, 98, 100–5, 107–9, 272, 292, 300–2, 352, 354
  Maoism 100–1, 104–5, 108
  post-Mao reform era 104
Māori 354
Marco Polo Bridge 106, 173
Margolis, Laura 240, 248–9, 251–2, 255–9, 263–4, 353
Marish, Ernest 273
Markus, Andrew 268

Marshall, George, US Army Chief of Staff 299, 301–2
Massachusetts Institute of Technology (MIT) 259
Massigli, René 323
Matkovsky, Mahail 142, 144
Matsuoka Yōsuke 198
Meilich, Ludwig 61
Melbourne 44, 60–2, 69–70, 90, 268, 273, 276–9, 281–2
  Bentleigh 277
  Caulfield 277
  Melbourne Age 275
  St Kilda 276–9
    Brighton Road State School 278
    Temple Beth Israel 279
  University of Melbourne 282
Menzies, Prime Minister Sir Robert 61, 67
Meyer, Hans 280
Meyrier, Jacques 323
migration 75, 77, 79, 87–8, 90–1, 154, 162, 209, 267–8, 270
migration, forced 193
Milosz, Czeslaw 227
Minsk 226
Moorabbin 276–7
  Moorabbin Hebrew Congregation 276
Moravia 270
Morocco 116
Moscow 141, 235
Moshinsky, Sam 138, 143
Mosse, George 254
Mossop, Sir Alan 340, 346
Mozambique 156
MS *St. Louis* 258, 263
Museum of London 335
Mussar movement 226, 228
Myanmar 356

Nagasaki 322
Nanjing 99, 105, 111, 180, 295, 325, 338
  Nanjing Massacre 101–2, 104, 107
Nansen, Fridtjof 133

Index

Nansen passports 17, 133–4, 146

National Socialist Party (Nazi) 13, 19, 22–4, 38, 68–9, 77–9, 85, 90, 97, 111, 115, 117, 120, 146, 193, 207–8, 210, 214–16, 230, 232, 240–1, 247–8, 253, 271

anti-Nazi 23, 55, 69, 85, 146

Nazi Germany 47, 133, 212, 217, 310, 353

de-Nazification, post-war 11

Nazi occupation 79, 193, 275, 5

Nazism 52, 68, 267

nationality 12, 28, 30, 57, 59, 112, 119–20, 143, 189, 192, 209, 214, 219, 247, 267, 344

Nationality Act, China (1929) 213–14

Netherlands 154, 158, 161

New South Wales 59, 164, 280

New Villages for the Commoners (NVC) 171, 173, 175–7, 180

New York 40, 85, 116, 134, 209, 211, 234, 238–9, 255

New York Times 219

Newcastle Art Gallery 62

Nicaragua 294

Ningbo 174

Nuremberg Laws (1935) 207, 210

Eleventh Decree (1935) 207

Odessa 233, 235

Ohel Moshe synagogue, Shanghai 1, 239

Opium Wars (1842) 187

Orthodox Judaism 136, 154–6, 225–30, 232–3, 235, 237, 240–2, 276, 353

Ottoman Turkish government 39

Ouchang 180

Ovid 19

Pacific region 2–5, 12, 23–5, 28, 32, 69, 235, 316, 351, 353

Palestine 70, 226, 228–9, 231, 233, 235

Panosyan, Murat 39–40

Paris 134, 178

Paris Peace Settlement (1919) 13

Partition of India (1947) 32

Pasteur Institute 315

Patton, General George 253

Pechkoff, Zinovi 322–3

Peking 137, 141, 336

Peking University 302

People's Liberation Army 292, 302

People's Republic of China (ROC) 113, 119, 121, 126–7, 187, 208–9, 211, 213, 215–17, 220, 290–1, 294, 296–9, 303

Peress, Gilles 47

Perry, Commodore Matthew 293

persecution 2, 4, 30, 38, 52, 82, 124, 152, 190, 193, 196, 212, 215–17, 253, 261, 263–4, 268, 352

Pétain, Philippe 308

Philippines, 120, 124–5, 293, 295

Plato 12

Poland 56, 214, 225, 226, 227, 230–2, 238–41, 353

Portnoy, Eliezer (Laizer) 232–3

post memory 39, 81–3

Potsdam declarations (1945) 102

Prager, Georg and Margarete 278

Preparatory Commission of the International Refugee Organization (PCIRO) 118, 120–1

propaganda 60, 108, 179, 195, 302

Qingdao 293, 301–2

Qinhuangdao 296

Queen Mary 52–3, 57, 59, 67, 69–71, 268–9, 280

Queensland 274

radical evil, Kantian notion of 21

Rancière, Jacques 18–19, 22, 31

Rangoon 297

368 *Index*

Rape of Nanjing *see* Nanjing, Nanjing Massacre
Reformed Government of the Republic of China 187
refugeedom 3, 29, 220, 242
refugees
  child 76, 90
  Chinese 112, 126–7, 170, 172, 174, 176, 177, 179, 182–3, 352
  German and Austrian 54, 70, 219, 352
  Hungarian 158
  Jewish 53, 55, 60, 116, 121, 123–5, 146, 154, 161, 186–4, 196–9, 207–20, 236–7, 248, 252, 255–7, 261, 264, 267–8, 273–4, 277, 282, 352, 354
  Refugee Committee, Shanghai 174–6
  Refugee Summer Olympic Games 178
  regime 30–2, 151–2, 156
  Russian 112, 119, 124, 151–3, 155, 157, 159–60, 166
  Singapore 55
  Soviet 164
  stateless 75, 112, 115, 117, 121, 157, 183, 187, 200, 220, 238, 256, 352, 354–5
  status 30, 177, 179, 183
Reichelt, Ernst 280
repatriation 30, 33, 114–26, 135, 140, 144–6, 153, 174, 176, 177, 182, 209, 216–18, 253, 255, 301, 315, 319, 322, 335–6, 341, 346
resettlement 33, 88, 115, 117–18, 121, 125, 152–7, 159–64, 166, 191, 214, 248, 251, 255
Returned Sailors', Soldiers', Airmen's Imperial League of Australia (RSSAILA) 60
Revolution of 1911 (Chinese) 339
rice riots (Tokyo) 173
Rich, Adrienne 39

Righteous Among the Nations 193, 199
rights, human 14, 217, 249–50
rights, natural 14, 134
rights, the right to have 16, 20, 82, 182, 210, 217, 220
Ristaino, Marcia 182
Rodeck, Ernst 280
Rohingya 356
Roosevelt, Franklin D. 296, 298–9, 303
  administration of 192
Rosengren, Camille 253–4
Rosengren, Frank 253
Rothstein, Arthur 356
Russia 1, 15, 17, 97, 124–5, 136, 153, 157–8, 160, 162, 166, 239, 294, 342
  Civil War 138, 152, 154, 162, 178
  emigrants 120, 122, 136, 138, 142–4
    Russian Emigrants' Committee and Relief Association 158
  Imperial 136–7, 139–41, 158
  Russian Fascist Party 138–9, 142, 144
  Russian Old Believers 165
  Russian Orthodox Church 136
  White 32, 113, 122, 125, 135, 138–9, 145, 157, 178, 182, 190, 220, 339

Sachsenhausen camp 54, 210, 278
Said, Edward 166
Saigon 122
Saint Petersburg 141, 341–2
Sakamoto, Pamela 199
Salgado, Sebastiao 47
Salvador, Angelina 336
Salvation Army 177, 179, 238
Samar (Philippines) 124–5
  Samar camp 125
San Antonio 259–60
  San Antonio Conservation Society 254
San Francisco 123, 160

Index

Sarawak 123
Savitsky, Kazimir 145
Schlesinger, Eve 57
Schlesinger, Gertrude 57
Schlesinger, Paul 53–4, 57, 61, 69
Schmeling, Max 229
Schreiabends (musical evenings in Melbourne) 278–9
Schwarcz, Vera 238
Scutari 40
Seefeld, Gerhard 53, 56, 60, 69
Seefeld, Professor Arthur 53
Shanghai 1, 3–5, 23–4, 53–4, 101, 111–14, 121–7, 138, 142–4, 153–8, 160–1, 163–4, 170–81, 183, 186–7, 190–5, 197–200, 207–12, 214–20, 224, 236–40, 247–8, 255–8, 263, 268–70, 272–9, 282–3, 290–5, 301, 309–14, 316–26, 334–40, 342–3, 346, 348, 351–7
    Cathay Hotel (Shanghai), 257
    Hongkew (district) 237
        Baikal Road 237
    Minhang district 173
    Nantao Safe Zone (Nantao refugee zone) 170–83
        Nantao Supervisory Committee 175
        Nantao trade unions 180
    Pudong (district) 173
    Zhabei (district) 173
Shanghai, Battle of (1937) 173, 187, 210
Shanghai Christian Warzone Relief Association 180
Shanghai Echo 217
Shanghai Herald 217
Shanghai International Rescue Society 179
Shanghai International Settlement and French Concession 111–12, 143, 172–4, 178, 187, 211–12, 236, 272, 293–4, 311–13, 338–9, 351
Shanghai Jewish Refugees Museum 1, 239, 352
Shanghai Jews 186, 188, 199–200, 209–10, 215, 217, 219, 237, 264, 282
Shanghai Municipal Council (SMC) 172, 211–12, 313
Shanghai Municipal Government 218
Shanghai Municipal Police 143, 339
    Special Branch 343
Shanghai Post and Mercury 111
Shanghai Preparation Committee of the Commoners' Residential Houses 173
Shanghai Truce Agreement (1932) 173
Shanghai Volunteer Corps 172
Shanghai Zionist Association 188
Shapiro, Marc 234
Shenzhen 180
Siberia 157, 239, 241–2
    Khabarovsk 341
Siegel, Manny 215–16
Siegelberg, Mira 17, 32
Singapore 1, 52–7, 60, 69–70, 108, 120, 123, 247, 268, 339–40, 353, 357
    German and Italian nationals in 55
    Sikh Police Barracks, Pearls Hill 56
Sino-American relations 290, 291–2, 298, 300–1
Sino-Japanese War 102, 187, 191–2, 199, 21
Smedley, Agnes 181
Society of Friends (Quakers) 61
Soloveitchik, Haim 241
Song Ziwen, ROC Foreign Minister 298
South America 151, 234
South China Patrol 293, 295
South China Sea 97
South Manchurian Railway Company (SMR) 194

370   *Index*

sovereignty 3, 20, 115, 143, 171,
174, 215–17, 220, 295,
298, 300, 303, 308–9, 338,
347, 352
  compromised 4
  non-sovereignty 20–1
  state 17, 32, 248, 292
Soviet Army 139, 144, 188, 230
Soviet Union 113, 122, 124–5, 135,
137–41, 143–5, 166, 195,
220, 302–3, 339
Spain 17, 255
Spanish Civil War 29
Spender, Percy 67
Spivak, Gayatri 22
Spreiregen, Paul 254
Stalin, Joseph 233, 296
statelessness
  1954 Convention Relating to the
Status of Stateless People
220
  refugees 38, 75, 112, 115, 117,
157, 183, 200, 238, 256,
352, 355
  stateless, nascent autonomy of
the 20, 23
  stateless people 4, 13–17, 23, 28,
39, 52, 82, 113, 172, 209,
217, 219–20, 257, 352,
354–6
  stateless Russians 121, 124,
142–4, 155
Stilwell, Joseph General 296–9,
303
Stimson, Secretary of War Henry
296
Stonebridge, Lyndsey 29
Straits Settlements 53–5, 60, 67, 70
Stratton, Jon 281
Strauss, Steven QC 282
Sugihara Chiune (Chuini) 198–9,
234
Sun Ke 188–9, 192, 212–14
Sun Yat-sen 187–8, 212–13
Surinam 234
Switzerland 154, 156–7, 160, 353
Sydney 57, 58, 62, 165, 268,
273–5, 278–9

Sydney Morning Herald 274
Syria 38, 40–1, 43

Tackaberry, Lt-Col. William 68–9
Taiping Civil War 339
Taiwan 102, 108, 126, 302
Talmud 224, 226–8, 230–2, 238–9,
353
Tatars 136, 139
Tatura 70, 354
  internment camp 52–4, 59, 279
  Tatura Melody 61
Telz 225
Terkels, Studs 97
Thailand 120
Thomson, Dr E. Laidlaw 56
Three Peoples' Principles Youth
Leagues 179, 213
Tianjin 123, 290, 292, 293–6,
301–2, 312–14, 317–18,
322, 338
Tokyo 101, 197–8, 211, 313, 325
Torah 63, 224–6, 228, 232,
236–41, 355
Toronto 18
totalitarianism 18, 133
Trakhtenberg, Vladimir 145
Trans-Siberian Railway 136, 207
Treaty of Wangxia (1844) 294
Trieste 270
Trouillot, Michel 252
Truman, President Harry S. 292,
301, 302
  administration 292, 302
Tsiang, Dr T. F. 117
Tubabo Island 124
Turkey 39–40

Ukraine 98, 153, 226–7
  Galicia 227
  Kharkov 226
  Poltav 226
United Council of Civilian Relief in
China 191
United Kingdom 118, 160, 163,
346
United Nations Campaign for
World Refugee Year 166

Index

United Nations Convention on Refugees (1951) 30, 152, 355
United Nations High Commissioner for Refugees (UNHCR) 17, 30–1, 113, 126–7, 151–4, 157, 159–61, 163–4
United Nations Relief and Rehabilitation Administration (UNRRA) 113–21, 215, 219, 248, 252, 260–2, 256
United States 17–18, 22, 39–40, 69, 86–8, 97, 100, 115, 118–19, 123–4, 137, 140, 146, 163, 186–7, 191–6, 198, 209, 211–12, 214, 218, 232–6, 239, 255, 257, 259, 272, 290, 292–8, 300, 302–3, 324, 337
  Army 293–4, 296, 298–9, 300
    Pocket Guide to China 296
  Army Airforce 252, 260, 290–2, 297
  Asiatic Fleet 293
  Consulate, in China 123, 256
  government 119, 123, 189–90, 294–5, 297–8, 300, 303
  Marine Corps 290, 293–6, 301–2, 337
  Marine III Amphibious Corps 300
  Military Police 158
  State Department 252, 255, 295
  Treasury Secretary 255
  War Department 295–6, 298, 303
United States Holocaust Memorial Museum (USHMM) 127, 254–5
USS *Hart* 295
USS *Panay* 295
USS *Susquehanna* 293
USS *Tutuila* 295
USS *Wake* 295
USSR 97, 100, 118, 139, 155, 230
Ut, Nick 47

Va'ad Hayeshivot 227, 341
VE Day 96
Velozhin 225
Vichy France, 308–12, 313, 322–3, 324–6
Victorian International Refugee Emergency Council 61
Vienna 53–4, 79, 85–6, 193, 270–3, 276–7, 280, 353
Vilna 116, 227, 230–6, 240–1
Vincent, Polly 347
Vincent, Sally 334
Vladivostok 136, 162, 207, 233–5

Wainhaus, Abraham 238
Walcott, Derek 39
Walkin, Chaya Leah 235–6
Walkin, Rabbi Shmuel David 237
Wang Jingwei Reformed government 308, 311–4, 317–18, 324
Wann, Nancy and Pamela 282
Waranga Basin 62
Ward Road gaol 340, 344
Warhaftig, Zorach 235, 300
Wedemeyer, General Albert 90, 299–300
Wentscher, Julius and Tina 53
Whitlam, Prime Minister Gough 282
William, Maurice 190–2
Wong, Jennings 121, 126
World Council of Churches (WCC) 154, 160
World War, First 13, 16–17, 78, 123, 152, 144, 174, 226, 231, 337, 339, 342
World War, Second 2–6, 12, 15, 17, 24, 29, 32, 53–4, 60, 77–9, 84, 96–7, 101–2, 109, 113, 116, 120, 127, 135, 139, 143–4, 146, 186, 192–4, 208, 219, 225–6, 249, 267–8, 283, 291–2, 294, 296, 302–3, 308, 336, 351–3
Wu Hung 104
Wu Nan-ju 116

Index

Wuhan *see* Hankou (Wuhan)
Wuppertal 270

Xiamen 313
Xie Xueshi 194
Xinjiang 302
Xu Beihong 105

Yan'an 101, 103, 105, 107–8
  Yan'an Forum on Literature and
    Art 103
Yangtze Patrol 293, 295
Yangtze River 293
Yass, Catherine 333–4
Yasue Norihiro, Colonel 193–8,
  200
Yeshiva 224–41
  Mir Yeshiva 224–6, 228–30,
    233–41, 353, 355
  Slobodka Yeshiva 225

Yeshiva Schools Council 231
Yu Hongjun 174
Yu Shengxiao 337
Yunnan Province 190–1, 292,
  297–300

Zaharovna, Natalia Andrevna
  337
Zauner, Herta 270
Zhang Zuolin 137, 141
Zhangzhou 180
Zhejiang Province 173
Zhu Jiahua 214
Zhu Maocheng 180
Zionism 188, 225, 229
  Zionist 21, 67, 188, 227, 231,
    233, 235, 257
Zisman, Samuel 248–9, 251–5,
  259–64
Zolberg, Aristide 28–9